KT-526-190

Effective Perl Programming

Ways to Write Better, More Idiomatic Perl

Second Edition

Joseph N. Hall
Joshua A. McAdams
brian d foy

PARK LEARNING CENTRE
UNIVERSITY OF GLOUCESTERSHIRE
PO Box 220, The Park
Cheltenham GL50 2RH
Tel: 01242 714333

✦✦ Addison-Wesley

Upper Saddle River, NJ • Boston • Indianapolis • San Francisco
New York • Toronto • Montreal • London • Munich • Paris • Madrid
Capetown • Sydney • Tokyo • Singapore • Mexico City

Many of the designations used by manufacturers and sellers to distinguish their products are claimed as trademarks. Where those designations appear in this book, and the publisher was aware of a trademark claim, the designations have been printed with initial capital letters or in all capitals.

The authors and publisher have taken care in the preparation of this book, but make no expressed or implied warranty of any kind and assume no responsibility for errors or omissions. No liability is assumed for incidental or consequential damages in connection with or arising out of the use of the information or programs contained herein.

The publisher offers excellent discounts on this book when ordered in quantity for bulk purchases or special sales, which may include electronic versions and/or custom covers and content particular to your business, training goals, marketing focus, and branding interests. For more information, please contact:

U.S. Corporate and Government Sales
(800) 382-3419
corpsales@pearsontechgroup.com

For sales outside the United States please contact:

International Sales
international@pearson.com

Visit us on the Web: informit.com/aw

Library of Congress Cataloging-in-Publication Data

Hall, Joseph N., 1966–
    Effective Perl programming : ways to write better, more idiomatic Perl / Joseph N. Hall, Joshua McAdams, Brian D. Foy. — 2nd ed.
        p.   cm.
    Includes bibliographical references and index.
    ISBN 978-0-321-49694-2 (pbk. : alk. paper)
    1. Perl (Computer program language) I. McAdams, Joshua. II. Foy, Brian D III. Title.
    QA76.73.P22H35 2010
    005.13'3—dc22
                                                            2010001078

Copyright © 2010 Pearson Education, Inc.

All rights reserved. Printed in the United States of America. This publication is protected by copyright, and permission must be obtained from the publisher prior to any prohibited reproduction, storage in a retrieval system, or transmission in any form or by any means, electronic, mechanical, photocopying, recording, or likewise. For information regarding permissions, write to:

Pearson Education, Inc.
Rights and Contracts Department
501 Boylston Street, Suite 900
Boston, MA 02116
Fax: (617) 671-3447

ISBN-13: 978-0-321-49694-2
ISBN-10:   0-321-49694-9
Text printed in the United States on recycled paper at Edwards Brothers in Ann Arbor, Michigan.
First printing, April 2010

3704261832

Effective Perl Programming

Second Edition

The Effective Software Development Series

Scott Meyers, Consulting Editor

Visit **informit.com/esds** for a complete list of available publications.

The **Effective Software Development Series** provides expert advice on all aspects of modern software development. Books in the series are well written, technically sound, and of lasting value. Each describes the critical things experts always do—or always avoid—to produce outstanding software.

Scott Meyers, author of the best-selling books *Effective C++* (now in its third edition), *More Effective C++*, and *Effective STL* (all available in both print and electronic versions), conceived of the series and acts as its consulting editor. Authors in the series work with Meyers to create essential reading in a format that is familiar and accessible for software developers of every stripe.

PEARSON

Addison-Wesley **Cisco Press** EXAM/**CRAM** **IBM** Press QUE PRENTICE HALL **SAMS** | Safari Books Online

Contents at a Glance

Contents

Foreword

When I first learned Perl more than a decade ago, I thought I knew the language pretty well; and indeed, I knew the *language* well enough. What I didn't know were the idioms and constructs that really give Perl its power. While it's perfectly possible to program without these, they represent a wealth of knowledge and productivity that is easily missed.

Luckily for me, I had acquired the first edition of Joseph N. Hall's *Effective Perl Programming*, and it wasn't to be found in my bookshelf. Instead, it had an almost permanent place in my bag, where I could easily peruse it whenever I found a spare moment.

Joseph's format for *Effective Perl Programming* was delightfully simple: small snippets of wisdom; easily digested. Indeed, it formed the original inspiration for our free Perl Tips (http://perltraining.com.au/tips/) newsletter, which continues to explore both Perl and its community.

A lot can change in a language in ten years, but even more can change in the community's understanding of a language over that time. Consequentially, I was delighted to hear that not only was a second edition in the works, but that it was to be written by two of the most prominent members of the Perl community.

To say that brian is devoted to Perl is like saying that the sun's corona is rather warm. brian has not only literally written volumes on the language, but also publishes a magazine (*The Perl Review*), manages Perl's FAQ, and is a constant and welcome presence on community sites devoted to both Perl and programming.

Josh is best known for his efforts in running *Perlcast*, which has been providing Perl news in audio form since 2005. Josh's abilities to consistently interview the brightest and most interesting people in the world not only make him an ideal accumulator of knowledge, but also have me very jealous.

As such, it is with great pleasure that I have the opportunity to present to you the second edition of this book. May it help you on your way to Perl mastery the same way the first edition did for me.

—*Paul Fenwick*
Managing Director
Perl Training Australia

Preface

Many Perl programmers cut their teeth on the first edition of *Effective Perl Programming*. When Addison-Wesley first published it in 1998, the entire world seemed to be using Perl; the dot-com days were in full swing and anyone who knew a little HTML could get a job as a programmer. Once they had those jobs, programmers had to pick up some quick skills. *Effective Perl Programming* was likely to be one of the books those new Perl programmers had on their desks along with the bibles of Perl, *Programming Perl*[1] and *Learning Perl*[2].

There were many other Perl books on the shelves back then. Kids today probably won't believe that you could walk into a bookstore in the U.S. and see hundreds of feet of shelf space devoted to computer programming, and most of that seemed to be Java and Perl. Walk into a bookstore today and the computer section might have its own corner, and each language might have a couple of books. Most of those titles probably won't be there in six months.

Despite all that, *Effective Perl Programming* hung on for over a decade. Joseph Hall's insight and wisdom toward the philosophy of Perl programming is timeless. After all, his book was about thinking in Perl more than anything else. All of his advice is still good.

However, the world of Perl is a lot different than it was in 1998, and there's a lot more good advice out there. CPAN (the Comprehensive Perl Archive Network), which was only a few years old then, is now Perl's killer feature. People have discovered new and better ways to do things, and with more than a decade of additional Perl experience, the best practices and idioms have come a long way.

---

1. Larry Wall, Tom Christiansen, and Jon Orwant, *Programming Perl, Third Edition* (Sebastopol, CA: O'Reilly Media, 2000).

2. Randal L. Schwartz, Tom Phoenix, and brian d foy, *Learning Perl, Fifth Edition* (Sebastopol, CA: O'Reilly Media, 2008).

Since the first edition of *Effective Perl Programming*, Perl has changed, too. The first edition existed during the transition from Perl 4 to Perl 5, so people were still using their old Perl 4 habits. We've mostly done away with that distinction in this edition. There is only one Perl, and it is major version 5. (Don't ask us about Perl 6. That's a different book for a different time.)

Modern Perl now handles Unicode and recognizes that the world is more than just ASCII. You need to get over that hump, too, so we've added an entire chapter on it. Perl might be one of the most-tested code bases, a trend started by Michael Schwern several years ago and now part of almost every module distribution. Gone are the days when Perlers celebrated the Wild West days of code slinging. Now you can have rapid prototyping and good testing at the same time. If you're working in the enterprise arena, you'll want to read our advice on testing. If you're a regular-expression fiend, you'll want to use all of the new regex features that the latest versions of Perl provide. We'll introduce you to the popular ones.

Perl is still growing, and new topics are always emerging. Some topics, like Moose, the post-modern Perl object system, deserve their own books, so we haven't even tried to cover them here. Other topics, like POE (Perl Object Environment), object-relational mappers, and GUI toolkits are similarly worthy, and also absent from this book. We're already thinking about *More Effective Perl*, so that might change.

Finally, the library of Perl literature is much more mature. Although we have endeavored to cover most of the stuff we think you need to know, we've left out some areas that are much better covered in other books, which we list in Appendix B. That makes space for other topics.

—*Joseph N. Hall, Joshua A. McAdams, and brian d foy*

Preface from the first edition

I used to write a lot of C and C++. My last major project before stepping into the world of Perl full time was an interpreted language that, among other things, drew diagrams, computed probabilities, and generated entire FrameMaker books. It comprised over 50,000 lines of platform-independent C++ and it had all kinds of interesting internal features. It was a fun project.

It also took two years to write.

It seems to me that most interesting projects in C and/or C++ take months or years to complete. That's reasonable, given that part of what makes an undertaking interesting is that it is complex and time-consuming. But it also seems to me that a whole lot of ideas that start out being mundane and uninteresting become interesting three-month projects when they are expressed in an ordinary high-level language.

This is one of the reasons that I originally became interested in Perl. I had heard that Perl was an excellent scripting language with powerful string-handling, regular-expression, and process-control features. All of these are features that C and C++ programmers with tight schedules learn to dread. I learned Perl, and learned to like it, when I was thrown into a project where most of my work involved slinging text files around—taking output from one piece of software and reformatting it so that I could feed it to another. I quickly found myself spending less than a day writing Perl programs that would have taken me days or weeks to write in a different language.

How and why I wrote this book

I've always wanted to be a writer. In childhood I was obsessed with science fiction. I read constantly, sometimes three paperbacks a day, and every so often wrote some (bad) stories myself. Later on, in 1985, I attended the Clarion Science Fiction & Fantasy Writers' workshop in East Lansing, Michigan. I spent a year or so occasionally working on short-story manuscripts afterward, but was never published. School and work began to consume more and more of my time, and eventually I drifted away from fiction. I continued to write, though, cranking out a technical manual, course, proposal, or paper from time to time. Also, over the years I made contact with a number of technical authors.

One of them was Randal Schwartz. I hired him as a contractor on an engineering project, and managed him for over a year. (This was my first stint as a technical manager, and it was quite an introduction to the world of management in software development, as anyone who knows Randal might guess.) Eventually he left to pursue teaching Perl full time. And after a while, I did the same.

While all this was going on, I became more interested in writing a book. I had spent the past few years working in all the "hot" areas—C++, Perl, the Internet and World Wide Web—and felt that I ought to be able to find something interesting in all that to put down on paper. Using and teaching Perl intensified this feeling. I wished I had a book that compiled the various Perl tricks and traps that I was experiencing over and over again.

Then, in May 1996, I had a conversation with Keith Wollman at a developers' conference in San Jose. I wasn't really trying to find a book to write, but we were discussing what sorts of things might be good books and what wouldn't. When we drifted onto the topic of Perl, he asked me, "What would you think of a book called *Effective Perl*?" I liked the idea. Scott Meyers's *Effective C++* was one of my favorite books on C++, and the extension of the series to cover Perl was obvious.

I couldn't get Keith's idea out of my head, and after a while, with some help from Randal, I worked out a proposal for the book, and Addison-Wesley accepted it.

The rest . . . Well, that was the fun part. I spent many 12-hour days and nights with FrameMaker in front of the computer screen, asked lots of annoying questions on the Perl 5 Porters list, looked through dozens of books and manuals, wrote many, many little snippets of Perl code, and drank many, many cans of Diet Coke and Pepsi. I even had an occasional epiphany as I discovered very basic things about Perl that I had never realized I was missing. After a while, a manuscript emerged.

This book is my attempt to share with the rest of you some of the fun and stimulation that I experienced while learning the power of Perl. I certainly appreciate you taking the time to read it, and I hope that you will find it useful and enjoyable.

—*Joseph N. Hall*
Chandler, Arizona
1998

Acknowledgments

For the second edition

Several people have helped us bring about the second edition by reading parts of the manuscript in progress and pointing out errors or adding things we hadn't considered. We'd like to thank Abigail, Patrick Abi Salloum, Sean Blanton, Kent Cowgill, Bruce Files, Mike Fraggasi, Jarkko Hietaniemi, Slaven Rezic, Andrew Rodland, Michael Stemle, and Sinan Ünür. In some places, we've acknowledged people directly next to their contribution.

Some people went much further than casual help and took us to task for almost every character. All the mistakes you don't see were caught by Elliot Shank, Paul Fenwick, and Jacinta Richardson. Anything left over is our fault: our cats must have walked on our keyboards when we weren't looking.

—*Joseph N. Hall, Joshua A. McAdams, and brian d foy*

From the first edition

This book was hard to write. I think mostly I made it hard on myself, but it would have been a lot harder had I not had help from a large cast of programmers, authors, editors, and other professionals, many of whom contributed their time for free or at grossly inadequate rates that might as well have been for free. Everyone who supported me in this effort has my appreciation and heartfelt thanks.

Chip Salzenberg and Andreas "MakeMaker" König provided a number of helpful and timely fixes to Perl bugs and misbehaviors that would have complicated the manuscript. It's hard to say enough about Chip. I've spent a little time mucking about in the Perl source code. I hold him in awe.

Many other members of the Perl 5 Porters list contributed in one way or another, either directly or indirectly. Among the most obviously helpful and insightful were Jeffrey Friedl, Chaim Frenkel, Tom Phoenix, Jon Orwant (of *The Perl Journal*), and Charlie Stross.

Randal Schwartz, author, instructor, and "Just Another Perl Hacker," was my primary technical reviewer. If you find any mistakes, e-mail him. (Just kidding.) Many thanks to Randal for lending his time and thought to this book.

Thanks also to Larry Wall, the creator of Perl, who has answered questions and provided comments on a number of topics.

I've been very lucky to work with Addison-Wesley on this project. Everyone I've had contact with has been friendly and has contributed in some significant way to the forward progress of this project. I would like to extend particular thanks to Kim Fryer, Ben Ryan, Carol Nelson, and Keith Wollman.

A number of other people have contributed comments, inspiration, and/or moral support. My friends Nick Orlans, Chris Ice, and Alan Piszcz trudged through several revisions of the incomplete manuscript. My current and former employers Charlie Horton, Patrick Reilly, and Larry Zimmerman have been a constant source of stimulation and encouragement.

Although I wrote this book from scratch, some of it by necessity parallels the description of Perl in the Perl man pages as well as *Programming Perl*. There are only so many ways to skin a cat. I have tried to be original and creative, but in some cases it was hard to stray from the original description of the language.

Many thanks to Jeff Gong, for harassing The Phone Company and keeping the T-1 alive. Jeff really knows how to keep his customers happy.

Many thanks to the sport of golf for keeping me sane and providing an outlet for my frustrations. It's fun to make the little ball go. Thanks to *Master of Orion* and *Civilization II* for much the same reasons.

Most of all, though, I have to thank Donna, my soulmate and fiancée, and also one heck of a programmer. This book would not have come into being without her seemingly inexhaustible support, patience, and love.

—*Joseph N. Hall*
1998

About the Authors

Joseph N. Hall, a self-professed "computer whiz kid," grew up with a TI programmable calculator and a Radio Shack TRS-80 Model 1 with 4K RAM. He taught his first computer class at the age of 14. Joseph holds a B.S. in computer science from North Carolina State University and has programmed for a living since 1984. He has worked in UNIX and C since 1987 and has been working with Perl since 1993. His interests include software tools and programming languages, piano and electronic keyboards, and golf.

Joshua A. McAdams has been an active member of the Perl community for nearly five years. He is the voice of *Perlcast*, hosted two YAPC::NAs in Chicago, conducts meetings for Chicago.pm, has spoken about Perl at conferences around the world, and is a CPAN (Comprehensive Perl Archive Network) author. Though this is his first book, he has authored Perl articles for *The Perl Review* and the Perl Advent Calendar. For a day job, Josh has the privilege to work at Google, where his day-to-day development doesn't always involve Perl, but he sneaks it in when he can.

brian d foy is the coauthor of *Learning Perl, Fifth Edition* (O'Reilly Media, 2008), and *Intermediate Perl* (O'Reilly Media, 2006) and the author of *Mastering Perl* (O'Reilly Media, 2007). He established the first Perl user group, the New York Perl Mongers; publishes *The Perl Review;* maintains parts of the Perl core documentation; and is a Perl trainer and speaker.

Introduction

"Learning the fundamentals of a programming language is one thing; learning how to design and write effective programs in that language is something else entirely." What Scott Meyers wrote in the Introduction to Effective C++ is just as true for Perl.

Perl is a Very High Level Language—a VHLL for the acronym-aware. It incorporates high-level functionality like regular expressions, networking, and process management into a context-sensitive grammar that is more "human," in a way, than that of other programming languages. Perl is a better text-processing language than any other widely used computer language, or perhaps any other computer language, period. Perl is an incredibly effective scripting tool for UNIX administrators, and it is the first choice of most UNIX CGI scripters worldwide. Perl also supports object-oriented programming, modular software, cross-platform development, embedding, and extensibility.

Is this book for you?

We assume that you already have some experience with Perl. If you're looking to start learning Perl, you might want to wait a bit before tackling this book. Our goal is to make you a better Perl programmer, not necessarily a new Perl programmer.

This book isn't a definitive reference, although we like to think that you'd keep it on your desktop. Many of the topics we cover can be quite complicated and we don't go into every detail. We try to give you the basics of the concepts that should satisfy most situations, but also serve as a starting point for further research if you need more. You will still need to dive into the Perl documentation and read some of the books we list in Appendix A.

There is a lot to learn about Perl.

Once you have worked your way through an introductory book or class on Perl, you have learned to write what Larry Wall, Perl's creator, fondly refers to as "baby talk." Perl baby talk is plain, direct, and verbose. It's not bad—you are allowed and encouraged to write Perl in whatever style works for you.

You may reach a point where you want to move beyond plain, direct, and verbose Perl toward something more succinct and individualistic. This book is written for people who are setting off down that path. *Effective Perl Programming* endeavors to teach you what you need to know to become a fluent and expressive Perl programmer. This book provides several different kinds of advice to help you on your way.

- **Knowledge, or perhaps, "Perl trivia."** Many complex tasks in Perl have been or can be reduced to extremely simple statements. A lot of learning to program effectively in Perl entails acquiring an adequate reservoir of experience and knowledge about the "right" ways to do things. Once you know good solutions, you can apply them to your own problems. Furthermore, once you know what good solutions look like, you can invent your own and judge their "rightness" accurately.
- **How to use CPAN.** The Comprehensive Perl Archive Network is modern Perl's killer feature. With over 5 gigabytes of Perl source code, major frameworks, and interfaces to popular libraries, you can accomplish quite a bit with work that people have already done. CPAN makes common tasks even easier with Perl. As with any language, your true skill is your ability to leverage what has already been done.
- **How to solve problems.** You may already have good analytical or debugging skills from your work in another programming language. This book teaches you how to beat your problems using Perl by showing you a lot of problems and their Perl solutions. It also teaches you how to beat the problems that Perl gives you, by showing how to efficiently create and improve your programs.
- **Style.** This book shows you idiomatic Perl style, primarily by example. You learn to write more succinct and elegant Perl. If succinctness isn't your goal, you at least learn to avoid certain awkward constructs. You also learn to evaluate your efforts and those of others.
- **How to grow further.** This book doesn't cover everything you need to know. Although we do call it a book on advanced Perl, not a whole lot of advanced Perl can fit between its covers. A real compendium of

advanced Perl would require thousands of pages. What this book is really about is how you can make yourself an advanced Perl programmer—how you can find the resources you need to grow, how to structure your learning and experiments, and how to recognize that you have grown.

We intend this as a thought-provoking book. There are subtleties to many of the examples. Anything really tricky we explain, but some other points that are simple are not always obvious. We leave those to stand on their own for your further reflection. Sometimes we focus on one aspect of the example code and ignore the surrounding bits, but we try to make those as simple as possible. Don't be alarmed if you find yourself puzzling something out for a while. Perl is an idiosyncratic language, and in many ways is very different from other programming languages you may have used. Fluency and style come only through practice and reflection. While learning is hard work, it is also enjoyable and rewarding.

The world of Perl

Perl is a remarkable language. It is, in our opinion, the most successful modular programming environment.

In fact, Perl modules are the closest things to the fabled "software ICs" (that is, the software equivalent of integrated circuits, components that can be used in various applications without understanding all of their inner workings) that the software world has seen. There are many reasons for this, one of the most important being that there is a centralized, coordinated module repository, CPAN, which reduces the amount of energy wasted on competing, incompatible implementations of functionality. See Appendix A for more resources.

Perl has a minimal but sufficient modular and object-oriented programming framework. The lack of extensive access-control features in the language makes it possible to write code with unusual characteristics in a natural, succinct form. It seems to be a natural law of software that the most-useful features are also the ones that fit existing frameworks most poorly. Perl's skeletal approach to "rules and regulations" effectively subverts this law.

Perl provides excellent cross-platform compatibility. It excels as a systems administration tool on UNIX because it hides the differences between different versions of UNIX to the greatest extent possible. Can you write cross-platform shell scripts? Yes, but with extreme difficulty. Most mere mortals should not attempt such things. Can you write cross-platform Perl scripts? Yes, easily. Perl also ports reasonably well between its UNIX birthplace and other platforms, such as Windows, VMS, and many others.

As a Perl programmer, you have some of the best support in the world. You have complete access to the source code for all the modules you use, as well as the complete source code to the language itself. If picking through the code for bugs isn't your speed, you have online support available via the Internet 24 hours a day, 7 days a week. If free support isn't your style, you can also buy commercial support.

Finally, you have a language that dares to be different. Perl is fluid. At its best, in the presence of several alternative interpretations, Perl does what you mean (sometimes seen as **DWIM**, "do what I mean"). A scary thought, perhaps, but it's an indication of true progress in computing, something that reaches beyond mere cycles, disk space, and RAM.

Terminology

In general, the terminology used with Perl isn't so different than that used to describe other programming languages. However, there are a few terms with slightly peculiar meanings. Also, as Perl has evolved, some terminology has faded from fashion and some new terminology has arisen.

In general, the name of the language is Perl, with a capital P, and `perl` is the name of the program that compiles and runs your source. Unless we are specifically referring to the interpreter, we default to using the capitalized version.

An **operator** in Perl is a nonparenthesized syntactical construct. (The arguments to an operator may, of course, be contained in parentheses.) A **list operator**, in particular, is an identifier followed by a list of elements separated by commas:

```
print "Hello", chr(44), " world!\n";
```

A **function** in Perl is an identifier followed by a pair of parentheses that completely encloses the arguments:

```
print("Hello", chr(44), " world!\n");
```

Now, you may have just noticed a certain similarity between list operators and functions. In fact, in Perl, there is no difference other than the syntax used. We will generally use the term "operator" when we refer to Perl built-ins like `print` and `open`, but may use "function" occasionally. There is no particular difference in meaning.

The proper way to refer to a subroutine written in Perl is just **subroutine**. Of course, "function," "operator," and even "procedure" will make acceptable literary stand-ins. Note that Perl's use of "function" isn't the same as the mathematical definition, and some computer scientists may shudder at Perl's abuse of the term.

All Perl **methods** are really subroutines that conform to certain conventions. These conventions are neither required nor recognized by Perl. However, it is appropriate to use phrases like "call a method," since Perl has a special method-call syntax that is used to support object-oriented programming. A good way of defining the (somewhat elusive) difference is that a method is a subroutine that the author intends you to call via method-call syntax.

A Perl **identifier** is a "C symbol"—a letter or underscore followed by one or more letters, digits, or underscores. Identifiers are used to name Perl variables. Perl variables are identifiers combined with the appropriate punctuation, as in `$a` or `&func`.

Although not strictly in keeping with the usage in the internals of Perl, we use the term **keyword** to refer to the small number of identifiers in Perl that have distinctive syntactical meanings—for example, `if` and `while`. Other identifiers that have ordinary function or operator syntax, such as `print` and `oct`, we call **built-ins**, if anything.

An **lvalue** (pronounced "ell value") is a value that can appear on the left-hand side of an assignment statement. This is the customary meaning of the term; however, there are some unusual constructs that act as lvalues in Perl, such as the `substr` operator.

Localizing a variable means creating a separate scope for it that applies through the end of the enclosing block or file. Special variables must be localized with the `local` operator. You can localize ordinary variables with either `my` or `local` (see Item 43 in Chapter 4). This is an unfortunate legacy of Perl, and Larry Wall wishes he had used another name for `local`, but life goes on. We say "localize with `my`" when it makes a difference.

Notation

In this book we use Joseph's PEGS (PErl Graphical Structures) notation to illustrate data structures. It should be mostly self-explanatory, but here is a brief overview.

Variables are values with names. The name appears in a sideways "picket" above the value. A scalar value is represented with a single rectangular box:

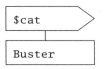

Arrays and lists have a similar graphical representation. Values are shown in a stack with a thick bar on top:

```
   @cats
  ┌────────────┐
  │ Buster     │
  ├────────────┤
  │ Mimi       │
  ├────────────┤
  │ Ginger     │
  ├────────────┤
  │ Ella       │
  └────────────┘
```

A hash is represented with a stack of names next to a stack of corresponding values:

```
   %microchips
  ┌──────────────┬────────┐
  │ Mimi      ╲  │ 9874   │
  ├──────────────┼────────┤
  │ Ginger    ╲  │ 5207   │
  ├──────────────┼────────┤
  │ Buster    ╲  │ 1435   │
  ├──────────────┼────────┤
  │ Ella      ╲  │ 3004   │
  └──────────────┴────────┘
```

References are drawn with dots and arrows as in those LISP diagrams from days of yore:

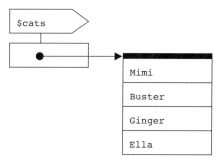

That's all there is to the basics.

Perl style

Part of what you should learn from this book is a sense of good Perl style.

Style is, of course, a matter of preference and debate. We won't pretend to know or demonstrate The One True Style, but we hope to show readers one example of contemporary, efficient, effective Perl style. Sometimes our style is inconsistent when that aids readability. Most of our preference comes from the *perlstyle* documentation.

The fact that the code appears in a book affects its style somewhat. We're limited in line lengths, and we don't want to write overly long programs that stretch across several pages. Our examples can't be too verbose or boring—each one has to make one or two specific points without unnecessary clutter. Therefore, you will find some deviations from good practice.

In some examples, we want to highlight certain points and de-emphasize others. In some code, we use . . . to stand in for code that we've left out. Assume that the . . . stands for real code that should be there. (Curiously, by the time this book hits the bookstores, that . . . should also be compilable Perl. Perl 5.12 introduces the "yadda yadda" operator, which compiles just fine, but produces a run time error when you try to execute it. It's a nice way to stub out code.)

Some examples need certain versions of Perl. Unless we specify otherwise, the code should run under Perl 5.8, which is an older but serviceable version. If we use a Perl 5.10 feature, we start the example with a line that notes the version (see Item 2 in Chapter 1):

```
use 5.010;
```

We also ignore development versions of Perl, where the minor version is an odd number, such as 5.009 and 5.011. We note the earliest occurrence of features in the first stable version of Perl that introduces it.

Not everything runs cleanly under `warnings` or `strict` (Item 3). We advise all Perl programmers to make use of both of these regularly. However, starting all the examples with those declarations may distract from our main point, so we leave them off. Where appropriate, we try to be `strict` clean, but plucking code out of bigger examples doesn't always make that practical.

We generally minimize punctuation (Item 18). We're not keen on "Perl golf," where people reduce their programs to as few characters as they can. We just get rid of the unnecessary characters and use more whitespace so the important bits stand out and the scaffolding fades into the background.

Finally, we try to make the examples meaningful. Not every example can be a useful snippet, but we try to include as many pieces of real-world code as possible.

Organization

The first two chapters generally present material in order of increasing complexity. Otherwise, we tend to jump around quite a bit. Use the table of contents and the index, and keep the Perl documentation close at hand (perhaps by visiting http://perldoc.perl.org/).

We reorganized the book for the second edition. Appendix B shows a mapping from Items in the first edition to Items in this edition. We split some first-edition Items into many new ones and expanded them; some we combined; and some we left out, since their topics are well covered in other books. Appendix A contains a list of additional resources we think you should consider.

The book doesn't really stop when you get to the end. We're going to keep going at http://effectiveperlprogramming.com/. There you can find more news about the book, some material we left out, material we didn't have time to finish for the book, and other Perl goodies.

1 | The Basics of Perl

If you are experienced in other languages but new to Perl, you are probably still discovering Perl's idiosyncrasies. This section deals with some of those idiosyncrasies. In particular, it addresses those that can bedevil newly minted Perl programmers who are still attuned to other languages.

For example, you should already know that a Perl variable is generally made up of some mark of punctuation like `$` or `@` followed by an identifier. But do you know whether different types of variables with the same name, such as `$a` and `@a`, are completely independent of one another? They are (see Item 5 in this chapter).

You should know that `@a` is an array, but do you know the difference between `$a[$i]` and `@a[$i]`? The latter is a slice (Item 9).

You should know that the number `0` is false, and that the empty string, `' '`, is false, but do you know whether the string consisting of a single space, `' '`, is false? It's true (Item 7).

Perl has many other interesting quirks that reflect its heritage of stealing the best from many other languages, with the addition of some uncommon ideas from its linguist creator, Larry Wall. Once you start to think as Perl thinks, however, these quirks make much more sense.

If you are an experienced Perl programmer, these basic items will be mostly review for you. However, you may find some interesting details that you haven't caught before, or perhaps other ways to explain concepts to your colleagues.

Item 1. Find the documentation for Perl and its modules.

Perl comes with a lot of documentation—more than you'd ever want to put on paper. You'd use a couple of reams of paper and a lot of toner to print it all. We lost count after the documentation got to be around 2,000 pages (on our virtual printer, so no trees harmed).

There is a huge amount of useful information in the documentation files, so it pays to be able to read them, but even more than that, to find information in them. Part of the ability to find what you need is knowledge, and part of it is tools.

The `perldoc` reader

The `perldoc` command searches the Perl tree for Perl modules (*.pm*) with embedded documentation, documentation-only *.pod* files (Item 82), and installed Perl programs. The `perldoc` command formats and displays the documentation it finds. To start, read `perldoc`'s own documentation:

```
% perldoc perldoc
PERLDOC(1) User Contributed Perl Documentation


NAME
        C<perldoc> - Look up Perl documentation in pod format.


SYNOPSIS
        C<perldoc> [-h] [-v] [-t] [-u] [-m] [-l]
... etc. ...
```

In general, you give `perldoc` the name of the documentation page you want to read. The *perltoc* is the table of contents that shows you all of the page names:

```
% perldoc perltoc
```

You might be interested in *perlsyn*, the page that discusses general Perl syntax:

```
% perldoc perlsyn
```

If you want to read about Perl built-ins, you look in *perlfunc*:

```
% perldoc perlfunc
```

You should read through *perlfunc* at least once just to see all that Perl has to offer. You don't have to remember everything, but you might later remember that Perl has a built-in to, say, interact with the /etc/passwd file even if you don't remember what that built-in is called. You'll also notice that it's extremely annoying to scroll through the output to find the built-in that you need. If you know the built-in that you want to read about, specify it along with the `-f` switch, which pulls out just the part for that function:

```
% perldoc -f split
```

You can also read module documentation with `perldoc`; just give it the module name:

```
% perldoc Pod::Simple
```

If you wonder where that module is installed, you can use the `-l` (letter ell) switch to get the file location:

```
% perldoc -l Pod::Simple
```

If you want to see the raw source, use the `-m` switch:

```
% perldoc -m Pod::Simple
```

The Perl documentation comes with several FAQ files that answer many common questions. You can read through them online, but `perldoc` also has a nice feature to search them with the `-q` switch. If you wanted to find answers that deal with random numbers, for example, you can try:

```
% perldoc -q random
```

Online documentation

As we write this, http://perldoc.perl.org/ is the best site for Perl documentation. It contains the core documentation that comes with the last several versions Perl as HTML and PDF, and it's smart enough to remember documentation that you've looked at before.

That site doesn't have all of the module documentation files, though. You can read those online at CPAN Search (http://search.cpan.org/) or Kobes's Search (http://kobesearch.cpan.org/), both of which give you a Web interface to CPAN. Some people find this documentation so convenient that they'll read it before they check their local systems.

CPAN Search is especially useful in that it provides "Other tools," a link that you'll find on each module page. One of those tools is a `grep`-like feature that lets you search the documentation inside a single distribution. That can be quite handy for tracking down the file giving you an error message, for instance.

AnnoCPAN (http://annocpan.org/) is another site for module documentation. On this site, any person can annotate the docs, leaving notes for the module authors or other people. This is especially handy when the documentation is missing information or has incorrect or incomplete information.

Local documentation

You can get some of the features of CPAN Search on your local system. The `CPAN::Mini::Webserver` provides a way to browse your MiniCPAN (Item 66). If you run an Apache Web server, the `Apache::Perldoc` module can act as your Web front end to the `perldoc` command.

The `Pod::POM::Web` module can also let you browse your local documentation. You can set it up under Apache as a mod_perl handler, as a CGI script, or as its own Web server:

```
% perl -MPod::POM::Web -e "Pod::POM::Web->server"
```

Things to remember

- Use `perldoc` to read Perl's documentation.
- Read uninstalled-module documentation on the Web.
- Set up a local documentation server to read local documentation with your Web browser.

Item 2. Enable new Perl features when you need them.

Starting with Perl 5.10, you must explicitly enable new features. This ensures that the latest release of Perl can be backward compatible while at the same time letting people start new work using all of the latest nifty features.

For instance, Perl 5.10 adds a `say` built-in that is just like `print` except that it adds the trailing newline for you. Not only is your string a couple of characters shorter, but you don't have to double-quote the string just for the newline:

```
say 'Hello!';  # just like print "Hello\n";
```

If someone had already created their own `say`, their program might break if they run it with Perl 5.10 using the now built-in with the same name. Fortunately, Perl doesn't enable new features by default:

```
% perl5.10.1 say.pl    # doesn't use new features

String found where operator expected at old_script.pl ⏎
   line 1, near "say "Hello!""
      (Do you need to predeclare say?)
```

If you want the new features, you can enable them with the new -E switch. It's just like the -e that lets you specify your program text on the command line, but it also brings in the all of the latest features for your version of Perl:

```
% perl5.10.1 -E say.pl   # use new features up to 5.10.1

% perl5.12.0 -E say.pl   # use new features up to 5.12.0
```

You can also enable the features inside the program text. With the `use` directive followed by a Perl version, not only do you ensure that people run your program with a compatible version (Item 83), but you also enable the new features for that version:

```
use 5.010; # use new features up to 5.10
```

Starting with Perl 5.12, you can automatically turn on strictures (Item 3) by requiring that version or later:

```
use 5.012; # automatically turns on strict
```

Whenever we want to use features specific to a version of Perl, we'll include a similar line in the example to let you know.

Another way to pull in features is with the `feature` pragma, also introduced with Perl 5.10. You can give it a "feature bundle" to tell it which set of features to enable:

```
use feature ':5.10';
```

You might not want to enable every new feature. You can control which new features you use with the `feature` pragma. For instance, you can limit `feature` to activating only `switch` and `say`:

```
use feature qw(switch say);
```

It's odd that you import `switch` although Perl's version of that idea uses the keywords `given-when` (Item 24). It's a holdover from C jargon.

Things to remember

- Starting with Perl 5.10, explicitly enable new features if you want to use them.
- Use the `-E` command-line switch to enable all new features.
- Use the `use VERSION` sequence to require at least that version of Perl and enable all new features as of that version.

Item 3. Enable strictures to promote better coding.

Perl is, by default, a very permissive language. You can quickly throw together some statements with a minimum of fuss. Perl takes care of most of the details with as little typing from you as possible. It's a feature.

That permissiveness, however, isn't so attractive a feature for larger programs where you'd like Perl to help you manage your coding. The `strict` pragma makes Perl much less permissive. In all of your Perl files, add this line:

```
use strict;
```

If you are using Perl 5.12 or later, you can automatically enable strictures by requiring that version or later (Item 2):

```
use 5.012;   # use strict enabled automatically
```

By enabling strictures, you've just caught most of the common errors that programmers make. Most of the rest you can catch with `warnings` (Item 99). These features might be annoying for a couple of weeks, but bit by bit your coding will improve, and `strict` will become less-and-less annoying until you don't even realize that it is there.

If you're translating legacy code that is not `strict`-safe, you might start by enabling it on the command line to see all of the errors before you commit to it:

```
perl -Mstrict program.pl
```

There are three parts to strictures: `vars`, `subs`, and `refs`. Normally you use all three of them together, but we will cover them separately.

Declare your variables

Misspellings are an all-too-common source of errors in Perl programs. You put your data in one variable, but then use the wrong variable name later. In the following example, you read into @temp but then try to iterate through @tmp. You're puzzled that you don't see any output, and no matter how much you look at the source, you can't see the problem:

```
my @temp = <FH>;
foreach (@tmp) {  # OOPS -- meant to use @temp
  print "Found $_\n";
}
```

The strict vars pragma catches and prevents such errors by making you declare all of your variables in some fashion. There are three ways you can declare a variable. You can declare it with my or our:

```
use strict 'vars';


my @temp;
our $temp;
```

Use the full package specification:

```
use strict 'vars';


$main::name = 'Buster';
```

Or list variables in use vars:

```
use strict 'vars';
use vars qw($bar);
$bar = 5;
```

You never have to declare the special variables—$_, %ENV, and so on. Additionally, strict ignores the global versions of $a and $b, which are special for sort (Item 22). Any other variable that Perl sees triggers a fatal error at compile time.

Be careful with barewords

Perl's default treatment of identifiers with no other interpretation as strings (sometimes called "poetry mode") is another potential source of errors that are hard to spot by visual inspection. Can you spot the error in the following code?

```
for ( $i = 0 ; $i < 10 ; $i++ ) {
  print $a[i];   # OOPS -- meant to say $a[$i]
}
```

The subscript i, which should have been $i, is interpreted as the string "i", which is interpreted in this context to have a numeric value of 0. Thus, the contents of $a[0] are printed ten times. Using strict 'subs' turns off poetry mode and generates errors for inappropriately used identifiers:

```
use strict 'subs';

for ( $i = 0 ; $i < 10 ; $i++ ) {
  print $a[i];   # ERROR
}
```

The strict 'subs' pragma gets along with the sanctioned forms of bare-word quoting—alone inside hash-key braces, or to the left of the fat arrow:

```
use strict 'subs';

$a{name} = 'ok';    # bareword as hash key is OK
$a{-name} = 'ok';   # also OK
my %h = (
  last  => 'Smith',   # bareword left of => is OK
  first => 'Jon'
);
```

Avoid soft references

The strict refs pragma disables soft references (Item 58). Soft references aren't often a source of bugs, but they aren't a widely used feature either. They happen when you try to dereference something that is really a string. Without strictures, Perl uses the value in the string as the name of the variable:

```
no strict 'refs';

$not_array_ref = 'buster';
@{$not_array_ref} = qw( 1 2 3 );   # really @buster
```

Things to remember

- By default, Perl is a very permissive programming language.
- Don't make Perl guess what you mean when you can be explicit.
- Enable `strict` to let Perl catch common programming problems.

Item 4. Understand what sigils are telling you.

Sigils are those funny characters you see at the fronts of Perl variable names and in dereferencing, and are often the source of people's confusion about Perl syntax. Programmers confuse themselves because they guess at what sigils tell them, read incorrect guesses about them on mailing lists, or have learned Perl from a tarot-card reader. People are afraid of them when, in reality, sigils are their best friends.

The sigil is only very loosely related to the variable type itself. In fact, you don't even need to have a variable. Don't think of them as variable type indicators at all.

The `$` means you are working with a single value, which can be a scalar variable or a single element accessed in an array or hash:

```
$scalar

$array[3]

$hash{'key'}
```

The `@` means you are working with multiple values, so you'll use it with arrays or hashes, since they are the only collection types Perl has:

```
@array

@array[0,2,6] # an array slice

@hash{ qw(key1 key2) } # a hash slice
```

The `%` sign is a bit special. It means you're treating something as a hash, and there is only one variable type and access method that can act as a hash, which is the whole hash itself:

```
%hash
```

Perl also has sigils for subroutines (`&`) and typeglobs (`*`), but they are used only for those types, so we won't bother with them here.

Now that you know not to use sigils to recognize variable types, how do you know what sort of variable you're looking at? There are three factors to consider: the sigil, the identifier, and possible indexing syntax for arrays or hashes. You can see all three in a single-element access to an array:

```
SIGIL   IDENTIFIER   INDEX

  $         name       [3]


  $name[3]
```

The sigil is $, the identifier is name, and the indexing is [3]. You know that the variable is name, and you know that it's an array variable because that's the only type that uses [ ] for indexing. You do the same thing for hashes:

```
SIGIL   IDENTIFIER    INDEX

  $         name      {'Buster'}


  $name{'Buster'}
```

You know that you are working with a hash variable because you use the { } for indexing and because you use a string for the index. The $ tells you only that this variable contains a single element from the hash.

If you don't see a single-element access, you can determine the variable type by looking at the sigil:

```
$scalar

@array

%hash
```

You also use sigils to dereference anonymous scalars, arrays, and hashes. You use the same rules to figure out the reference type (Item 59).

Things to remember

- Sigils relate to the data, not necessarily the variable type.
- The $ indicates a single element.
- The @ indicates a list of elements.

Item 5. Know your variable namespaces.

There are seven separate kinds of package variables or variable-like elements in Perl: scalar variables, array variables, hash variables, subroutine names, format names, filehandles, and directory handles.

Each of these different kinds of package variables has its own namespace. Changing the value of one kind of variable does not in any way affect the value of another kind of variable with the same name. For example, the scalar variable $a is independent of the array variable @a:

```
my $a = 1;              # set scalar $a = 1
my @a = ( 1, 2, 3 );    # @a = (1,2,3) but $a is still 1
```

Also, each package in a Perl program defines its own set of namespaces. For example, $a in package main is independent of $a in package foo:

```
$a = 1;        # set scalar $main::a = 1
package foo;   # default package is now foo
$a = 3.1416;   # $foo::a is 3.1416; $main::a still 1
```

You have to look to the right as well as the left of an identifier, as Perl does, to determine what kind of variable the identifier refers to. For example, the syntax for accessing single elements of arrays and hashes begins with $, not @ or %. The $ means that the result is a scalar value, not that you are referring to a scalar variable (Item 4):

```
my $a = 1;
my @a = ( 1, 2, 3 );
my %a = ( a => 97, b => 98 );
$a[3]    = 4;   # $a is still 1; @a is (1,2,3,4) now
$a{'c'} = 99;   # $a, @a still the same;
                # %a has three key-value pairs now
```

Not all variable-like items in Perl are prefixed with punctuation characters. Subroutine names can be prefixed with ampersand (&), but the ampersand is generally optional. The parentheses around subroutine arguments can also be omitted in some cases, as in the following example.

Define a subroutine named "hi" to see the different ways you can call it:

```
sub hi {
  my $name = shift;
  return "hi, $name\n";
}
```

You can call the subroutine using the "old-style" syntax, including the ampersand and the parentheses:

```
print &hi("Fred");
```

This style isn't seen as often in new code. Instead, you'll see subroutines called with only parentheses:

```
print hi("Fred");
```

The parentheses give perl enough information to know that hi is a subroutine. If hi has been declared or defined before you use it, even the parentheses are optional:

```
print hi "Fred";
```

Filehandles, format names, and directory handles are not prefixed with punctuation characters, but are recognized in context. The filehandle, directory handle, and format name are independent of one another, even though they are all named TEST:

```
open TEST, '>', "$$.test"   # open filehandle TEST
print TEST "test data\n";    # print to filehandle TEST

opendir TEST, ".";           # directory handle named TEST

# format named TEST
format TEST = @<<<<<<<<<<<<< @<<<< @<<<<
$name, $lo, $hi
.
```

If this seems like it can get confusing, it can. Luckily, it is now common for people to store filehandles and directory handles in objects, thanks to IO::File and IO::Dir.

Things to remember

- Each variable type has its own namespace.
- Different types of variables with the same name don't affect each other.
- Variables in different packages can have the same name but not affect each other.

Item 6. Know the difference between string and numeric comparisons.

Perl has two completely different sets of comparison operators, one for comparing strings and one for comparing numbers. It's worthwhile to know the difference and to keep them straight, since using the wrong comparison operator can be a source of hard-to-find bugs.

The operators used to compare strings use letters and look like words, or like FORTRAN. Strings are compared character-by-character—that is, by comparing the values of the characters in the strings (or by the current locale, if you have use locale), including case, spaces, and the like:

```
'a' lt 'b'              # TRUE
'a' eq 'A'              # FALSE -- capitalization
"joseph" eq "joseph "  # FALSE -- spaces count
```

Numeric comparison operators use punctuation and look like algebra, or like C:

```
0   <   5   # TRUE
10 == 10.0  # TRUE
```

String-comparison operators should not be used for comparing numbers since they don't compare numbers properly (unless your definition of "properly" puts "10" before "2"). The same applies for numeric operators used to compare strings:

```
'10' gt '2'     # FALSE -- '1' sorts before '2'
"10.0" eq "10"  # FALSE -- different strings
'abc' == 'def'  # TRUE -- both look like 0 to ==
```

The kind of mistake this leads to is conditionals that are true when you don't want them to be since both operands turn into numbers:

```
my $hacker = 'joebloe';

if ( $user == $hacker ) {  # WRONG -- == used on strings
  deny_access();
}
```

Perl's sort operator uses string comparisons by default. Don't use string comparisons to sort numbers (Item 22)!

One way around the confusion of eq and == is to avoid both of them. Instead of getting it right, let Perl think about it for you by using the smart match operator, ~~ (Item 23). It looks on either side and figures out what to do. It also uses the idea of "numish" strings—strings that look like numbers.

These comparisons are really numeric comparisons because the smart match sees a number on the righthand side, or it sees a number on the lefthand side and a numish string on the righthand side, causing the comparison to be performed with the == operator:

```
use 5.010;

if ( 123      ~~ '456' ) { ... } # Number and numish: FALSE
if ( '123.0' ~~ 123 )   { ... } # String and number: TRUE
if ( 'Mimi'   ~~ 456 )   { ... } # String and number: FALSE
```

Otherwise, the smart match will make a string comparison using the eq operator:

```
if ( 'Mimi' ~~ 'Mimi' ) { ... }  # String and string: TRUE
```

This can be a little tricky. Numish strings on both sides are still a string comparison (eq operator):

```
if ( '123.0' ~~ '123' ) { ... } # numish and numish: FALSE
```

You need to be careful when you use variables with smart match, since their history in the program matters. If you previously did something to $var to trigger a conversion (Item 8), you might get unexpected results as the smart match chooses the wrong comparison type. In the following cases, you start with a string but convert it to a number by using it with a numeric operator, forcing a numeric comparison with the == operator:

```
use 5.010;

if ( ( '123' + 0 ) ~~ '123.0' ) { # Number and numish: TRUE
  say "Matched 1!";
}

my $var = '123';
if ( ( $var + 0 ) ~~ '123.0' ) { # Number and numish: TRUE
  say "Matched 2!";
}
```

```
my $var2 = '123';
$var2 + 0;
if ( $var2 ~~ '123.0' ) {  # Number and numish: TRUE
  say "Matched 3!";
}
```

However, if you start with a number but make it into a string, Perl sees it only as a string and forces `eq` semantics on it.

```
use 5.010;

my $var3 = 123;
$var3 = "$var3";
if ( $var3 ~~ '123.0' ) {  # string and numish, eq, FALSE
  say "Matched 4!";
}
```

Things to remember

- Remember that strings and numbers compare and sort differently.
- Use the letter comparison operators to compare strings.
- Use the symbol comparison operators to compare numbers.

Item 7. Know which values are false and test them accordingly.

Since numeric and string data in Perl have the same scalar type, and since Boolean operations can be applied to any scalar value, Perl's test for logical truth has to work for both numbers and strings.

The basic test is this: `0`, `'0'`, `undef`, and `''` (the empty string) are false. Everything else is true.

More precisely, when you use a quantity in **Boolean context** (a term sometimes used to refer to conditionals in control expressions, such as the `?:` operator, `||`, and `&&`), it is first converted to a string (Item 8). Perl then tests the string result. If the result is the empty string, or a string consisting exactly of the single character `'0'`, the result is false. Otherwise, the result is true. Note that this rule means that `undef` will evaluate as false, since it always looks like `0` or the empty string to everything except the `defined` operator.

This generally works very well. If problems arise, it's probably because you tested a quantity to see if it is false when really you should have tested to see if it is defined:

```
while ( my $file = glob('*') ) {   # WRONG
  do_something($file);
}
```

That `glob` works well almost all of the time. Each time through the loop, the `glob('*')` produces another filename from the current directory, which goes into `$file`. Once `glob` has gone through all the filenames in the directory, it returns `undef`, which appears to be the empty string and therefore false, causing the while loop to terminate.

There is one problem, though. If there is a file named `0` in the current directory, it also appears to be false, causing the loop to terminate early. To avoid this, use the `defined` operator to test specifically for `undef`:

```
while ( defined( my $file = glob('*') ) ) {   # CORRECT
  do_something($file);
}
```

The situation is exactly the same for the line-input operator, `<>`, although Perl does this for you automatically. It looks like you're testing the line from STDIN in this `while`:

```
while (<STDIN>) {
  do_something($_);
}
```

However, this is a special case in which Perl automatically converts to check `$_` for definedness:

```
while ( defined( $_ = <STDIN> ) ) {   # implicitly done
  do_something($_);
}
```

You can verify this for yourself with `B::Deparse`, which undoes the result of `perl`'s compilation so you can see what it thought of your code:

```
% perl -MO=Deparse \
    -e 'while( <STDIN> ) { do_something($_) }'
while (defined($_ = <STDIN>)) {
    do_something($_);
```

```
}
-e syntax OK
```

If you want to use another variable to hold the line you just read, you have to do the `defined` check yourself:

```
while ( defined( my $line = <STDIN> ) ) {
  do_something($line);
}
```

The end of the array

The mere fact that an array element is not defined doesn't mean that you've gone beyond the bounds of the array. Normally, Perl is very tolerant of out-of-bounds accesses that make other languages cranky:

```
my @cats = qw( Buster Roscoe Mimi );
my $favorite = $cats[8];  # there's no cat there, so undef
```

It's perfectly fine to have an `undef` value in the middle of an array, too:

```
my @cats = qw( Buster Roscoe Mimi );
$cats[1] = undef;  # R.I.P. Roscoe
```

You don't want to use the value to decide whether you have gone through each element of the array:

```
while ( defined( my $cat = shift @cats ) ) {  # WRONG
  print "I have a cat named $cat\n";
}
```

Instead, ensure that you go through all of the elements by using `foreach`, and skip those that aren't defined:

```
foreach my $cat (@cats) {
  next unless defined $cat;
  print "I have a cat named $cat\n";
}
```

If you need to know the last element of the array, don't look for `undef` values. The `$#cats` syntax gives you the last element.

```
for ( my $i = 0 ; $i <= $#cats ; $i += 2 ) {
  next unless defined $cat[$i];
  print "I have a cat named $cat[$i]\n";
}
```

Hash values

You may also need to use a different testing strategy to check whether an element is present inside a hash, as `undef` is a perfectly acceptable value in a hash. Suppose `%hash` is undefined to start. Checking for the key `foo` results in false as a value, with `defined`, and with `exists`:

```
my %hash;

if ( $hash{'foo'} )          { ... }  # FALSE
if ( defined $hash{'foo'} ) { ... }  # also FALSE
if ( exists $hash{'foo'} )  { ... }  # also FALSE
```

Once you assign to a key, even with a false or undefined value, the key exists:

```
$hash{'foo'} = undef;  # assign an undef value

if ( $hash{'foo'} )          { ... }  # still FALSE
if ( defined $hash{'foo'} ) { ... }  # still FALSE
if ( exists $hash{'foo'} )  { ... }  # now TRUE

print keys %hash;                     # ('foo')
```

Assigning a defined value, even if it is false, makes the value defined:

```
$hash{'foo'} = '';

if ( $hash{'foo'} )          { ... }  # still FALSE
if ( defined $hash{'foo'} ) { ... }  # now TRUE
if ( exists $hash{'foo'} )  { ... }  # now TRUE
```

Before you test hash-element access, figure out what you really want to test. There isn't one right answer; it depends on how you want to handle the value.

Things to remember

- There are four false values: `undef`, `''`, `0`, and `'0'`.
- Everything other than the four false values is true.
- Ensure you test for the type of value that you want, not just truth.

Item 8. Understand conversions between strings and numbers.

Perl's scalar variables can contain either string or numeric data. They can also contain both at the same time, usually as the result of converting string data to a number, or vice versa.

Perl automatically converts values from numeric to string representation, or vice versa, as required. For example, if a string appears next to a numeric operator like +, Perl converts the string value to a number before proceeding with the arithmetic. If a number is the object of a pattern match, Perl first converts the number to a string.

Places where Perl expects strings are called **string contexts**, and places where Perl expects numbers are called **numeric contexts**. These are nice terms to know, but we won't use them very often in this book, since it rarely makes any real difference.

The function Perl uses to convert numbers to strings is the C standard library's `sprintf()` with a format of `"%.20g"`. If you need to use a particular format, use Perl's `sprintf`:

```
my $n = sprintf "%10.4e", 3.1415927;   # "3.1416e+00"
```

The function used for converting strings to numbers is the C standard library's `atof()`. Any leading white space is ignored. Perl uses whatever leading part of the string appears number-like and ignores the rest. Perl converts anything that doesn't look like a number to 0. For example:

```
my $n = 0 + "123";        # 123
my $n = 0 + "123abc";     # also 123 -- trailing stuff
                          # ignored
my $n = 0 + "\n123";      # also 123 -- leading whitespace
my $n = 0 + "a123";       # 0 -- no number at beginning
my $n = 0 + "\x{2165}";   # 0 -- Roman numerals aren't
                          # numbers
```

The conversion process does not recognize octal or hexadecimal. Use the `oct` operator to convert octal or hexadecimal strings:

```
my $n = 0 + "0x123";        # 0 -- looks like number 0
my $n = 0 + oct("0x123");   # 291 -- oct converts octal
                            # and hex to decimal

print "mode (octal): ";     # prompt for file mode
```

```
chmod <STDIN>, $file;          # WRONG -- string from STDIN
                               # is interpreted as decimal,
                               # not octal

print "mode (octal): ";        # prompt for file mode
chmod oct(<STDIN>), $file;     # RIGHT -- mode string converted
                               # to octal
```

When Perl automatically converts a number to a string or vice versa, it keeps both representations until the value of the variable is changed.

Strings and numbers at the same time

Usually, it does not matter whether a variable contains a string or a numeric value, but there are a few occasions when it does. For example, the bitwise numeric operators act on the whole numeric value if applied to a number, but character-wise if applied to a string:

```
my $a = 123;
my $b = 234;
my $c = $a & $b;   # number 106

$a = "$a";
$b = "$b";
my $d = $a & $b;   # string "020"
```

You can see this at work with the Devel::Peek module. Start with a string that has a value that partially converts to a number, and then use it in a numerical operation (without changing it):

```
use Devel::Peek qw(Dump);

my $a = '12fred34';   # converts to 12

print STDERR "Before conversion: ";
Dump($a);

my $b = $a + 0;

print STDERR "After conversion: ";
Dump($a);

print STDERR "\n$a\n";
```

The Dump output shows you what Perl is tracking. Although we're not going to get into Perl internals, you can see that before the conversion, Perl has a PV slot where it stores the actual string value. After the conversion, it also has IV and NV slots where it stores the converted numeric value:

```
Before conversion: SV = PV(0x801038) at 0x80e770
  REFCNT = 1
  FLAGS = (PADMY,POK,pPOK)
  PV = 0x204c10 "12fred34"\0
  CUR = 8
  LEN = 12

After conversion: SV = PVNV(0x8023c0) at 0x80e770
  REFCNT = 1
  FLAGS = (PADMY,IOK,NOK,POK,pIOK,pNOK,pPOK)
  IV = 12
  NV = 12
  PV = 0x204c10 "12fred34"\0
  CUR = 8
  LEN = 12
```

The error variable $! is an example of a variable with a "magic" property. It returns the value of the system variable errno when it is used in a numeric context, but it returns the string from the perror() function (or some equivalent for your system) in a string context:

```
open "";        # invalid file name; should produce
                # an error
print "$!\n";   # "No such file or directory"
print 0 + $!, "\n";   # "2" (or whatever)
```

This issue also affects the smart match operator (Item 23) that is implicitly used by given-when (Item 24). Since the smart match guesses what sort of comparison it needs to do, it might make unexpected choices. In this example, you test two strings using the smart match operator, expecting that it will match only the same string:

```
use 5.010;

for my $s ( '137', ' 137' ) {
  given ($s) {
    when ('137')  { say "$s matches '137'"; continue }
```

```
    when (' 137') { say "$s matches ' 137'" }
  }
}
```

The output shows that the strings match only exactly themselves:

```
137 matches '137'
 137 matches ' 137'
```

However, a slight modification to the program changes the results. If you use the string in an arithmetic expression, even without changing the string explicitly, the smart match does a numeric comparison instead of a string comparison:

```
use 5.010;

for my $s ( '137', ' 137' ) {
  my $t = $s + 0;
  given ($s) {
    when ('137')  { say "$s matches '137'"; continue }
    when (' 137') { say "$s matches ' 137'" }
  }
}
```

Now you get more matches than you expect:

```
137 matches '137'
137 matches ' 137'
 137 matches '137'
 137 matches ' 137'
```

Create your own dualvar

You don't need to use Perl's internal conversion to create "dualvars"—variables that have different string and numeric values depending on context. Here's a subroutine that returns both a numeric error code and an error string, all in one normal scalar value:

```
use Scalar::Util qw(dualvar);

sub some_sub {

  # ...
```

```
  if ($error) {
    return dualvar( -1,
      'You are not allowed to do that' );
  }
}

my $return_value = some_sub();
```

The variable `$return_value` keeps its distinct numeric and string values until you change it. However, now that you know this, don't start using it everywhere. Save it for very special situations, like impressing people at conferences and cocktail parties.

Things to remember

- Perl uses a scalar as a string or number based on context.
- Perl converts a string to a number using its best guess.
- If a string doesn't look like a number, Perl converts it to 0.

Item 9. Know the difference between lists and arrays.

Lists and arrays are different things. If you can recognize when you have one or the other, along with the rules that apply to each, you'll be far ahead of most people (and even most Perl books, for that matter). Some of the most powerful idioms in Perl depend on this difference.

A list is an ordered collection of scalars. You can construct lists yourself, get them as return values from built-ins and subroutines, or extract them from other lists.

An array is a variable that contains a list, but isn't the list itself. It's a container for the list.

Part of the confusion comes from a shared syntax. You can extract single elements from both a list and an array using the same syntax:

```
(localtime)[5];  # the year

$array[5];
```

You can also slice both a list and an array with the same syntax:

```
(localtime)[ 5, 4, 3 ];  # the year, month, and day


@array[ 5, 4, 3 ];
```

The comma operator

Although you can have an array, which is a variable, in a scalar context, there's no such thing as a list in scalar context. If you use an array in a scalar context, you get the number of elements in the array:

```
my @array = qw( Buster Mimi Roscoe );
my $count = @array;                      # 3
```

A list is always only a list. It has no scalar interpretation. Consider how you construct a list. You separate a series of scalars with the comma operator (yes, it's an operator):

```
( 'Buster', 'Mimi', 'Roscoe' )
```

Is that a list? Well, you really don't know yet. You have to use that series of scalars in an expression that expects a list. Assigning it to an array or using it in a `foreach` loop provides a list context:

```
my @cats = ( 'Buster', 'Mimi', 'Roscoe' );


foreach ( qw( Buster Mimi Roscoe ) ) {
   ...;
}
```

(The `qw()` quoting doesn't change anything. It's just a syntactic shortcut.)

What if you assign the same literal text to a scalar variable? Do you have a list then? What shows up in `$scalar`?

```
my $scalar = ( 'Buster', 'Mimi', 'Roscoe' );
my $scalar = qw( Buster Mimi Roscoe );
```

Many people guess that `$scalar` gets the value 3 because they think they have a three-item list. But they don't have a list on the righthand side; they have a series of scalars separated by the comma operator. The comma operator in scalar context returns its rightmost element. Perl assigns the value `Roscoe` to `$scalar`.

People mess up this concept because they test it incorrectly. What's a common list to try?

```
my $scalar = ( 1, 2, 3 );
```

In this case, the number of scalars on the righthand side just happens to be the same as the last element on the righthand side, but you still do not have a list.

Assignment in list context

Another dark corner of Perl is the assignment operator. Most people think they understand it, but don't realize that it has a result just like any other operator. In list context, the assignment operator returns the number of elements on the righthand side. It doesn't *assign* that; it's just the return value, which hardly anyone ever uses for anything:

```
my $elements = my @array = localtime;
```

The assignment operator is right associative, so the rightmost assignment operator does its work first, assigning the list produced by `localtime` to `@array`. This part of the operation has its own result that it then assigns to `$elements`. If you had written it with grouping parentheses to show the order of the operation, it would look like:

```
my $elements = ( my @array = localtime );
```

The rule at work is that a list *assignment* in scalar context returns the number of elements on the righthand side of the assignment. It's true; read about it in *perlop*. This is such an important concept that you should read it again: A list assignment in scalar context returns the number of elements on the righthand side.

Knowing this rule, you can use it to your advantage. If you want to count the number of elements from something that produces a list, you first assign it to a list, then assign that to a scalar, just as in the previous `localtime` example. However, since the rule is right associative, you can actually provide *no* elements in the list in the middle that you are assigning to:

```
my $elements = () = localtime;
```

Sometimes this is known as the **goatse operator** and written without spaces so it resembles a goat's head (or maybe something else):

```
my $elements =()= localtime;
```

This comes in handy when you want to count the number of elements a global match or a `split` would produce without doing anything with those elements. You assign to the empty list to set the context, then save the result of the assignment:

```
my $count =()= m/(...)/g;


my $count =()= split /:/, $line;
```

Things to remember

- A list is a collection of scalars.
- An array is a container variable that stores a list.
- Although many operations look the same for lists and arrays, some are different.

Item 10. Don't assign `undef` when you want an empty array.

Uninitialized scalar variables in Perl have the value `undef`, a special value that stands for the absence of value. You can reset scalar variables to their uninitialized state by assigning `undef` to them or by using the `undef()` function:

```
my $toast = undef;
undef $history;
```

Uninitialized array variables, however, have the value `()`, the empty list. If you assign `undef` to an array variable, what you actually get is a list of one element containing `undef`. Don't assign `undef` to an array variable! Since a single-element list evaluates to true in Perl, even if that single element is `undef`, you can create some hard-to-find problems in your code:

```
@still_going = undef;
if (@still_going) { ... }
```

The simplest way to avoid this is to assign the empty list `()` to array variables when you want to clear them:

```
my @going_gone = ();
```

You can also use the `undef` function:

```
undef @going_gone;
```

The `defined` operator is the only way to distinguish `undef` from `0` or the empty string `' '`. The `defined` operator will work on any value, and will return true as long as the variable is not undefined:

```
if ( defined($a) ) { ... }
if ( defined(@a) ) { ... }
```

You can assign `undef` to an element of an array, but that doesn't change the size of the array, it just replaces the value for a given element or set of elements, creating a potentially sparse array:

```
$sparse[3] = undef;
@sparse[ 1, 5, 7 ] = ();
```

You can eat up quite a bit of memory by adding undefined values to an array:

```
@sparse[ 0 .. 99 ] = ();
```

Note that `undef` is a perfectly reasonable element value. You cannot shorten an array by assigning `undef` values to elements at the end of the array.

```
my @a = 1 .. 10;
$a[9] = undef;
print scalar(@a), "\n";  # "10"
```

To actually shorten an array without assigning a whole new value to it, you must use one of the array operators like `pop`:

```
my $val = pop @a;
print scalar(@a), "\n"  # "9"
```

Or `splice`:

```
splice @a, -2;
print scalar(@a), "\n";  # "7"
```

Or assign to `$#array_name`:

```
$#a = 4;
print scalar(@a), "\n";  # "5"
```

As with arrays, you cannot undefine a hash by assigning `undef` to it. In fact, assigning any list with an odd number of elements to a hash results in a warning message:

```
    Odd number of elements in hash assignment ⏎
      at program.pl ...
```

You can assign the empty list () to create an empty hash:

```
%gone = ();
if ( keys %gone ) {
  print "This will never print\n";
}
```

Or you can use the `undef` operator to reset the hash to a pristine state.

```
my %nuked = ( U => '235', Pu => 238 );
undef %nuked;
if ( keys %nuked ) {
  print "This won't print either\n";
}
if ( defined %nuked ) {
  print "Nor will this\n";
}
```

As with arrays, you cannot shorten or remove elements from a hash by assigning `undef` values to them. In order to remove elements from a hash you must use the `delete` operator, which you can use on hash slices as well as single elements:

```
my %spacers = (
  husband  => "george",
  wife     => "jane",
  daughter => "judy",
  son      => "elroy",
);

delete $spacers{'husband'};

if ( exists $spacers{'husband'} ) {
  print "Won't print because 'husband' is gone\n";
}

delete @spacers{ 'daughter', 'son' };
```

Things to remember

- Remember that `undef` is a scalar value.
- Don't assign `undef` to an array to clear it out; it makes a one-element list.
- Use `exists` to check whether a key is in a hash; don't trust its value.

Item 11. Avoid a slice when you want an element.

Is `@a[1]` an array element or an array slice? It's a slice. One of the counterintuitive factors encountered by people just beginning to learn Perl is the difference between array elements and array slices. Even after you know the difference, it's not hard to accidentally type `@` instead of `$`.

An introductory book or course about Perl will typically begin by telling you that scalar variable names begin with `$` and array variable names begin with `@`. This is, of course, a gross oversimplification (Item 4).

To access element `$n` of array `@a`, you use the syntax `$a[$n]`, not `@a[$n]`. This may seem peculiar. However, it is a consistent syntax. Scalar values, not variables, begin with `$`, even when those values come from an array or hash.

Therefore, `@a[$n]` doesn't mean element `$n` of array `@a`. Rather, it is something different, called a **slice**. A slice is a shortcut way of accessing several elements at once. Instead of repeating the same variable with different indexes:

```
my @giant = qw( fee fie foe fum );
my @queue = ( $giant[1], $giant[2] );
```

You can use a slice to accomplish the same task in a much easier-to-read manner:

```
my @giant = qw( fee fie foe fum );
my @queue = @giant[ 1, 2 ];
```

You can even use an array to provide indexing:

```
my @fifo = ( 1, 2 );
my @queue = @giant[ @fifo ];
```

Now, `@a[1]` is as much a slice as are `@a[1, 2]`, `@a[2, 10]`, `@a[5, 3, 1]`, `@a[3..7]`, and so on: `@a[1]` is a list, not a scalar value. It is just a list of one element.

Watch out for single-element slices. They are dangerous critters if not used properly. A slice used in a scalar context returns the last value in the slice, which makes single-element slices work like scalar values in some cases. For example:

```
my $jolly = @giant[3];
```

Probably what was intended here was `my $jolly = $giant[3]`. The single-element slice `@giant[3]` is still okay, sort of, since `@giant[3]` in a scalar context evaluates to its last (and in this case only) element, `$giant[3]`.

Although single-element slices work somewhat like array elements on the righthand side of assignments, they behave very differently on the lefthand side of assignments. Since a single-element slice is a list, an assignment to a single element slice is a list assignment, and therefore, the righthand side of the assignment is evaluated in a list context.

If you have warnings turned on (and why don't you? Item 99), Perl warns you about this case:

```
use warnings;

my @giant = qw( fee fie foe fum );

my $jolly = @giant[3];
```

Though the result of the operation is what you expected, assigning "fum" to `$jolly`, it was not for the right reason. Because of this, you get a warning message that tells you that you might have an unintended use of a slice:

```
        Scalar value @giant[3] better written as ⏎
          $giant[3] at ...
```

Lvalue slices

A slice has all the characteristics of a list of variable names on the lefthand side of an assignment. You can even use it on the lefthand side of an assignment expression, or in other places where lvalues are required. Using named variables rather than a slice for a lefthand expression looks very different, but accomplishes the same task:

```
( $giant[1], $giant[2] ) = ( "tweedle", "dee" );
@giant[ 1, 2 ] = ( "tweedle", "dee" );
```

Unintentionally evaluating an operator in a list context can produce dramatic (and unfortunate) results. A good example is the line-input operator, which assigned to a slice or even assigned in list context causes the entirety of STDIN to be evaluated immediately:

```
@info[0] = <STDIN>;
( $info[0] ) = <STDIN>;
```

This reads all the lines from standard input, assigns the first one to element 0 of @info, and ignores the rest! Assigning <STDIN> to @info[0] evaluates <STDIN> in a list context. In a list context, <STDIN> reads all the lines from standard input and returns them as a list.

Don't confuse slices and elements

One more difference between slices and elements is that the expression in the brackets of an element access is evaluated in a scalar context, whereas for slices it is evaluated in a list context. This leads to another example of bizarre behavior that is more difficult to explain.

Suppose you want to add a line containing 'EOF' to the end of the array @text. You could write this as $text[@text] = 'EOF'. What if you write @text[@text] instead? You'll end up making a seriously wrong, but very innocent-looking, mistake:

```
chomp( @text = <STDIN> );
@text[@text] = 'EOF';
```

Perl interprets the array @text inside the brackets in a list context. In a scalar context it returns the number of elements in @text, but in a list context it returns the contents of the array itself. The result is a slice with as many elements are there are lines.

The contents of the lines are interpreted as integer indices—if they're text they will likely all turn out to be zero, so the slice will look like @text[0, 0, 0, 0, 0, ...]. Then EOF is assigned to the first element of the slice, and undef to all the rest, which means that this will probably just overwrite the first element of @text with undef, leaving everything else alone.

What a mess!

Get in the habit of looking for single-element slices like @a[0] in your programs. Single-element slices are generally not what you want (though they're handy for tricks now and then), and a single-element slice on the lefthand side of an assignment is almost certainly wrong. `Perl::Critic` (Item 112) is a tool that can help you find these cases.

Slicing for fun and profit

Beginning Perl programmers generally do not (intentionally) use slices, except to select elements from a resulting list:

```perl
my ( $uid, $gid ) = ( stat $file )[ 4, 5 ];

my $last = ( sort @list )[-1];

my $field_two = ( split /:/ )[1];
```

However, slices can be put to some pretty interesting (and weird) uses. For example, here are two slightly different ways to reverse elements 5 through 9 of `@list`:

```perl
@list[ 5 .. 9 ] = reverse @list[ 5 .. 9 ];
@list[ reverse 5 .. 9 ] = @list[ 5 .. 9 ];
```

Slices provide a handy way to swap two elements:

```perl
@a[ $n, $m ] = @a[ $m, $n ];   # swap $a[$m] and $a[$n]
@item{ 'old',    'new' } =
  @item{ 'new', 'old' };        # swap $item{old} and
                                # $item{new}
```

Use slices to reorder arrays

Slices are also used in sorting (Item 22).

Given two parallel arrays `@uid` and `@name`, this example sorts @name according to the numerical contents of `@uid`. The `sort` orders the indices in `@name`, uses that sorted list as a slice, then assigns the slice back to `@name`:

```perl
@name =
  @name[ sort { $uid[$a] <=> $uid[$b] } 0 .. $#name ];
```

Although this works, it's not a particularly nice thing to do to your coworkers.

Create hashes quickly and easily

You can use hash slices to create hashes from two lists, to overlay the contents of one hash onto another, and to subtract one hash from another.

Creating a hash with 26 elements keyed "A" through "Z" with values of 1 through 26 is easy:

```
@char_num{ 'A' .. 'Z' } = 1 .. 26;
```

Overlaying all of the matching elements from an existing hash with those from a new one, while also adding any elements that exist only in the new hash, is simple:

```
@old{ keys %new } = values %new;
```

This task can be accomplished more tersely, but also less efficiently:

```
%old = ( %old, %new );
```

"Subtracting" one hash from another is just a matter of deleting from a hash using a list of keys:

```
delete @name{ keys %invalid };
```

The preceding one-line statement replaces the more wordy:

```
foreach $key ( keys %invalid ) {
  delete $name{$key};
}
```

Things to remember

- Use a slice to select multiple elements from a list, array, or hash.
- Don't use a slice when you know you need exactly one element.
- Remember that an lvalue slice imposes list context on the righthand side.

Item 12. Understand context and how it affects operations.

Larry Wall, Perl's creator, is a linguist at heart, and his creation reflects that. Just as two people talking to each other rely on their shared context to understand the conversation, Perl uses information about the operators to decide how to handle the data. Pay more attention to what you are doing than what you are doing it to.

You can also make your own context-sensitive code (Item 45).

Number and string context

In Perl, context tells operations how to treat data and evaluate expressions. Sometimes this context is completely determined by the operator. The arithmetic operators treat data as numbers, while the string operators treat data as strings:

```
my $result = '123' + '345';  # 468

my $result = 123 . 345;      # '123456'
```

You must use the correct operator in comparisons (Item 6). If you try to compare numbers as strings, you can get funny results. As a string, '12' is less than '2' because the string comparators work character-by-character, and '1' is less than '2':

```
if ( '12' lt '2' ) { print "12 is less than 2!\n"; }
```

Likewise, comparing strings with numeric comparators may give you puzzling results. As numbers, foo and bar both convert to 0 (Item 8), so they are numerically equal:

```
if ( 'foo' == 'bar' ) { print "Oh noes! foo is bar!\n" }
```

Scalar and list context

Perl enforces scalar context when the operation expects to work with single items. It enforces list context when the operation expects to work with multiple items.

The additive operators (numeric and string) are scalar operators because they expect single items on either side:

```
1 + 2
'foo' . 'bar'
```

List operators expect to work with multiple elements. The print operator takes a list of items and outputs them:

```
print reverse( 1 .. 10 ), "\n";
```

The while condition is in scalar context, but the foreach condition is in list context, because that is the way they are defined:

```
while ( SCALAR CONTEXT HERE ) { ... }

foreach ( LIST CONTEXT HERE ) { ... }
```

This means that the two do different things with the line-input operator. Consider iterating over a filehandle to process lines, stopping once you find the __END__ token. With a `while` loop, you read one line per iteration, and when you are done with the loop, you can still read another line from that filehandle:

```
while (<STDIN>) {
  last if /__END__/;
  ...;
}

my $next_line = <STDIN>;
```

If you used `foreach`, you would have a problem. Since `foreach` imposes list context, it reads all of STDIN, leaving no lines to read after you are done, even though you stop the loop early:

```
foreach (<STDIN>) {
  last if /__END__/;
  ...;
}

my $next_line = <STDIN>;  # Oops -- no more lines!
```

It's normally bad form to read in lines before you need them, so it is generally better to use `while` anyway.

Context by assignment

The assignment operator supplies context. It knows whether it is going to assign to a single element or a list of elements. If the assignment operator knows it is assigning to a list, it supplies list context to its righthand side. All of these are list assignments:

```
my ($n)       = ( 'a', 'b', 'c' );  # $n is 'a'

my ($n, $m)   = ( 'a', 'b', 'c' );  # $n is 'a', $m is 'b'

my @array     = ( 'a', 'b', 'c' );

my @lines     = <STDIN>;            # reads all lines
```

Note that a list of a single element, like `my ($n)`, is just as good as a list with any other number of items. It's still a list. The parentheses around the scalars make it a list operation even when there is a single scalar.

Assigning to a bare scalar (no surrounding parentheses on the lefthand side) supplies **scalar context**.

```
my $single_line = <STDIN>;   # read only one line
```

That can be really tricky sometimes. What is `$n` in this case?

```
my $n = ( 'a', 'b', 'c' );   # $n is 'c'
```

To understand this odd result, know the difference between lists and arrays (Item 9).

Void context

There is also a **void context**, in which you call a subroutine or use an operator but don't save or use the result:

```
some_sub(@args);


grep { /foo/ } @array;


1 + 2;
```

In some cases, Perl can tell that the operation is useless. For instance, does it really need to do that `grep` when you don't save the result?

In some cases, like that `1 + 2;`, you get a warning when you have warnings enabled (Item 99):

```
Useless use of a variable in void context
```

Things to remember

- Perl determines context by what you are doing.
- Perl interprets scalars according to number or string context.
- List context can have completely different results than scalar context.

Item 13. Use arrays or hashes to group data.

Perl has two built-in types to make your coding life easier: the array and the hash. These are **collection** types designed to group related data.

Don't use numbered variables

From the beginner who knows about scalars but hasn't learned about arrays, you'll often see code that uses separate scalars to store a series of values:

```
my $fib_0 = 1;
my $fib_1 = 1;
my $fib_2 = 2;
my $fib_3 = 3;
my $fib_4 = 5;
```

The next programmer is almost there, having essentially reinvented arrays the hard way:

```
$fib[0] = 1;
$fib[1] = 1;
$fib[2] = 2;
$fib[3] = 3;
$fib[4] = 5;
```

The easy way is to store the values in an array directly:

```
my @x = ( 1, 1, 2, 3, 5 );
```

It's even easier with the quotewords operator, qw():

```
my @x = qw( 1 1 2 3 5 );
```

A more-complicated variation on this involves pairs of values stored in separate variables—for instance, two-dimensional coordinates:

```
my $x0 = 1;
my $y0 = 1;
my $x1 = 2;
my $y1 = 4;
```

You can store those in an array, too, but to keep each point's data together you must store them as **tuples**, where each point gets its own array reference:

```
my @points = ( [ 1, 1 ], [ 2, 4 ] );
```

It's then easy to go through all of your points:

```
foreach my $point (@points) {
  print "x: $point->[0] y: $point->[1]\n";
}
```

Avoid groups of variables

Another common beginner pattern uses several different variables to record information that logically goes together. To work with the data for a person, a new programmer might create three separate scalar variables:

```
my $person_name = 'George';
my $person_id   = '3';
my $person_age  = 29;
```

Although this beginner has used three variables, the data are actually connected to a single person, and the variables themselves are connected with the common prefix person. Anytime the beginner had to work with that data, it would be necessary to pass each of the values separately, hoping the variables are used in the correct order:

```
some_sub( $person_name, $person_id, $person_age );
```

When you see this sort of pattern, convert it to a hash. The part of the variable name after person becomes the hash key:

```
my %person = (
  id   => 3,
  name => 'George',
  age  => 29,
);
```

Now you don't have to worry about how you pass around everything you know about George, since you can always just pass a reference to the hash:

```
some_sub( \%person );
```

If you have a list of persons, you can collect them in an array:

```
my @persons = ( \%person1, \%person2 );
```

That example has the same problem the beginner had at the start: a series of variable names for each hash. You don't need to construct named hashes if you create the hash references as the elements of the array:

```
my @persons = ( { id => 1, ... }, { id => 2, ... }, ... );
```

Things to remember

- Avoid series of like-named scalar variables to group data.
- Use collection variable types to group data that go together.
- Use hashes to key data to their meanings.

Item 14. Handle big numbers with `bignum`.

Although Perl tries to hide its underlying architectural details from you, in some cases, such as with the highest (or lowest) number it can represent, it has to let those details leak through. Compilations to 32-bit `perl` are still common, and their integer range is limited to 32 bits. Try this Perl one-liner:

```
% perl -le 'print 12345678901234567890012345';
```

Instead of the number you may expect, you get something in exponential notation:

```
1.23456789012346e+24
```

Try this program that computes a factorial:

```
my $factorial = 1;
foreach my $num ( 1 .. $ARGV[0] ) {
  $factorial *= $num;
}


print "$factorial\n";
```

On a 32-bit `perl`, this falls into exponential notation at 18!:

```
% perl factorial.pl 17
355687428096000
```

```
% perl factorial.pl 18
6.402373705728e+15
```

Those are still the right, exact numbers, but at 21! (51,090,942,171,709, 440,000), `perl` starts losing digits:

```
% perl factorial.pl 21
5.10909421717094e+19
```

Get all of the digits

You can fix `perl`'s imprecision by using the `bignum` pragma:

```
use bignum;

my $factorial = 1;
foreach my $num ( 1 .. $ARGV[0] ) {
  $factorial *= $num;
}


print "$factorial\n";
```

Now your program can deal with much-larger numbers:

```
% perl factorial.pl 100
93326215443944152681699238856266700490715968264381621
46859296389521759999322991560894146397615651828625369
7920827223758251185210916864000000000000000000000000
```

You can now process arbitrarily large numbers, limited only by the resources of your system. Integers and floating-point values are handled automatically by choosing the right type of object for each, and converting when necessary. You might pay a run time penalty for stepping outside of the bounds of the hard-wired data types native to the underlying system, but that's what you get for wanting correct answers.

Limiting `bignum`'s effect

With the `bignum` pragma, all of your number and math operations use the big numbers. Sometimes you may not want that, since `bignum` converts numbers to objects of either `Math::BigInt` or `Math::BigFloat`. That can have a significant impact on performance, as all math now requires method calls.

If you want `bignum` for most of the program, you can turn it off within a scope with `no`:

```
{
  no bignum;

  # numbers in here are the regular sort
  my $sum = $n + $m;
}
```

If you want to use `bignum` for a small portion of the program, you can enable it lexically:

```
{
  use bignum;

  # numbers in here are the bignum sort
  my $sum = $n + $m;
}
```

If you need `bignum` for only certain objects in your program, you can create those objects yourself and deal with them as you would any other object, so their special handling applies only to certain numbers:

```
use Math::BigInt;

my $big_factorial = Math::BigInt->new(1);
foreach my $num ( 1 .. $ARGV[0] ) {
  $big_factorial *= $num;
}


print "$big_factorial\n";
```

When you create the objects yourself, all of the other numbers in your program still use the built-in sizes.

Things to remember

- Perl's built-in number precision is limited by the local architecture.
- The `bignum` pragma gives you numbers with arbitrary precision.
- Use `bignum` selectively to apply it to only part of your program.

2 | Idiomatic Perl

Perl is a language designed by a linguist, and as much as any human language, Perl is a language of idioms.

What we call idiomatic Perl is the mixture of elegance and custom that comes naturally to Perl programmers, or we hope at least the majority of them, after experience and experimentation.

Exactly what is idiomatic and what is purely a matter of style or opinion is debatable. There are many different ways to express both simple and complex algorithms in Perl. Some ways, however, are clearly more "right" than others. Although Perl's motto may be "There's More Than One Way To Do It," the corollary is, "But Most of Them Are Wrong," or "Some Ways Are Better Than Others."

Idiom and convention are very important in Perl. They are less important in simple languages like C and Bourne or C shell. There are not too many tricks you need to learn in C programming. You may think we're crazy to say that, but if you take a look at your local bookstore's programming section, you will see that all the books on how to do clever things in C are fairly skinny. It's the books on C++ that are thick. And although there are a lot of details to be learned in support of shell programming, a thorough how-to book on shell programming is also a slim volume.

Not so with Perl. Perl is an expressive language, and often a succinct one. Larry Wall designed the language to allow frequently used constructs to be coded very compactly. Sometimes Perl programmers will talk about Perl's **Huffman coding**: the most-frequent constructs take the fewest keystrokes. Perl's very high level features like <>, regular expressions, and grep are particularly potent. For example:

```
# swap $a and $b
( $a, $b ) = ( $b, $a );

# read lines from files or standard input
# and print them out in sorted order
```

```
print sort <>;

# print all the lines containing the word joebloe
print grep /\bjoebloe\b/, <>;

# copy all the numbers in @n evenly
# divisible by 5 into @div5
my @div5 = grep { not $_ % 5 } @n;

# one way of turning "123.234.0.1"
# into the integer 0xb7ae0010
$bin_addr = pack 'C4', split /\./, $str_addr;
```

You can code all of these examples in other ways, but when you write them in the style of some other language, your result is longer and less efficient. You could, say, reproduce the functionality of <> explicitly in Perl, but the result would be a fairly long Perl program that would obscure the "interesting" part of the program. The resulting program would also be harder to debug and maintain simply because of its greater length and complexity.

To a certain extent, idiom and style overlap. Some idioms, like print sort <>, are inarguable, but there are certainly gray areas:

```
# print key-value pairs from %h one per line
foreach my $key ( sort keys %h ) {
  print "$key: $h{$key}\n";
}

# another way to print key-value pairs
print map "$_: $h{$_}\n", sort keys %h;
```

The first example above is very plain Perl. It is efficient and readable, and uses only basic features of the language. The second example is shorter and, some might argue, has a higher "cool factor" because it uses the nifty map operator and a list context in place of the mundane foreach loop. However, you should consider yourself and your potential audience before leaving code like the second example for posterity, as it is definitely more obscure (but not *that* obscure) and might even be less efficient.

Every Perl programmer needs to master a number of basic idioms and should learn to recognize a number of others. Programmers should always use those idioms that produce efficient, succinct, and readable code. Other, more-complex idioms may or may not be appropriate, depending on the programmer, the audience, and the nature of the program being written.

In this chapter (were you wondering when it would ever really get started?), we'll show you a number of Perl idioms. You will definitely want to learn and use the simpler ones. Beyond those, you will have to consider the tradeoffs between "plain" and "nifty."

How your Perl looks is up to you. You can write very plain Perl if you like. Writing plain Perl is like building a house as much as possible out of masonry blocks. It works, it's simple, it's a little dull, and it's hard to create intricate shapes.

On the other hand, you may want to try using all the nifty features that Perl gives you. Continuing the house analogy, you may be the kind of builder who spends more time at Home Depot looking at power tools than pounding nails on the job. You may like to build all kinds of cool features using the latest technology. This is fine, so long as you realize that sometimes a hammer is all you need.

Or maybe after a while you will wind up somewhere in-between.

Sometimes you need `s/\G0/ /g`, and sometimes you just need `$a = $b`.

Item 15. Use $_ for elegance and brevity.

"Dollar underscore," or `$_`—you may love it, or you may hate it, but either way, if you're going to be a proficient Perl programmer, you need to understand it.

`$_` is a default argument for many operators, and also for some control structures. Here are some examples:

```
# $_ as a default argument
print $_;  # default argument for print
print;     # ... same thing

print "found it"
  if $_ =~ /Rosebud/;  # matches and substitutions
print "found it"
  if /Rosebud/;         # same thing
```

```
$mod_time = -M $_;        # most filehandle tests
$mod_time = -M;           # same thing

foreach $_ (@list) { do_something($_) }  # foreach
foreach (@list)     { do_something($_) }  # same thing

while ( defined( $_ = <STDIN> ) ) {
  # while; a special case
  print $_;
}
while (<STDIN>) { print }  # same thing
```

As also seen in Item 7, the last example illustrates the special case where using the line-input operator `<filehandle>` alone as the condition of a `while` loop is a shortcut for reading a line from the file into `$_` until the end-of-file is reached. It automatically checks that it returned something, since the line input operator tells you it's done by returning `undef`.

This may seem a bit capricious and random, but it's easy to keep track of what does what with `$_` by checking the Perl documentation. You don't have to memorize the complete list, because you can just look it up. For example, does `split` have special behavior with `$_`? Just look it up.

`$_` is a normal scalar variable—mostly. You can use it, print it, change its value, and so on, just as if it were an ordinary scalar. There are a couple of things to watch out for, though.

`$_` and the `main` package

Before Perl 5.10, `$_` was always in the package `main`. This applied even, or especially, if you were in some other package:

```
package foo;
$_ = "OK\n";  # this still means $main::_

package main;
print;          # prints "OK"
```

In fact, all special variables (`[$@%]`-punctuation and a few others) have this property. You can use a variable like `$foo::_` if you like, but it has no special properties and isn't *the* `$_`.

Localizing $_

Before Perl 5.10, you could only localize $_ with `local`. Most times when you work with special variables, you want to limit their effects so your changes don't live beyond your intent. With `local`, you have your own $_ until the end of the current scope:

```
{
  local $_;

  # ... do stuff with your version of $_

  some_sub();  # uses your $_
}
```

With `local`, your change affects everything until the end of the scope, including any subroutines you call. Your version of $_ is visible throughout the entire program.

As of Perl 5.10, you can have a lexical $_ so that your changes affect only the code that's in scope, and nothing outside that scope can see it. Even though you call `some_sub` in the same scope, it doesn't see the value of the lexically-scoped $_:

```
{
  my $_;

  #... do stuff with your version of $_

  some_sub();  # doesn't use your $_
}
```

Programming style and $_

Oddly enough, when you use $_, you may not see much of it. Can you count how many times it *doesn't* show up in this code?

```
while (<>) {  # 1
  foreach (split) {  # 2 and 3
    $w5++ if /^\w{5}$/  # 4
  }
}
```

```
# find files ending in .txt and less than 5000 bytes long
@small_txt =
  grep { /\.txt$/ and (-s) < 5000 } @files;  # 5 and 6
```

Some Perl programmers may feel that `$_` is more an aid to obfuscation than to elegance. There is even one book[1] that says, "Many Perl programmers write programs that have references to `$_` running like an invisible thread through their programs. Programs that overuse `$_` are hard to read and are easier to break than programs that explicitly reference scalar variables you have named yourself." However, which of these is easier on the eyes?

```
while ( defined( $line = <STDIN> ) ) {
  print $line if $line =~ /Perl/;
}


while (<STDIN>) { print if /Perl/ }
```

There's no obfuscation here. If you learn a little Perl and know how to use the documentation, any confusion should be short-lived.

Things to remember

- Perl uses `$_` as the default variable for many operations.
- Avoid temporary variables by using the default variables when you can chain operations.
- Localize `$_` before you use it so you don't disturb other code.

Item 16. Know Perl's other default arguments.

`$_` is not the one-and-only default argument in Perl. There are several others. Just as with `$_`, reading and referring to the documentation is always your best guide.

@_ as a default

Inside a subroutine, `shift` uses `@_` as a default argument. When you `shift` with no arguments in your subroutine, you are really pulling the left-most element from `@_`:

---

1. David Till, *Teach Yourself Perl 5 in 21 Days* (Berkeley, CA: Sams Publishing, 1996).

```
sub foo {
  my $x = shift;
  ...;
}
```

One interesting quirk in Perl syntax shows up when you try to `shift` an array argument passed by reference and convert that reference into an array in one statement:

```
bar( \@bletch );

sub bar {
  my @a = @{shift};
  ...;
}
```

In this example, `@{shift}` refers to the variable `shift` and not to the function. If you have `strict` enabled (Item 3), Perl will catch this for you:

```
Global symbol @shift requires explicit package name ...
```

You have to put something else inside the braces to let Perl know that the identifier isn't a variable name. Since `shift` is a function, you can call shift with parentheses to let `perl` know:

```
my @a = @{ shift() };
```

Alternatively, you can use the unary + operator. In this case it serves as a no-op (a placeholder that performs no operation), but it does let `perl` know that `shift` is not a regular string:

```
my @a = @{ +shift };
```

However, if you don't attempt inline dereferencing and instead separate your work, you don't ever have to work around this ambiguous syntax.

@ARGV as a default

Outside of a subroutine, `shift` uses `@ARGV` as its default. Knowing this, you can write custom command-line argument handling—for example, processing any string that starts with a hyphen as a command-line option and everything else as a file:

```
foreach (shift) {
  if (/^-(.*)/) {
```

```
      process_option($1);
    }
    else {
      process_file($_);
    }
  }
```

Of course, you shouldn't do this yourself. Instead, you should use one of the many available argument processors, like `Getopt::Long`.

Also note that the `shift` operator always uses `@ARGV` or `main::@_` even if your default package is something other than `main`.

Other functions that use $_

Several other built-ins use `$_` by default: `-X` filetests (except for `-t`), `abs`, `alarm`, `chomp`, `chop`, `chr`, `chroot`, `cos`, `defined`, `eval`, `exp`, `glob`, `hex`, `int`, `lc`, `lcfirst`, `log`, `lstat`, `oct`, `ord`, `pos`, `print`, `quotemeta`, `read-link`, `ref`, `require`, `reverse` in scalar context only, `rmdir`, `say`, `sin`, `split`, `sqrt`, `stat`, `study`, `uc`, `ucfirst`, and `unlink`.

STDIN as a default

Unlike the rest of the file-test operators, which use `$_` as a default, the `-t` operator uses the filehandle `STDIN` as a default. `-t` tests a filehandle in the manner of the UNIX `isatty()` function to determine whether the filehandle is interactive—that is, whether its input is from a human typing at a keyboard or from some other, most likely automated, source. These two calls to `-t` are equivalent:

```
print "You're alive!" if -t STDIN;
print "You're alive!" if -t;
```

Use the `-t` operator to help modify the behavior of a program depending on whether it is running interactively. For example, you could use `-t` in a CGI script to start it up in a special debugging mode if the script is being run from the command line. You might also want to check out the `IO::Interactive` module, which does the same thing but handles a couple of special cases, too.

The `getc` function, which reads a character from a filehandle, uses `STDIN` by default:

```
my $char = getc STDIN;
my $char = getc;
```

Other defaults

Just to round out this Item, Table 2-1 shows the other defaults that Perl built-ins use.

Things to remember

- Some operations use a default argument other than `$_`.
- Some default arguments change based on context, like those for `shift`.
- You don't have to use the defaults when you specify your argument.

Table 2-1 The Default Arguments to Perl's Built-Ins that Do Not Use `$_`

Perl built-in	Default argument
chdir	$ENV{HOME}, $ENV{LOGDIR}, or $ENV{SYS$LOGIN}
close	default filehandle
dump	top of program
eof	last file read or end of ARGV
exit	0
getpgrp	$$
gmtime	time
localtime	time
open	$FILEHANDLE
pop	@ARGV outside of a subroutine or @_ in a subroutine
rand	1
reverse	$_ in scalar context
select	current filehandle
shift	@ARGV outside of a subroutine or @_ in a subroutine
tell	last file read
write	current filehandle

Item 17. Know common shorthand and syntax quirks.

Perl is a "human" language in that it has a context-dependent syntax. You can take advantage of this by omitting things that the interpreter can assume—default arguments, $_, optional punctuation, and so on. Perl figures out from the context what you really mean (usually).

Perl is also a very high level language with an extremely rich and diverse syntax, but sometimes the various syntactical features don't fit together as well as they might. In some cases, you may have to help Perl along by resorting to a syntactical gimmick of one kind or another. Along these lines, here are some suggestions, and some things to watch out for.

Swap values with list assignments

Perl doesn't have a special operator to swap values in two variables, but you can always use a list assignment to the same effect. Perl evaluates the righthand side before it does the assignment:

```
( $b, $a ) = ( $a, $b );   # swap $a and $b


( $c, $a, $b ) = ( $a, $b, $c );   # rotate $a, $b and $c
```

Slices give you a convenient syntax for permuting the contents of an array:

```
@a[ 1, 3, 5 ] = @a[ 5, 3, 1 ];   # shuffle some elements
```

You can rearrange the indices so you swap the even- and odd-numbered elements in an array:

```
@a[ map { $_ * 2 + 1, $_ * 2 } 0 .. ( $#a / 2 ) ] = @a;
```

Force a list context with [ ] or ( )[]

In some cases, you may need to force Perl to evaluate an expression in list context. For example, if you want to split a string captured by a regular expression capture, you might first write:

```
# split $_ on + up to :
my ($str) = /([^:]*)/;
my @words = split /\+/, $str;
```

To write this in a single expression without the use of the temporary $str, you have to resort to trickery, since the pattern match would not return the right kind of value in the scalar context imposed by `split`. The inside of a literal slice is in list context:

```
my @words = split /\+/, (/([^:]*)/)[0];
```

If you want to take a reference to a list literal in a single step, use the anonymous array constructor `[]`. The reference operator `\` applied to a list literal actually creates a list of references, not a reference to an array (Item 61):

```
my $wordlist_ref = \( split /\++/, $str );   # WRONG

my $wordlist_ref = [ split /\++/, $str ];    # CORRECT
```

Use => to make key-value pairs

The `=>` (fat arrow) operator is a synonym for the comma operator. There is one minor difference in functionality: if the lefthand argument to `=>` is an identifier by itself, Perl always treats it as a string and will not interpret it as a function call. Thus, you can use things such as `time` to the left of `=>` without fear:

```
my @a = ( time => 'flies' );  # "time" is taken literally
print "@a\n";                 # "time flies"

my @b = ( time, 'flies' );    # time operator
print "@b\n";                 # "862891055 flies"
```

Use `=>` to make initializers prettier, if you like. This is especially appropriate when creating initializers for hashes. They help you make clear columns that show the keys and values of a hash:

```
my %elements = (
   'Ag' => 47,
   'Au' => 79,
   'Pt' => 78,
);
```

It's a little nicer when you don't have to quote the keys:

```
my %elements = (
  Ag => 47,
  Au => 79,
  Pt => 78,
);
```

Sometimes you don't need the => at all. You can use the quote-words operator (Item 21) if your keys and values have no whitespace in them:

```
my %elements = qw(
  Ag   47
  Au   79
  Pt   78
);
```

Use the => operator to simulate named parameters

You can simulate named parameters for function calls. You can set up your subroutine to work with a hash of parameters. To quickly construct that hash, put your default values at the front and the subroutine arguments at the end. In this example, %params has a default value for align:

```
sub img {
  my %params = ( align => 'middle', @_ );

  # write out the keys and values of the
  # hash as an HTML tag
  print "<img ",
    (
    join ' ', map { "$_=\"$param{$_}\"" }
      keys %param
    ),
    ">";
}
```

When you call the img subroutine, you pass in the key-value pairs for the settings that you want:

```
img( src => 'icon.gif', align => 'top' );
```

In this case, you pass in align => 'top', which replaces the default setting in %params, and you get your correctly aligned img tag:

```
<img src="icon.gif" align="top" />
```

Don't follow our simple example for creating HTML in real applications, though. Use one of the HTML modules instead.

Use => to show direction

Finally, here's another interesting use of => as syntactic "sugar." With rename, you can show the direction from the original filename to the new one:

```
rename "$file.c" => "$file.c.old";
```

Don't confuse => with ->, which you use for subscripting references (Item 58) or method calls.

Watch what you put inside { }

Parentheses, square brackets, angle brackets, and curly braces all have multiple meanings in Perl. Perl uses the contents of the braces (or whatever) and the surrounding context to figure out what to do with them. Usually the result makes sense, but at times it may surprise you.

Be especially careful with braces, perhaps two of the most hard-working characters in Perl. Braces are used to enclose blocks, delimit variable names, create anonymous hashes, and in hash element and dereferencing syntax. It's dizzying if you think about it too hard. It's pretty scary that the interpreter can tell the difference between an anonymous hash constructor and a block!

If you see a plus sign inside braces for no apparent reason, there probably *is* a reason for it. Perl's unary plus has no effect on its argument, but it does provide a fix for some syntactical problems. Suppose you have a subroutine that returns a reference to an array. If you put just the subroutine name in {}, you create a soft reference (catch that with strict: Item 3):

```
my @a = @{func_returning_aryref};  # WRONG!
```

These uses do what you probably mean, since you give Perl a hint that func_returning_aryref is a subroutine name:

```
my @a = @{ func_returning_aryref() };  # OK -- parentheses

my @a = @{ &func_returning_aryref };    # OK -- ampersand

my @a = @{ +func_returning_aryref };    # OK -- unary plus
```

If you're unlucky, you might also run into a situation where a hash constructor is confused with a block. Suppose you have a subroutine that returns a list of key-value pairs that you want to use in an anonymous hash constructor. Since the curly brace is one of the most overloaded characters in Perl, you might have to give Perl some extra hints to show it which use you want. As part of a larger expression, Perl knows `key_value_pairs()` must be in a hash constructor:

```
my $hashref = eval {
   return { key_value_pairs() }  # OK
};
```

You can use a unary + to give Perl a hint that your opening brace is the start of an anonymous hash constructor:

```
my $hashref = eval {
   +{ key_value_pairs() }        # OK
};
```

By itself, however, Perl guesses that `key_value_pairs()` is in a block, which is unfortunately an incorrect guess in this case:

```
my $hashref = eval {
   { key_value_pairs() }  # probably not okay
};
```

And, finally, Perl thinks an identifier appearing all alone (possibly surrounded by whitespace) inside braces is a string. If it is the name of a function, the function is not called unless there is something other than just an identifier present:

```
${shift} = 10;  # sets $shift = 10

sub soft { ${ +shift } = 10; }  # soft reference!
soft 'a';                       # sets $a = 10
```

Because of this confusion, you shouldn't use these constructs yourself, and when you encounter someone else using them, give them a proper thrashing.

Use @{[ ]} or eval {} to make a copy of a list

Sometimes you may want to perform a destructive operation on a copy of a list rather than on the original. For instance, if you want to find which

.h files that are missing, you can change the names of the .c files to .h files and check which ones exist:

```
my @cfiles_copy = @cfiles;
my @missing_h =
  grep { s/\.c$/\.h/ and not -e } @cfiles_copy;
```

Perl doesn't give you a function for making copies of things, but if you need to make an unnamed copy of a list, you can put the list inside the anonymous list constructor [ ], then immediately dereference it:

```
my @missing_h =
  grep { s/\.c$/\.h/ and !-e } @{ [@cfiles] };
```

Another way to make a copy of something is to put it inside an `eval` block, which returns the result of its last evaluated expression:

```
my @missing_h =
  grep { s/\.c$/\.h/ and !-e } eval { @cfiles };
```

Use the block form of `eval` in situations like this, not the string form, since the block form is much more efficient.

Consider if you really need to make a copy, though. In these simple examples, you did that extra work to avoid a little messiness inside the `grep`. You could just as well save the element to another variable in the `grep`:

```
my @missing_h = grep {
  my $h = $_;
  $h =~ s/\.c$/\.h/ and !( -e $h )
} @cfiles;
```

Note that all of these techniques make only shallow copies. If any of the list elements are references, the copy might share data with the original. If you need a completely disconnected, deep copy, use `dclone` from `Storable`:

```
use Storable qw(dclone);

my $copy_ref = dclone( \@array );
```

Now `$copy_ref` has nothing in common with `@array`.

You have to decide which way makes more sense for your problem, but often the mechanics of copying a list obscures what you are doing.

Things to remember

- Perl's syntax is a blend from many sources, so it has many quirks.
- Use the => to show the relationships between data.
- Use `dclone` to make deep copies of arrays.

Item 18. Avoid excessive punctuation.

Perl programs tend to be filled with punctuation, often to the point where they have an intimidating, busy appearance. Excessive punctuation makes programs less readable, and wise programmers will take advantage of changes in Perl that make it possible to write programs with considerably less punctuation than before.

Call subroutines without parentheses

You can call a subroutine with varying levels of punctuation: prefixed with an ampersand, without an ampersand but with parentheses after the function name, or without an ampersand or parentheses. The last style works only if the function has been declared or defined before the function call is encountered.

```
&myfunc( 1, 2, 3 );

myfunc( 1, 2, 3 );

myfunc 1, 2, 3;
```

The traditional & syntax has its uses: it's the only way to call a subroutine whose name is a keyword, such as `&for`. "List operator" syntax, without ampersand or parentheses, works if the definition or declaration of the function appears lexically before the function call. This is generally fine, but there are some pitfalls.

You can't use the subroutine with the list operator syntax unless Perl has already seen the subroutine definition:

```
myfunc 1, 2, 3;  # ERROR
sub myfunc { }
```

Also, the definition must lexically appear before its use, since that's the order that Perl sees it and parses it in. You can't trick `perl` with a `BEGIN` block:

```
myfunc 1, 2, 3;  # ERROR

BEGIN {
  sub myfunc { }
}
```

Also, the definition of the subroutine needs to be there at compile time, so a definition inside an `eval` is not going to work:

```
eval "sub myfunc {}";
myfunc 1, 2, 3;  #  ERROR
```

A `BEGIN` block that comes lexically before your subroutine call makes it all work out, even if it is a bit strange:

```
BEGIN { eval "sub myfunc {}" }  # works -- but strange
myfunc 1, 2, 3;
```

You can also forward-declare the subroutine name, and define it later. Perl now knows that `myfunc` is a subroutine, so it can parse the source correctly:

```
use subs qw(myfunc);

myfunc 1, 2, 3;
sub myfunc { }
```

Use and and or instead of && and ||

Another helpful feature is the addition of the super-low precedence short-circuit logical operators `and` and `or`. Nothing in the precedence table is lower than these operators. (There's also the less exciting `not` and the generally useless `xor`.) These allow you to get rid of parentheses in a variety of situations, since you don't have to group expressions.

The lowest-precedence `and` and `or` operators allow you to omit parentheses around list operators, assignment, and binding. Which one looks nicer to you in each case?

```
print("hello, ") && print "goodbye.";
print "hello, " and print "goodbye.";

( my $size = -s $file ) || die "$file has zero size.\n";
my $size = -s $file or die "$file has zero size.\n";
```

```
( my $word =~ /magic/ ) || $mode = 'peon';
my $word =~ /magic/ or $mode = 'peon';


open( my ($fh), '>', $file )
  || die "Could not open $file: $!";
open my ($fh), '>', $file
  or die "Could not open $file: $!";
```

Remember that you can always eliminate a semicolon preceding a closing brace. This is probably a good idea in a block consisting of a single statement, especially as an argument to map, grep, do, eval, and the like:

```
my @caps = map { uc $_; } @words;  # unnecessary semicolon
my @caps = map { uc $_ } @words;   # looks cleaner
```

One more way to get rid of extra parentheses and braces is to use the expression modifier, or "backwards conditional," syntax. It's handy once you get used to it:

```
if (/^__END__$/) { last }  # mundane

last if /^__END__$/;       # doesn't this look better?
```

Things to remember

- Avoid overusing parentheses or braces.
- Use the list operator syntax for Perl subroutines.
- Use the low precedence and or or to avoid precedence problems.

Item 19. Format lists for easy maintenance.

Although we told you to avoid excessive punctuation (Item 18), there's at least one part of Perl that especially wants you to use extra punctuation. Larry Wall, when designing Perl, wanted to make a language that tolerates some of the frequent syntax errors from other languages. If people keep making the same error over and over, sometimes the solution is to make it not be an error anymore.

Perl lets you add a trailing comma after the last item in a list:

```
my @cats = ( 'Buster Bean', 'Mimi', );  # not an error
```

When you add another item, you don't have to remember to add the comma, because it is already there:

```
my @cats = ( 'Buster Bean', 'Mimi', 'Roscoe' );
```

This makes more sense when you format your lists so that each element gets its own line:

```
my @cats = (
    'Buster Bean',
    'Mimi',
    'Roscoe',
);
```

If you need to add or delete an element, you don't need to change any other line or interfere with any other element as long as you always put a comma after every element. You can even comment out an item temporarily:

```
my @cats = (
    'Buster Bean',
    # 'Mimi',
    'Roscoe';
);
```

This works even better with hashes, which you construct with lists. You put one key-value pair on a line, and align the columns:

```
my %spacers = (
    husband  => "George",
    wife     => "Jane",
    daughter => "Judy",
    son      => "Elroy",
);
```

If your list elements don't have whitespace, you can also use the quote-words operator so you don't have to type the commas or quotes:

```
my %spacers = qw(
    husband   George
    wife      Jane
    daughter  Judy
    son       Elroy
);
```

Things to remember

- Use one line per list element to make data easier to read and edit.
- Use a trailing comma in your lists so you don't forget to add it when you add more elements.
- Align hash keys and values as columns to make them easier to maintain.

Item 20. Use `foreach`, `map`, and `grep` as appropriate.

There are several different ways of iterating over elements in a list in Perl.

There is a strong tendency among Perl programmers to avoid using a C-style `for` loop and subscripts when iterating through a list. Loops that use subscripts tend to be slower than loops that don't, since subscripts take a significant amount of time for Perl to evaluate. The C style is too much work:

```
for ( my $i = 0 ; $i <= @array ; $i++ ) {
  print "I saw $array[$i]\n";
}
```

Most programmers use `foreach`, `map`, or `grep` instead. The capabilities of `foreach`, `map`, and `grep` overlap somewhat, but each is designed for its own primary purpose. These constructs are easy to abuse—you can write pretty much any kind of loop with any one of them—but doing so can confuse you, and anyone else who visits your code in the future. You should use them appropriately.

Use `foreach` to iterate read-only over each element of a list

If all you want to do is to cycle over the elements in a list, use `foreach`:

```
foreach my $cost (@cost) {
  $total += $cost;
}

foreach my $file ( glob '*' ) {
  print "$file\n" if -T $file;
}
```

Remember that `foreach` uses `$_` as a control variable by default if none is specified:

```
foreach ( 1 .. 10 ) {  # print the first 10 squares
  print "$_: ", $_ * $_, "\n";
}
```

Also, you can always use the shorter keyword for instead of `foreach`—Perl knows what you mean:

```
for (@lines) { # print the first line beginning with From:
  print, last if /^From:/;
}
```

Use `map` to create a list based on the contents of another list

If you want to create a transformed copy of a list, use `map`. The following two lines turn a list of filenames into a list of file sizes. Remember that most file test operators use `$_` by default (Item 51):

```
my @sizes = map { -s } @files;
```

```
my @sizes = map -s, @files;
```

`map` evaluates its transform expression or block in list context. Sometimes it can be useful to return an empty list or a list of more than one element. Using a match operator can be elegant.

Both of the following examples use the match operator `m//` and parentheses inside `map`. In a list context, `m//` returns a list of the substrings captured in regular expression capture, or the empty list if the match fails.

This `map` finds all of the filenames (without the extensions) that end in .txt. Since the match operator is in list context, it returns the list of things that match in the parentheses:

```
my @stem = map { /(.*)\.txt$/ } @files;
```

This `map` does a similar thing to find the `From:` address in a list of e-mail headers. It returns only for those elements where the match succeeds:

```
my ($from) = map /^From:\s+(.*)$/, @message_lines;
```

For efficiency, `$_` is actually an alias for the current element in the iteration. If you modify `$_` within the transform expression of a `map`, you modify the input data. This is generally considered to be bad style, and—who knows?—you may even wind up confusing yourself this way. If you want to modify the contents of a list, use `foreach`. (More on this later.)

You should also make sure that map is returning a sensible value—don't use map as just a control structure. The next example breaks three of the rules concerning map. First, tr/// modifies $_ and thus @elems. Second, the return value from map is a nonsensical list of values from tr///—the number of digits deleted by tr/// in each element. Third, you don't do anything with the output list, the whole point of map:

```
map { tr/0-9//d } @elems;   # PROBABLY WRONG
```

This returns a sensible value, but tr/// still modifies @elems (Item 114):

```
my @digitless = map { tr/0-9//d; $_ } @elems;   # BAD STYLE
```

If you must use tr///, s///, or something similar inside map, use a lexical variable to avoid changes to $_. In this example, you save the value of $_ in $x so you can modify it:

```
my @digitless = map {
  ( my $x = $_ ) =~ tr/0-9//d;
  $x
} @elems;
```

Use foreach to modify elements of a list

If you actually want to modify the elements in a list, use foreach. As with map and grep, the control variable is an alias for the current element in the iteration. Modifying the control variable modifies that element:

```
# multiply all the elements of @nums by 2
foreach my $num (@nums) {
  $num *= 2;
}

# strip digits from elements of @ary
foreach (@ary) { tr/0-9//d }

# slower version using s///
foreach (@elems) { s/\d//g }

# uppercase $str1, $str2 and $str3
foreach ( $str1, $str2, $str3 ) {
  $_ = uc $_;
}
```

Use grep to select elements in a list

The grep operator has a particular purpose, which is to select or count elements in a list. You wouldn't know this, though, looking at some of the more creative abuses of grep, usually from programmers who feel that a foreach loop isn't quite as cool as a grep. As you try to write effective Perl, we hope you will stay closer to the straight and narrow.

Here's a conventional use of grep in a list context:

```
print grep /joseph/i, @lines;
```

By the way, Perl evaluates the "selection" expression or block argument to grep in a scalar context, unlike map's transform expression. This will rarely make a difference, but it's nice to know.

In a scalar context, grep returns a count of the selected elements rather than the elements themselves:

```
my $has_false = grep !$_, @array;
my $has_undef = grep !defined($_), @array;
```

Things to remember

- Use map when you need to transform one list into another.
- Use grep to filter a list.
- Use foreach when you want to modify the variable in-place.

Item 21. Know the different ways to quote strings.

Perl gives you a plethora of different ways to quote strings.

There are single quotes, where everything is left "as-is" except for escaped backlashes and single quotes:

```
'Isn\'t she "lovely"?'  # Isn't she "lovely"?
```

Double quotes, on the other hand, support several kinds of escape sequences. There are the usual \t, \n, \r, and so on from C:

```
"Testing\none\n\two\n\three"   # Testing
                               # one      wo
                               #      hree
```

There are the octal and hex ASCII escapes like \101 and \x41:

```
"\x50\x65\x72\x6c\x21"  # Perl!
```

You can specify Unicode code points with \x{} (Item 74):

```
"There be pirates! \x{2620}";
```

And you can use Unicode character names if you use the `charnames` module:

```
use charnames;

my $str = "There be pirates! \N{SKULL AND CROSSBONES}";
```

Double quotes also support the interpolation of the contents of variables and subscript expressions beginning with $ and @.

```
foreach $key ( sort keys %hash ) {
   print "$key: $hash{$key}\n";
}
```

The elements of arrays and slices are interpolated by joining them with the contents of the $" special variable—normally a single space:

```
my @n = 1 .. 3;
print "testing @n\n";  # testing 1 2 3
```

If your variable name appears next to other legal identifier characters, you can use {} to delimit the name:

```
print "testing @{n}sies\n";  # testing 1 2 3sies
```

The \u, \U, \l, \L, \E escapes work to change the case of characters in a double-quoted string:

```
my $v = "very";
print "I am \u$v \U$v\E tired!\n"; # I am Very VERY tired!
```

This doesn't begin to cover all the nuances of double-quote interpolation. A full description, with all the gory details, is in the *perlop* documentation.

Alternative quoting: q, qq, and qw

Sometimes it is helpful to be able to use characters other than single or double quotes to enclose strings, especially when those characters show up as literal text in the string. Naturally, Perl allows you to use any punctuation character to enclose strings. Just prefix your favorite character with q for a single-quoted string, or qq for a double-quoted string:

```
q*A 'starring' role*    # A 'starring' role
qq|Don't "quote" me!|   # Don't "quote" me!
```

If you use your new delimiter in the string, you still have to escape it, although you avoid this situation if you can choose a different delimiter:

```
q*Make this \*bold\**    # Make this *bold*
```

If you use a "matchable" delimiter (either (, [, <, or {), then the end of the string is the corresponding closing delimiter. These are all the same:

```
qq<Don't "quote" me!>
qq[Don't "quote" me!]
qq{Don't "quote" me!}
qq(Don't "quote" me!)
```

Perl keeps track of nesting when looking for the closing delimiter:

```
qq<Don't << quote >> me!>    # Don't << quote >> me!
```

Use q{} and/or qq{} to quote source code

The delimiter you choose can give other programmers hints about what you are doing. Use the curly braces when your string is really source code, such as snippets for Benchmark:

```
use Benchmark;

our $b = 1.234;
timethese(
  1_000_000,
  {
    control => q{ my $a =       $b },
    sin     => q{ my $a = sin $b },
    log     => q{ my $a = log $b },
  }
);
```

Create comma-less, quote-less lists with `qw( )`

Finally, as a shorthand way of creating a list of strings, you can quote with
`qw` ("quote words"). Perl splits a string inside `qw` quotes on whitespace,
returning a list of strings:

```
@ISA = qw( Foo Bar Bletch );
```

That is functionally equivalent to quoting the values yourself and separating them with commas:

```
@ISA = ( 'Foo', 'Bar', 'Bletch' );
```

Don't make the mistake of unintentionally including commas inside `qw`
quotes, because they will be considered part of the quoted strings. In this
example you end up with "Foo,", "Bar,", and "Bletch", all but "Bletch"
having extra commas:

```
@ISA = qw( Foo, Bar, Bletch );
```

When you do this with `warnings` enabled (Item 99), you get something
like this:

```
Possible attempt to separate words with commas ...
```

Alternative quoting: "here doc" strings

Perl's **here doc** or **here document** strings provide yet another way to quote
text. Many of you may be familiar with here docs already—Perl's here doc
feature is derived from the UNIX shell feature of the same name. Here
docs are useful for quoting long passages of text or source code.

A here doc string begins with << followed by an identifier, and ends when
that identifier appears on a line by itself somewhere later in the text. The
string begins on the line after <<. If the identifier is quoted (with single,
double, or back quotes), the type of quotes determines the type of string
enclosed in the here doc. The default is a double-quoted string:

```
print <<EOT;  # ; ends statement = comment ignored!
Dear $j $h,

You may have just won $m!
EOT
```

If you want a single-quoted string, you use the single tick (') around the here-doc identifier:

```
print <<'XYZZY';  # single-quoted this time ...
Dear $j $h,

You may have just won $m!
XYZZY
```

Sometimes the here doc can look quite odd because you can use more than one at the same time. The contents stack on each other:

```
print <<"HERE", <<"THERE";
This is in the HERE here doc
HERE
This is in the THERE here doc
THERE
```

Here docs can also look odd as arguments to subroutines, since the text appears outside of the subroutine call:

```
some_sub( <<"HERE", <<"THERE" );
This is in the HERE here doc
HERE
This is in the THERE here doc
THERE
```

Although you can do that, it's pretty confusing for other humans to read it, so you should probably avoid it.

Things to remember

- Use q() or qq() for generalized quoting.
- Use qw() to quote a list automatically.
- Use here docs to quote multi-line strings.

Item 22. Learn the myriad ways of sorting.

At its most basic, sorting in Perl is simplicity itself. Perl's sort operator takes a list of elements and returns a copy of that list in order:

```
my @elements = sort qw(
  hydrogen
  helium
  lithium
);
```

The sort order Perl uses is the UTF-8 collation order (unless you specify use locale or use bytes), meaning that the items are sorted by comparing the UTF-8 values (well, really just the numeric values of the encoding) of the first, second, third, and following characters of each element as necessary. Make sure you know what a character is, though (Item 77).

This leads to some interesting and unexpected results with numbers and case:

```
print join ' ', sort 1 .. 10;
print join ' ', sort qw( my Dog has Fleas );
```

If the default UTF-8 comparison isn't what you want, you need to write your own comparison subroutine.

Comparison (sort) subroutines

A Perl sort subroutine is not an entire sorting algorithm. A better name might be "comparison subroutine."

Sort subroutines are different from ordinary subroutines in that the arguments are passed in via the hard-coded package variables $a and $b rather than as elements of @_. $a and $b are localized for the sort subroutine, as if there were an implicit local($a, $b) at the beginning of the subroutine (but don't do that yourself).

$a and $b get a "bye" from use strict vars—they do not have to be declared explicitly (Item 3). They belong to the current package, not the main package like special variables.

Perl calls the sort subroutine repeatedly during sorting. Its job is to compare $a and $b and return -1, 0 or 1 depending on whether $a sorts less than, equal to, or greater than $b.

Perl's built-in sorting behavior is as though the elements were compared with the cmp operator. Here you have used a named subroutine, utf8ly, to specify the sorting order:

```
sub utf8ly { $a cmp $b }
my @list = sort utf8ly @list;
```

A more concise way of using a `sort` subroutine is to write it as a `sort` block. Just place the body of the subroutine right where the name of the `sort` subroutine would go:

```
my @list = sort { $a cmp $b } ( 16, 1, 8, 2, 4, 32 );
```

To change the sorting order, change the way that `$a` and `$b` are compared. For example, replace the `cmp` operator with `<=>` to sort numerically:

```
my @list = sort { $a <=> $b } ( 16, 1, 8, 2, 4, 32 );
```

You can sort with case-insensitivity by lowercasing each string before you do the comparison:

```
my @list = sort { lc($a) cmp lc($b) } qw(This is a test);

# ('a', 'is', 'test', 'This')
```

You can turn an ascending sort into a descending one by swapping `$a` and `$b`:

```
my @list = sort { $b cmp $a } @list;
```

You can even use `$a` and `$b` to compute values to use for the comparison, like sorting filenames based on their modification times:

```
my @list = sort { -M $a <=> -M $b } @files;
```

Something that comes up from time to time is the need to sort the keys of a hash according to their corresponding values. There is a neat idiom for doing this by using `$a` and `$b` to access the value:

```
my %elems = ( B => 5, Be => 4, H => 1, He => 2, Li => 3 );

sort { $elems{$a} <=> $elems{$b} } keys %elems;
```

Finally, you may want to sort on multiple keys. There is a standard idiom using the `or` operator for this. Here's a slightly contrived example that sorts on first name if the last names are the same:

```
my @first = qw(John Jane Bill Sue Carol);
my @last  = qw(Smith Smith Jones Jones Smith);

my @index = sort {
  $last[$a] cmp $last[$b]   # last name, then
```

```
      or
    $first[$a] cmp $first[$b] #  first name
  } 0 .. $#first;

  for (@index) {
    print "$last[$_], $first[$_]\n";  # Jones, Bill
  }   # Jones, Sue
      # Smith, Carol, etc.
```

In the preceding example, you are actually sorting a list of indices. This is a fairly common thing to do. Note the use of the short-circuit Boolean operator or in the sort subroutine. Each time Perl calls the sort subroutine, it first evaluates the part of the expression to the left of the or. If it evaluates to a non-zero "true" value—in this case, meaning that $a doesn't compare equal to $b—then or returns that value and you're done. Otherwise Perl evaluates the comparison on the righthand side and returns that value.

Note that this wouldn't work if Perl's or operator (or its higher-precedence cousin, ||) returned only 1 or 0. It's the fact that or returns the actual value computed on the lefthand or righthand side that makes this work.

Advanced sorting: the mundane ways

Sometimes it takes a significant amount of processing to compare two keys. For example, let's sort on the third field, the uid, of a password entry:

```
  open my ($passwd), '<', '/etc/passwd' or die;
  my @by_uid =
    sort { ( split /:/, $a )[2] <=> ( split /:/, $b )[2] }
    <$passwd>;
```

This seems okay at first glance. It does indeed sort the lines in the required order. However, it also performs the relatively complex split operation twice each time it calls the sort subroutine.

sort typically calls the subroutine many times for each key. Comparison-based sorting algorithms perform on the order of $n \log n$ comparisons per sort, where n is the number of elements sorted. In order to make your sorts run quickly, you have to make the comparisons run quickly. If your keys require significant transformation before comparison, you should find a way to cache the result of the transformation.

In the preceding example, you could create a hash of the comparison values before performing the `sort`, and then sort the hash by its values:

```
open my ($passwd), '<', '/etc/passwd' or die;
my @passwd = <$passwd>;

# key is whole line, value is uid
my %lines = map { $_, ( split /:/ )[2] } @passwd;

my @lines_sorted_by_uid =
  sort { $lines{$a} <=> $lines{$b} } keys %lines;
```

Advanced sorting: the cool ways

Through design, or perhaps trial, or maybe just by accident, Perl programmers have come up with some convenient idioms for implementing complex sorting transforms.

One of the things that is less than ideal in the preceding examples is the need for a separate statement to set up an array or hash of transformed keys. One way of getting around this is something I have nicknamed the **Orcish Maneuver** ("|| cache"). It uses the little-known ||= operator. Let's revisit the example of sorting filenames by modification date that we saw a little earlier.

Sorting with the Orcish Maneuver

Here's the old way to sort files by their modification ages, inefficiencies included. This sort has to call -M many, many times:

```
my @sorted = sort { -M $a <=> -M $b } @files;
```

Here it is using the Orcish Maneuver:

```
my @sorted =
  sort { ( $m{$b} ||= -M $b ) <=> ( $m{$b} ||= -M $b ) }
  @files;
```

Wow! What the heck is going on here? First of all, look at that ||=:

```
$m{$a} ||= -M $a
```

The ||= has the same semantics as writing it out:

```
$m{$a} = $m{$a} || -M $a
```

The first time the sort subroutine encounters a particular filename $a, $m{$a} has the value undef, which is false, and thus the righthand side of the ||, -M $a, has to be evaluated. Since this is Perl, not C, the || operator returns the actual result of the righthand side, not a simple 0 or 1 ("true" or "false") value. This value now gets assigned to $m{$a}.

Subsequent tests against the same filename will use the modification time value cached in $m{$a}.

The hash %m is temporary and should be empty or undefined when this sort statement is encountered. You may want to wrap this line of code in braces and make %m a my variable to limit its scope, something like:

```perl
{
    my %m;
    @sorted = sort ...
}
```

The Schwartzian Transform

The most concise, all-around sorting technique, though, is the **Schwartzian Transform**, named after Randal Schwartz. A Schwartzian Transform is a sort bracketed by maps.

The best way to show a Schwartzian Transform is to build it up by pieces. Use the prior example of the modification time sorting, but do it more efficiently. First, start with the filenames:

```perl
my @names = glob('*');
```

And now, turn the names into a same-length list of two-element anonymous lists:

```perl
my @names_and_ages = map { [ $_, -M ] } @names;
```

Each element is now a reference to a two-element array—a tuple (Item 13). The first element of each tuple is the original name (from $_), while the second element is the modification age in days (from -M, with an implied $_ argument).

In the next step, sort this list of references using a sort block:

```perl
my @sorted_names_and_ages =
    sort { $a->[1] <=> $b->[1] } @names_and_ages;
```

Within the `sort` block, `$a` and `$b` represent elements of the `@names_and_ages` list, which are array references. Thus, `$a->[1]` represents the second element of a selected tuple, containing the age in days. The net result is that you sort the tuples numerically (note the <=> "spaceship" operator) by ascending ages.

This gets you most of the way there; now all you need to do is to extract the original names from each tuple. Simple enough, with one more map:

```
my @sorted_names =
  map { $_->[0] } @sorted_names_and_ages;
```

And that's it. But that's much too wordy for the seasoned Perl hacker, so here it is all put together as a Schwartzian Transform:

```
my @sorted_names =
  map  { $_->[0] }     # 4. extract original names
  sort { $a->[1]
          <=>
         $b->[1] }     # 3. sort [name, key] tuples
  map  { [ $_, -M ] } # 2. create [name, key] tuples
  @files;              # 1. the input data
```

Just read this from bottom to top, and you'll see it's made up of the same steps as you had in the previous case—but they're all strung together.

Simple sorts involving a single key and transformation can use a similar pattern, changing only the rightmost map and, if necessary, the comparison operator. Here's the password file sorted by the third field using a Schwartzian Transform:

```
open my ($passwd), '<', '/etc/passwd' or die;
my @by_uid =
  map  { $_->[0] }
  sort { $a->[1] <=> $b->[1] }
  map  { [ $_, ( split /:/ )[2] ] } <$passwd>;
```

Note how much more concise this is. You got rid of the hash `%key` used to temporarily store the transformed keys. You were also able to eliminate the `@passwd` array and take the input to the Schwartzian Transform directly from the filehandle.

Things to remember

- Perl sorts according to UTF-8 by default.
- You can give `sort` your own comparison routine.
- For complex sorting situations, you can used a cached-key sort.

Item 23. Make work easier with smart matching.

Perl 5.10 introduced the smart match operator, ~~. It looks at the operands on both sides to decide what to do. You can set up some powerful conditions with minimal typing. Complete details are in the *perlsyn*, but here are some examples to whet your appetite. Smart matching is mostly used with `given-when` (Item 24).

If you want to use smart matching, make sure you are using at least Perl 5.10.1. The original smart match behavior changed from commutative to non-commutative (meaning that the order of operands now matters). Just to be clear, this section specifies the point release of Perl for its examples:

```
use 5.010001;
```

First, consider the simple task of checking that a key exists in a hash, or an element in an array. It's easy to make these conditions:

```
if ( exists $hash{$key} ) { ... }

if ( grep { $_ eq $name } @cats ) { ... }
```

A smart match makes them look a bit nicer, and more consistent, even though it handles different tasks:

```
use 5.010001;  # ~~ changed behavior in 5.10.1

if ( $key ~~ %hash ) { ... }

if ( $name ~~ @cats ) { ... }
```

Next, consider how you would check that some key in a hash matches a regex. You would have to go through all of the keys yourself:

```
my $matched = 0;

foreach my $key ( keys %hash ) {
  do { $matched = 1; last } if $key =~ /$regex/;
}
```

```
if ($matched) {
  print "One of the keys matched!\n";
}
```

That's too much work. You could hide all of that in a subroutine to make the program flow more pleasing, but in Perl 5.10, that work is already built in:

```
use 5.010001;


if ( %hash ~~ /$regex/ ) {
  say "One of the keys matched!";
}
```

If you want to check if an array element matches a regex, the condition looks almost the same:

```
use 5.010001;


if ( @array ~~ /$regex/ ) {
  say "One of the elements matched!";
}
```

Several other operations that would otherwise take a lot of work become almost trivial with the smart match:

```
%hash1  ~~ %hash2      # the hashes have the same keys

@array1 ~~ @array2     # the arrays are the same

%hash   ~~ @keys       # one the elements in @keys is a
                       # key in %hash

$scalar ~~ $code_ref   # $code_ref->( $scalar ) is true
```

The full table for the smart match operator behavior is in the *perlsyn* documentation.

Things to remember

- Use the smart match operator to encapsulate complex behavior.
- Remember that the smart match operator does different things based on its operands.
- Use at least Perl 5.10.1 to get the stable behavior for smart matching.

Item 24. Use `given-when` to make a switch statement.

Almost since Perl came to life, Perl programmers have been complaining about the only thing Perl didn't seem to steal from C: its `switch` statement. As of Perl 5.10, Perl not only fixes that, but as with most things Perl, it makes it a heck of a lot better.

Type less

Perl gives `switch` a new name, calling it `given-when`. As with most of its design, Perl thinks about how people talk to each other: "If I'm `given` this, `when` it is this, I do this." You might already do this as a series of `if-elsif-else` statements:

```
my $dog = 'Spot';

if    ( $dog eq 'Fido'  ) { ... }
elsif ( $dog eq 'Rover' ) { ... }
elsif ( $dog eq 'Spot'  ) { ... }
else                      { ... }
```

You want to test `$dog` for different possibilities, and then run some code when you find the right condition. You have to repeat the structure of the code for every branch. That's too much work for a high-level language such as Perl. Instead, you can use `given-when`, which handles most of typing for you:

```
use 5.010;

given ($dog) {
  when ('Fido')  { ... }
  when ('Rover') { ... }
  when ('Spot')  { ... }
  default        { ... };
};
```

That's a lot less typing! Perl handles some of the tricks for you. First, it **topicalizes** `$dog`, which is Perl's way of saying that it sets the default variable `$_` to the value for `$dog`. That way, you don't type `$dog` over and over again as you did in the first example. Second, Perl automatically compares the topic, `$_`, to the item that you provided. It's the same as doing it yourself, if you like doing extra work:

```
use 5.010;

given ($dog) {
  my $_ = $dog;
  when ( $_ eq 'Fido' ) { ... }
  when ( $_ eq 'Rover' ) { ... }
  when ( $_ eq 'Spot' )  { ... }
  default { ... };
};
```

Smart matching

The `given-when` construct is much more powerful than just a chain of conditions. The previous example uses the `eq` string comparison. In the example before that, though, how does Perl know to use that comparison? Unless you have an explicit comparison in `when`, Perl's really using smart matching, the `~~` (Item 23):

```
use 5.010;

given ($dog) {
  when ( $_ ~~ 'Fido' ) { ... }
  when ( $_ ~~ 'Rover' ) { ... }
  when ( $_ ~~ 'Spot' )  { ... }
  default { ... };
};
```

Smart matching figures out how to compare its two operands by what they are. In this case, Perl sees a scalar variable, `$_`, and a literal string, `'Fido'`. Perl assumes that you want a string comparison and that's what it does. You can use smart matching anywhere, but `when` uses it when you don't specify your own comparison.

If you use something else in the smart match, you get a different comparison. The *perlsyn* documentation has a table of all of the possibilities, but here are some interesting ones:

```
$dog  ~~ /$regex/   # $dog matches the regex
```

```
$dog   ~~ %Dogs      # $dog is a key in %Dogs

$dog   ~~ @Dogs      # $dog is an element in @Dogs

@Dogs ~~ /$regex/   # one item in @Dogs matches regex

%Dogs ~~ /$regex/   # one key in @Dogs matches regex
```

The when block adds the extra magic of assuming that the operand on the lefthand side is the topic, $_. These two are the same:

```
when (RHS) { ... }

when ( $_ ~~ RHS ) { ... }
```

Multiple branches

By default, when a when block matches, that's it. Perl won't try any of the other when blocks. That's just what you would expect of an `if-elsif-else` construct. There is an implicit `break` at the end of each when block that tells it to break out of the loop:

```
use 5.010;

given ($dog) {
   when ('Fido')  { ...; break }
   when ('Rover') { ...; break }
   when ('Spot')  { ...; break }
   default        { ... };
};
```

However, with a `continue`, you can run one when block and then try the next one, too. In this example, you can test the name in $dog in each when:

```
use 5.010;

my $dog = 'Spot';

given ($dog) {
   when (/o/) { say 'The name has an "o"'; continue }
   when (/t/) { say 'The name has a "t"'; continue }
   when (/d/) { say 'The name has a "d"'; continue }
```

```
};
```

Intermingling code

Once of the other drawbacks of `if-elsif-else` is that you can't run interstitial code between the conditions. You have to match a condition before you run any code. With `given-when`, you can insert any code you like around the when portions, including code that changes the topic:

```
use 5.010;

my $dog = 'Spot';

given ($dog) {
   say "I'm working with [$_]";
   when (/o/) { say 'The name has an "o"'; continue }

   say "Continuing to look for a t";
   when (/t/) { say 'The name has a "t"'; continue }

   $_ =~ tr/p/d/;
   when (/d/) { say 'The name has a "d"'; continue }
};
```

Switching over a list

You can use when in a `foreach` loop, too. It does the same thing as in a given, although you get to try the condition for each item in the input list:

```
use 5.010;

my $count = 0;

foreach (@array) {
   when (/[aeiou]$/)  { $vowels_count++ }
   when (/[^aeiou]$/) { $count++ }
}

say "\@array contains $count words ending in consonants and
   $vowel_count words ending in vowels";
```

Things to remember

- Use `given-when` if you want a switch statement.
- The smart match operator in `when` uses `$_` by default.
- Use `when` in other looping constructs besides `given`.

Item 25. Use do `{}` to create inline subroutines.

The do `{}` syntax lets you group several statements as a single expression. It's a bit like an inline subroutine. For example, to quickly read in an entire file, you can localize the input record separator `$/` (Item 43), open the file with a lexical filehandle (Item 52), read the data, and store it in a scalar, all in one block:

```perl
my $file = do {
   local $/;
   open my ($fh), '<', $filename or die;
   <$fh>;
};
```

With the do block, `local` and `my` are scoped to just that block; they don't affect anything else. The last evaluated expression, `<$fh>`, is the return value of the block, just as it would be for a conventional subroutine. You assign that value once to `$file`, which you declare outside the block to give it the proper scope.

Consider the same thing without do `{}`. You want to make some things short term inside the block, but you have to end up with the contents outside the block. You have to do some extra work to assign the `$file`, which you have to type twice:

```perl
my $file;
{
   local $/;
   open my ($fh), '<', $filename or die;
   $file = join '', <$fh>;
}
```

You can save some code in chains of `if-elsif-else` blocks that you might use simply to set the right values. Suppose you need to select the localization for thousands and decimal separators. You could declare some variables, and then assign to those variables based on the right conditions:

```
my ( $thousands_sep, $decimal_sep );
if ( $locale eq 'European' ) {
  ( $thousands_sep, $decimal_sep ) = qw( . , );
}
elsif ( $locale eq 'English' ) {
  ( $thousands_sep, $decimal_sep ) = qw( , . );
}
```

That's a bit sloppy, because you have to type the variables several times, making the code dense and obscuring the task. With a do, you can use the fact that the last evaluated expression is the result, so you can get rid of the extra variable typing:

```
my ( $thousands_sep, $decimal_sep ) = do {
  if    ( $locale eq 'European' ) { qw( . , ) }
  elsif ( $locale eq 'English' )  { qw( , . ) }
};
```

Sometimes you might want to use a do to move some error handling out of the way to de-emphasize it. For instance, if you have to go through a list of files but don't want to stop because you can't open one of them, you can catch the failure in open and run an expression on the righthand side of the or:

```
foreach my $file (@files) {
  open my ($fh), '<', $file or do { warn ...; next };
  ... do stuff ...;
}
```

If your do {} gets much longer than a couple of statements, you're better off moving it into its own subroutine, so don't overuse the idiom.

There's another use for do, although it's rather rare. Sometimes you want to run your while block before you test the condition for the first time. Consider prompting users for a string, and continuing to prompt them until they type it correctly. You need to get their first input before you can test it, so you repeat some code:

```
print "Type 'hello': ";
chomp( my $typed = <STDIN> );
```

```
while ( $typed ne 'hello' ) {
  print "Type 'hello': ";
  chomp( $typed = <STDIN> );
}
```

You can eliminate the duplicate code by using `while` as an expression modifier for a do `{}` when you need run some code before you check the condition:

```
my $typed;
do {
  print "Type 'hello': ";
  chomp( $typed = <STDIN> );
} while ( $typed ne 'hello' );
```

You did need to declare `$typed`, which is a bit ugly, but it's not as ugly as the previous example.

Things to remember

- A do block returns the last evaluated expression.
- Fit the do anywhere you can use an expression.
- Use the scope of the do block to localize variables.

Item 26. Use `List::Util` and `List::MoreUtils` for easy list manipulation.

One of the keys to grokking Perl is knowing how to work with lists. Indeed, in his preface to *Higher Order Perl*, Mark Jason Dominus says that Perl is more like Lisp than it is like C. Perl has the built-ins like `map`, `grep`, and `foreach` that you can use to build up complex list handling. Some list operations are so common that you can use fast, C implementations of them in either `List::Util` or `List::MoreUtils`.

Find the maximum value quickly

If you need to find the maximum number in a list, you can easily do it yourself in pure Perl:

```
my @numbers = 0 .. 1000;
my $max     = $numbers[0];
```

```
foreach (@numbers) {
  $max = $_ if $_ > $max;
}
```

But in pure Perl that's relatively slow. The `List::Util` module, which comes with Perl, provides a `max` routine implemented in C that does it for you:

```
use List::Util qw(max);


my $max_number = max( 0 .. 1000 );
```

The `maxstr` routine does the same thing for strings:

```
use List::Util qw(maxstr);


my $max_string = maxstr( qw( Fido Spot Rover ) );
```

Similarly, you could easily sum a list of numbers yourself in pure Perl:

```
my $sum = 0;
foreach ( 1 .. 1000 ) {
  $sum += $_;
}
```

But it's much easier and faster with `List::Util`'s `sum`:

```
use List::Util qw(sum);


my $sum = sum( 1 .. 1000 );
```

Reduce a list

There's another way to sum numbers. `List::Util`'s `reduce` function, again implemented in C, can do it for you much faster and with a more-pleasing syntax:

```
use List::Util qw(reduce);


my $sum = reduce { $a + $b } 1 .. 1000;
```

`reduce` takes a block just like `sort`, but works differently. It shifts off the first two elements in its input list and aliases them to `$a` and `$b`. The input list is now two elements shorter. `reduce` takes the result of the operation, in this case addition, and unshifts it onto the input list. It starts the process over and finally stops when it has only one element, which becomes the result of the `reduce`—in this case, $sum.

Knowing that, you can come up with other reductions that don't already have their own functions, such as taking the product of all of the numbers:

```
my $product = reduce { $a * $b } 1 .. 1000;
```

Determine if any element matches

In pure Perl, it's annoying to find the *first* element in a list that matches some condition. It's easy to find that *any* element matches a condition. For instance, you can easily check that `@list` contains an element that is greater than 1,000:

```
my $found_a_match = grep { $_ > 1000 } @list;
```

However, what if `@list` has 100 million elements, and the first element is 1,001? The preceding code will still check every item even though you already have your answer. You could fix this by terminating the loop yourself, but do you really want to write that much code?

```
my $found_a_match = 0;
foreach my $elem (@list) {
  $found_a_match = $elem if $elem > 1000;
  last if $found_a_match;
}
```

`List::Util`'s `first` routine does all of this for you, and also tells you what the value was. It has the advantage, however, of stopping once it knows the answer. It doesn't need to scan the entire list to see if one of the numbers is larger than 1,000:

```
use List::Util qw(first);
```

```
my $found_a_match = first { $_ > 1000 } @list;
```

In the `List::MoreUtils` module, which you have to install from CPAN yourself in most cases, there are additional convenience functions:

```
use List::MoreUtils qw(any all none notall);
```

```
my $found_a_match = any  { $_ > 1000 } @list;
my $all_greater   = all  { $_ > 1000 } @list;
```

```
my $none_greater  = none  { $_ > 1000 } @list;
my $all_greater   = notall { $_ % 2   } @list;
```

Iterate over more than one list at a time

Sometimes you have several lists that correlate with one another, and you
want to iterate through them simultaneously. You could do the usual thing
by using an index, which wraps the interesting parts of your code with
some structural code. If you wanted a new list, `@c`, with the sum of corresponding elements in `@a` and `@b`, you could iterate over the indices and
add the corresponding values in each array:

```
my @a = (...);
my @b = (...);
my @c;

foreach my $i ( 0 .. $#list ) {
  my ( $a, $b ) = ( $a[$i], $b[$i] );
  push @c, $a + $b;
}
```

Instead of all that extra code to handle the arrays, use the `pairwise` routine in `List::MoreUtils`:

```
use List::MoreUtils qw(pairwise);
```

```
my @c = pairwise { $a + $b } @a, @b;
```

The `pairwise` routine is fine if you have two arrays, but if you have more
than two, you can make an iterator with `each_array`, which brings back
a little of the work but is still easier:

```
use List::MoreUtils qw(each_array);
```

```
my $ea = each_array( @a, @b, @c );
```

```
my @d;
while ( my ( $a, $b, $c ) = $ea->() ) {
  push @d, $a + $b + $c;
}
```

Merge arrays

If you need to merge two or more arrays, you can do it the hard way, but
List::MoreUtils can make it easy with its mesh routine:

```
use List::MoreUtils qw(mesh);

my @odds  = qw/1 3 5 7  9/;
my @evens = qw/2 4 6 8 10/;

my @numbers = mesh @odds, @even;  # returns 1 2 3 4 ...
```

And more much

You've seen only a few examples of what the List::Util and
List::MoreUtils modules can do for you to reduce the amount of code
that you type as well as to show other programmers your intent. Check
out their documentation to see what else these modules can do for you.

Things to remember

- Use the List::Utils and List::MoreUtils modules for common
  list operations.
- Select items from a list with List::MoreUtils' all, any, none, or
  notall.
- Work with multiple lists at the same time with pairwise or
  each_array.

Item 27. Use autodie to simplify error handling.

Many of Perl's built-in functions are system calls that might fail through
no fault of your program, so you have to check that they've succeeded. For
instance, when you try to open a file, you have to ensure that the open
worked before you try to use the filehandle:

```
open my ($fh), '<', $file
  or die "Could not open $file: $!";
```

All of the error checking clutters your code, but you do it over and over
again. To save yourself the typing, you can use the autodie pragma

(included with Perl starting with 5.10.1, but also on CPAN so you can install it yourself):

```
use autodie;

open my ($fh), '<', $file;  # automatically dies for you
```

By itself, `autodie` applies to all of the functions it handles, mostly all of the built-ins that interact with the system. If you want it to apply only to certain functions, you can tell autodie to handle those specific functions only, or all of the functions in a group:

```
use autodie qw(open close);  # only specific functions

use autodie qw(:filesys);    # all functions from group
```

You don't have to apply `autodie` to your entire file either. It's a lexical pragma, like `strict`, that applies only within its scope:

```
{
  use autodie;

  open my ($fh), '<', $file;  # automatically dies for you
}
```

Alternatively, you can apply `autodie` to the entire file and turn it off within a scope:

```
use autodie;

{
  no autodie;  # back to normal in this scope

  chdir('/usr/local') or die "Could not change to $dir";
}
```

When `autodie` raises an error for you, it sets `$@`, the `eval` error variable, to an instance of an `autodie::exception` object:

```
use autodie;

eval { open my ($fh), '<', $file };
my $error = $@;  # always save $@ right away
                 # in case it changes
```

You can query the error to see where it came from. `autodie` is smart enough to know how to classify the errors so you have some flexibility in how you handle them. The `autodie::exception` object knows how to deal with the smart match operator (Item 23), so you can have a hierarchy of handlers going from specific to general. You can match against the specific sort of error or the error type (these are listed in the `autodie` documentation):

```
use 5.010;
use autodie;

eval { open my ($fh), '<', $file };
my $error = $@;  # always save $@ right away
                 # in case it changes
given ($error) {
  when (undef)  { say "No error"; }
  when ('open') { say "Error from open"; }
  when (':io')  { say "Non-open, IO error."; }
  when (':all') { say "All other autodie errors." }
  default       { say "Not an autodie error at all." };
}
```

If you don't have Perl 5.10, you have to do a bit more work to handle the `autodie` errors:

```
# from the autodie documentation
if ( $error and $error->isa('autodie::exception') ) {
  if ( $error->matches('open') ) {
    print "Error from open\n";
  }
  if ( $error->matches(':io') ) {
    print "Non-open, IO error.\n";
  }
}
elsif ($error) {  # A non-autodie exception.
  ...;
}
```

Things to remember

- Use `autodie` to handle errors from built-ins automatically.
- Specify subsets of `autodie` to limit its effect.
- Catch `autodie` exceptions with `eval`.

3 | Regular Expressions

Perl's regular expressions are a language unto themselves, and that language seems almost as complex as Perl, perhaps even more so.

You don't have to use everything, but there are some features of regular expressions that will make your life much easier. This chapter shows you some of their more-popular features.

Although Perl's regular-expression engine contains many optimizations for efficiency, it's possible—and easy at times—to write matches and substitutions that run much more slowly than they should.

Efficiency may not always be your primary objective. In fact, efficiency should rarely be your primary objective in software development. Generally, a programmer's first priority should be to develop adequate, robust, and correct solutions to problems. It doesn't hurt, though, to keep efficiency in mind.

Now that Perl handles Unicode, Perl's regular expressions have many features to deal with not only bytes but characters and graphemes, too. Not only that: Regular expressions can deal with character properties. We save most of this issue for Chapter 8, "Unicode," so you'll find quite a bit of regex stuff there, too.

Item 28. Know the precedence of regular expression operators.

The "expression" in "regular expression" is there because regular expressions are constructed and parsed using grammatical rules similar to those used for arithmetic expressions. Regular expressions serve a very different purpose, true; but understanding the similarities between them will help you write better regular expressions, and hence better Perl.

Regular expressions are made up of atoms and operators. **Atoms** are generally single-character matches. For example:

```
a      # matches the letter a
\$     # matches the character $
```

```
\n       # matches newline
[a-z]    # matches a lowercase letter
.        # matches any character except \n
\1       # arbitrary length--backreference to 1st capture
```

There are also special "zero-width" atoms. For example:

```
\b       # word boundary--transition from \w to \W
^        # matches start of a string
\A       # absolute beginning of string
\Z       # end of a string or newline at end --
         # might or might not be zero-width
\z       # absolute end of string with nothing after it
```

Atoms are modified or joined together by regular-expression operators. As in arithmetic expressions, there is an order of precedence among these operators.

Regular expression precedence

Fortunately, there are only four precedence levels. Imagine if there were as many as there are for arithmetic expressions!

Parentheses and the other grouping operators have the highest precedence. Table 3-1 shows the precedence order of regular-expression operators.

A repetition operator binds tightly to its argument, which is either a single atom or a grouping operator:

```
ab*c       # matches ac, abc, abbc, abbbc, etc.
abc*       # matches ab, abc, abcc, abccc, etc.
ab(c)*     # same thing and capture the c
ab(?:c)*   # same thing but don't capture the c
abc{2,4}   # matches abcc, abccc, abcccc
(abc)*     # matches empty string, abc, abcabc, etc.
```

Table 3-1 Regular Expression Operator Precedence, from Highest to Lowest

Precedence	Operators	Description
Highest	() (?:) etc.	Parentheses and other grouping
	? + * {m,n} +? ++ etc.	Repetition
	^ $ abc \G \b \B [abc]	Sequence, literal characters, character classes, assertions
Lowest	a|b	Alternation

Placement of two atoms side-by-side is called **sequence**. Sequence is a kind of operator, even though it is written without punctuation. To illustrate this, let's suppose that sequence were actually represented by a bullet character (•). The above examples would look like:

```
a•b*•c           # matches ac, abc, abbc, abbbc, etc.
a•b•c*           # matches ab, abc, abcc, abccc, etc.
a•b•(c)*         # same thing and capture the c
a•b•(?:c)*       # same thing but don't capture the c
a•b•c{2,4}       # matches abcc, abccc, abcccc
(a•b•c)*         # matches empty string, abc, abcabc, etc.
```

Is the precedence of the operators more apparent now?

The last entry in the precedence chart is alternation. Let's continue to use the "•" notation for a moment:

```
e•d|j•o          # matches ed or jo
(e•d)|(j•o)      # same thing
e•(d|j)•o        # matches edo or ejo
e•d|j•o{1,3}     # matches ed, jo, joo, jooo
```

The zero-width atoms like ^ and \b group the same way as do other atoms:

```
^e•d|j•o$        # matches ed at beginning, jo at end
^(e•d|j•o)$      # matches exactly ed or jo
```

It's easy to forget about precedence. Removing excess parentheses is a noble pursuit, especially within regular expressions, but be careful not to remove too many:

```
# who sent me this email?
/^Sender|From:\s+(.*)/; # WRONG! -- this would match:
                        # X-Not-Really-From: faker
```

The pattern was meant to match `Sender:` and `From:` lines in a mail header, but it actually matches something somewhat different. Here it is with some parentheses added to clarify the precedence:

```
/(^Sender)|(From:\s+(.*))/;
```

Adding a pair of parentheses, or perhaps capture-free parentheses, (?:) (Item 32), fixes the problem:

```
# better, this time
/^(Sender|From):\s+(.*)/;      # $1 contains Sender or From
/^(?:Sender|From):\s+(.*)/;    # $1 contains the data
```

Double-quote interpolation

Perl regular expressions are subject to the same kind of interpolation as double-quoted strings are. Variable names, and string escapes like \U and \Q, are not regular-expression atoms, and are never seen by the regular-expression parser. Interpolation takes place in a single pass that occurs before Perl parses a regular expression:

```
/te(st)/;        # matches test in $_
/\Ute(st)/;      # matches TEST
/\Qte(st)/;      # matches te(st)
$x = 'test';
/$x*/;           # matches tes, test, testt, etc.
/test*/;         # same thing as above
```

Double-quote interpolation and the separate regular-expression parsing phase combine to produce a number of common "gotchas." For example, here's what can happen if you forget that an interpolated variable is not an atom:

```
# read in a pattern and match it twice
chop( $pat = <STDIN> );  # for example, bob
print "matched\n" if /$pat{2}/;       # WRONG--/bob{2}/
print "matched\n" if /($pat){2}/;     # CORRECT--/(bob){2}/
print "matched\n" if /$pat$pat/;      # brute force way
```

In this example, if the user typed in bob, the first regular expression would match bobb, since the contents of $pat are expanded before the regular expression is interpreted.

All three of the preceding regular expressions have another potential pitfall. Suppose the user types in the string hello :-). This will generate a fatal run time error. The result of interpolating this string into /($pat){2}/ is /(hello :-)){2}/, which, aside from being nonsense, has unbalanced parentheses. Perl tells you where your regex error is:

```
Unmatched ) in regex; marked by <-- HERE in ↵
   m/(hello :-)) <-- HERE {2}/
```

You can catch this with qr// (Item 40).

If you don't want special characters like parentheses, asterisks, periods, and the like interpreted as regular-expression metacharacters, use the quotemeta operator, or the escape \Q. Both quotemeta and \Q put a back-slash in front of any character that isn't a letter, digit, or underscore.

In the following code, you read a string from standard input, quote it, then use that string for matching. If the string that was input were **hello :-)**, it would become **hello\ \:\-\)** after quoting, making it safe to use in a regular-expression match.

```
chomp( $pat = <STDIN> );
my $quoted = quotemeta $pat;
print "matched\n" if /($quotemeta){2}/;
```

Alternatively, you can do the meta-quoting in the expression itself with \Q and \E:

```
chomp( $pat = <STDIN> );
print "matched\n" if /(\Q$pat\E){2}/;
```

As with seemingly everything else pertaining to regular expressions, tiny errors in quoting metacharacters can result in strange bugs:

```
# this actually means /hello \ \:\-\)\{2\}/--fatal error
print "matched\n" if /(\Q$pat){2}/;  # WRONG! no \E
```

Things to remember

- Watch out for regular-expression precedence.
- Use parentheses to group parts of a regular expression.
- Use \Q or quotemeta to use metacharacters as literal characters.

Item 29. Use regular expression captures.

Although regular expressions are handy for determining whether a string looks like one thing or another, their greatest utility is in helping you parse the contents of strings. To break apart strings with regular expressions, you use regular-expression captures.

The capture variables: $1, $2, $3 . . .

Most often, parsing with regular expressions involves the use of the regular expression capture variables $1, $2, $3, and so on. **Capture variables** are associated with parentheses inside regular expressions, also known as

capture buffers. Each pair of parentheses in a regular expression "captures" what its contents match and "memorizes" it in a capture variable. For example, you can pick apart a URL, separating the host from the path:

```
$_ = 'http://www.perl.org/index.html';
if (m#^http://([^/]+)(.*)#) {
  print "host = $1\n";   # www.perl.org
  print "path = $2\n";   # /index.html
}
```

Only successful matches affect the capture variables. An unsuccessful match leaves the capture variables alone, even if it appears that part of a match might be succeeding. Continuing with the preceding code example, a new, unsuccessful match leaves $1 and $2 with the values they contained before the evaluation of the following expression:

```
$_ = 'ftp://ftp.uu.net/pub/';
if (m#^http://([^/]+)(.*)#) {
  print "host = $1\n";   # still www.perl.org
  print "path = $2\n";   # still /index.html
}
```

When an expression inside a pair of parentheses matches several different places in a string, the corresponding capture variable contains the last match:

```
$_ = 'ftp://ftp.uu.net/pub/systems';
if (m#^ftp://([^/]+)(/[^/]*)+#) {
  print "host = $1\n";        # ftp.uu.net
  print "fragment = $2\n";   # /systems
}
```

The capture variables are assigned in the order of the opening parentheses, regardless of nesting. In cases involving nested parentheses, count left parentheses to determine which capture variable a particular set of parentheses refers to:

```
$_ = 'ftp://ftp.uu.net/pub/systems';
if (m#^ftp://([^/]+)((/[^/]*)+)#) {
  print "host = $1\n";        # ftp.uu.net
  print "path = $2\n";        # /pub/systems
  print "fragment = $3\n";   # /systems
}
```

The "count left parentheses" rule applies for all regular expressions, even ones involving alternation:

```
$_ = 'ftp://ftp.uu.net/pub';
if (m#^((http)|(ftp)|(file)):#) {
  print "protocol = $1\n";   # ftp
  print "http     = $2\n";   # empty string
  print "ftp      = $3\n";   # ftp
  print "file     = $4\n";   # empty string
}
```

The $+ special variable contains the value of the last non-empty buffer:

```
print "\$+ = $+\n";   # ftp, from $3
```

And the parade of frills continues! Capture variables are automatically localized by each new scope. In a unique twist, these localized variables receive copies of the values from the outer scope. This is in contrast to the usual reinitializing of a localized variable:

```
$_ = 'ftp://ftp.uu.net/pub';
if (m#^([^:]+)://(.*)#) {
  print "\$1, \$2 = $1, $2\n";     # ftp, ftp.uu.net/pub
  {
    # $1 and $2 start with the values from outside
    print "\$1, \$2 = $1, $2\n";   # ftp, ftp.uu.net/pub
    if ( $2 =~ m#([^/]+)(.*)# ) {
      print "\$1, \$2 = $1, $2\n";# ftp.uu.net, /pub
    }
  }

  # on exit from the block, the old $1 and $2 are back
  print "\$1, \$2 = $1, $2\n";     # ftp, ftp.uu.net/pub
}
```

The localizing mechanism used is `local`, not `my` (Item 43).

Numbered backreferences

Regular expressions can make use of the capture buffers with backreferences. The atoms \1, \2, \3, etc. match the contents of the corresponding buffers.

An obvious (but not necessarily useful) application of backreferences is in solving simple word puzzles. For example, this expression matches a doubled word character:

```
/(\w)\1/;
```

An this matches two or more repeated word characters:

```
/(\w)\1+/;
```

It is important to keep count of your nested parentheses. For instance, this expression, which matches consecutive pairs of repeated word characters, must backreference \2 because of the nesting:

```
/((\w)\2){2,}/;
```

You can reuse backreferences. The following example finds occurrences where the same vowel is repeated four times. The first line illustrates the long way so you can see repeated backreferences. The second line is more idiomatic:

```
/([aeiou]).*\1.*\1.*\1/;
/([aeiou])(.*\1){3}/;
```

Although you may not find yourself using them all that often, backreferences are a powerful feature. They can sometimes be handy for dealing with delimiters in a simplified way. You can find matching quotes with them:

```
q/"stuff"/ =~ /(['"]).*\1/;
```

You probably don't want greedy regular expressions, because you'll end up eating up too many quotes. A nongreedy (Item 34) version works better:

```
q/"stuff","more"/ =~ /(['"]).*?\1/;
```

You can even get really fancy and handle escaped quotes:

```
q/"stuff\"more/ =~ /(['"])(\\\1|.)*?\1/;
```

Unfortunately, this approach breaks down quickly: You can't use it to match parentheses (even without worrying about nesting), and there are faster ways to deal with embedded escapes.

Captures in substitutions

Capture and match variables are often used in substitutions. The variables $1, $2, $&, and so forth within the replacement string of a substitution refer to the capture buffers from the match part, not from an earlier statement. Knowing this, you can perform such functions as swapping two words using a substitution:

```
s/(\S+)\s+(\S+)/$2 $1/;
```

Try some simple HTML entity escaping, using a hash of mapped escape values:

```
my %ent = { '&' => 'amp', '<' => 'lt', '>' => 'gt' };
$html =~ s/([&<>])/&$ent{$1};/g;
```

You can even use substitution to collapse words, in this case "abbreviating" a newsgroup name:

```
$newsgroup =~ s/(\w)\w*/$1/g;
```

You don't need capture variables in some substitutions if you look at what to throw away rather than what to keep. Between these two methods of eliminating leading whitespace, use the second version, since it does less work:

```
s/^\s*(.*)/$1/; # WASTEFUL
```

```
s/^\s+//;        # better
```

You can use the /e (eval) option to help solve some tricky problems where you need to compute the replacement string during substitution. Here, you replace all of the names of nonexistent files with a "not found" message:

```
s/(\S+\.txt)\b/-e $1 ? $1 : "<$1 not found>"/ge;
```

Substitutions using /e can sometimes be more legibly written using matching delimiters, and possibly the /x option (Item 37):

```
s{
  (\S+\.txt)\b  # all the filenames ending in .txt
}{
  -e $1 ? $1 : '<$1 not found>'
}gex;
```

Matching in list context

In list context, the match operator returns a list of values corresponding to the contents of the capture buffers. If the match is unsuccessful, the match operator returns an empty list. This doesn't change the behavior of the capture variables: $1, $2, $3, and so on are still set as usual.

This is one of the most-useful features of the match operator. It allows you to scan and split apart a string in a single step. This makes tasks like splitting RFC 2822 headers easy and compact:

```
my ( $name, $value ) = /^([^:]*):\s*(.*)/;
```

You can be selective about what is returned. This code returns a Subject: line minus any Re: portion:

```
my ( $bs, $subject ) = /^subject:\s+(re:\s*)?(.*)/i;
```

The result can be sliced to provide just the information you want:

```
my $subject = (/^subject:\s+(re:\s*)?(.*)/i)[1];
```

Alternatively, you can just make the parentheses around the Re: match noncapturing:

```
my ($subject) = /^subject:\s+(?:re:\s*)?(.*)/i
```

Using a match inside a map is even more succinct. Here you pull the date with a very compact line of code:

```
my ($date) = map { /^Date:\s+(.*)/ } @msg_hdr;
```

Note how it turns out to be extremely handy that a failed match returns an empty list.

Tokenizing with regular expressions

Tokenizing a string—dividing it into lexical elements like whitespace, numbers, identifiers, operators, and so forth—offers an interesting application for regular-expression captures.

If you have written (or tried to write) computer-language parsers in Perl, you may have discovered that Perl seems to be missing some features that would make the task easier. In fact, it can seem downright difficult at times. The problem is that when you are "lexing" a string, what you want is to find out which of several possible patterns matches the beginning of a string. What Perl is good at, though, is finding out where in a string a single pattern matches. The two don't map onto one another very well.

Take the example of parsing simple arithmetic expressions containing numbers, parentheses, and the operators +, -, *, and /. Let's ignore whitespace, assuming you would have substituted it out beforehand.

One way to parse arithmetic might be via a series of conditions that each pushes its match into an array:

```
my @tokens;

while ($_) {
  if (/^(\d+)/) {
    push @tokens, 'num', $1;
  }
  elsif (/^([+\-\/*()])/) {
    push @tokens, 'punct', $1;
  }
  elsif (/^([\d\D])/) {
    die "invalid char $1 in input";
  }
  $_ = substr( $_, length $1 );
}
```

This turns out to be moderately efficient, even if it looks ugly. Regular expressions that are anchored with ∧ execute very quickly, since Perl tries matching only at the start of the string rather than potentially at every position in it.

However, if you start feeding long strings to a lexer like this, it will slow down considerably because of the substr operation at the end. You might think of keeping track of the current starting position in a variable named $pos, and then doing something like:

```
if ( substr( $_, $pos ) =~ /^(\d+)/ ) { ... }
```

That probably won't be much faster, and may even be slower on short strings.

One approach that works reasonably well, and is not affected unduly by the length of the text to be lexed, relies on the behavior of the match operator's /g option in a scalar context. Each time a /g match is executed in scalar context, the regular-expression engine starts looking for a match after the end of the preceding match. This allows you to use a single regular expression, and it frees you from having to keep track of the current position explicitly:

```
# the m//g method
while (
    /
    (\d+)          |   # number
    ([+\-\/*()])   |   # punctuation
    (\D)               # something else
    /xg
  )
{
  if ( $1 ne "" ) {
    push @tok, 'num', $1;
  }
  elsif ( $2 ne "" ) {
    push @tok, 'punct', $2;
  }
  else {
    die "invalid char $3 in input";
  }
}
```

Things to remember

- Use the capture variables only after a successful match.
- Save a list of captures by using the match operator in list context.

Item 30. Use more precise whitespace character classes.

Whitespace is a tricky subject that seems simple, but has plenty of gotchas that can trip you up. There is horizontal whitespace, which we generally think of as word separators, and various types of typographical whitespace that make text easy to read.

Similarly, our concept of "lines" is often defined by some sort of vertical whitespace. Computers don't particularly care about lines, and programs know about them only because they group characters together based on a character that the program decides is the line separator.

Perl's regular expressions have a variety of ways for you to specify exactly the type of whitespace that you need to match.

Horizontal whitespace

Prior to Perl 5.10, you had two predefined character classes that dealt with whitespace. The \s matched all whitespace, and its complement \S matched everything that wasn't whitespace. With this sweeping classification of whitespace, you could easily find yourself manipulating characters unintentionally if you weren't paying attention. Suppose you want to replace runs of whitespace with a single space. You might try just matching \s+:

```
my $string = <<'HERE';
This    is    a         line
This    is      another line
And a      final    line
HERE


$string =~ s/\s+/ /g;
```

Since the line endings are whitespace, too, you end up replacing each with a single space. Instead of four lines of single-spaced words, you end up with one line:

```
This is a line This is another line And a final line
```

To avoid this, you could specify exactly the characters you want:

```
$string =~ s/[ \t]+/ /g;
```

You might think that replacing all spaces and tabs with spaces would do the job, but what if the string includes any of the several other horizontal whitespace characters in the Unicode Character Set? You won't remove those spaces with such a restrictive substitution.

As of Perl 5.10, you can use the \h character class to match any horizontal whitespace:

```
use 5.010;


$string =~ s/\h+/ /g;
```

Now you can collapse all of your horizontal whitespace while keeping your line endings in place.

Like Perl's other character-class shortcuts, \h has a converse, \H, which matches everything that is not horizontal whitespace, including vertical whitespace and all nonwhitespace characters.

Vertical whitespace

Just as you have situations where you want to match only horizontal white-space, you may find yourself needing to match only vertical whitespace. This includes the carriage return, newline, form feed, vertical tab, and Unicode line and paragraph separators. If you want to check whether you have a multi-line string, for example, you can match any vertical whitespace with \v:

```
use 5.010;


if ( $string =~ m/\v/ ) {
   say 'Found a multiline string';
}
```

To break your multiline string into lines no matter the separator, you can use \v in your `split` pattern:

```
my @lines = split /\v/, $multi_line_string;
```

The converse of \v, \V, matches all nonvertical whitespace, including horizontal whitespace and all nonwhitespace characters.

Any line ending

Line endings are a long-standing annoyance of computing. There's the newline and there's the carriage return. Some files use just the newline to terminate a line, and some files use a carriage return followed by a newline. Many network protocols also expect a carriage return-newline pair. Unicode introduces additional line-ending characters.

Say your job is to handle any line ending, or even all of them at the same time. You could match sequences of optional carriage returns followed by newlines so you can normalize each line ending to a single newline:

```
$string =~ s/(?:\r?\n)/\n/g;
```

However, that doesn't quite work, since the \r and \n are really logical characters that don't necessarily map to the same bits on every system (Mac Classic, we're looking at you). You might change the expression to use a character class, so you can match a single occurrence or two consecutive occurrences of either character:

```
$string =~ s/[\r\n]{1,2}/\n/g;
```

However, that might turn \n\n, which should end two separate lines, into one line. Also, it still doesn't handle Unicode line endings.

To handle all sorts of line endings, you could use a quite-complicated regular expression that includes some characters you may not have thought of as line endings, such as the vertical tab, 0x0B, and the form feed, 0x0C:

```
$string =~
    s/(?>\x0D\x0A?|[\x0A-\x0C\x85\x{2028}\x{2029}])/\n/g;
```

Rather than making you go through all of that, Perl 5.10 introduces the \R character class, which does the same thing:

```
use 5.010;


$string =~ s/\R/\n/g;
```

Now, each of your line endings is just a newline.

Non-newlines

Perl 5.12 introduces a new character-class shortcut for non-newlines, \N. Normally, you can match any non-newline with . as in:

```
if ( $string =~ m/(.+)/ ) { ... }
```

If someone adds the /s flag, however, perhaps in a blind conversion to "best practices," the . suddenly matches newlines and breaks your code:

```
if ( $string =~ m/(.+)/xsm ) { ... } # BROKEN!
```

If you know that you want only non-newlines, you can match them explicitly with \N rather than relying on side effects from /s:

```
use 5.012;


if ( $string =~ m/(\N+)/ ) { ... }
```

The complement of \N is, curiously, not a character-class shortcut. It's just \n, the newline. Remember this for your next Perl Trivia Challenge.

Things to remember

- Match horizontal whitespace with \h.
- Match vertical whitespace with \v.
- Match non-newlines with \N.

Item 31. Use named captures to label matches.

Wouldn't it be grand if you didn't have to remember all of those numbered variables to get the parts of the string you matched? Consider the annoyances you've had to tolerate. For instance, say you write a regular expression to match a couple of names:

```
$_ = 'Buster and Mimi';
if (/(\S+) and (\S+)/) {
  my ( $first, $second ) = ( $1, $2 );
  ...;
}
```

Later, the requirements change and you have to add some more parentheses, but you forget about the change in the number variables. It happens to all of us:

```
$_ = 'Buster or Mimi';
if (/(\S+) (and|or) (\S+)/) {
  my ( $first, $second ) = ( $1, $2 );  # OOPS!
  ...;
}
```

Imagine this example with several more captures added.

What if you didn't have to remember which number went with which capture? If you have Perl 5.10 or later, you're in luck, since you can use named capture syntax. Instead of just parentheses, you use the (?<LABEL>) syntax. Your matches show up in the %+ hash, with the labels as keys:

```
use 5.010;

$_ = 'Buster and Mimi';
if (/(?<first>\S+) and (?<second>\S+)/) {
```

```
      my ( $first, $second ) = ( $+{first}, $+{second} );
      ...;
  }
```

Now, if you add another set of parentheses, nothing goes wrong, because the matches don't depend on order:

```
  use 5.010;

  $_ = 'Buster and Mimi';
  if (/(?<first>\S+) (and|or) (?<second>\S+)/) {
    my ( $first, $second ) = ( $+{first}, $+{second} );
    ...;
  }
```

This works for backreferences, too. Instead of using \1, \2, and so on, you use \k<label> to refer to a named capture:

```
  use 5.010;

  $_ = 'Buster and Buster';
  if (/(?<first>\S+) (and|or) \k<first>/) {
    say 'I found the same name twice!';
  }
```

Even though you have given labels to some of these captures, Perl still tracks them in the numbered variables, so you can use either after the match.

Perl 5.10 also introduces relative backreferences, so you don't have to remember the absolute position of each capture. With \g, you can specify the absolute number corresponding to the capture you want:

```
  if (/(?<first>\S+) (and|or) \g1/) {
    say 'I found the same name twice!';
  }
```

In that case, you still must count the captures to ensure that you get the right one. Better are relative backreferences. If you know the match you want is two captures back, you can use a negative number to refer to its position, although you have to wrap curly braces around the number:

```
  if (/(?<first>\S+) (and|or) \g{-2}/) {
    say 'I found the same name twice!';
  }
```

Things to remember

- Staring with Perl 5.10, you can label your captures.
- Find your labeled capture results in the %+ hash.
- Use relative backreferences to avoid counting absolute capture positions.

Item 32. Use noncapturing parentheses when you need only grouping.

Parentheses in Perl regular expressions serve two different purposes: grouping and capture. While this is usually convenient, or at least irrelevant, it can get in the way sometimes. For instance, if you want to match the Subject: line of an e-mail, ignoring possible reply prefixes, you might use two sets of parentheses:

```
my ( $bs, $subject ) = /^subject:\s+(re:\s*)?(.*)/i
```

You need the first set of parentheses for grouping (so the ? will work correctly), but they get in the way, capture-wise. What you would like to have is the ability to group without captures.

Perl offers a feature for this specific purpose. Capture-free parentheses (?:) group like parentheses, but don't create backreferences or capture variables. If you are using parentheses for grouping alone, you don't need a copy of what the parentheses matched. You can save the time required to make the copy by using Perl's capture-free parentheses:

```
my ($subject) = /^subject:\s+(?:re:\s*)?(.*)/i;
```

Some patterns use nested parentheses, as you might if trying to match a host name with (\w+(\.\w+)*). There's no point in remembering the contents of the inner parentheses in this pattern, so if you want to save a little time, use capture-free parentheses:

```
my ($host) = m/(\w+(?:\.\w+)*)/;
```

The time you save isn't generally all that much unless the parentheses match large chunks of text, and capture-free parentheses don't exactly improve readability. But sometimes, every little bit of speed helps. To see just how much, benchmark your regular expressions (Item 41).

Capture-free parentheses are also handy in the match-inside-map construct, where you use the match in list context so it returns a list of its captures:

```
my @subjects =
  map { /^subject:\s+(?:re:\s*)?(.*)/i } @headers;
```

You can also use capture-free parentheses to disable the **separator-retention mode** in `split`. Normally, captures in the pattern you give to `split` also show up in the output list:

```
my $string = '1:2:3:4';
my @items = split /(:)/, $string;
```

With separator-retention mode, you get the captures, too. In this example, `@items` now contains the list `qw(1 : 2 : 3 : 4)`, including both the digits and the colons. This can be useful when you want to know what was between the elements, but more often it's a mistake.

Suppose you want to break up the string by either : or ;, surrounded by optional whitespace. You must use parentheses to set off the , | ; so you can trim whitespace on both sides:

```
my $string = '1:2; 3: 4 ;5';
my @items = split /\s*(,|;)\s*/, $string;
```

You probably didn't mean to keep those separators, but now you have them! Oops. To leave them out of the output list, use the noncapturing parentheses:

```
my @items = split /\s*(?:,|;)\s*/, $string;
```

Things to remember

- Use noncapturing parentheses when you only need to group elements.
- Use noncapturing parentheses in `split` to avoid separator-retention mode.

Item 33. Watch out for the match variables.

The match variables (`$``, `$&`, and `$'`) impose a speed penalty on your Perl programs because they cause Perl to perform some extra bookkeeping. After a successful match, they represent the part of the string that comes before the match, the part that matched, and the part that follows the match, respectively:

```
'My cat is Buster Bean' =~ m/Buster/;

print <<"HERE";
 Prematch: $`
    match: $&
Postmatch: $'
HERE
```

In the output you see the parts of the string surrounding the match:

```
  Prematch: My cat is
     match: Buster
Postmatch:  Bean
```

Match variables can help with text manipulation when a you need to compute a replacement string. For instance, suppose you want to replace HTML comments:

```
# replacing certain html comments
while (<OLD>) {
  if ( /<!--\s*(.*?)\s*-->/ and ok_to_replace($1) ) {
    $_ = $` . html_data($1) . $';
  }
  print NEW $_;
}
```

Performance issues

Some people complain that using match variables makes Perl programs run more slowly. This is true—they do complain.

But the match variables actually do pose a performance problem. They might be useful for a particular match, but any time Perl sees one of these variables anywhere in your source, it turns on the special accounting it needs for remembering these parts, and it does that for every match, whether you want it or not. This extra works slows down your program significantly.

```
'My cat is Buster Bean' =~ m/Buster/;
print "I matched $&\n";

while (<>) {
  next unless /Bean/;  # penalty on every match!
}
```

You might even get these variables when you don't intend to use them. For instance, the `English` module that provides long names equivalent to Perl's special variables uses `$``, `$&`, and `$'`. Just loading the module is enough to trigger the problem:

```
use English;  # Oops! Now all are slower
```

When you use that module, you can tell it not to handle those match vars:

```
use English qw(-no_match_vars);
```

Use the /p flag

Perl 5.10 introduced a new way to do the same thing but apply it to only one match operator rather than to all of them. When you use `/p` with the match operator, Perl sets the `${^PREMATCH}`, `${^MATCH}`, and `${^POSTMATCH}` variables, but only for that match. You don't suffer the global penalty:

```
use 5.010;

'My cat is Buster Bean' =~ m/\s\w+\sBean/p;
say "I matched ${^MATCH}";

while (<>) {
  next unless /Bean/;  # no penalty!
}
```

Things to remember

- Avoid using the match variables, which degrade performance.
- Don't accidently use the match variables when you use `English`.
- Use the `/p` flag to enable the per-match variables in Perl 5.10.

Item 34. Avoid greed when parsimony is best.

Greed isn't about money, at least where regular expressions are concerned. It's the term used to describe the matching behavior of most regular-expression engines, Perl's included.

A general rule is that a Perl regular expression will return the "leftmost longest" match it can find, at the first position in a string where it can find a match of any length. Repetition operators like * and + "gobble up" characters in the string until matching more characters causes the match to fail:

```
$_ = "Greetings, planet Earth!\n";
/\w+/;          # matches Greetings
/\w*/;          # matches Greetings
/n[et]*/;       # matches n in Greetings
/n[et]+/;       # matches net in planet
/G.*t/;         # matches Greetings, planet Eart
```

This is normally a desirable behavior, but not always. What if you want to match just the text between single quotes? In this example, you match too much:

```
# match a single-quoted string--not!
$_ = "This 'test' isn't successful?";
my ($str) = /('.*')/;  # matches "test' isn"
```

Perl keeps matching beyond what appears to be the end of your pattern. It isn't really, though: The . matches ' characters, ending at the last occurrence of '.

You can fix the single-quoted string example by excluding single quote from the characters allowed inside the match string:

```
# match a single-quoted string, the old-fashioned way
$_ = "This 'test' isn't successful?";
my ($str) = /('[^']*')/;  # matches 'test'
```

Fortunately, Perl has nongreedy repetition operators. This is a powerful and enormously helpful feature that allows you to write simple regular expressions for cases that previously required complex or even impossibly difficult regular expressions.

You can make any repetition operator (*, +, {m,n}) **nongreedy** by following it with a question mark (?). The operator will then match the shortest string that results in a pattern match, rather than the longest. This makes the examples above trivially simple:

```
# match a single-quoted string the nongreedy way
$_ = "This 'test' isn't successful?";
my ($str) = /('.*?')/;  # matches 'test'
```

You can now attempt more ambitious operations, like matching a double-quoted string that contains character escapes (let's support \", \\, and \123):

```
# a double-quoted string
$_ = 'a "double-quoted \"string\042"';
my ($str) = /("(\\["\\]|\\\d{1,3}|.)*?")/;
print $str;  # "double-quoted \"string\042"
```

The only problem with nongreedy matching is that it can be somewhat slow. Don't use nongreedy operators unnecessarily, but do use them to avoid having to write complex regular expressions that might or might not work correctly.

Things to remember

- Remember that Perl's quantifiers match the longest strings they can.
- Avoid writing patterns that match more than you intend.
- Make your quantifiers nongreedy with ?.

Item 35. Use zero-width assertions to match positions in a string.

Sometimes you need to match a condition, rather than characters, in a string. You can match word boundaries, the start or end of the string, or the starts or ends of lines in a string. Perl's regular expressions have **anchors** that constrain the match to these positions. These anchors are also called **zero-width assertions** because they specify a condition but don't consume any characters.

Use \b for word boundaries

Consider the following pattern match, which wants to extract the username and terminal from the output of the who command:

```
# innocuous at first ...
my @who = `who`;
$_ = pop @who;
my ( $user, $tty ) = /(\w+)\s+(\w+)/;
```

This works fine on input like joebloe ttyp0 ... but will not match at all on strings like webmaster-1 ttyp1 ... and will return a strange result on joebloe pts/10. You probably should have matched any nonwhitespace instead:

```
my ( $user, $tty ) = /(\S+)\s+(\S+)/;
```

There is probably something wrong in your regular expression if you have \w adjacent to \s, or \W adjacent to \S. At the least, you should examine such regular expressions very carefully.

Another thing to watch out for is "words" containing punctuation characters. Suppose you want to search for a whole word in a text string:

```
print "Enter a word to search for: ";
my $word = <STDIN>;
print "found\n" if $text =~ /\b\Q$word\E\b/;
```

This works fine for input like `hacker` and even `Perl5-Porter`, but fails for words like `goin'`, or any word in general that does not begin and end with a \w character. It will also consider `isn` a matchable word if `$text` contains `isn't`. The \b matches transitions between \w and \W characters—not transitions between \s and \S characters. If you want to support searching for words delimited by whitespace, you have to write something like this instead:

```
print "Enter a word to search for: ";
my $word = <STDIN>;
print "found\n" if $text =~ /(^|\s)\Q$word\E($|\s)/;
```

The word boundary anchor, \b, and its inverse, \B, are zero-width assertions. They are not the only zero-width assertions (^, \A, etc. are others), but they are the easiest to get wrong. If you are not sure what \b and \B will match in your string, try substituting for them:

```
my $text = q(What's a "word" boundary?);
( my $btext = $text ) =~ s/\b/:/g;
( my $Btext = $text ) =~ s/\B/:/g;
print "$btext\n$Btext\n";
```

When you run that program, you see a colon everywhere Perl thinks it sees a word boundary:

```
% tryme
:What:':s:  :a:  ":word:"  :boundary:?
W:h:a:t's  a  :"w:o:r:d":  b:o:u:n:d:a:r:y?:
```

The results at the ends of the string should be especially interesting to you. Note that if the last (or first) character in a string is not a \w character, there is no word boundary at the end of the string. The beginnings and ends of the strings are virtual nonword characters. Note also that there are not-word boundaries between consecutive \W characters (like space and double-quote) as well as consecutive \w characters.

Match the beginning with ^ or \A

The ^ anchor normally matches at the beginning of a string. Many people incorrectly learn that it's the "beginning-of-line" anchor, because they only ever use it on single-line strings. This regex will match only the first word, even though it has the /g flag:

```perl
my $string = <<'HERE';
This is a line
That is another line
And a final line
HERE

my (@matches) = $string =~ m/^(\w+)/g; # only 'This'

print "@matches\n";
```

The output shows that you've made only one match:

```
This
```

If you want to match all of the lines' first words, you can use the /m flag to turn on **multiline mode**. The /m changes the ^ anchor to match at the beginning of the string or after a line ending:

```perl
my (@matches) = $string =~ m/^(\w+)/mg;
```

Now the output shows all of the words of the beginnings of the lines:

```
This That And
```

In multiline mode, if you want to match only at the beginning of the string, use the \A anchor. In this example, you match a word that starts with a T at the beginning of the string or a word that doesn't start with a T at the beginning of any other line:

```perl
my (@matches) = $string =~ m/
    (           # start of $1
        (?:     # noncapturing parens
        \A T    # start of string then T
        |       # --or--
```

```
     ^ [^T]   # start of line and not a T
     )
  \w+          # the rest of the word
  )            # end of $1
```

```
  /xmg;
```

The output shows that you match just two words, one for each type of anchor:

```
  This And
```

You can also do some things that are a bit more clever with a beginning-of-line anchor, such as initializing the `%scores` hash by matching two fields per line from a here document:

```
  my %scores = <<'EOF' =~ /^(.*?):\s*(.*)/mg;
  fred: 205
  barney: 195
  dino: 30
  EOF
```

Match the end with $ or \Z

The `$` normally matches the end of a string, although it leaves room for a possible newline at the end:

```
  if ( "some text\n" =~ /text$/ ) {
    print "Matched 'text'\n";
  }
```

The preceding example matches as if newline weren't there. It still works if you omit the newline from the string:

```
  if ( "some text" =~ /text$/ ) {
    print "Matched 'text'\n";
  }
```

However, if what you really want is the absolute end of a string, you need to be explicit, perhaps using a negative lookahead to ensure that there isn't a newline left over:

```
  if ( "some text\n" =~ /text(?!\n)$/ ) {   # fails
    print "Matched 'text'\n";
  }
```

Here, the `(?!\n)` ensures that there are no newline characters after the `$`, and this is enough to force `$` to its end-of-string meaning.

You don't need to go that far, however, since the `\z` anchor does the same thing. This match fails because there's a newline after `text`, so `text` is not at the absolute end of the string:

```
if ( "some text\n" =~ /text\z/ ) {   # fails
  print "Matched 'text'\n";
}
```

You could also use the `\Z` anchor, which matches at the end of the string but also allows a possible newline, just like `$`. The string matches because `\Z` can ignore the newline:

```
if ( "some text\n" =~ /text\Z/m ) {   # works again
  print "Matched 'text'\n";
}
```

By adding the `/m` suffix to the regular expression, a `$` can also match just before intermediate newlines:

```
print "fred\nquit\ndoor\n" =~ /(..)$/mg;
```

Both the preceding and the following examples print `editor` (the last two characters of each line):

```
print "fred\nquit\ndoor" =~ /(..)$/mg;   # Same
```

Things to remember

- Use `\b` to match boundaries between word and nonword characters.
- Use `\A` or `\z` to match the absolute beginning or end of a string.
- Use `^` or `$` to match the beginning or end of each line in multiline mode.

Item 36. Avoid using regular expressions for simple string operations.

Regular expressions are wonderful, but they are not the most-efficient way to perform every string operation. Although regular expressions can be used to perform string operations such as extracting substrings or translating characters, they are better suited for more-complex operations. Simple string operations in Perl should be handled by special-purpose operators like `index`, `rindex`, `substr`, and `tr///`.

Bear in mind that all regular-expression matches, even simple ones, must manipulate capture variables. If all you need is a comparison or a substring, manipulating capture variables is a waste of time. For this reason, if no other, you should prefer special-purpose string operators to regular-expression matches whenever possible.

Compare strings with string-comparison operators

If you have two strings to compare for equality, use string-comparison operators, not regular expressions:

```
# the fast way
if ( $answer eq 'yes' ) { something_wonderful() }
```

The string-comparison operators are at least twice as fast as regular-expression matches, especially if you don't use anchors:

```
# the slow way
if ( $answer =~ /^yes$/ ) { something_wonderful() }


# even slower (and probably wrong) without anchors
if ( $answer =~ /yes/ ) { something_wonderful() }
```

Some more-complex comparisons are also faster if you avoid regular expressions. You don't need a regular expression just for case-insensitivity, for example:

```
# this is faster ...
if ( lc($answer) eq 'yes' ) { something_wonderful() }


# ... than this
if ( $answer =~ /^yes$/i ) { something_wonderful() }
```

Find substrings with `index` and `rindex`

The `index` operator locates an occurrence of a shorter string in a longer string. The `rindex` operator locates the rightmost occurrence, but still counts character positions from the left:

```
# find position of $little_str in $big_str, 0-based
my $pos = index $big_str, $little_str;

# find rightmost $little_str in $big_str
my $pos = rindex $big_str, $little_str;
```

The `index` operator is very fast—it uses a Boyer-Moore algorithm for its searches. Perl will also compile `index`-like regular expressions into Boyer-Moore searches. You could use a match operator, and then look at the length of `$'`, the part of the string before the match (although match operators will be slower):

```
$big_str =~ /\Q$little_str/;   # Don't do this
my $pos = length $';

# yes, the pos operator does have uses; still slow
$big_str =~ /\Q$little_str/g;   # or /og, maybe
my $pos = pos($big_str) - length($big_str);
```

The overhead associated with using a regular-expression match makes `index` several times faster than `m//` for short strings, even if the match uses the `/o` option.

Extract and modify substrings with `substr`

The `substr` operator extracts a portion of a string, given a starting position and length. If no length is provided, then the remainder of the string is extracted.

```
# extract "Perl"
my $perl = substr "It's a Perl World", 7, 4;

# extract "Perl World"
my $perl_world = substr "It's a Perl World", 7;
```

The `substr` operator is much faster than a regular expression written to do the same thing:

```
# the slow way
my ($perl) = ( "It's a Perl World" =~ /^.{7}(.{4})/ );
```

The neatest thing about `substr` is that you can make replacements with it by using it on the left side of an expression. The text referred to by `substr` is replaced by the string value of the righthand side:

```
# change the world
my $world = "It's a Perl World";
substr( $world, 7, 4 ) = "Mad Mad Mad Mad";
```

You can combine `index` and `substr` to perform `s///`-like substitutions, but for this purpose, `s///` is usually faster:

```
# look for Perl, then replace it:
substr( $world, index( $world, Perl ), 4 ) =
  "Mad Mad Mad Mad";


# less noisy and probably faster
$world =~ s/Perl/Mad Mad Mad Mad Mad/;
```

Transliterate single characters

If you want to change all occurrences of a character to another character, you don't need the substitution operator, which requires all the overhead of the regular-expression engine and has additional side effects you don't care about:

```
$string =~ s/a/b/g;
```

Don't forget about Perl's `tr///` operator. It doesn't use regular expressions because it changes literal characters to other characters. You don't need a /g flag (`tr///` doesn't have one) because it always changes all characters:

```
$string =~ tr/a/b/;
```

The transliteration operator matches corresponding characters on each side to perform a one-for-one replacement. You can even use ranges to specify the characters. Here's a Perly version of ROT-13, moving every letter over 13 places in the alphabet:

```
$string =~ tr/a-mA-Mn-zN-Z/n-zN-Za-mA-M/;
```

If you want to transliterate only part of a string, you can combine it with `substr` as an lvalue:

```
substr( $string, 0, 10 ) =~ tr/a/b/;
```

Things to remember

- Don't use regular expressions to solve every problem.
- Use Perl's many string operators to do their jobs.
- Use the transliteration operator to replace single characters.

Item 37. Make regular expressions readable.

Regular expressions are often messy and confusing. There's no denying it—regular expressions have a very compact and visually distracting appearance. They are a "little language" unto themselves. However, this little language isn't made up of words like `foreach` and `while`. Instead, it uses atoms like `\w`, `[a-z]`, and +.

The concept of regular expressions is confusing all by itself. Ordinary programming chores generally translate more-or-less directly into code. You might think "count from 1 to 10," and write a `foreach` loop like the following:

```
foreach my $i ( 1 .. 10 ) {
   print "$i\n";
}
```

A regular expression that accomplishes a particular task may not look a whole lot like a series of straightforward instructions. You might think "find me a single-quoted string," and wind up with something like:

```
/'(?:\\'|.)*?'/
```

You can make regular expressions more (human-) readable, which is especially important if you intend to share your programs with others, or if you plan further work on them yourself. Keeping regular expressions simple is a start, but there are a couple of Perl regex features you can use to help make even complex regular expressions more understandable.

Add whitespace and comments to regular expressions

Normally, whitespace encountered in a regular expression is significant. In this example, the literal space in the regex matches space in the string:

```
my ( $a, $b, $c ) = /^(\w+) (\w+) (\w+)/;
```

Literal newlines in the following patterns match newlines in the string:

```
$_ = "Testing
one
two";  # $_ contains embedded newlines
```

```
s/
/<lf>/g;   # replace newlines with <lf>

print "$_\n";   # Testing<lf>one<lf>two
```

The /x flag, which you can apply to both pattern matches and substitutions, tells the regular-expression parser to ignore whitespace (so long as it isn't preceded by a backslash), including comments. You can use this to spread out the logical parts of your expression and group the parts of the regex. This pattern to find a single-quoted string, including any escaped quote, looks much better when you can easily see the parts of the pattern:

```
my ($str) = /( ' (?: \\' | . )*? ' )/x;
```

This can be especially helpful when a regular expression includes a complex alternation and a couple of levels of grouping. With /x, you can format the regular expression to show its structure, explain the purpose of each part, and show an example of the text you want to match. When literal whitespace is not significant, you can add Perl comments inside the pattern:

```
my ($str) = m/
        (               # start of $1
        "               # start of double-quoted string

    (?:
        \\\W              | # special char, \+
        \\x[0-9a-fA-F]{2} | # hex,          \xDE
        \\[0-3][0-7]{2}   | # octal         \0377
        [^"\\]              # ordinary char
    )*

        "
    )                   # end of $1

    /x;
```

Break complex regular expressions into pieces

Regular expressions are subject to double-quote interpolation (Item 28). You can use this feature to write regular expressions that are built up out of variables. In some cases, this may make them easier to read. With qr//

(Item 40), you can create the subpatterns that you compose into a larger regular expression:

```perl
my $num   = qr/[0-9]+/;
my $word  = qr/[a-zA-Z_]+/;
my $space = qr/[ ]+/;

$_ = "Testing 1 2 3";
my @split = /($num | $word | $space)/gxo;
print join( ":", @split ), "\n";   # Testing: :1: :2: :3
```

The pattern this example creates is /([0-9]+ | [a-zA-Z_]+ | [ ])/gxo. We used the /o ("compile once") flag (Item 39), since there is no need for Perl to compile this regular expression more than once.

You can rewrite the double-quoted string example from earlier, this time using subpatterns to represent the parts, and then composing them into the final regex in $whole:

```perl
my $whole = do {

  # escaped char like \", \$
  my $spec_ch = qr/\\ \W/x;

  # hex escape: \xab
  my $hex_ch = qr/\\x [0-9a-fA-F]{2} /x;

  # oct escape: \123
  my $oct_ch = qr/\\  [0-3][0-7]{2} /x;

  # ordinary char
  my $char = qr/[^\"\\]/;

  qr/
        (
            "
            (?: $spec_ch | $hex_ch | $oct_ch | $char) *
            "
        )
        /xo;
};
```

```
#... and here's the actual regular expression ...
my ($str) = /$whole/o;
```

If you are curious as to exactly what a regular expression built up in this manner looks like, print out `$whole`. The regular-expression object stringifies it for you:

```
print "The regex is----\n$whole\n----\n";
```

This is a fairly straightforward example of using variables to construct regular expressions. See the book *Mastering Regular Expressions*[1] for a much more complex example—a regular expression that can parse an RFC 2822 address.

Things to remember

- Use the /x flag to add insignificant whitespace and comments to regular expressions.
- Format your regular expressions to emphasize their structure.
- Build up regular expressions from smaller regular expressions.

Item 38. Avoid unnecessary backtracking.

Alternation in regular expressions is generally slow. Because of the way Perl's regular-expression engine works, each time an alternative in a regular expression fails to match, the engine has to "backtrack" in the string and try the next alternative:

Suppose you want to match one of several possible names. You might try an alternation that includes each name:

```
while (<>) {
  print
    if /\b(george|jane|judy|elroy)\b/;
}
```

The pattern match finds a word boundary, and then tries to match `george`. If that fails, it backs up to the boundary and tries to match `jane`; if that

---

1. Jeffrey E.F. Friedl, *Mastering Regular Expressions, Third Edition,* (Sebastopol, CA: O'Reilly Media, 2006).

fails, judy, then elroy. If one of those names matches, it looks for another word boundary.

Backtracking is especially bad when many of the alternations look similar. Consider this contrived example, where the alternations start with the same prefix:

```
'aaabbbccg' =
    ~/\b(aaabbbccc|aaabbbccd|aaabbbcce|aaabbbccf)\b/;
```

The match operator tries the first alternation and tests it all the way until the final c before it discovers that it doesn't match the last character. It then backs up all the way and starts the second alternation, again getting all the way to the end before it fails. It backs up again, and keeps trying all of the alternations, eventually failing. That's a lot of work.

There's a way around this, though, by building a **trie** (as in **retrie**val). That's a tree that uses the common prefixes from all of the alternations to construct an optimized alternation that minimizes backtracking. The Regexp::Trie module handles the details for you:

```
use Regexp::Trie;

my $rt = Regexp::Trie->new;
foreach (qw/foobar foobah fooxar foozap fooza/) {
  $rt->add($_);
}

my $alternation = $rt->regexp;

print "$alternation\n";
```

The output shows the regular expression that the module created to efficiently scan the string with a minimum of backtracking:

```
(?-xism:foo(?:ba[hr]|xar|zap?))
```

When you want to use this in the match operator, you just interpolate it into the match operator:

```
$string =~ m/$alternation/;
```

As of Perl 5.10, the regular-expression engine automatically modifies each string-literal alternations into a trie, so in some cases you don't have to handle the details yourself.

Use a character class (`[abc]`) instead of alternation

There are some instances where alternation is completely unnecessary and should be avoided. For example, using an alternation instead of a character class can impose a tremendous speed penalty on a pattern match. You might try to find a Perl variable name by using an alternation to match the sigil:

```
while (<>) {
    push @var, m'(($|@|%|&)\w+)'g;
}
```

Since you're trying to match a single character, you should use a character class instead:

```
while (<>) {
    push @var, m'([$@%&]\w+)'g;
}
```

Avoid unnecessary backtracking from quantifiers

Consider the pattern `/\b(\w*t|\w*d)\b/`, which matches words ending in either `t` or `d`. Each time you use this pattern, the engine will look for a word boundary. It then tries the first alternation, looking for as many word characters in a row as possible. Then it looks for a `t`. It won't find one, since it already has read all the word characters, so it will have to back up a character. If that character is a `t`, that's great—now it can look for a word boundary, and then it's all done. If there was no match, the engine keeps backing up and trying to find a `t`. If it runs all the way back to the initial word boundary, then the engine tries the second half of the alternation, looking for a `d` at the end.

You can see that this is a very laborious process. While the regular-expression engine is meant to do complicated work, this particular pattern makes that work much more complicated than it needs to be.

An obvious shortcoming is that if the engine starts out at the beginning of a word that ends in `d`, it has to go all the way to the end and back-search fruitlessly for a `t` before it even starts looking for a `d`. You can fix this by getting rid of the alternation:

```
/\b\w*[td]\b/
```

This is an improvement. Now, the engine will scan the length of the word only once, regardless of whether it ends in `t`, `d`, or something else.

This doesn't completely solve the backtracking issue, though. Notice that there is no need for the regular-expression engine to backtrack more than a single character from the end of a word. If that character isn't a t or d, there's no point in continuing, since even if it did find one earlier in the string, it wouldn't be what you are looking for, a t or d at the end of the word.

You can approach the problem in a slightly different manner. Ask yourself: "If I were looking for words ending in t or d, what would I be looking at?" More than likely, you'd look just at the ends of words:

```
/[td]\b/
```

Now, this is interesting. This little regular expression does everything that the other two do, though it may not be obvious at first. Think about it: To the left of the t or d there will be zero or more \w characters. You don't care what sorts of \w characters they are, so, tautologically if you will, once you have a t or d to the left of a word boundary, you have a word ending in t or d. This is a general issue with the * quantifier at the beginning of a pattern: Since it can always match zero instances, it's the same as not being there at all.

Naturally, this little regular expression runs much faster than either of the two preceding it—about twice as fast, in fact. And obviously there's not much backtracking, since the expression matches only a single character!

Nonbacktracking, possessive quantifiers

One way to avoid backtracking is to tell Perl not to do it. Perl 5.10 introduces a "possessive" form of the regular-expression quantifiers. Put a + after any quantifier, and it will not backtrack. The quantifier will match as much as possible and never give anything back. If the portion of the regex after the quantifier can't match where the regex left off, the match fails.

Suppose you want to find something interesting in a string representing a DNA sequence. You write a regular expression that matches as many groups of three letters as you can, then a GCG, followed by any two characters, and then a G. Maybe this is DNA gibberish or represents a mutant alien, but it illustrates backtracking quite well:

```
my $string = 'GCGGCCGCAGCUGCCGCUGCAGCCGCCGCUGCCGCCGCG';

if ( $string =~ /^(?:GC.)*GCG(..G)/ ) {
```

```
    print "Matches GCG with XXG afterward!\n";
  }
```

To see all the steps this goes through, you can use the `re` pragma to turn on regex debugging. You can run the following program yourself to see its lengthy output:

```
use re 'debugcolor';

my $string = 'GCGGCCGCAGCUGCCGCUGCAGCCGCCGCUGCCGCCGCG';

if ( $string =~ /^(?:GC.)*GCG(..G)/ ) {
  print "Matches GCG with XXG afterward!\n";
}
```

In this example, the * is greedy, so it matches as much as it can, almost to the end of the string. It discovers that although there is a GCG at the end, there isn't anything after it. It starts backtracking, trying the match three characters back, failing, backtracking again, failing, and so on, all the way back to the beginning. It finds GCG at the beginning, but all of that work is a waste, because you really wanted it to fail after it matched the last GCG in the string. That's not so bad in this short example, but imagine it with a much longer strand of DNA, or repeated on millions or billions of strings.

You can get rid of the backtracking with the possessive +, which applies to any of the quantifiers. Add it to any quantifier and that quantifier will never backtrack. Now the match fails much more quickly:

```
if ( $string =~ /^(?:GC.)*+GCG(..G)/ ) {
  print "Matches GCG with XXG afterward!\n";
}
```

As a side note, you might also write the pattern with a negated character class so you don't match a G in the first group:

```
/^(?:GC[^G])*GCG(..G)/
```

Things to remember

- Turn alternations into tries for faster matching.
- Use character classes to represent multiple possibilities for single characters.
- Use possessive quantifiers to avoid regular-expression backtracking.

Item 39. Compile regexes only once.

The regular expressions for most pattern matches and substitutions are compiled into Perl's internal form only once—at compile time, along with the rest of the surrounding statements. In the following example, Perl compiles the pattern `/\bmagic_word\b/` only once, since it is a constant pattern. Perl reuses the compiled form again and again during run time:

```
# count occurrences of magic_word in @big_long_list
foreach (@big_long_list) {
  $count += /\bmagic_word\b/;
}
```

When a pattern contains interpolated variables, as in `/\b$magic\b/`, older `perls` recompile it every time it executes the match operator. It doesn't know whether the variable has changed (although in modern `perls`, it does):

```
print "Give me the magic word: ";
chomp( my $magic = <STDIN> );

# count occurrences of the magic word in @big_long_list
foreach (@big_long_list) {
  $count += /\b$magic\b/;
}
```

Recompiling such a pattern each time it is used in a match is grossly wasteful. If you know `$magic` isn't going to change, you can tell Perl as much by using the `/o` flag on the match operator.

```
print "Give me the magic word: ";
chomp( my $magic = <STDIN> );

# count occurrences of the magic word in @big_long_list
foreach (@big_long_list) {
  $count += /\b$magic\b/o;  # compile once
}
```

Now Perl will compile the regular expression only once. If you change `$magic`, the match operator will not notice.

The `/o` flag also works for substitutions. The replacement string in the substitution continues to work normally—it can vary from match to match:

```
print "Give me the magic word: ";
chomp( my $magic = <STDIN> );

foreach (@big_long_list) {
  s/\b$magic\b/random_word()/eo;
}
```

The /o flag works with regular-expression quoting, too (Item 40), which also allows you to pre-compile regular expressions.

Things to remember

- Be careful when you interpolate variables into regular expressions.
- Use the /o flag to compile a regular expression only once.

Item 40. Pre-compile regular expressions.

Quick—how many components do you see in this Perl expression?

```
/abc/
```

There are two parts to the expression: the match operator and the regular expression inside the match operator. The match operator applies the regex to its target, but the operator and the regex inside it aren't inseparable.

You can create compiled regular expressions outside of the match or substitution operator with qr//. Its syntax is just like that of any other generalized quoting (Item 21):

```
my $name  = 'Buster';
my $regex = qr/\b$name\b/;
```

As with normal string interpolation in the match operator, regular-expression metacharacters are special. The value in $regex becomes a virtual reference to a compiled regular expression. It's really just a string with some magic attached to it. It looks like a reference to ref, but if you dereference it, you just get undef. However, if you print it out and take a look, the output resembles the regular expressions that you know and love:

```
(?-xism:\bBuster\b)
```

You can still use any of the flags that affect the pattern, such as /i, /m, and /s. This regular expression is case-insensitive, and lets the . match a newline, so the two names can appear across lines:

```
my $regex = qr/Buster(.*)Mimi/si;
```

You can compile `$regex` into your match or substitution operators just as you could with strings:

```
# count occurrences of the magic word in @big_long_list
foreach (@big_long_list) {
  $count += /$regex/;  # compiled once
}
```

You don't even need the match operator explicitly, although it looks a bit weird without it:

```
$string =~ $regex;
```

You can also use `qr//` to test that a regular expression compiles before you try to use it. You don't have to wait until you try to apply the regular expression to find out whether it will work. Compile the regex in an `eval`:

```
my $name = '(';
my $regex = eval { qr/\b$name\b/ }
  or die "Regex failed: $@";
```

For instance, if `$name` had an unbalanced `(`, you could catch the error. Perl helpfully tells you what confused it:

```
Unmatched ( in regex; marked by <-- HERE in m/( <-- HERE /
```

Things to remember

- Pre-compile a regular expression with `qr//`.
- Interpolate pre-compiled regular expressions into the match operator.
- Use `eval` to try matches that might not interpolate into valid regular expressions.

Item 41. Benchmark your regular expressions.

As with many other things in Perl, one of the best ways to determine how to make a pattern match run quickly is to write alternative implementations and compare them to one another.

Use the `Benchmark` module to see how much of a difference capture-free parentheses (Item 32) can really make. Here's a small program to test a

regular expression that extracts the requesting host from the line of an
Apache *access_log* in the common log format, which looks like:

```
www.example.com - - [01/Dec/2009:21:09:42 -0600] "POST / ↵
  HTTP/1.1" 200 30447
```

To pull out the hostname at the front of that entry, you could try two regular expressions along with a control:

```
use Benchmark qw(timethese);
my @data = <>;

timethese(
  $ARGV[0] || 100,
  {
    control => q{
        foreach (@data) {
            my ($host) = 'www.example.com'
        }
    },

    mem => q{
        foreach (@data) {
            my ($host) = m/(\w+(\.\w+)+)/;
        }
    },

    memfree => q{
        foreach (@data) {
            my ($host) = m/(\w+(?:\.\w+)+)/;
        }
    },
  }
);
```

When we tested this under Perl 5.10.0 on a MacBook Air using a 100,000
line Apache *access_log*, the capture-free parentheses performed about 22%
faster:

```
Benchmark: timing 100 iterations of control, mem, memfr↵
  ee...
    control:  2 secs ( 2.05 usr +  0.02 sys =  2.07 CPU)
```

```
      mem: 25 secs (24.36 usr +  0.12 sys = 24.48 CPU)
  memfree: 20 secs (19.18 usr +  0.12 sys = 19.30 CPU)
```

Your results may vary, so you should always test your benchmarks using your target platform and setup.

Maybe you're not satisfied with just 22% improvement. The first two regular expressions tried were basically the same idea with a variation. Sometimes the answer is to completely rethink the pattern and describe it in another way. In this case, you're looking for a hostname at the beginning of a line:

```
timethese(
  $ARGV[0] || 100,
  {
    # same as before...
    anchor => q{
        foreach (@data) { my ($host) = m/^(\S+)/; }
    },
  }
);
```

The new regular expression is much faster than the previous one:

```
Benchmark: timing 100 iterations of anchor, control, ⏎
  mem, memfree...
    anchor: 11 secs (10.78 usr +  0.07 sys = 10.85 CPU)
   control:  2 secs ( 2.02 usr +  0.01 sys =  2.03 CPU)
       mem: 25 secs (24.69 usr +  0.19 sys = 24.88 CPU)
   memfree: 20 secs (19.34 usr +  0.14 sys = 19.48 CPU)
```

Sometimes elements like an anchor or a less-specific pattern can make a big difference.

Things to remember

- Compare regular-expression performance with `Benchmark`.
- Use a control as a reference point for comparison.
- Consider a completely different approach when small optimizations are insufficient.

Item 42. Don't reinvent the regex.

Finding numbers in text seems easy; you could start with something simple like /\d+/. But what about decimal places? In that case, there are possible thousands separators. Oh—and what about the positive or negative sign, or exponential notation? It doesn't take long for a simple problem to get out of hand.

Other than as a mental exercise, why would you want to write a regular expression to trim white space or to find e-mail addresses? Solutions to these and many other common problems are nicely packaged in the Regexp::Common module on CPAN, which contains the patterns already created for you:

```
use Regexp::Common;
my $text =
   'Absolute zero is -459.67 on the Fahrenheit scale';
print "$1 is [beyond] freezing!\n"
   if $text =~ /$RE{num}{real}{-keep}/;
```

Regexp::Common exports the %RE hash, which contains prebuilt regular expressions ready for you to use, like the $Re{num}{real} expression in this example. The final {-keep} key is a little bit of magic that Regexp::Common provides to capture the matched text.

There is even an object-oriented interface for those so inclined. To access the keys you need and call the match method. The object-oriented interface tends to blow away captures, but maybe that doesn't bother you for the profanity filter you need:

```
use Regexp::Common;

my $text = 'shpx';
$text =~ tr/A-Za-z/N-ZA-Mn-za-m/;

while (<>) {
  print "Kiss your mother with that mouth?\n"
    if $RE{profanity}->matches($text);
}
```

In this case, you read the input and scold people for saying things they shouldn't. By the way, if you are looking for some middle-school giggles, looking at the source code for the profanity regex won't provide you with any. The author was kind enough to do a little obfuscation to make the code G-rated.

It can be difficult to find the regex you need in `Regexp::Common` because they are divided among many sub-modules. This can be a pain when you want to see what is available, but it does have some real benefits. For instance, you can selectively choose not to load some of the regular expressions in order to reduce your load time and memory footprint.

Also, you can install "plug-in" modules that aren't distributed with the core `Regexp::Common`. For instance, the `Regexp::Common::Email::Address` is a separate module, but `Regexp::Common` can load it:

```
use Regexp::Common qw(Email::Address);

my $text =
    'my email address is josh+spam@example.com, okay';

if ( $text =~ /$RE{Email}{Address}{-keep}/ ) {
  $text = $RE{ws}{crop}->subs($1);
  print "$text\n";
}
```

Things to remember

- Use `Regex::Common` instead of creating complex regular expressions yourself.
- Load plug-ins to expand the regular expressions available in `Regex::Common`.

4 | Subroutines

A big part of Perl's power as a dynamic language comes from its malleable subroutines. You don't have to do much to define a subroutine. You don't have to tell it how many parameters it will receive, or what types of data you will give it. You can pass a subroutine any list that you like and figure out what to do with it later. Although Perl is very permissive and gives you plenty of flexibility to decide things as late as possible. Despite that, there is a lot that you can do to keep yourself from being *too* flexible.

You don't even have to define subroutines ahead of time, either. You can make new ones at run time and you can even redefine them later. You can write subroutines that create other subroutines. Each of those subroutines can keep its own private data. You can store these subroutines as references, passing them around like any other data.

Many complicated problems become quite simple when you use the power of Perl subroutines.

Item 43. Understand the difference between `my` and `local`.

The difference between `my` and `local` is one of the more subtle and difficult aspects of Perl. It's subtle because the occasions where you can observe functional differences between `my` and `local` are somewhat infrequent. It is difficult because the differences in behavior that do result can be unexpected and very hard to understand.

People sometimes state the difference between `my` and `local` as something like, "`my` variables affect only the subroutine they're declared in, while `local` variables affect all the subroutines called from that subroutine." But this is wrong: `my` has nothing to do with subroutines, `local` has nothing to do with subroutines, and of course the difference between them has nothing to do with subroutines. It may look that way, but the truth—as you will see—is something else entirely. Nevertheless, we are treating `local` and `my` in this section because their use in subroutines is extremely important.

Global variables

In Perl, all variables, subroutines, and other entities that can be named have package scope (or just "global scope") by default. That is, they exist in the symbol table of the current package. Braces, subroutines, or files alone do not create `local` variables.

In most cases, Perl puts global names in the appropriate package symbol table during the compilation phase. Names that Perl cannot see at compile time it inserts during execution. Let's run a program named *tryme* to see:

```
print join " ", keys %::;
$compile_time;  # created at compile time
${"run_time"};  # soft ref, at run time
```

When you run the program, you see a list of everything that Perl is tracking in the symbol table:

```
ARGV 0 FileHandle:: @ stdin STDIN " stdout STDOUT $
stderr STDERR _<perlmain.c compile_time DynaLoader::
_<tryme ENV main:: INC DB:: _ /
```

Notice, in this example, that the identifier `compile_time` is present in the symbol table before the variable `$compile_time` is actually reached during execution. If you were unsure of Perl's compiler-like nature before, an example like this should confirm it for you.

You've probably been told since the beginning of your programming career (or hobby, or however you prefer to describe it) that global variables are bad. Good programs shouldn't use a lot of global variables, because global variables create hidden interfaces, make code difficult to read and modify, and even make it hard for compilers to optimize your code.

If you have written programs of more than a few hundred lines, especially as part of a team effort, you'll agree with this at least partially. You should see the need for a mechanism to support local variables in Perl.

Of course, Perl does support local variables, and in fact is more generous in its support than most languages. Most languages give you only a single mechanism for creating local variables. Perl gives you two different mechanisms.

Lexical (compile-time) scoping with my

Perl's my operator creates variables with lexical scope. A variable created with my exists from the point of declaration through the end of the enclosing scope. An enclosing scope is a pair of braces, a file, or an `eval` string. The scope is lexical in that it is determined solely by an inspection of the program text during compilation. Another way of saying this is that the scope of a `my` variable can be determined by simply looking at the source code. This code uses both a global and lexical `$a`:

```
$a = 3.1415926;  # global
{
  my $a = 2.7183;  # lexical
  print $a;        # 2.7183
}
print $a;          # 3.1415926
```

Here, the variable `$a` in use outside the braces is the global `$a`. The variable `$a` inside the braces is the lexical `$a`, which is scoped to those braces.

This is the way most commonly used programming languages handle scopes. But this is Perl, and you shouldn't be surprised to hear that there are a few wrinkles. In fact, there are more than a few wrinkles.

Revisit your inspection of the symbol table. Here's a program similar to the one at the beginning of this Item but with things reordered a bit. This time use `my`:

```
my $compile_time;  # a lexical variable
$compile_time;
print join " ", keys(%::);
```

This time, when you run it, you don't see `compile_time` in the output:

```
ARGV 0 FileHandle:: @ stdin STDIN " stdout STDOUT $ stderr
STDERR _<perlmain.c DynaLoader::  _<tryme ENV main:: INC
DB:: _ /
```

Let's look at something else:

```
$compile_time;      # not a my variable
my $compile_time;   # but this is a my variable
print join " ", keys(%::);
```

When you run this example, you now see `compile_time` in the output:

```
ARGV 0 FileHandle:: @ stdin STDIN " stdout STDOUT $
stderr STDERR _<perlmain.c compile_time DynaLoader::
_<tryme ENV main:: INC DB:: _ /
```

These examples demonstrate that my variables do not "live" in the symbol table. In the example with my `$compile_time` first, there is only one variable named `$compile_time` in the file, and it never gets into the package symbol table. In the other example, there are two separate variables named `$compile_time`: the global one in the symbol table, and my `$compile_time`, which is not in a symbol table.

You can always access the value of package variables via qualified names. Qualified names (those containing `::`) always refer to variables in the symbol table. For example:

```perl
# qualified names vs. my variables
{
   my $a = 3.1416;
   $main::a = 2.7183;
   print "(inside) a = $a\n";
   print "(inside) main::a = $main::a\n";
   print "(inside) ::a = $::a\n";
}
print "(outside) a = $a\n";
```

The output shows what Perl thinks `$a` is at each step:

```
(inside) a = 3.1416
(inside) main::a = 2.7183
(inside) ::a = 2.7183
(outside) a = 2.7183
```

Symbol tables are also used for a variety of other things, including soft references and typeglobs. Since my variables are not in a symbol table, you can't get at them using either technique. Here's a demonstration involving soft references, which always use the symbol table variable even when the lexical variable is in scope:

```perl
# soft references vs. my variables
my $a = 3.1416;
${'a'} = 2.7183;
print "my a = $a\n";
print "{a} = ${'a'}\n";
```

When you run this, you see the different versions of `$a` that Perl uses in each print:

```
my a = 3.1416
{a} = 2.7183
```

Typeglobs work the same way. In fact, as this example demonstrates, type-globs, soft references, and qualified variable names never refer to lexical (my) variables:

```
# typeglobs vs. my variables
$a = 2.7183;
my $a = 3.1416;
*alias = *a;
print "my a = $a\n";
print "alias = $alias\n";
print "{a} = ${'a'}\n";
print "::a = $::a\n";
```

The output shows what Perl thinks $a is at each step:

```
my a = 3.1416
alias = 2.7183
{a} = 2.7183
::a = 2.7183
```

Notice that the *alias typeglob refers to the global *a, even though the typeglob assignment comes after my $a. It makes no difference where the assignment comes—a typeglob always refers to an entry in the symbol table, and my variables aren't going to be there.

The rest of the "wrinkles" have to wait until you see more about local variables.

Run time scoping with local

Perl's other scoping mechanism is local, which has been around a lot longer than my. In fact, my was introduced only in Perl 5. What, you may wonder, is so wrong with local that Larry Wall felt it worthwhile to add an entirely different scoping mechanism to supplant it?

To answer this question, let's look at how local works. At some point, you will start to see the virtues of my.

local is a run time scoping mechanism. Unlike my, which basically creates new variables in a private symbol table during compilation, local has a run time effect: it saves the values of its arguments on a run time stack, and then restores them when the thread of execution leaves the containing scope.

At first glance, local and my appear to do very similar things. Here's an example similar to the one in the last section, with the my replaced by local:

```
# your basic use of 'local'
$a = 3.1416;
{
  local $a = 2.7183;
    print $a;   # 2.7183;
}
    print $a;     # 3.1416;
```

Although this looks like the example with my and produces the same output, something very different is going on in the innards of Perl.

In the case of my, as you have seen, Perl creates a separate variable that is not accessible by name during run time. In other words, it never appears in a package symbol table. During the execution of the inner block, the global $a on the outside continues to exist, with its value of 3.1416, in the symbol table.

In the case of local, however, Perl saves the current contents of $a on a run time stack. Perl replaces the contents of $a with the new value. When the program exits the enclosing block, Perl restores the values saved by local. There is only one variable named $a throughout the entire example.

To better illustrate this, use a soft reference to take a peek into the symbol table:

```
$a = $b = 3.1416;
{
  local $a = 2.7183;
  my $b = 2.7183;
  print "IN: local a = $a, my b = $b\n";
  print "IN: {a} = ${'a'}, {b} = ${'b'}\n";
}
    print "OUT: local a = $a, my b = $b\n";
```

Running this produces:

```
IN: local a = 2.7183, my b = 2.7183
IN: {a} = 2.7183, {b} = 3.1416
OUT: local a = 3.1416, my b = 3.1416
```

How interesting. The trick of using the soft reference to look at the global `$a` that worked with my seems to have no effect with local. This is as it should be. my creates a different variable, while local temporarily saves the value of the existing one.

Since local is a run time, not a compile-time, mechanism, the changes that local makes to global variables you can observe outside the lexical scope containing the local operator. The most notorious example of this is the nested subroutine call:

```
$a = 3.1416;
sub print_a { print "a = $a\n" }

sub localize_a {
  print "entering localize_a\n";
  local $a = 2.7183;
  print_a();
  print "leaving localize_a\n";
}
print_a();
localize_a();
print_a();
```

Running this yields:

```
a = 3.1416
entering localize_a
a = 2.7183
leaving localize_a
a = 3.1416
```

This is the oft-cited example that leads to describing local as having something to do with subroutine calls, which, as shown earlier, it does not.

When to use my

In general, you should use my rather than local if you have a choice. One reason for this is that my is faster than local. It takes some time to save a value on the stack:

```
use Benchmark;
timethese(
  1_000_000,
  {
    'local' => q{ local $a = $_; $a *= 2; },
    'my'    => q{    my $a = $_; $a *= 2; },
  }
);
```

The output shows that my is quite speedy:

```
Benchmark: timing 1000000 iterations of local, my...
    local:  ( 0.98 usr +  0.01 sys =  0.99 CPU) ⌐
        @ 1010101.01/s
       my:  ( 0.55 usr + -0.00 sys =  0.55 CPU) ⌐
  @ 1818181.82/s
```

my is also easier to understand and doesn't create the strange "nonlocal" side effects that local does.

Yet another reason to use my is that the lexical variables it creates form the basis for closures in Perl (Item 49).

When to use `local`

One compelling reason to use local, or at least to be familiar with it, is that there is a lot of ancient, Perl 4-style code out there that uses it. Replacing local with my isn't as easy as a search-and-replace with a text editor— you will have to examine each use of local individually to see whether it takes advantage of one of the "features" of local. It is probably better to leave code that uses local alone so long as it is performing well.

Also, some things have to be done with `local`.

Most $-punctuation variables—or other variables that Perl handles specially—can only be localized with local (although Perl 5.10 introduces a lexical $_: Item 15). It is an error to attempt to localize a special variable with my:

```
my $contents = do { my $/; open ... };   # ERROR!
```

You can use local in a number of other situations where you can't use my, such as on a variable in another package:

```
package foo;
$a = 3.1416;
{
  package main;
  local $foo::a = 2.7183;

  package foo;
  print "foo::a = $a\n";
}

package foo;
print "foo::a = $a\n";


% tryme foo::a=2.7183 foo::a=3.1416
```

You can also use local on elements of arrays and hashes. Yes, it's strange, but true. You can even use local on a slice:

```
@a = qw(Jolly Green Giant);
{
  local ( @a[ 0, 1 ] ) = qw(Grumbly Purple);
  print "@a\n";
}
print "@a\n";
```

This gives:

```
Grumbly Purple Giant
Jolly Green Giant
```

You can also use local on typeglobs (Item 118). In theory, local could be made to work on almost any value, but there are limitations in the current implementation. For example, as of this writing, you cannot use local on a dereferenced value like $$a.

local and my as list operators

One way in which local and my are the same is their syntax; you can apply both to single scalars, arrays, and hashes:

```
# some examples of local and my
local $scalar;
```

```
my @array;
local %hash;
```

You can initialize a variable while localizing it:

```
local $scalar = 3.1416;
my @array = qw(Mary had a little lamb);
local %hash = ( H => 1, He => 2, Li => 3 );
```

If you use parentheses around the arguments to `my` and `local`, the arguments become a list, and Perl evaluates the assignments in list context:

```
local ( $foo, $bar, $bletch ) = @a;   # 1st 3 elems from @a
```

Watch out for the usual list assignment "gotchas":

```
# WRONG -- don't forget the parens!
# $bletch gets size of @a; only $foo is localized!
local $foo, $bar, $bletch = @a;


# WRONG -- localizes @a, @b but only @a gets values
my ( @a, @b ) = @c;


# WRONG -- reads all of standard input
my ($a) = <STDIN>;
```

Things to remember

- Use `my` to create lexical variables that are private to a scope.
- Use `local` to give global variables temporary values.
- Use `local` with most special variables.

Item 44. Avoid using @_ directly unless you have to.

Unlike many programming languages, Perl has no built-in support for named or "formal" parameters. The arguments to a subroutine are always passed in via a single array variable called `@_`. It is up to the author of the subroutine to give the arguments names and check them for consistency.

In general, you should always start off a subroutine by copying its arguments and giving them names. The preferred method is to use `my`:

```
sub digits_gone {
  my ($str) = @_;
  $str =~ tr/0-9//d;   # remove digits from a string
  $str;                # return translated string
}
```

The idiomatic way to read arguments passed to a subroutine is to use shift to get them one at a time or a list assignment to read them all:

```
sub char_count {
  my $str   = shift;
  my @chars = @_;
  my @counts;
  for (@chars) {
    push @counts, eval "\$str =~ tr/$_//";
  }
  @counts;  # return list of counts
}
```

The elements of @_ are actually aliases for the values you passed in. Modifying an element of @_ modifies the corresponding subroutine argument—a sort of "call by reference" semantics. Not only can subroutines modify their arguments, but attempts to do so can fail if the arguments are read-only:

```
sub txt_file_size {
  $_[0] .= '.txt' unless /\.txt$/;
  -s $_[0];
}
```

If you try to call this subroutine as txt_file_size "test", it fails with an error message, as it tries to modify the read-only value "test."

Sometimes this aliasing "feature" turns out to be genuinely useful. For example, you can write subroutines that modify their argument, which is especially useful to clean up data:

```
sub normalize_in_place {
  my $max = 0;
  for (@_) { $max = abs($_) if abs($_) > $max }
  return unless $max;
```

```
    # note that $_ is an "alias of an alias" -- works fine!
    for (@_) { $_ /= $max }
    return;  # void return
}


my ( $x, $y, $z ) = 1 .. 3;
normalize_in_place $x, $y, $z;
printf( ( "%.2g " x 3 ) . "\n", $x, $y, $z );
```

The output shows that your call to `normalize_in_place` affects the values of $x, $y, and $z:

```
0.33 0.67 1
```

If you want to optimize for speed, it might be faster for you to use @_ without copying it, since copying values takes a significant amount of time. If you do so, remember that array subscripting tends to be slow, so try to use constructs like `foreach`, `grep`, and `map` that allow you to iterate over an array without having to subscript its elements repeatedly. The best approach, of course, would be to write two or more different versions and `Benchmark` them.

Even though subroutine arguments are passed as aliases, any array arguments are "flattened" into a list. You can modify the elements of an array argument, but not the array itself:

```
sub no_bad {
  for $i ( 0 .. $#_ ) {
    if ( $_[$i] =~ /^bad$/ ) {
      splice @_, $i, 1;
      print "in no_bad: @_\n";
      return;
    }
  }
  return;
}


my @a = qw(ok better fine great bad good);
no_bad @a;
print "after no_bad: @a\n";
```

The output shows that you are able to change @_ inside `no_bad`, but once the subroutine returns, @a is back to its original value:

```
in no_bad: ok better fine great good
after no_bad: ok better fine great bad good
```

Finally, on a slightly different topic, a subroutine that you call with no arguments usually has empty @_s. However, if you call a subroutine with an ampersand and no parentheses, it inherits the current @_:

```
sub inner {
  print "\@_ = @_\n";
}

sub outer {
  &inner;  # this is the only syntax that works
}

outer 1 .. 3;  # prints @_ = 1 2 3
```

Things to remember

- Avoid changing the values in @_ since that changes the original data.
- Don't copy data in @_ into variables if you don't need to change them.

Item 45. Use `wantarray` to write subroutines returning lists.

You probably know already that subroutines can return either scalar or list values. Perhaps you have written both kinds of subroutine. You also probably understand the significance of scalar and list contexts (Item 12). In an idle moment, you may have even wondered how something like the following works:

```
sub sorted_text_files {
  my $dir = shift;
  opendir my ($dh), $dir or die "eh?: $!";

  # not relevant to wantarray, but we have to
  # add the directory prefix here to make this work
  my @files = grep { -T } map { "$dir/$_" } readdir $dh;
  sort @files;
}
```

You can get a sorted list of files by using `sorted_text_files` in a call to `print`:

```
print join ' ', sorted_text_files '/etc';
```

Since the output is what you expect, you probably don't see anything magical about it. However, things are different if you use `sorted_text_files` in scalar context:

```
print join ' ', scalar( sorted_text_files '/etc' );
```

In this case, you get no output.

Maybe what's going will become more apparent if you change the last line, `sort @files`, to read `@files = sort @files`. Now, instead of nothing at all, you get a number.

What you are seeing is the result of the way that Perl evaluates the return value of a subroutine. The context—list or scalar—of the return value of a subroutine is determined by the context in which you call the subroutine. Perl notes the context when you call the subroutine and it applies that context to whatever expression winds up as the return value.

In cases where you need to know the calling context, you can use the `wantarray` operator, which returns true if the subroutine call appeared in a list context (yes, `wantarray` is poorly named, since it implies it must be an array). Say that you want to modify the `sorted_text_files` subroutine so that it returns a `joined` list of filenames if evaluated in a scalar context. You could rewrite it like this:

```
sub sorted_text_files {
  my $dir = shift;
  opendir my ($dh), $dir or die "eh?: $!";

  # not relevant to wantarray, but we have to
  # add the directory prefix here to make this work
  my @files = grep { -T } map { "$dir/$_" } readdir $dh;
  if (wantarray) {  # list or scalar context?
    sort @files;    # list context -- return a list
  }
  else {
    join ' ', sort @files;  # scalar -- return a string
  }
}
```

`wantarray` is also occasionally useful for answering questions. If you want to find out whether `grep`'s block argument was evaluated in a scalar or list context, you can use something like the following:

```
sub how { print wantarray ? "arrayish" : "scalarish" }
grep { how() } 1;
```

Its output pretty much settles the question:

```
scalarish
```

Void context

There's a third context, the void context, where you do nothing with the return value of the subroutine:

```
sorted_text_files('/etc');
```

In this case, `sorted_text_files` doesn't really need to do any work, since nothing is going to happen with the result. In that case, `wantarray` returns `undef` and you can `return` immediately to skip all the work:

```
sub sorted_text_files {
  return unless defined wantarray;
  # same as before
}
```

Even finer control

If you want to even know more about what's happening with the data you are sending back from your subroutine, you can use `Contextual::Return`. Through the magic of Damian Conway, you can find out more about what's going to happen to your data. Here's an excerpt from its documentation:

```
use Contextual::Return;

sub handle_everything {
  return SCALAR { 'thirty-twelve' }
  BOOL         { 1 }
  NUM          { 7 * 6 }
  STR          { 'forty-two' }
```

```
    LIST            { 1, 2, 3 }

    HASHREF         { { name => 'foo', value => 99 } }
    ARRAYREF        { [ 3, 2, 1 ] }

    GLOBREF         { \*STDOUT }
    CODEREF {
      die "Don't use this result as code!";
    };
  }
```

Although `Contextual::Return` is very cool, don't overuse it.

Things to remember

- Allow your subroutines to respond to context.
- The `wantarray` function tells you the context of your subroutine.
- For greater control over return values, try `Contextual::Return`.

Item 46. Pass references instead of copies.

Two disadvantages of the "plain old" method of subroutine argument passing are that (1) even though you can modify its elements, you can't modify an array or hash argument itself, and (2) copying an array or hash into @_ takes time. You can overcome both of these disadvantages with references (Item 58).

Passing reference arguments

When you pass arguments to a subroutine, Perl aliases @_ to them. It does this for efficiency. When you store them in variables, Perl then makes a copy. The more arguments you pass, the more work Perl has to do. For instance, you can write a subroutine to sum a list of numbers. It takes the list directly from the arguments:

```
sub sum {
  my @numbers = @_;   # now makes a copy
  my $sum     = 0;
  foreach my $num (@numbers) { $sum += $num }
  $sum;
}
```

What if someone wants to call that subroutine with a lot of numbers?

```
sum( 1 .. 100_000 );
```

Perl has to copy 100,000 elements in `@numbers` in `sum`, although it doesn't change any of the values. Perl does a lot of work for no good reason. If you could pass only one thing, a reference to the array, Perl wouldn't have to do all of that work. A small change to the subroutine fixes that:

```
sub sum {
  my ($numbers_ref) = @_;  # now makes a copy
  my $sum           = 0;
  foreach my $num (@$numbers_ref) { $sum += $num }
  $sum;
}
```

Since Perl's argument list is always a flat list, the subroutine doesn't know anything about the original structure. If you make the argument list from two or more arrays, the subroutine sees only the whole list. To maintain their identities, you can pass them as array references:

```
process_arrays( \@arrayA, \@arrayB );
```

In the subroutine, you'll get a list of array references, which you can process independently:

```
sub process_arrays {
  my (@array_refs) = @_;  # refs to all arrays

  foreach my $ref (@array_refs) {
    ... process array ...;
  }
}
```

You can do this with any reference types that you like. Your subroutine just has to do the right thing with the arguments that it gets:

```
process_refs( \@array, \%hash, \&sub_name );
```

This isn't only for arrays and hashes, though. If you have very large strings, you can pass references to scalars to avoid copying the strings in the subroutine. This example processes a string in-place in the subroutine without ever making the copy:

```
process_big_string( \$string );

sub process_big_string {
  my $string_ref = shift;

  $string_ref =~ s/\bPERL\b/Perl/g;
}
```

Returning reference arguments

The same copying problem goes in the other direction, too. When you return values, the caller just gets a flat list. You return references to any of the types. You can do this especially when the data structures are large. Here's a subroutine that reads in an entire file and returns a reference to the scalar that has its contents:

```
my $string_ref = slurp_file($file);
print "The file was:\n$$string_ref\n";

sub slurp_file {
  my $file = shift;

  open my ($fh), '<', $file or die;
  local $/;
  my $string = <$fh>;

  \$string;
}
```

You can return more than one thing from a subroutine, too, and they can keep their identities, just like passing arguments to a subroutine:

```
my ( $array_ref, $hash_ref ) = make_data_structure();

sub make_data_structure {
  # ...
  return \@array, \%hash;
}
```

Passing typeglobs for speed

In the days before references, programmers sometimes resorted to passing typeglobs (Item 118) when it was necessary to pass an array or hash by value. Here's an example of using typeglobs to construct a subroutine that takes two arrays by reference:

```
sub two_arrays {
  local *a1 = shift;  # create a private a1 and a2
  local *a2 = shift;

  # now, do whatever it is to @a1 and @a2 ...
}


our @a = 1 .. 3;
our @b = 4 .. 6;
two_arrays *a, *b;
```

There is no reason to write code like this any more, but if you deal with a lot of legacy code, you may run into something like it.

Using `local` * on reference arguments

Subroutines that take arguments by reference for speed sometimes lose some of their speed advantage as they continually dereference those arguments. The syntax can become distracting or hard to follow for some people.

Here's a subroutine that takes two arrays and returns a list made up of the largest elements from the arrays, compared pairwise:

```
sub max_v {
  my ( $a, $b ) = @_;
  my $n = @$a > @$b ? @$a : @$b;  # no. of items
  my @result;
  for ( my $i = 0 ; $i < $n ; $i++ ) {
    push @result, $$a[$i] > $$b[$i] ? $$a[$i] : $$b[$i];
  }
  @result;
}
```

Those doubled dollar signs aren't very pretty, are they?

One way to get around this problem is to alias variables to the arrays. Assigning a reference to a typeglob has the effect of creating an aliased variable of the type appropriate to the reference:

```
sub max_v_local {
  local ( *a, *b ) = @_;
  my $n = @a > @b ? @a : @b;
  my @result;
  for ( my $i = 0 ; $i < $n ; $i++ ) {
    push @result, $a[$i] > $b[$i] ? $a[$i] : $b[$i];
  }
  @result;
}
```

This subroutine is somewhat easier to read once you know what the first assignment means, and it will probably execute faster than the first version. When I tested this example, I saw about a 10% speed increase—not enormous, but significant.

Things to remember

- Use references to avoid excessive copying when you pass large data structures or strings.
- Pass references to subroutines to work with the original data.
- Pass references when you need to pass arrays or hashes intact.

Item 47. Use hashes to pass named parameters.

Although Perl provides no method of automatically naming parameters in the function to which you pass them (in other words, no "formal parameters" [Item 48]), there's a variety of ways that you can call functions with an argument list that provides both names and values.

All of these mechanisms require that the function you call do some extra work while processing the argument list. In other words, this feature isn't built into Perl either, but it's a blessing in disguise. Different implementations of named parameters are appropriate at different times. Perl makes it easy to write and use almost any implementation you want.

A simple approach to named parameters constructs a hash out of the argument list:

```perl
sub uses_named_params {
  my %param = (
    foo => 'val1',
    bar => 'val2',
  );
  my %input = @_;  # read in args as a hash

  # combine params read in with defaults
  @param{ keys %input } = values %input;

  # now, use $param{foo}, $param{bar}, etc.
  ...
}
```

You would call `uses_named_params` with key-value pairs just as if you were constructing a hash:

```perl
uses_named_params( bar => 'myval1', bletch => 'myval2' );
```

That wasn't very many lines of code, was it? And they were all fairly simple. This is a natural application for hashes.

You may want to allow people to call a subroutine with either positional parameters or named parameters. The simplest thing to do in this case is to prefix parameter names with minus signs. Check the first argument to see if it begins with a minus. If it does, process the arguments as named parameters. Here's one straightforward approach:

```perl
sub uses_minus_params {
  my %param = ( -foo => 'val1', -bar => 'val2' );
  my %input;

  if ( substr( $_[0], 0, 1 ) eq '-' ) {
    # read in named params as a hash
    %input = @_;
  }
  else {
    my @name = qw(-foo -bar);
    # give positional params names and save in a hash
    %input = map { $name[$_], $_[$_] } 0 .. $#_;
  }
```

```
    # overlay params on defaults
    @param{ keys %input } = values %input;


    # use $param{-foo}, $param{-bar}
}
```

You can call this subroutine with either named or positional parameters (although it's better to choose one method and stick with it):

```
uses_minus_params( -foo => 'myval1', -xtra => 'myval2' );
uses_minus_params( 'myval1', 'myval2' );
```

Stay away from single character parameter names—for example, -e and -x. In addition to being overly terse, those are file test operators (Item 51).

If you use this method for processing named parameters, you refer to the arguments inside your subroutine by using a hash whose keys are prefixed with minus signs (e.g., $param{-foo}, $param{-bar}). Using identifiers preceded by minus signs as arguments or keys may look a little funny to you at first ("Is that really Perl?"), but Perl actually treats barewords preceded by minus signs as though they were strings beginning with minus signs.

This is generally convenient, but this approach does have a couple of drawbacks. First, although an identifier with a leading minus sign gets a little special treatment from Perl, the identifier isn't forcibly treated as a string, as it would be to the left of => or alone inside braces. Thus, you have to quote a parameter like -print, lest it turn into -1 (while also printing the value of $_). Second, if you want to use the positional argument style and need to pass a negative first argument, you have to supply it as a string with leading whitespace or do something else equally ungainly.

There are plenty of applications where these issues don't present a problem, but there are plenty more where one or both do. In this case, you may want to resort to yet another technique, which is to pass named parameters in an anonymous hash:

```
sub uses_anon_hash_params {
  my %param = ( foo => 'val1', bar => 'val2' );
  my %input;


  if ( ref $_[0] eq 'HASH' ) {
    # read in named params as a hash
    %input = %{ shift() };
  }
```

```perl
    else {
      my @name = qw(foo bar);
      # give positional params names and save in a hash
      %input = map { $name[$_], $_[$_] } 0 .. $#_;
    }

    # overlay params on defaults
    @param{ keys %input } = values %input;

    # use $param{foo}, $param{bar} ... for example:
    for ( keys %param ) {
      print "$_: $param{$_}\n";
    }
  }
```

The syntax for using named and positional parameters now looks like:

```perl
uses_anon_hash_params( { foo => 3, test => 10 } );
uses_anon_hash_params( -123, 345 );

# or even ...
uses_anon_hash_params { foo => 3, test => 10 };
```

This is a pretty complicated piece of boilerplate to have at the beginning of a subroutine. If you have several subroutines that accept named parameters, you will probably want to create a subroutine that does most of the work. Here is a subroutine that implements the anonymous hash technique:

```perl
sub do_params {
  my ( $arg, $default ) = @_;
  my %param = @$default;
  my %input;

  if ( ref $$arg[0] eq 'HASH' ) {
    # named params -- turn 'em into a hash
    %input = %{ $$arg[0] };
  }
  else {
    # positional params -- name 'em
    %input =
      map { $$default[ $_ * 2 ], $$arg[$_] } 0 .. $#_;
  }
```

```
    # overlay defaults
    @param{ keys %input } = values %input;
    \%param;
}
```

And here's how you might use it:

```
sub uses_anon_hash_params {

  # ref to arg list and defaults
  my $param = do_params \@_,
    [ foo => 'val1', bar => 'val2' ];

  # do_params returned a hash ref
  # now, use $$param{foo}, $$param{bar}-- for example:
  for ( keys %$param ) {
    print "$_: $$param{$_}\n";
  }
}
```

Each of the techniques illustrated here has its own advantages and drawbacks. Use the technique that best suits your application, or, if none is quite right, adapt one as necessary.

Things to remember

- Use hashes to name subroutine arguments.
- Set default values for parameters by merging hashes.
- Choose either positional or named parameters, and stick with your choice.

Item 48. Use prototypes to get special argument parsing.

Perl supports subroutine prototypes, but they are not named, typed formal parameters along the lines of those in most languages. Rather, they are a mechanism that allows programmers to write subroutines whose arguments are treated like those of built-in functions. Don't think of Perl's prototypes as a way to validate data; they are there to give Perl hints on how to parse your code.

Your own pop

Consider implementing a `pop2` function that removes and returns two elements from the end of an array. Suppose you want to be able to use it like the built-in `pop`:

```
my @a    = 1 .. 10;
my $item = pop @a;
```

You want your version to work similarly by removing two elements from the array you pass it:

```
my ( $item1, $item2 ) = pop2 @a;
```

Normally, if you wanted to implement something like `pop2`, you would use references so you could modify the argument (Item 46):

```
sub pop2_ref { splice @{ $_[0] }, -2, 2 }
```

But you have to call this with a reference to an array, not the name of the array:

```
my @a = 1 .. 10;
my ( $item1, $item2 ) = pop2_ref \@a;
```

You have to use prototypes in order to write a function that gets the same special treatment of its argument list that a built-in operator like `pop` does.

A prototype appears at the beginning of a subroutine declaration or definition:

```
sub pop2 (\@) { splice @{ $_[0] }, -2, 2 }
```

Prototypes are made up of prototype atoms. Prototype atoms are characters, possibly preceded by backslashes, indicating the type of argument(s) to be accepted by a subroutine. In this example, the `\@` atom indicates that the subroutine `pop2` is to take a single named array argument. A backslashed atom, like `\$` or `\@`, tells Perl to pass a reference to the corresponding argument, so in this case the array argument to `pop2` will be passed as a reference, not as a list of values.

Prototypes also invoke argument type and number checking where appropriate. For example, if you try to invoke `pop2` on a non-array value it doesn't work:

```
my @popped = pop2 %hash;
```

Table 4-1 Subroutine Prototype Characters and Their Meanings

Prototype characters	Meaning
\$, \@, \%, \&, *	Returns reference to variable name or argument beginning with $, @, %, etc
$	Forces scalar context
@, %	Gobbles the rest of the arguments; forces list context
&	Coderef; sub keyword optional if first argument
*	Typeglob
;	Separate mandatory from optional arguments

The result is a compile-time error, because Perl knows that a hash doesn't belong there:

```
Type of arg 1 to main::pop2 must be array ↵
   (not private hash)
```

Table 4-1 shows the characters you can use in a prototype.

Multiple array arguments

How about a subroutine that takes two array arguments and "blends" them into a single list? Take one element from the first array, then one from the second, then another from the first, and so on:

```
sub blend (\@\@) {
  local ( *a, *b ) = @_;  # faster than lots of derefs
  my $n = $#a > $#b ? $#a : $#b;
  my @res;
  for my $i ( 0 .. $n ) {
    push @res, $a[$i], $b[$i];
  }

  # could have written this:
  # map { $a[$_], $b[$_] } 0..$n;
  # but for and push turn out to be faster
  @res;
}

# sample usage
blend @a, @b;
blend @{ [ 1 .. 10 ] }, @{ [ 11 .. 20 ] };
```

Along the same lines, you can write a subroutine that iterates through the elements of a list like `foreach`, but *n* at a time:

```perl
# for_n: iterate over a list n elements at a time
sub for_n (&$@) {
  my ( $sub, $n, @list ) = @_;
  my $i;
  while ( $i < $#list ) {
    &$sub( @list[ $i .. ( $i + $n - 1 ) ] );
    $i += $n;
  }
}


# sample usage
@a = 1 .. 10;
for_n { print "$_[0], $_[1]\n" } 2, @a;
```

Be careful when using atoms like `\@` and `\%` in code that you are going to share with the world, since other programmers may not expect subroutines to take arguments by reference without an explicit backslash. Document such behavior thoroughly.

By the way, you don't need your own `blend` or `for_n`, since `List::MoreUtils`' `mesh` and `natatime` can do those for you (Item 26).

Things to remember

- Use prototypes to create your own array or hash operators.
- Use prototypes to create subroutines that take separate arrays as arguments.
- Avoid overusing prototypes, especially when they would confuse people.

Item 49. Create closures to lock in data.

In Perl, **closures** are subroutines that refer to lexical variables that have gone out of scope. The data does not disappear, because the subroutines still have references to them. You can use closures to limit data to a named subroutine or new anonymous subroutines.

Private data for named subroutines

Sometimes your subroutines need some data that only they can see. As with any data, you want to limit their visibility to the smallest scope that you can compose. You could just put your data directly inside the subroutine:

```
sub some_sub {
  my $application_root = '/path/to/my/app';


  # do stuff with %hash
}
```

If you do that, Perl has to recreate the scalar every time that you call the subroutine. If you don't need to change the data, that's a waste. Maybe it doesn't affect performance that much, but it's just philosophically ugly and needless.

You can define `$application_root` outside of the subroutine, but you still want to limit its scope. You do that by wrapping a block around the definition of `$application_root` and the subroutine. You need to define `$application_root` before you define the subroutine so the subroutine can refer to it, so you need to wrap it in a BEGIN block:

```
BEGIN {
  my $application_root = '/path/to/my/app';

  sub some_sub {
    ...;
  }
}
```

In Perl 5.10 and later, you can get the same thing with a `state` variable. This is such a common pattern that it's now a feature. The first time you run the subroutine, Perl defines the `state` variable and assigns its value. On subsequent calls, Perl ignores that line and the variable keeps the value it had from the previous run of the subroutine:

```
use 5.010;

sub some_sub {
  state $application_root = '/path/to/my/app';

  # do stuff with $application_root
}
```

The `state` variable is more useful for maintaining a variable's value between calls to the subroutine:

```
use 5.010;

sub show_letter {
  state $letter = 'a';

  print "Letter is ", $letter++, "\n";
}

foreach ( 0 .. 5 ) {
  show_letter();
}
```

The output shows the progression of `$letter`:

```
Letter is a
Letter is b
Letter is c
Letter is d
Letter is e
Letter is f
```

Private data for subroutine references

Anonymous closures are almost the same thing as using `state` variables, but they can be much more useful because you can create as many closures as you like and you can set up each subroutine just the way you need it. If you wanted to make an anonymous closure doing the same as the previous example, you do mostly the same thing although it all happens at run time:

```
my $session = do {
  my $application_root = '/path/to/my/app';

  sub {
    ...;
  }
};
```

More useful, however, is something that creates the closure on demand. Even though you have an anonymous subroutine, you still did all of the same work you did to set up the named subroutine. That's not very flexible. Instead, you can use a **factory** that makes subroutines:

```
my $session = closure_factory('/path/to/my/app');

sub closure_factory {
    my $application_root = shift;

    sub {
        ...;
    }
}
```

You can create as many of these as you like. Consider a set of independent counters that you create from the same factory subroutine (a fancy name for a subroutine that creates other subroutines):

```
sub make_cycle {
    my ( $min, $max ) = @_;

    my @numbers = $min .. $max;
    my $cursor  = 0;

    sub { $numbers[ $cursor++ % @numbers ] }
}

my $cycle_5_10 = make_cycle(  5,   9 );
my $cycle_f_m  = make_cycle( 'f', 'm' );
```

When you call one of your closures, it doesn't affect any of the other closures that you created from the same factory:

```
foreach ( 0 .. 10 ) {
    print $cycle_5_10->(), $cycle_f_m->();
}
```

The output shows the closures operating independently as they interlace their output:

```
5f6g7h8i9j5k6l7m8f9g5h
```

Closures can share data

You don't have to limit your out-of-scope data to a single closure. As long as you create the subroutines while those data are in scope, they will share the references. Consider the `File::Find::Closures` module, which supplies convenience subroutines to work with `File::Find`. The `find` subroutine expects a reference to a subroutine to do its magic:

```
use File::Find qw(find);
use File::Find::Closures qw(find_by_regex);

my ( $wanted, $reporter ) = find_by_regex(qr/*.pl/);

find( $wanted, @search_dirs );

my @files = $reporter->();
```

The `find_by_regex` handles two important details for you, each handled by its own closure. First, it creates the callback function that `find` needs. In the same scope, it defines the `@files` array to store the list of files that it collects. To access that array, it creates a second closure:

```
# From File::Find::Closures
sub find_by_regex {
  require File::Spec::Functions;
  require Carp;
  require UNIVERSAL;

  my $regex = shift;

  unless ( UNIVERSAL::isa( $regex, ref qr// ) ) {
    Carp::croak "Argument must be a regular expression";
  }

  my @files = ();

  sub {
    push @files,
      File::Spec::Functions::canonpath($File::Find::name)
      if m/$regex/;
  }, sub { wantarray ? @files : [@files] }
}
```

Things to remember

- Use lexical variables to make data private to subroutines.
- In Perl 5.10 or later, use `state` variables for private data.
- Make generator ("factory") subroutines that create new subroutines for you.

Item 50. Create new subroutines with subroutines.

If you are often calling the same subroutine with some of the same arguments, you can create a new subroutine that remembers some of the arguments for you. This is known as **currying** a subroutine.

Suppose that you have a subroutine that filters a list for elements matching a pattern, and then sorts the results:

```perl
sub my_sorted_grep {
  my ( $pattern, $array_ref ) = @_;

  my @results = sort grep /$pattern/o, @$array_ref;

  wantarray ? @results : scalar @results;
}
```

When you call it, you have to supply both the pattern and the input list:

```perl
my @results = my_sort_grep qr/.../, \@input;
```

That's not such a big deal, but what if you want to do that several times throughout your code with the same pattern? You have to type all that out over and over again. That's no good; you have the same pattern scattered throughout the code, so wrap it in a subroutine that remembers the pattern for you:

```perl
my $find_buster = sub {
  my ($array_ref) = shift;
  my_sorted_grep( qr/Buster/i, @$array_ref );
};
```

Now you have a way to call it without going through all of the details:

```perl
my @results = $find_buster->( \@input );
```

You can also use functions to create new functions out of old ones. We could devote an entire book to these **higher-order functions** in Perl, but fortunately, Mark Jason Dominus has already written *Higher Order Perl*.

Here's a short example, though. Suppose you have a set of subroutines that transform a string:

```
sub my_uc      { uc $_[0] }
sub my_ucfirst { ucfirst $_[0] }
sub trim_front { my $s = shift; $s =~ s/^\s+//; $s }
sub trim_back  { my $s = shift; $s =~ s/\s+$//; $s }
```

Now, given a string, you want to trim the whitespace at the front and end of the string and make the first character uppercase. You could call all of the needed subroutines individually, assigning their results back to the original scalar:

```
my $string = '';
$string = trim_front($string);
$string = trim_back($string);
$string = my_ucfirst($string);
```

You could also skip the intermediate steps by using the result of one step as the input for the next, but that's a bit messy:

```
$string = my_ucfirst( trim_back( trim_front($string) ) );
```

Instead, you can compose the functions into a new subroutine:

```
my $ucfirst_and_trim = sub {
  my $string = shift;
  my_ucfirst( trim_back( trim_front($string) ) );
};
```

Now you can use your composed subroutine anywhere you want to perform all three operations:

```
$string = $ucfirst_and_trim->($string);
```

This isn't much different than writing a normal subroutine, where you create a bit of reusable code, except that you are now doing it at run time.

Take it one step further by writing a factory subroutine that creates the composed subroutine for you. Maybe you don't know which operations you'll need until run time, so you don't know what to put inside the anonymous subroutine. This composing subroutine takes a list of sub-routine references and gives back a single subroutine that returns their combined result:

```perl
sub composer {
  my (@sub_refs) = @_;

  sub {
    my $string = shift;
    foreach my $sub_ref (@sub_refs) {
      $string = $sub_ref->($string);
    }
    return $string;
  };
}
```

You compose your new subroutine any way that you like. In this case, you list the operations you want in the order that you want them in:

```perl
my $ucfirst_and_trim =
  composer( \&trim_front, \&trim_back, \&my_ucfirst );


$string = $ucfirst_and_trim->($string);
```

Your composing subroutine can do anything you need it to do, as long as it returns a code reference (or maybe more than one code reference).

Things to remember

- Create new subroutines based on program state during run time.
- Wrap subroutines to provide default arguments.
- Use generator subroutines to create higher-order functions.

5 | Files and Filehandles

It's easy to work with files in Perl. Its heritage includes some of the most powerful utilities for processing data, so it has the tools it needs to examine the files that contain those data and to easily read the data and write them again.

Perl's strength goes beyond mere files, though. You probably think of files as things on your disk with nice icons. However, Perl can apply its filehandle interface to almost anything. You can use the filehandle interface to do most of the heavy lifting for you. You can also store filehandles in scalar variables, and select which one you want to use later.

Item 51. Don't ignore the file test operators.

One of the more frequently heard questions from newly minted Perl programmers is, "How do I find the size of a file?" Invariably, another newly minted Perler will give a wordy answer that works, but requires quite a bit of typing:

```
my (
   $dev,   $ino,     $mode, $nlink, $uid,
   $gid,   $rdev,    $size, $atime, $mtime,
   $ctime, $blksize, $blocks
) = stat($filename);
```

Or, perhaps they know how to avoid the extra variables that they don't want, so they use a slice (Item 9):

```
my ($size) = ( stat $filename )[7];
```

When you are working this hard to get something that should be common, stop to think for a moment. Perl is specifically designed to make the common things easy, so this should be really easy. And indeed, it is if you use the -s file test operator, which tells you the file size in bytes:

```
my $size = -s $filename;
```

Many people overlook Perl's file test operators. Maybe they are old C programmers, maybe they've seen only the programs that other people write, or they just don't trust them. This is a shame; they are succinct and efficient, and tend to be more readable than equivalent constructs written using the `stat` operator. Curiously, the file test operators are the first functions listed in *perlfunc*, because they are under the literal -X. If you want to read about them, you tell `perldoc` to give you the function named -X:

```
% perldoc -f -X
```

File tests fit into loops and conditions very well. Here, for example, is a list of the text files in a directory. The -T file test decides if the contents are text by sampling part of the file and guessing.

Almost all file tests use $_ by default:

```
my @textfiles = grep { -T } glob "$dir_name/*";
```

The -M and -A file tests return the modification and access times of the file, but in days relative to the start of the program. That is, Perl takes the time the program was started, subtracts the time the file was modified or accessed, and gives you back the result in days. Positive values are in the past, and negative values indicate times after the start of the program. That seems really odd, but it makes it easy to measure age in terms a human can understand. If you want to find the files that haven't been modified in the past seven days, you look for a -M value that is greater than 7:

```
my $old_files = grep { -M > 7 } glob '*';
```

If you want to find the files modified after your program started, you look for negative values. In this example, if -M returns something less than zero, `map` gives an anonymous array that has the name of the file and the modification age in days; otherwise, it gives the empty list:

```
my @new_files = map { -M < 0 ? [ $_, -M ] : () } glob '*';
```

Reusing work

If you want to find all of the files owned by the user running the program that are executable, you can combine the file tests in a `grep`:

```
my @my_executables = grep { -o and -x } glob '*';
```

The file test operators actually do the stat call for you, figure out the answer, and give it back to you. Each time you run a file test, Perl does another stat. In the last example, Perl did two stats on $_.

If you want to use another file test operator on the same file, you can use the virtual _ filehandle (the single underscore). It tells the file test operator to not call stat and instead reuse the information from the last file test or stat. Simply put the _ after the file test you want. Now you call only one stat for each item in the list:

```
my @my_executables = grep { -o and -x _ } glob '*';
```

Stacked file tests

Starting with Perl 5.10, you can stack file test operators. That is, you test the same file or filehandle for several properties at the same time. For instance, if you want to check that a file is both readable and writable by the current user, you list the -r and -w file tests before the file:

```
use 5.010;

if ( -r -w $file ) {
  print "File is readable and writable\n";
}
```

There's nothing especially magic about this, since it's a syntactic shortcut for doing each operation independently. Notice that the equivalent long form does the test closest to the file first:

```
if ( -w $file and -r $file ) {
  print "File is readable and writable\n";
}
```

Rewriting the example from the previous section, you'd have:

```
my @my_executables = grep { -o -x } glob '*';
```

Things to remember

- Don't call stat directly when a file test operator will do.
- Use the _ virtual filehandle to reuse data from the last stat.
- Stack file test operators in Perl 5.10 or later.

Item 52. Always use the three-argument open.

A long time ago, in a Perl far, far away, you had to specify the filehandle mode and the filename together:

```
open( FILE, '> output.txt' ) || die ...;   # OLD and WRONG
```

That code isn't so bad, but things can get weird if you use a variable for the filename:

```
open( FILE, $read_file ) || die ...;   # WRONG and OLD
```

Since the data in `$read_file` can do two jobs, specify the mode and the filename, someone might try to pull a fast one on you by making a weird filename. If they put a > at the beginning of the filename, all of a sudden you've lost your data:

```
$read_file = '> birdie.txt';   # bye bye birdie!
```

The two-argument form of `open` has a **magic** feature where it interprets these redirection symbols. Unfortunately, this feature can leave your code open to exploits and accidents.

Imagine that the person trying to wreak havoc on your files decides to get a little more tricky. They think that you won't notice when they open a file in read-write mode. This allows the input operator to work on an open file, but also overwrites your data:

```
$read_file = '+> important.txt';
```

They could even sneak in a pipe, which tells `open` to run a command:

```
$read_file = 'rm -rf / |';   # that's gonna hurt!
```

And now, just when you think you have everything working, the software trolls come out at three in the morning to ensure that your pager goes off just when you get to sleep.

Since Perl 5.6, you can use the three-argument `open` to get around this problem. By "can," we mean, "you always will from now on forever and ever."

When you want to read a file, you ensure that you *only* read from a file:

```
open my ($fh), '<', $read_file or die ...;
```

The filename isn't doing double duty anymore, so it has less of a chance of making a mess. None of the characters in $read_file will be special. Any redirection symbols, pipes, or other funny characters are literal characters.

Likewise, when you want to write to a file, you ensure that you get the right mode:

```
open my ($fh), '>',  $write_file  or die ...;
open my ($fh), '>>', $append_file or die ...;
```

The two-argument form of open protects you from extra whitespace. Part of the filename processing magic lets Perl trim leading and trailing whitespace from the filename. Why would you ever want whitespace at the beginning or end? We won't pretend to know what sorts of crazy things you want. With the three-argument open, you can keep that whitespace in your filename. Try it sometime: make a filename that starts with a newline. Did it work? Good. We'll let you figure out how to delete it.

Things to remember

- Use the three-argument form of open when you can.
- Use lexical scalars to store filehandle references.
- Avoid precedence problems by using or to check the success of open.

Item 53. Consider different ways of reading from a stream.

You can use the line input operator <> to read either a single line from a stream in a scalar context or the entire contents of a stream in a list context. Which method you should use depends on your need for efficiency, access to the lines read, and other factors, like syntactic convenience.

In general, the line-at-a-time method is the most efficient in terms of time and memory. The implicit while (<>) form is equivalent in speed to the corresponding explicit code:

```
open my ($fh), '<', $file or die;

while (<$fh>) {
  # do something with $_
}
```

```
while ( defined( my $line = <$fh> ) ) { # explicit version
    # do something with $line
}
```

Note the use of the `defined` operator in the second loop. This prevents the loop from missing a line if the very last line of a file is the single character 0 with no terminating newline—not a likely occurrence, but it doesn't hurt to be careful.

You can use a similar syntax with a `foreach` loop to read the entire file into memory in a single operation:

```
foreach (<$fh>) {
    # do something with $_
}
```

The all-at-once method is slower and uses more memory than the line-at-a-time method. If all you want to do is step through the lines in a file, you should use the line-at-a-time method, although the difference in performance will not be noticeable if you are reading a short file.

All-at-once has its advantages, though, when combined with operations like sorting:

```
print sort <$fh>;   # print lines sorted
```

If you need access to more than one line at a time, all-at-once may be appropriate. If you want to look at previous or succeeding lines based on the current line, you want to already have those lines. This example prints three adjacent lines when it finds a line with "Shazam":

```
my @f = <$fh>;
foreach ( 0 .. $#f ) {
  if ( $f[$_] =~ /\bShazam\b/ ) {
    my $lo = ( $_ > 0 )   ? $_ - 1 : $_;
    my $hi = ( $_ < $#f ) ? $_ + 1 : $_;
    print map { "$_: $f[$_]" } $lo .. $hi;
  }
}
```

You can still handle many of these situations with line-at-a-time input, although your code will definitely be more complex:

```
my @fh;
@f[ 0 .. 2 ] = ("\n") x 3;
```

```
for ( ; ; ) {
  # queue using a slice assignment
  @f[ 0 .. 2 ] = ( @f[ 1, 2 ], scalar(<$fh>) );
  last if not defined $f[1];
  if ( $f[1] =~ /\bShazam\b/ ) {  # ... looking for Shazam
    print map { ( $_ + $. - 1 ) . ": $f[$_]" } 0 .. 2;
  }
}
```

Maintaining a queue of lines of text with slice assignments makes this slower than the equivalent all-at-once code, but this technique works for arbitrarily large input. The queue could also be implemented with an index variable rather than a slice assignment, which would result in more complex but faster running code.

Slurp a file

If your goal is simply to read a file into memory as quickly as possible, you might consider clearing the line separator character and reading the entire file as a single string. This will read the contents of a file or stream much faster than either of the earlier alternatives:

```
my $contents = do {
  local $/;
  open my ($fh1), '<', $file1 or die;
  <$fh>;
};
```

You can also just use the `File::Slurp` module to do it for you, which lets you read the entire file into a scalar to have it in one big chunk or read it into an array to have it line-by-line:

```
use File::Slurp;

my $text  = read_file('filename');
my @lines = read_file('filename');
```

Use `read` or `sysread` for maximum speed

Finally, the `read` and `sysread` operators are useful for quickly scanning a file if line boundaries are of no importance:

```
open my ($fh1), '<', $file1 or die;
open my ($fh2), '<', $file2 or die;

my $chunk = 4096;  # block size to read
my ( $bytes, $buf1, $buf2, $diff );

CHUNK: while ( $bytes = sysread $fh1, $buf1, $chunk ) {
  sysread $fh2, $buf2, $chunk;
  $diff++, last CHUNK if $buf1 ne $buf2;
}


print "$file1 and $file2 differ" if $diff;
```

Things to remember

- Avoid reading entire files into memory if you don't need to.
- Read entire files quickly with `File::Slurp`.
- Use `read` of `sysread` to quickly read through a file.

Item 54. Open filehandles to and from strings.

Since Perl 5.6, you can open filehandles on strings. You don't have to treat strings any differently from files, sockets, or pipes. Once you stop treating strings specially, you have a lot more flexibility about how you get and send data. Reduce the complexity of your application by reducing the number of cases it has to handle.

And this change is not just for you. Though you may not have thought that opening filehandles on strings was a feature, it is. People tend to want to interact with your code in ways that you don't expect.

Read from a string

If you have a multiline string to process, don't reach for a regex to break it into lines. You can open a filehandle on a reference to a scalar, and then read from it as you would any other filehandle:

```
my $string = <<'MULTILINE';
Buster
Mimi
```

```
Roscoe
MULTILINE

open my ($str_fh), '<', \$string;

my @end_in_vowels = grep /[aeiou]$/, <$str_fh>;
```

Later, suppose you decide that you don't want to get the data from a string that's in the source code, but you want to read from a file instead. That's not a problem, because you are already set up to deal with filehandles:

```
my @end_in_vowels = grep /[aeiou]$/, <$other_fh>;
```

It gets even easier when you wrap your output operations in a subroutine. That subroutine doesn't care where the data come from as long as it can read from the filehandle it gets:

```
my @matches = ends_in_vowel($str_fh);
push @matches, ends_in_vowel($file_fh);
push @matches, ends_in_vowel($socket);

sub ends_in_vowel {
  my ($fh) = @_;

  grep /[aeiou]$/, <$fh>;
}
```

Write to a string

You can build up a string with a filehandle, too. Instead of opening the string for reading, you open it for writing:

```
my $string = q{};

open my ($str_fh), '>', \$string;

print $str_fh "This goes into the string\n";
```

Likewise, you can append to a string that already exists:

```
my $string = q{};

open my ($str_fh), '>>', \$string;

print $str_fh "This goes at the end of the string\n";
```

You can shorten that a bit by declaring $string at the same time that you take a reference to it. It looks odd at first, but it works:

```
open my ($str_fh), '>>', \my $string;
```

```
print $str_fh "This goes at the end of the string\n";
```

This is especially handy when you have a subroutine or method that normally expects to print to a filehandle, although you want to capture that output in memory. Instead of creating a new file only to read it back into your program, you just capture it directly.

seek and tell

Once you have a filehandle to a string, you can do all the usual filehandle sorts of things, including moving around in this "virtual file." Open a string for reading, move to a location, and read a certain number of bytes. This can be really handy when you have an image file or other binary (non–line-oriented) format you want to work with:

```
use Fcntl qw(:seek);  # for the constants
my $string = 'abcdefghijklmnopqrstuvwxyz';

my $buffer;
open my ($str_fh), '<', \$string;

seek( $str_fh, 10, SEEK_SET ); # move ten bytes from start
my $read = read( $str_fh, $buffer, 4 );
print "I read [$buffer]\n";
print "Now I am at position ", tell($str_fh), "\n";

seek( $str_fh, -7, SEEK_CUR );  # move seven bytes back
my $read = read( $str_fh, $buffer, 4 );
print "I read [$buffer]\n";
print "Now I am at position ", tell($str_fh), "\n";
```

The output shows that you are able to move forward and backward in the string:

```
I read [klmn]
Now I am at position 14
I read [hijk]
Now I am at position 11
```

You can even replace parts of the string if you open the filehandle as read-write, using +< as the mode:

```
use Fcntl qw(:seek);  # for the constants
my $string = 'abcdefghijklmnopqrstuvwxyz';

my $buffer;
open my ($str_fh), '+<', \$string;

# move 10 bytes from the start
seek( $str_fh, 10, SEEK_CUR );
print $str_fh '***';
print "String is now:\n\t$string\n";

read( $str_fh, $buffer, 3 );
print "I read [$buffer], and am now at ",
  tell($str_fh), "\n";
```

The output shows that you've changed the string, but can also read from it:

```
String is now:
    abcdefghij***nopqrstuvwxyz
I read [nop], and am now at 16
```

You could do this with substr, but then you'd limit yourself to working with strings. When you do it with filehandles, you can handle quite a bit more.

Things to remember

- Treat strings as files to avoid special cases.
- Create readable filehandles to strings to break strings into lines.
- Create writeable filehandles to strings to capture output.

Item 55. Make flexible output.

When you use hard-coded (or assumed) filehandles in your code, you limit your program and frustrate your users. Some culprits look like these:

```
print "This goes to standard output\n";
print STDOUT "This goes to standard output too\n";
print STDERR "This goes to standard error\n";
```

When you put those sorts of statements in your program, you reduce the flexibility of the code, causing people to perform acrobatics and feats of magic to work around it. They shouldn't have to localize any filehandles or redefine standard filehandles to change where the output goes. Despite that, people still code like that because it's quick, it's easy, and mostly, they don't know how easy it is to do it better.

You don't need an object-oriented design to make this work, but it's a lot easier that way. When you need to output something in a method, get the output filehandle from the object. In this example, you call `get_output_fh` to fetch the destination for your data:

```
sub output_method {
   my ( $self, @args ) = @_;

   my $output_fh = $self->get_output_fh;

   print $output_fh @args;
 }
```

To make that work, you need a way to set the output filehandle. That can be a set of regular accessor methods. `get_output_fh` returns STDOUT if you haven't set anything:

```
sub get_output_fh {
   my ($self) = @_;

   return $self->{output_fh} || *STDOUT{IO};
 }

sub set_output_fh {
   my ( $self, $fh ) = @_   ;

   $self->{output_fh} = $fh;
 }
```

With this as part of the published interface for your code, the other programmers have quite a bit of flexibility when they want to change how your program outputs data:

```perl
$obj->output_method("Hello stdout!\n");

# capture the output in a string
open my ($str_fh), '>', \$string;
$obj->set_output_fh($str_fh);
$obj->output_method("Hello string!\n");

# send the data over the network
socket( my ($socket), ... );
$obj->set_output_fh($socket);
$obj->output_method("Hello socket!\n");

# output to a string and STDOUT at the same time
use IO::Tee;
my $tee =
  IO::Tee->new( $str_fh, *STDOUT{IO} );
$obj->set_output_fh($tee);
$obj->output_method("Hello all of you!\n");

# send the data nowhere
use IO::Null;
my $null_fh = IO::Null->new;
$obj->set_output_fh($null_fh);
$obj->output_method("Hello? Anyone there?\n");

# decide at run time: interactive sessions use stdout,
# non-interactive session use a null filehandle
use IO::Interactive;
$obj->set_output_fh( interactive() );
$obj->output_method("Hello, maybe!\n");
```

It gets even better, though. You almost get some features for free. Do you want to have another method that returns the output as a string? You've already done most of the work! You just have to shuffle some filehandles around as you temporarily make a filehandle to a string (Item 54) as the output filehandle:

```perl
sub as_string {
  my ( $self, @args ) = @_;

  my $string = '';
  open my ($str_fh), '>', \$string;
```

```
    my $old_fh = $self->get_output_fh;
    $self->set_output_fh($str_fh);
    $self->output_method(@args);

    # restore the previous fh
    $self->set_output_fh($old_fh);

    $string;
    }
```

If you want to have a feature to turn off all output, that's almost trivial now. You just use a null filehandle to suppress all output:

```
$obj->set_output_fh( IO::Null->new )
    if $config->{be_quiet};
```

Things to remember

- For flexibility, don't hard-code your filehandles.
- Give other programmers a way to change the output filehandle.
- Use `IO::Interactive` to check if someone will see your output.

Item 56. Use `File::Spec` or `Path::Class` to work with paths.

Perl runs on a couple hundred different platforms, and it's almost a law of software engineering that any useful program that you write will migrate from the system you most prefer to the system you least prefer. If you have to work with file paths, use one of the modules that handle all of the portability details for you. Not only is it safer, it's also easier.

Use `File::Spec` for portability

The `File::Spec` module comes with Perl, and the most convenient way to use it is through its function interface. It automatically imports several subroutines into the current namespace:

```
use File::Spec::Functions;
```

To construct a new path, you need the volume (maybe), the directory, and the filename. The volume and filename are easy:

```
my $volume = 'C:';
my $file   = 'perl.exe';
```

You have to do a bit of work to create the directory from its parts, but that's not so bad. The `rootdir` function gets you started, and the `catdir` puts everything together according to the local system:

```
my $directory =
    catdir( rootdir(), qw(strawberry perl bin) );
```

If you are used to Windows or UNIX, you may not appreciate that some systems, such as VMS, format the directory portion of the path the same as the filename portion. If you use `File::Spec`, however, you don't have to worry too much about that.

Now that you have all three parts, you can put them together with `catpath`:

```
my $full_path =
    catpath( $volume, $directory, $file );
```

On UNIX-like filesystems, `catpath` ignores the argument for the volume, so if you don't care about that portion, you can use `undef` as a placeholder:

```
my $full_path =
    catpath( undef, $directory, $file );
```

This might seem like a silly way to do that if you think that your program will ever run only on your local system. If you don't want to handle the portable paths, just don't tell anyone about your useful program, so you'll never have to migrate it.

`File::Spec` has many other functions that deal with putting together and taking apart paths, as well as getting the local representations to common paths such as the parent directory, the temporary directory, the devnull device, and so on.

Use `Path::Class` if you can

The `Path::Class` module is a wrapper around `File::Spec` and provides convenience methods for things that are terribly annoying to work out yourself. To start, you construct a file or a directory object. On Windows, you just give `file` your Windows path, and it figures it out. The `file` function assumes that the path is for the local filesystem:

```
use Path::Class qw(file dir);

my $file = file('C:/strawberry/perl/bin/perl.exe');
```

This path doesn't have to exist. The object in `$file` doesn't do anything to verify that the path is valid; it just deals with the rules for constructing paths on the local system.

If you aren't on Windows but still need to work with a Windows path, you use `foreign_file` instead:

```
my $file = foreign_file( 'Win32',
  'C:/strawberry/perl/bin/perl.exe' );
```

Now `$file` does everything correctly for a Windows path. If you need to go the other way and translate it into a path suitable for another system, you can use the `as_foreign` method:

```
# /strawberry/perl
my $unix_path = $file->as_foreign('Unix');
```

Once you have the object, you call methods to interact with the file.

To get a filehandle for reading, call `open` with no arguments. It's really just a wrapper around `IO::File`, so it's just like calling `IO::File->new`:

```
my $read_fh = $file->open
  or die "Could not open $file: $!";
```

If you want to create a new file, you start with a `file` object. That doesn't create the file, since the object simply deals with paths. When you call `open` and pass it the `>`, the file is created for you and you get back a write filehandle:

```
my $file = file('new_file');

my $fh = $file->open('>');

print $fh "Put this line in the file\n";
```

You can get the directory that contains the file, and then open a directory handle:

```
my $dir = $file->dir;
my $dh = $dir->open or die "Could not open $dir: $!";
```

If you already have a directory object, it's easy to get its parent directory:

```
my $parent = $dir->parent;
```

You read from the directory handle with `readdir`, as normal, and get the name of the file. As with any `readdir` operation, you get only the filename, so you have to add the directory portion yourself. That's not a problem when you use `file` to put it together for you:

```
while ( my $filename = readdir($dh) ) {
  next if $filename =~ /^\.\.?$/;
  my $file = file( $dir, $file );
  print "Found $file\n";
}
```

Things to remember

- Don't hard-code file paths with operating system specific details.
- Use `File::Spec` or `Path::Class` to construct portable paths.

Item 57. Leave most of the data on disk to save memory.

Datasets today can be huge. Whether you are sequencing DNA or parsing weblogs, the amount of data that is collected can easily surpass the amount of data that can be contained in the memory of your program. It is not uncommon for Perl programmers who work with large data sets to see the dreaded "Out of memory!" error.

When this happens, there are a few things you can do. One idea is to check how much memory your process can use. The fix might be as simple as having your operating system allocate more memory to the program.

Increasing memory limits is really only a bandage for larger algorithmic problems. If the data you are working with can grow, you're bound to hit memory limits again.

There are a few strategies that you can use to reduce the memory footprint of your program.

Read files line-by-line

The first and most obvious strategy is to read the data you are processing line-by-line instead of loading entire data sets into memory. You could read an entire file into an array:

```
open my ($fh), '<', $file or die;
my @lines = <$fh>;
```

However, if you don't need all of the data at once, read only as much as you need for the next operation:

```
open my ($fh), '<', $file or die;

while (<$fh>) {
  #... do something with the line
}
```

Store large hashes in DBM files

There is a common pattern of problem in which you have some huge data set that you have to cycle through while looking up values keyed in another potentially large data set. For instance, you might have a lookup file of names by ID and a log file of IDs and times when that ID logged in to your system. If the set of lookup data is sufficiently large, it might be wise to load it into a hash that is backed by a DBM file. This keeps the lookups on the filesystem, freeing up memory. In the `build_lookup` subroutine in the example below, it looks like you have all of the data in memory, but you've actually stored it in a file connected to a tied hash:

```
use Fcntl;  # For O_RDWR, O_CREAT, etc.

my ( $lookup_file, $data_file ) = @ARGV;

my $lookup = build_lookup($lookup_file);

open my ($data_fh), '<', $data_file or die;

while (<$data_fh>) {
  chomp;
  my @row = split;
```

```perl
    if ( exists $lookup->{ $row[0] } ) {
      print "@row\n";
    }
}

sub build_lookup {
  my ($file) = @_;
  open my ($lookup_fh), '<', $lookup_file or die;

  require SDBM_File;
  tie( my %lookup, 'SDBM_File', "lookup.$$",
    O_RDWR | O_CREAT, 0666 )
    or die
    "Couldn't tie SDBM file 'filename': $!; aborting";

  while (<$lookup_file_handle>) {
    chomp;
    my ( $key, $value ) = split;
    $lookup{$key} = $value;
  }

  return \%lookup;
}
```

Building the lookup can be costly, so you want to minimize the number of times that you have to do it. If possible, prebuild the lookup DBM file and just load it at run time. Once you have it, you shouldn't have to rebuild it. You can even share it between programs.

SDBM_File is a Perl implementation of DBM that doesn't scale very well. If you have NDBM_File or GDBM_File available on your system, opt for those instead.

Read files as if they were arrays

If key-based lookup by way of a hash isn't flexible enough, you can use Tie::File to treat a file's lines as an array, even though you don't have them in memory. You can navigate the file as if it were a normal array. You can access any line in the file at any time, like in this random fortune printing program:

```
use Tie::File;


tie my @fortunes, 'Tie::File', $fortune_file
  or die "Unable to tie $fortune_file";


foreach ( 1 .. 10 ) {
  print $fortunes[ rand @fortunes ];
}
```

Use temporary files and directories

If these prebuilt solutions don't work for you, you can always write temporary files yourself. The `File::Temp` module helps by automatically creating a unique temporary file name and by cleaning up the file after you are done with it. This can be especially handy if you need to completely create a new version of a file, but replace it only once you're done creating it:

```
use File::Temp qw(tempfile);


my ( $fh, $file_name ) = tempfile();


while (<>) {
  print {$fh} uc $_;
}


$fh->close;


rename $file_name => $final_name;
```

`File::Temp` can even create a temporary directory that you can use to store multiple files in. You can fetch several Web pages and store them for later processing:

```
use File::Temp qw(tempdir);
use File::Spec::Functions;
use LWP::Simple qw(getstore);


my ($temp_dir) = tempdir( CLEANUP => 1 );


my %searches = (
  google      => 'http://www.google.com/#hl=en&q=perl',
```

```
  yahoo      => 'http://search.yahoo.com/search?p=perl',
  microsoft => 'http://www.bing.com/search?q=perl',
);

foreach my $search ( keys %searches ) {
  getstore( $searches{$search},
    catfile( $temp_dir, $search ) ) );
}
```

There's one caution with `File::Temp`: it opens its files in binary mode. If you need line-ending translations or a different encoding (Item 73), you have the use `binmode` on the filehandle yourself.

Things to remember

- Store large hashes on disk in DBM files to save memory.
- Treat files as arrays with `Tie::File`.
- Use `File::Temp` to create temporary files and directories.

6 | References

Learning references is one of the major rites of passage in Perl. Introduced in Perl 5, references opened the way for complex data structures and object-oriented programming. References are the key to organizing data and passing it around as a unit. If you want to move to the next level in Perl, you need references.

Although this chapter shows you some reference tricks, your greatest benefit will come from your effective creation and manipulation of data structures. You'll develop those skills with practice, so don't be afraid to start using them.

Item 58. Understand references and reference syntax.

A reference is a scalar value. You can store a reference in a scalar variable or as an element of an array or hash, just as you can with numbers and strings.

You can think of a reference as a "pointer" to some other object in Perl. References can point to any kind of object, including other scalars (even references), arrays, hashes, subroutines, and typeglobs.

Aside from a general pointer-like behavior, however, references do not have very much in common with pointers in C or C++. You can create only references to existing objects; you cannot modify them afterward to do something like pointing to the next element of an array.

You can convert references into strings or numbers, but Perl doesn't have a built-in way to convert a string or number back into a reference. Although a reference is treated syntactically like any other scalar value, a reference "knows" what type of object it points to. Finally, each reference to a Perl object increments that object's reference count, preventing the object from being scavenged by Perl's garbage collector.

Creating references

You can create references in several different ways. The simplest is to use the backslash operator (or "take a reference" operator) on a variable:

```
my $a          = 3.1416;
my $scalar_ref = \$a;
```

The backslash operator creates a reference pointing at the value of the argument of the backslash. In the PEGS notation, that looks like:

The backslash operator works on any kind of variable name:

```
my $array_ref = \@a;
my $hash_ref  = \%a;
my $sub_ref   = \&a;
my $glob_ref  = \*a;
```

It also works on array and hash elements:

```
$array_elem_ref = \$a[0];
$hash_elem_ref  = \$a{'hello'};
```

It even works on literal values, although references to literal values are read-only:

```
$one_ref  = \1;
$mode_ref = \oct('0755');
```

The backslash works in a very strange way on a list of values, returning a list of references rather than a reference to a list. It decides what references to return using a seemingly arbitrary heuristic.

Take this `val` subroutine:

```
sub val { return 1 .. 3 }
```

When you create a reference using the ampersand, you get back a CODE reference to the `val` subroutine itself:

```
my $ref1 = \(&val);
```

If you create a reference after calling `val`, you get a SCALAR back:

```
my $ref2 = \( val() );
```

Since this particular statement does the assignment in scalar context, the reference is to the last value returned by `val`, which is **3**.

If you change the assignment to list context, you get a SCALAR reference to the first value returned by `val`, which is **1**.

```
my ($ref3) = \( val() );
```

You would think that the behavior of getting references from lists returned from subroutines would carry over to literal lists—and it does. Both of these cases return a scalar reference to the value **3**:

```
my $ref4 = \( 1 .. 3 );
```

```
my $ref5 = \( 1, 2, 3 );
```

References and reference syntax can get a little complex, so even if you understand what's going on, it's likely that the next person who has to touch your code will not, so be as clear as possible.

The anonymous array constructor, which looks like an ordinary list except that you enclose the contents within brackets instead of parentheses, creates an unnamed array in memory and returns a reference to it. This is the customary method of creating a reference to a list of items.

```
my $a_ref = [ 1 .. 3 ];
```

`$a_ref` is now an ARRAY reference to an unnamed array containing the values **1**, **2**, and **3**:

```
print ref $a_ref, " @$a_ref";
```

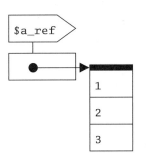

The anonymous hash constructor, which uses braces rather than brackets, works similarly:

```
my $h_ref = { anonymous => 'user' };
$h_ref->{'joe'}  = 'bloe';
$h_ref->{'john'} = 'public';
```

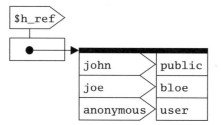

A subroutine definition without a name returns a reference to an anonymous subroutine.

References to subroutines are sometimes called **coderefs**. Here you store a coderef in `$greetings` and then execute the reference code:

```
my $greetings = sub { print "hello, world!\n" };
$greetings->();
```

This style of subroutine creation is often used in signal handling, as in this interrupt handler:

```
$SIG{INTR} = sub { print "not yet--I'm busy\n" };
```

References to anonymous subroutines are very useful (Item 50). They are somewhat like function pointers in C. However, since anonymous subroutines are created dynamically, not statically, they have peculiar properties that are more like something from LISP.

References to scalars can be very efficient when you need to pass around large strings. In the next example, the first call to `some_sub()` makes a copy of the entire contents of `$string`, while the second call copies only the reference to the string:

```
my $string = 'a' x 1_000_000;


some_sub($string);


some_sub( \$string );
```

This works through "autovivification," discussed later in this Item.

Using references

Dereferencing uses the value that a reference points to. There are several different forms of dereferencing syntax.

The canonical form of dereferencing syntax is to use a block returning a reference in a place where you could otherwise use a variable or a subroutine identifier. Whereas using an identifier would give you the value of the variable with that name, using a block returning a reference gives you the value that the reference points to.

In this example, you have an ordinary scalar, $a, and then create a reference to that scalar, $s_ref. You can work with this reference just as you would any regular scalar value:

```
my $a    = 1;
my $s_ref = \$a;
print ${$s_ref};
${$s_ref} += 1;
```

Array references work in a similar manner. Here you have an array, @a, and create a reference to it, $a_ref. Both supply the same data to print. Changes made to either are visible when accessing either the array or the reference to the array.

```
my @a    = 1 .. 5;
my $a_ref = \@a;
print "@a";
print "@{$a_ref}";
push @{$a_ref}, 6 .. 10;
```

The code inside the block can be arbitrarily complex, so long as the result of the last expression evaluated yields a reference. In this contrived example, you return the third value of one of two different arrays based on the value of the variable $hi:

```
my $ref1 = [ 1 .. 5 ];
my $ref2 = [ 6 .. 10 ];
my $val  = ${
  if ($hi) { $ref2; }
  else { $ref1 }
  }[2];
print $val;  # either 3 or 8
```

If the reference value is in a scalar variable, you can dispense with the braces and just use the name of the scalar variable, with the leading $, instead. You can use more than one $ if it's a reference to a reference. This example uses a reference to a scalar and a reference to a reference to print the word `testing` twice:

```
my $a         = 'testing';
my $s_ref     = \$a;
my $s_ref_ref = \$s_ref;
print "$$s_ref $$$s_ref_ref";
```

This even applies to references to hashes:

```
my $h_ref = { 'F' => 9, 'Cl' => 17, 'Br' => 35 };
print "The elements are ", join ' ', keys %$h_ref, "\n";
print "F's atomic number is is $$h_ref{'F'}\n";
```

Expressions like `$$h_ref{'F'}`, or the even-more-awkward equivalent `${$h_ref}{'F'}`, occur frequently. There is a more visually appealing "arrow" syntax that you can use to write subscripts for array and hash references:

```
${$h_ref}{'F'} # canonical form
$$h_ref{'F'}   # scalar variable form
$h_ref->{'F'}  # arrow form
```

You can cascade arrows. Furthermore, if on the left and right sides of an arrow are both subscripts, you can omit the arrow. Both of these `print` statements print the word `joe`:

```
$student->[1] = { 'first' => 'joe', 'last' => 'bloe' };
print $student->[1]->{'first'};
print $student->[1]{'first'};
```

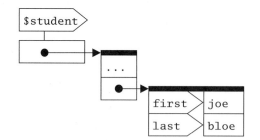

Be careful about leaving out too many arrows or braces. For example, if you omit the first arrow, you get an array of hashrefs, which is different:

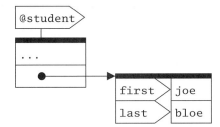

Finally, Perl handles all references, no matter what their type, like ordinary scalars—they have no special "type" that distinguishes them syntactically from other scalars. However, a reference value contains information about the type of object it points to. You can get to this information with the `ref` operator.

This reference to a scalar value results in **SCALAR** being printed:

```
my $s_ref = \1;
print ref $s_ref;
```

And this subroutine reference causes **CODE** to be printed:

```
my $c_ref = sub { 'code!' };
print ref $c_ref;
```

Autovivification

If you use a scalar with an undefined value as if it were a reference to another object, Perl automatically creates an object of the appropriate type and makes that scalar a reference to that type. This is called **autovivification**. For example, the following code creates an array of four elements and makes `$ref` a reference to it:

```
undef $ref;
$ref->[3] = 'four';
```

This can be especially handy for deep data structures, saving you the work of creating each level:

```
use Data::Dumper;

my $ds;
```

```
$ds->{top}[0]{cats}[1]{name} = 'Buster';

print Dumper($ds);
```

With a little bit of code, you've created a quite complex structure:

```
$VAR1 = {
  'top' => [ {
    'cats' => [
      undef,
      {
        'name' => 'Buster'
      }
    ]
  } ]
};
```

Item 60 presents a longer example of autovivification.

Soft references

If you dereference a string value, Perl will return the value of the variable with the name given in the string. The variable will be created if necessary. This is called a **soft reference**.

Soft references can be the results of variable interpretation:

```
my $str = 'pi';
${$str} = 3.1416;
print "pi = $pi\n";
```

You might even use literal strings to create the soft reference:

```
${ 'e' . 'e' } = 2.7183;
print "ee = $ee\n";   # 2.7183
```

Such a variable name does not have to be a legal identifier, which means that you can create variables out of whitespace and even null characters:

```
${}       = 'space';
${' '}  = 'space';
${'   '} = 'two space';
${"\0"} = 'null';
```

Note that soft references have nothing to do with reference counts. Only ordinary "hard" references increment reference counts.

Turning on `strict refs` disables soft references (Item 3), and with good reason: there is almost always a better way to do things.

Things to remember

- Take a reference to a variable using the reference operator, \, or with anonymous array, [ ], or hash, {}, constructors.
- Dereference a reference to get the value it points to.
- Don't treat a normal scalar as a reference; that creates a soft reference.

Item 59. Compare reference types to prototypes.

Once you start passing references as subroutine arguments, you'll want to verify that you got the type that you were expecting.

```
sub count_matches {
  my ( $regex, $array_ref ) = @_;

  my $matches = grep /$regex/, @$array_ref;
}
```

If you pass the wrong sort of arguments to `count_matches`, everything blows up. If you use an array instead of an array reference in your call, Perl will complain:

```
my $matches = count_matches( qr/.../, @array );
```

You get an error like:

```
Not an ARRAY reference at ...
```

Likewise, if you pass a string instead of a regex reference, you get another sort of error if the string isn't a valid regex but one with, say, an unmatched parenthesis:

```
my $matches = count_matches( '(...', \@array );
```

You get an error that points at the problem with the regex:

```
Unmatched ( in regex; marked by <-- HERE in ⏎
  m/( <-- HERE / at ...
```

The `ref` operator

To find out the reference type that you have, use `ref`:

```
my $array_ref = \@array;

my $type = ref $array_ref;  # $type is 'ARRAY';
```

For the basic types, you will get one of: **SCALAR**, **ARRAY**, **HASH**, **CODE**, **GLOB**, or **Regexp**.

Comparing types

Some people will match the type returned by `ref` against the literal type they hard-code:

```
sub count_matches {
  my ( $regex, $array_ref ) = @_;

  die "First argument needs to be a regex reference"
    unless ref $regex eq 'Regexp';
  die "Second argument needs to be an array reference"
    unless ref $regex eq 'ARRAY';

  my $matches = grep /$regex/, @$array_ref;
}
```

However, it's easy to make a mistake by hard-coding the values. For instance, it's easy to forget that the reference type for a regular expression doesn't follow the pattern of the other types; it's mixed case and there is a trailing p:

```
die '...' unless ref $regex eq 'REGEX';  # WRONG
die '...' unless ref $regex eq 'Regex';  # WRONG
```

You don't have to remember the literal values, though. You can use a prototype of the reference that you want to generate the string you need, assigning it to a scalar with an uppercase name to denote that it is a constant:

```
# ref of empty anonymous array
my $ARRAY_TYPE = ref [];

# ref of empty anonymous regex
my $REGEX_TYPE = ref qr//;
```

```
# ref of empty anonymous hash
my $HASH_TYPE = ref {};

# ref of empty anonymous sub
my $CODE_TYPE = ref sub { };
```

Now you'll get the same type that Perl returns, and save yourself the risk of mistyping that literal string, and there's nothing to memorize:

```
die '...' unless ref $regex eq $REGEX_TYPE;
die '...' unless ref $array eq $ARRAY_TYPE;
```

You could do the same thing with the `constant` or `Readonly` modules:

```
use constant ARRAY_TYPE => ref [];

use Readonly;
Readonly my $ARRAY_TYPE => ref [];
```

If you need to do more complex validation of your subroutine arguments, check out `Params::Validate`.

Things to remember

- Verify references' types before you dereference them.
- Use prototypical values to compare reference types.
- Turn prototypical values into constants.

Item 60. Create arrays of arrays with references.

Perl has no lists of lists per se, but an array containing array references does the trick. This is commonly called an **array of arrays** or just **AoA**. Remember that the parentheses or brackets you use for the subscripts must match the type of structure you want to create (Item 61).

You can construct the AoA directly:

```
# an array of refs to arrays
my @a = ( [ 1, 2 ], [ 3, 4 ] );
print $a[1][0];  # gives 3

# a ref to an array of refs to arrays
my $a = [ [ 1, 2 ], [ 3, 4 ] ];
print $a->[1][0];  # gives 3
```

You can also build up the data structure programmatically. For instance, you can generate a matrix that represents a multiplication table, using a couple of C-style `for` loops to go through the indices:

```
my $max = 5;
my $matrix;
for ( my $i = 1 ; $i < $max ; $i++ ) {
  for ( my $j = 0 ; $j < $max ; $j++ ) {
    $matrix->[$i][$j] = $i * $j;
  }
}
```

It's not too hard to print an AoA nicely, either. Most of the work is in just setting up the format rather than accessing the data structure:

```
my $format = ' %2d' x @{$matrix};

printf " i/j $format\n", 0 .. $max;
for my $i ( 0 .. $max - 1 ) {
  printf "%2d:  $format\n", $i, @{ $matrix->[$i] };
}
```

The output is your nicely formatted multiplication table:

```
i/j   0  1  2  3  4
0:    0  0  0  0  0
1:    0  1  2  3  4
2:    0  2  4  6  8
3:    0  3  6  9 12
4:    0  4  8 12 16
```

If you want to get a particular element, you just use the right indices:

```
my $two_squared = $matrix->[2][2];
```

Remember to be careful with the first subscript. You need the `->` after `$matrix` because it's a reference. After the first index, you can omit the `->` because two subscripts next to each other imply a reference (Item 58).

Consider another example. Suppose you want quick access to lines of text:

```
my @lines;
while (<>) {
  chomp;
```

```
    push @lines, [split];
}
```

Once you have the data structure, you can quickly get to any word on any line. If you want, say, the third word on the seventh line, you just need to get the indices correct. In this case, `@lines` is an array (not a reference), so you don't use a leading `->`:

```
my $third_on_seventh = $lines[6][2];
```

How many words are on line 15 in the file? The array element is a reference to an array, so you can dereference it and assign it to a scalar to get the count of its elements (Item 9):

```
my $count = @{ $lines[14] };
```

Which line has the most words? You can use a Schwartzian Transform (Item 22) to sort the indices for `@lines` to avoid creating a copy of your data. Since you need only one index to get the line with the most words, assign it to a list that has one scalar variable:

```
my ($most_words) =
  map   { $_->[0] }
  sort  { $b->[1] <=> $a->[1] }
  map   { [ $_, scalar @{ $lines[$_] } ] } 0 .. $#lines;

print "Line $most_words is the longest with ",
  scalar @{ $lines[$most_words] }, " words\n";
```

That's a little verbose. You could do it as one long list operation, and you might enjoy puzzling out this variation on the Schwartzian Transform:

```
use 5.010;

printf "Line %s is the longest with %s words\n",
  map   { @$_ }
  sort  { $b->[1] <=> $a->[1] }
  map   { state $l = 0; [ $l++, scalar @$_ ] }
  map   { [split] }
  <>;
```

You can see more examples in the *perldsc* (Perl Data Structures Cookbook) or the *perllol* documentation.

Things to remember

- Use array references to create arrays of arrays in Perl.
- Use arrays of arrays to represent matrices.
- Ensure you know if your variable is a regular array or a reference.

Item 61. Don't confuse anonymous arrays with list literals.

The anonymous array constructor, [], looks very much like the parentheses that surround list literals. Superficially, they both seem to serve the same purpose—building lists. However, anonymous array constructors differ from list literals in significant ways.

An anonymous array constructor returns a reference, not a list. The purpose of an anonymous array constructor is to allow you to create a reference to an array object without having to create a named array:

```
# If you didn't have [], you might try:
{ my @arr = 0 .. 9; $aref = \@arr }
print $$aref[4];  # gives 4


# or perhaps:
my $aref = do { \( my @arr = 0 .. 9 ) };


# But you do have []:
my $aref = [ 0 .. 9 ];
```

You can assign the array references created by anonymous array constructors to array variables, but it's probably not what you want. Be careful to use array variables with lists, and scalar variables with anonymous array constructors:

```
# meant to use parentheses, maybe?
my @files = [ glob '*.c' ];
print "@files\n";  # something like ARRAY(0xa4600)


# another classic -- yields the enigmatic
# ARRAY(0xa45d0),ARRAY(0xa4654),ARRAY(0xa4558)
my @two_d_array = [ [ 1 .. 3 ], [ 4 .. 6 ], [ 7 .. 9 ] ];
foreach my $row (@two_d_array) {
  print join( ',', @$row ), "\n";
}
```

Operators and functions create list and scalar contexts. The anonymous array constructor is an operator. Parentheses aren't. Just putting parentheses around something will not change a scalar context into a list context (Item 12).

You can see this for yourself:

```
sub arrayish { print "arrayish\n" if wantarray }

my $foo    = arrayish();          # nope
my $foo    = ( arrayish() );      # not yet
my $foo    = ( arrayish(), () );  # dang, it's stubborn
my $foo    = [ arrayish() ];      # score!
my ($foo) = arrayish();           # this works too
```

This is part but not all of the problem that results if you mistakenly assign a would-be list literal instead of an anonymous array constructor to a scalar variable. The other part of the problem is that when you dereference the scalar variable, Perl takes whatever weird value wound up in the scalar and dereferences it—perhaps interpreting it as a soft reference. Of course, what you are going to get is total nonsense anyway, but these two effects can combine to make the debugging process difficult by treating you to some very strange behaviors up front. For example:

```
# meant to use brackets this time, I bet
my $file_list_ref = ( glob '*.c' );
print "@$file_list_ref\n";  # prints nothing?
print "$file_list_ref\n";   # prints foo.c or something
```

With all this in mind, a clever reader should be able to figure out what's going on here:

```
my $aref = ( 1 .. 10 );
print $$aref;  # prints nothing?
print $aref;   # also prints nothing?
```

Things to remember

- Use the anonymous array constructor, [ ], to create a reference.
- Remember that the anonymous array constructor imposes list context.
- Assign lists to arrays, but anonymous arrays to scalars.

Item 62. Build C-style `structs` with anonymous hashes.

People often ask whether Perl has "real data structures, like C." Well, it sort of does. You already know that there are only a few data types in Perl: scalars, arrays, hashes, subroutines, plus a few other odds and ends like filehandles. Structures, like those used in C or Pascal, are not among those types. So in one sense, Perl doesn't have structures. But on the other hand, hashes provide a very similar effect:

```
$student{'last'}  = 'Smith';
$student{'first'} = 'John';
$student{'bday'}  = '01/08/72';
```

When referring to an element of a hash, you can omit the quotation marks around the key so long as it is a valid Perl identifier:

```
$student{last} = 'Smith';
```

This looks somewhat like an element of a structure, doesn't it?

Your first reaction to this might be something like, "Yuck! That's using a string to look up a member of a structure! That's horribly inefficient! A real structure would use some kind of numeric offset computed by the compiler." However, this is wishful thinking where Perl is concerned, and you shouldn't let it bother you at all. Perl is an interpreted language. Accessing variables and elements of arrays and hashes is relatively slow no matter what. The time required to look up an element of a hash is of little consequence in the grand scheme of things.

You can even pass these "structures" to subroutines:

```
sub student_name {
  my %student = @_;
  return "$student{first} $student{last}";
}


print student_name(%student);
```

Now, this may look useful, but it is not particularly efficient. When you pass a hash as an argument, you are actually unrolling the hash into a list of elements, and then reading those elements back into an entirely new hash inside the subroutine. There are also some syntactic limitations. You can't easily pass two hashes this way. Since Perl unrolls the hashes into a single list when it calls the subroutine, it doesn't know how to split the list back into two hashes. In this case, all of the key-value pairs get eaten up by `%roomie1`:

```
sub roommates {
  my ( %roomie1, %roomie2 ) = @_;
    ...
}
```

So, while hashes are the right general idea, they aren't perfect. What works better is using references to hashes, and in particular, using anonymous hash constructors to create them:

```
my $student = {
  last  => 'Smith',
  first => 'John',
  bday  => '01/08/72'
};
```

You can also create an empty structure and fill it in a piece at a time. Using the arrow syntax to access the members of your "structures" makes things look even more like C or C++:

```
$student           = {};
$student->{last}  = 'Smith';
$student->{first} = 'John';
$student->{bday}  = '01/08/72';
```

Since you are now manipulating scalars, not hashes, passing them into subroutines is more efficient, and passing more than one at a time is no problem:

```
sub roommates {
  my ( $roomie1, $roomie2 ) = @_;
    ...
}

roommates( $student1, $student2 );
```

This technique is the basis for the way that Perl constructs objects in most classes.

Things to remember

- Uses hashes to simulate C structs.
- Pass hash references, not hashes, to subroutines to avoid copying.
- Pass hash references to subroutines to retain hash identity.

Item 63. Be careful with circular data structures.

Perl currently uses a reference-counting approach to memory management. Each time an object acquires a name or a new reference, Perl increments that object's reference count. Whenever an object loses a name or a reference, Perl decrements its reference count. Once an object's reference count reaches zero, Perl deletes the object and reclaims the storage used by it.

Reference counting fails when objects point to one another in a circular or self-referential fashion. Consider the following example:

```perl
package Circular;

sub new {
  my $class = shift;
  return bless { name => shift }, $class;
}

sub DESTROY {
  my $self = shift;
  print "$self->{name}: nuked\n";
}

package main;
{
  my $a = Circular->new('a');
  my $b = Circular->new('b');
  $a->{next} = $b;
  $b->{next} = $a;
}

print "the end\n";
```

The block inside the `main` package creates two objects belonging to the class `Circular`, each one containing a reference to the other. The situation looks like this just before the end of the block:

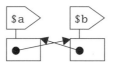

Each object has a reference count of two: one due to its name, and the other due to the reference from the other object. The lexical variables `$a` and `$b` go out of scope once the block exits, and then you have:

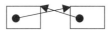

You can no longer get at these objects, since neither has a name and you have no external references to either of them. They are just taking up space. Unfortunately, there's nothing Perl can do to help you, since both objects still have a reference count of one. These objects will continue to hang around until the entire program exits.

Perl eventually destroys these objects. At the very end of a thread of execution, Perl makes a pass with a "mark-sweep" garbage collector. This final pass destroys all of the objects created by the interpreter, accessible or otherwise. If you run the example above, you will see the final pass in action:

```
the end
b: nuked
a: nuked
```

As you might expect, Perl destroys the objects after it executes the last statement in the normal flow of the program.

This final pass is important. You can use Perl as an embedded language. If you used the interpreter repeatedly within the same process to execute code like the above, it would leak memory if there were not a sure-fire means of destroying all the objects created during that thread.

Short of terminating execution, there is no way to clean up this mess once you get into it, but you can prevent it by the careful application of brute force. You have to implement a technique for explicitly breaking the circular references. One solution that would work in the previous case would be:

```
package main;
{
  my $a = Circular->new('a');
  my $b = Circular->new('b');
  $a->{next} = $b;
  $b->{next} = $a;
  $head      = $a;
}
undef $head->{next};
undef $head;
```

Here, we save a link into the circular data structure in the variable $head. Since there is only a single cycle in the structure, breaking a single link is enough to allow Perl to reclaim all the objects in it. If this doesn't seem thorough enough, you can handle them all yourself:

```
while ($head) {
  my $next = $head->{next};
  undef $head->{next};
  $head = $next;
}
undef $head;
print "the end\n";
```

Here you traverse the structure and explicitly destroy every one of the troublesome references. You are destroying references to the objects you want to delete so that their reference counts go to zero. There is no way to explicitly destroy an object in Perl regardless of its reference count; if there were, it could be a horrendous source of bugs and crashes.

Another approach is to do the work in two passes, in a fashion somewhat like that of a mark-sweep collector. First, acquire a list or "catalog" of the references that you need to destroy:

```
my $ptr = $head;
do {
  push @refs, \$head->{next};
  $head = $head->{next};
} while ( $ptr != $head );
$ptr = $head = undef;
```

This loop traverses the self-referential structure and collects a list of references to all the references you need to destroy. The next pass just traverses the list and destroys them:

```
foreach (@refs) {
  print "preemptive strike on $$_\n";
  undef $$_;
}
```

A two-pass approach is extravagant in the case of a simple circular list like this one, but in the case of a graph-like structure containing many cycles, it may be the only alternative.

Things to remember

- Perl manages memory with reference counting.
- Avoid circular references, which Perl can't reclaim.
- If you create circular references, you have to break them yourself.

Item 64. Use `map` and `grep` to manipulate complex data structures.

Sometimes it's useful to take a "slice" of a multidimensional array or hash, or to select slices that have certain characteristics. Conversely, you may need to assemble a collection of lists into a two-dimensional array, or perhaps assemble a collection of two-dimensional arrays into a three-dimensional array. Perl's `map` and `grep` operators are perfect choices for chores like these.

Slicing with `map`

Begin with a program that reads a file of three-dimensional coordinates into memory. The example file has these data:

```
# point data
1 2 3
4 5 6
9 8 7
```

This program reads a file of 3-D coordinates into memory. Each line of the file will contain the *x*, *y*, and *z* coordinates of a single point, separated by whitespace. For example:

```
open my ($points), '<', 'points'
   or die "couldn't read points data: $!\n";

while (<$points>) {
  next if /^\s*#.*$/;   # skip comments
  push @xyz, [split];
}

foreach my $pt (@xyz) {
  print "point ", $i++,
    ": x = $pt->[0], y = $pt->[1], ",
    "z = $pt->[2]\n";
}
```

This program prints:

```
point 1: x = 1, y = 2, z = 3
point 2: x = 4, y = 5, z = 6
point 3: x = 9, y = 8, z = 7
```

The point data is read into a structure that looks like:

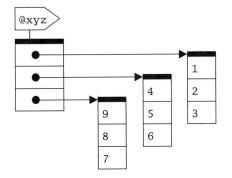

Now, suppose you would like to have just the *x* (0th) element from each point, as indicated by the shading in the PEGS diagram. You could write a loop using an explicit index, or perhaps a C-style `for` loop:

```
for ( $i = 0 ; $i < @xyz ; $i++ ) {
  push @x, $xyz[$i][0];
}
```

But, really, this is a natural application for `map`:

```
my @x = map { $_->[0] } @xyz;
```

Nesting with `map`

On the other hand, suppose that you are starting out with parallel arrays @x, @y, and @z containing vectors of points:

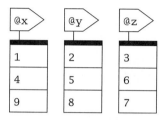

Now, you would like to assemble them into a single three-dimensional structure like the one shown earlier. Once again, you could use some sort of explicit looping structure to turn @x, @y, and @z into @xyz, the slow and tedious way:

```
for ( $i = 0 ; $i < @x ; $i++ ) {
  $xyz[$i][0] = $x[$i];
  $xyz[$i][1] = $y[$i];
  $xyz[$i][2] = $z[$i];
}
```

However, `map` provides a much more elegant alternative. Use [ ] inside `map` to create more deeply nested structures:

```
my @xyz = map { [ $x[$_], $y[$_], $z[$_] ] } 0 .. $#x;
```

You can no doubt envision a host of variations on the slicing and nesting themes. For example, switching the *x* (0th) and *y* (1st) coordinates:

```
my @yxz = map { [ $_->[1], $_->[0], $_[2] ] } @xyz;
```

You can do the same thing with a slice that rearranges the elements, which is a bit nicer to look at:

```
my @yxz = map {
  [ @$_[ 1, 0, 2 ] ]
} @xyz;
```

The data look much different from the separate arrays:

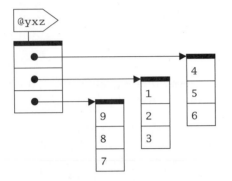

Or, perhaps you create a new list containing the magnitudes of the points:

```
my @mag = map {
   sqrt( $_->[0] * $_->[0] +
         $_->[1] * $_->[1] +
         $_->[2] * $_->[2] )
} @xyz;
```

The Schwartzian Transform (Item 22) is an application that uses both slicing and nesting operations with `map`:

```
my @sorted_by_mtime =
   map  { $_->[0] }                # slice
   sort { $a->[1] <=> $b->[1] }
   map  { [ $_, -M $_ ] }          # nest
   @files;
```

Selecting with `grep`

Suppose that you would like to filter `@xyz` so that it contains only points whose *y* coordinates are greater than their *x* coordinates. You could write a loop (how did you guess we were going to say that?):

```
foreach $pt (@xyz) {
   if ( $pt->[1] > $pt->[0] ) {
      push @y_gt_x, $pt;
   }
}
```

But this time, you have a task that is perfectly suited to grep:

```
my @y_gt_x = grep { $_->[1] > $_->[0] } @xyz;
```

Of course, you can combine map and grep—for example, to gather the *x* coordinates of the points with *y* greater than *x*:

```
my @x = map { $_->[0] }
   grep { $_->[1] > $_->[0] } @xyz;
```

```
my @x = map { $_->[0] > $_->[1] ? ( $_->[0] ) : () } @xyz;
```

Things to remember

- Use map to transform elements of a data structure into a new structure.
- Use grep to select elements from complex data structures.
- Use map and grep together for complex operations.

7 | CPAN

The Comprehensive Perl Archive Network (CPAN) is a repository of all things Perl, including the `perl` source code, Perl libraries and modules, and Perl applications. The skill of Perl programmers is largely judged by their ability to effectively use CPAN. As we write this, CPAN is over 6 GB, with 16,835 modules from 7,758 authors.

In 1993, Tim Bunce, Jarkko Hietaniemi, and Andreas König organized the *perl-packrats* mailing list. Larry Wall was working on Perl 5, a major upgrade to Perl that would allow people to extend the language through modules. As Perl was becoming more and more popular, people were creating very useful libraries, but they didn't have a formal way to distribute them. If you knew about a library and could find it on the author's Web site, you could download it yourself. If that library needed another library, you had to go find that one, and so on until you had everything installed.

In 1995, Jarkko set up an FTP repository (ftp://ftp.cpan.org/pub/CPAN) to collect all the Perl that was floating around so that people could get it all in one place.

Around the same time, Andreas König set up PAUSE, the Perl Authors Upload Server, to manage modules. People upload their work to PAUSE, which creates some indices from what it finds, then the master CPAN site mirrors PAUSE to add the modules/ and authors/ directories. Even though the authors/ directory forms most of CPAN, by size and attention, it's not all of CPAN, which really does aim to be comprehensive.

There is a ring of servers that mirror directly from the CPAN master server. The master server syncs with PAUSE, and then the public-use mirrors sync with the master. It's all just a big repository copied onto several hundred servers across the globe. CPAN itself doesn't do anything else for you.

On top of that, however, is the CPAN toolchain, which is how most people experience CPAN. You probably have already used `CPAN.pm` or `CPANPLUS`, which both know how to read the PAUSE index files, connect to a CPAN server, and download and install distributions for you.

Over the years, the term "CPAN" has taken on many meanings, though. It's as overloaded a term as the braces in Perl syntax. Some people consider CPAN to be a site, like Graham Barr's CPAN Search (http://search.cpan.org/), or Randy Kobes's (http://kobesearch.cpan.org/). Those Web sites provide an interface to the CPAN repository but add a lot to the presentation, such as information from CPAN Testers (http://testers.cpan.org/), CPAN Ratings (http://cpanratings.perl.org/), the CPAN RT issue tracker (http://rt.cpan.org/), and much more.

Item 65. Install CPAN modules without admin privileges.

If you can create files, you can install modules. "But, but, but . . ." you say. No, if you can create files, you can install modules. You can even install `perl` itself (Item 110) without special privileges. That's not to say that you aren't limited by some sort of restrictive social situation, but that's not a problem that technology can solve.

Perl modules aren't anything special. They are just files, and you can tell Perl where to find your modules. You just need to know how to get them there.

First, you have to choose where you want to put them. For your own use, you can put them into a lib directory under your home directory; that's as good a place as any. Assume your home directory is /Users/snuffy for the rest of this Item.

Doing it yourself

Everyone should install distributions the hard way at least once, just so they can appreciate the time-saving miracles of the CPAN tools. You may get only halfway through the process before you give up, but that's good enough.

Say you've already downloaded and unpacked a distribution, and you're in the distribution directory ready to get down to business. You need to run the right build script to install the modules.

For `MakeMaker`-based distributions, you use `INSTALL_BASE`:

```
% perl Makefile.PL INSTALL_BASE=/Users/snuffy
% make test install
```

For `Module::Build`-based distributions, you use `--install_base`:

```
% perl Build.PL --install_base /Users/snuffy
% ./Build test
% ./Build install
```

No matter which one you use, you end up with some directories under /Users/snuffy/lib, which is just the base directory. Your modules will end up in something like /Users/snuffy/lib/perl5; that's the directory that you need to add to your module search path (Item 69). You might also see directories such as /Users/snuffy/bin and /Users/snuffy/man.

Configuring `CPAN.pm`

The easiest way to install modules where you want is to just tell `CPAN.pm` where you want them.

You can set the options `CPAN.pm` passes to both `ExtUtils::MakeMaker` and `Module::Build`. You can start up the `CPAN.pm` shell by calling the `cpan` utility with no arguments. Earlier versions of `CPAN.pm` made you explicitly commit your changes, so you may have to commit them explicitly:

```
% cpan
cpan> o conf makepl_arg INSTALL_BASE=/Users/snuffy
cpan> o conf mbuild_arg --install_base /Users/snuffy
cpan> o conf commit
```

Before you rush off to install your modules, check that your configuration stuck around. Start up the shell again and check the value you just set, just to be sure:

```
% cpan
cpan[1]> o conf makepl_arg
    makepl_arg              [INSTALL_BASE=/Users/snuffy]
```

If you'd rather just edit a file by hand, look for the `CPAN::Config` or `CPAN::MyConfig` modules.

Once you have everything set up in the tools, simply install the modules:

```
% cpan Set::CrossProduct IO::Interactive Getopt::Whatever
```

Configuring CPANPLUS

If you like to use CPANPLUS, another distribution installation tool, you can edit your $HOME/.cpanplus/lib/CPANPLUS/Config/User.pm, which has your user settings. You can also go through its shell configuration, entering the same values you used before for CPAN.pm. Choose the "Setup installer settings":

```
% cpanp
CPAN Terminal> s reconfigure
=================>        MAIN MENU        <=================

Welcome to the CPANPLUS configuration. Please select which
parts you wish to configure

Defaults are taken from your current configuration.
If you would save now, your settings would be written to:

    CPANPLUS::Config::User


   1> Select Configuration file
   2> Setup CLI Programs
   3> Setup CPANPLUS Home directory
   4> Setup FTP/Email settings
   5> Setup basic preferences
   6> Setup installer settings

 Section to configure: [1]: 6
```

Once you get that far, just follow the instructions. When you have everything set up, install the modules normally:

```
% cpanp i XML::Twig
```

Using `local::lib`

The `local::lib` module takes some of the guesswork out of the process for you. By default, it sets up the modules directory in your home directory. Just by loading it, you set up a modules directory under your home directory:

```
% perl -MCPAN -Mlocal::lib \
    -e 'CPAN::install(Net::MAC::Vendor)'
```

CPAN.pm installs the Net::MAC::Vendor module in ~/perl5/lib/perl5. You don't have to know where local::lib puts it, though, because you when use the local::lib module in your program, it automatically puts the right directories in @INC:

```
#!/usr/bin/perl

use local::lib;

use Net::MAC::Vendor;
```

If you really want to see all of the details, you can load local::lib by itself. When you do that, it prints its settings:

```
% perl -Mlocal::lib
export MODULEBUILDRC="/Users/snuffy/perl5/.modulebuildrc"
export PERL_MM_OPT="INSTALL_BASE=/Users/snuffy/perl5"
export PERL5LIB="/Users/snuffy/perl5/lib/perl5:/Users/⏎
    snuffy/perl5/lib/perl5/darwin-2level:$PERL5LIB"
export PATH="/Users/snuffy/perl5/bin:$PATH"
```

The local::lib module also lets you explicitly specify your own directory. See its documentation for the details.

Things to remember

- Install Perl modules even if you don't have administrative privileges.
- Use the lib or local::lib modules to tell perl where your modules are.
- Configure cpan or cpanp to install modules in custom locations.

Item 66. Carry a CPAN with you.

You don't need to connect to a network to get the benefits of CPAN. You can install modules from CPAN even though you are on a plane flying over an ocean, in the middle of a desert, or even at a conference with broken Wi-Fi.

The repository is getting pretty big. It's been around since around 1994, and the rate at which it's growing is not slowing. As we write this, all of CPAN is just under 7 GB. You can't even fit it on a DVD anymore.

However, the immediately usable portion of CPAN is much smaller. Through the toolchain, you deal only with the latest versions of any module. When you take out the older versions of everything, the size drops to about 1 GB. That size has been growing, too, showing that even just the bleeding edge of CPAN is getting bigger.

Setting up a MiniCPAN

The `CPAN::Mini` module provides the `minicpan` program, which copies the latest versions of the modules to your local computer. You can call it from the command line, using one of the mirrors that you find at http://mirrors.cpan.org/:

```
% minicpan -l /MiniCPAN -r http://cpan.example.com
```

Of course, `/MiniCPAN` doesn't have to permanently be on your local computer. You can mirror to an external device, like a thumb drive, and have a CPAN with you wherever you go.

Running `minicpan` manually is easy. More useful, however, is a constantly updating MiniCPAN. Add that command to your crontab (or whatever periodically runs programs on your system).

You can also set options in the `minicpan` configuration file. Put a .minicpanrc in your home directory:

```
# ~/.minicpanrc
local:   /MiniCPAN
remote: http://cpan.example.com
```

You don't have to just pull down the latest versions of everything, either. If the `minicpan` tool isn't flexible enough for you, write your own script using `CPAN::Mini`. For instance, you might not want a full MiniCPAN, so you can filter what you mirror with `path_filters` or `module_filters`. Either tells `CPAN::Mini` what it can skip:

```
use CPAN::Mini;

CPAN::Mini->update_mirror(
  remote => "http://cpan.example.com",
  local  => "/MiniCPAN",

  # skip paths matching regex or where the
```

```
# sub returns true
# path like B/BD/BDFOY/Mac-iTunes-1.23.tar.gz
path_filters =>
  [ qr/BDFOY/, sub { $_[0] =~ /JMCADA/ } ],

# skip modules matching the regex:
module_filters => [qr/Acme/i],
);
```

Using your MiniCPAN

Now that you have set up your MiniCPAN, you have to tell your tools where to find it. For CPAN.pm, you have to set the urllist configuration. Start the shell with cpan to configure it:

```
% cpan
cpan[1]> o conf urllist push file:///MiniCPAN
Please use 'o conf commit' to make the config permanent!

cpan[2]> o conf commit

cpan[3]> o conf urllist
    urllist
        0 [file:///MiniCPAN]
```

In CPANPLUS, start up the shell, and follow the directions for s reconfigure:

```
% cpanp
CPAN Terminal> s reconfigure
```

Follow the menus to select the "Select Hosts" option, and then the "Custom" option.

Once you've set up your favorite tool, it should draw directly from your MiniCPAN instead of from a public repository.

Injecting your own modules

Another great feature of a MiniCPAN is that you can inject your own non-public modules into the MiniCPAN and install them using the standard CPAN tools. You'll do the injecting with CPAN::Mini::Inject.

The first thing that you'll want to do is set up a configuration file for CPAN::Mini::Inject. This file is similar to the one that you created for CPAN::Mini, only it is located at $HOME/.mcpani/config. A sample file might look like:

```
local: /Users/clara/cpan
remote: ftp://ftp.cpan.org/pub/CPAN
repository: /Users/clara/internal-modules
passive: yes
dirmode: 0755
```

Here we have told CPAN::Mini::Inject that we want to store our MiniCPAN at /Users/clara/cpan, want to mirror our public modules from ftp://ftp.cpan.org/, and want to store our private modules at /Users/clara/internal-modules.

Now that you have a configuration file for CPAN::Mini::Inject, you'll want to build a private module to install in your MiniCPAN. Assuming you have a distribution coded and ready to build, all you have to do is ask your build tool to make the distribution file. If you are using ExtUtils::MakeMaker:

```
% make dist
```

Or with Module::Build (Item 79):

```
% ./Build dist
```

These commands create a .tar.gz file containing all of the files that make up your distribution. This is the file that you would typically upload to CPAN (Item 70).

If your distribution is Foo-Bar and is at version 0.01, then the distribution file that would be created is Foo-Bar-0.01.tar.gz. Knowing this, you can tell CPAN::Mini::Inject to add your modules to the set of modules that it knows about. If you aren't doing anything too fancy, you should be able to get by with the mcpani utility that is installed with CPAN::Mini::Inject:

```
% mcpani --add module Foo::Bar \
    --authorid JMCADA --modversion 0.01 \
    --file Foo-Bar-0.01.tar.gz
```

Next, you need to tell mcpani to update your mirror from the public repository and inject your modules afterward. You can do this in two steps:

```
% mcpani --mirror
% mcpani --inject
```

Or all in one swoop:

```
% mcpani --update
```

After you are done, you should have a MiniCPAN with both your private and all public modules ready to be installed from it.

Things to remember

- Use CPAN::Mini to maintain a personal CPAN mirror.
- Configure your CPAN tools to point at your local repository.
- Use CPAN::Mini::Inject to host your private modules in MiniCPAN.

Item 67. Mitigate the risk of public code.

Think before you download that CPAN module! It might look simple enough at first, but what else do you have to do? Are there fragile dependencies, an unresponsive maintainer, or many unresolved bugs? What are you getting yourself into by committing to that module?

It might seem like heresy to suggest that you *not* use a CPAN module, but that's not really what's going on here. No one else can make your decision for you, since they probably don't know everything that goes into your problem. Your economic inputs might be different from somebody else's. Providing real-time financial data to a trader has different requirements than offline analysis of Web server traffic, and with that comes a different risk tolerance.

Everything is a trade-off. By reusing a module that somebody has already written, you save yourself development time. In many cases, the original author thought deeply about the problem and implemented a robust solution. That doesn't mean, however, that your boss or customers will absolve you of any responsibility when things go wrong.

You don't need a Ferrari to drive to the store

People often think that processing dates is a simple matter, but how many of them have taken the pains that Dave Rolsky did with DateTime to support time zones, leap seconds, and the many other dimensions that most people don't even know about? In those cases, using DateTime might be a win.

Yes, *might be*. DateTime handles everything, and you're sure to get the right answer using it, but do you need all of that support to format an epoch time into YYYYMMDD? What if you have to do that task millions of times as you process a log file? Do you want the extra overhead for all the features that you won't use? Maybe you do, but do you *know* that you do, or are you guessing?

Do you really need that upgrade?

There's a lot of stuff under the hood of a CPAN module, and you've probably experienced that long line of dependencies that stack up as you install a module. Have you ever tried to install a complicated module by hand, tracking each new dependency you need to download? It gets messy quickly.

CPAN has one outstanding design flaw: PAUSE tracks only the latest version of a module, and that version number has almost no consistency between different distributions throughout CPAN. When you use CPAN.pm or CPANPLUS to upgrade a module, the tool recognizes that a module has dependencies. It checks the version of what you have installed already and what the latest version on CPAN is. Even though you never asked to upgrade the dependencies, the tool might do it for you, silently and without asking. What was stable for you previously might be broken by something you didn't explicitly ask to install.

For instance, in CGI.pm version 2.64, Lincoln Stein changed the default separator for query parameters from & to ;. The semicolon is the modern way to do it, but plenty of old code expects the & because that was part of the published interface. When applications upgraded to the latest CGI.pm, despite the fact that they didn't want (or even know about) the new features, they broke.

We're not telling you not to upgrade; just don't throw away your thinking cap. You know there's a risk, so upgrade a development machine first to see if anything breaks.

Capstone modules

Michael Schwern, the maintainer of the Test::More and ExtUtils::Makemaker modules, can effectively break all of CPAN for everyone with even the slightest mistake (although he takes great pains not to). Most modern distributions rely on `Test::More` to handle the test suite, but if `Test::More` doesn't work, modules can't pass their tests, and the tool-chain doesn't install modules that fail their tests.

To a smaller extent, other modules that you depend on can break your application. They might introduce bugs, change the interface slightly, give different output, or do many other things that work differently enough that your application doesn't work correctly anymore. It's inevitable; it either has happened to you or is going to happen to you. Consider this before you risk that upgrade, and don't upgrade your production machine first.

Test drive before you buy

Mitigate the risk by trying the module before you stake your project on it. The Perl community provides a wealth of extra information about distributions. You don't have to go into it blindly.

Check CPAN Testers

The CPAN Testers (Item 97) collect test reports for all distributions uploaded to CPAN, and it's not uncommon for distributions to have hundreds of test reports from different systems and versions of Perl. You can check out a distribution at http://testers.cpan.org/, but you can also see a summary of the reports on the distribution's page at CPAN Search (http://search.cpan.org/).

Along with dependency information, David Cantrell was able to figure probabilities of successful installation of most CPAN distributions based on platform and Perl version. Check CPANdeps (http://deps.cpantesters.org/) before you decide to upgrade or try a new module. If you don't see green boxes, especially for the version of `perl` and operating system that you are targeting, tread carefully.

Check the Google juice

If you wonder if anyone else uses a module, find your favorite search engine and see what you can find. It might seem like an obvious thing to do, but not so many people do it, apparently. Are there mailing lists? When people ask questions about the modules, do other people answer? How quickly do they answer? In 15 minutes, the same day, two weeks later? How many answers are there? How many different people gave those answers? Quick answers from several different people are a sign of vitality and popularity. Delayed answers that are always from the same person might mean you'll have a lonely life using that module.

Separate development from production

You shouldn't test your code in production, using live customers as your test subjects. Try deploying your code with upgraded modules to a test server first, so you can ensure that it works and its performance is acceptable. You don't even need new hardware for this when you use virtual machines.

Upgrade less frequently

Do you really need to upgrade your modules every day? Maybe you truly need that fix in the latest release, but any time you upgrade, you're going to spend a little time managing that. Many upgrades also require newer versions of dependencies that you may not care about directly, and those indirect upgrades have chances to create problems. Frequent upgrades can suck away your time from the task at hand. Consider scheduling all upgrades at the same time, say quarterly, so you can concentrate your integration effort.

Use a DPAN to manage your dependencies

Sometimes CPAN is just too risky for you. If you want more control, consider setting up a DPAN, or (Distributed|Decentralized|Dark) Perl Archive Network. This is a private CPAN-like repository that your normal CPAN toolchain can use instead of the public repositories. You decide what goes in your repository, and what version of it goes into your repository. The `MyCPAN::App::DPAN` can help you set it up.

Things to remember

- Remember that publicly available code can be risky.
- Research modules before you use them.
- Create your own CPAN substitute (or "DPAN") to control the modules and versions you use.

Item 68. Research modules before you install them.

CPAN is a gold mine of code, but as with a real-life gold mine, there is a lot of dirt that you have to sift through to get to the good stuff. Fortunately, the Perl community has a wealth of resources to help you find the gold.

CPAN Search

The best place to start looking for information about a module or distribution is CPAN Search (http://search.cpan.org/). Find the module you are interested in, and navigate to its distribution page. At the top of that page, you'll see links to many of the resources the community provides, as shown in the figure below. It's a great place to start your research.

Bugs

From the distribution page on CPAN Search, you see a link to view and report bugs that takes you to the Request Tracker (RT) ticketing system for CPAN modules (http://rt.cpan.org/). You can see how many out-standing bugs the distribution has, and just as importantly, how many bugs the maintainers have fixed. This helps you get a feel for the quality of the module, but there are some questions that you should consider.

For instance, if there are no bugs filed, does that mean that the code is really solid, or does it mean that nobody is using the module? Conversely, if there are scores of bugs, is the module unstable, or are there just a lot of people using it? If there are bugs filed, but no responses, does that mean that the module has been abandoned, or does it just mean that the author uses a different system of bug tracking than CPAN's Request Tracker?

CPAN Testers

Another important link on the distribution page is for CPAN Testers (Item 97). The CPAN Testers are a group of dedicated individuals who run auto-mated tests on distributions across a range of platforms and then send the reports of those test runs back for the world to see. The information they provide is summarized in three groups: a pass count, a fail count, and an unknown-state count.

Don't let a few failures or unknowns get you down. The testers operate on multiple platforms and test versions of Perl that are years old. The distribution that you are researching could be failing its tests on platforms you don't use or on a Perl that retired years ago. Click on the report details and test matrix links to get a good understanding of where a distribution's issues really are.

CPAN Ratings

You also see a five-star rating system for the distribution, and if someone has rated it, you see some of the stars highlighted. The more stars, the better the rating the module has. There is also a link for any reviews people have written for this distribution. Read a sampling of the reviews to see if the praise or criticism has any bearing on your decision to install the distribution.

These ratings and reviews are all subjective, so they shouldn't be your only factor in deciding whether or not to use the distribution; however, they are still useful for your research.

Other considerations

When was the last release, and how many releases have there been? These two facts can let you know if a module has gone stale or been abandoned. Then again, it could just be that the module is stable and does not need regular updating.

Often there is a link to the source control repository for the code. Poke around in the repository and get a feel for how the development of the distribution is going. You might even become a committer!

CPANTS Kwalitee

The CPAN Testers provide another bit of trivia for you to consider when checking out a distribution. You can visit the CPAN Testing Service (http://cpants.perl.org/), find the distribution that you are interested in, and see the "kwalitee" of that distribution. There's a saying that we don't have a way to judge the true quality of a distribution, but we can measure something that is close, just like "kwalitee" is close to "quality."

Kwalitee boils down to a checklist of items that the Perl community thinks are important factors in judging the quality of a module. For instance, does the distribution have tests and documentation, and does it follow current best practices?

Of course, you can write a perfectly horrible piece of code that passes kwalitee checks. Most good distributions pass most kwalitee checks, and that's the sign of a detail-oriented maintainer. Be a little wary of any distribution that fails too many of the kwalitee checks.

Read the code

Perl is an open-source language. Perl code, especially the code on CPAN, is just text that you can read yourself. Examine some of the code that you are about to download. You should be able to tell if the developer knows what he or she is doing, and you might even learn a thing or two.

As you read the code, think about how easy it is to tell what is going on. Maybe you don't understand all of the features, but can you follow the program flow? If you had to work on that code, would you go crazy? Remember, if you use that code, you might have to deal with one of its bugs.

Things to remember

- Research modules before you install and rely on a distribution.
- Use different data sources to judge CPAN distributions.
- Examine the code you download to get a feel for what you will be using.

Item 69. Ensure that Perl can find your modules.

Perl modules are just files that the use directive loads into your programs. How does Perl find these files given just the module name?

The include path

Perl searches an **include path**, which is a list of directories stored in the global variable @INC.

The default include path is built into the Perl executable when Perl is compiled. There are a number of ways to see exactly what the include path is. One, of course, is to write a little script that prints it out. From the command line, this will do the trick:

```
% perl -e 'print "include is @INC\n"'
```

A slightly easier-to-type alternative is to check Perl's configuration with the -V command line option:

```
% perl -V
Summary of my perl5 (revision 5 version 10 subversion 0) ⏎
  configuration:
...blah blah blah...

Characteristics of this binary (from libperl):
  Compile-time options: PERL_DONT_CREATE_GVSV ⏎
    PERL_MALLOC_WRAP USE_LARGE_FILES USE_PERLIO
  Built under darwin
  Compiled at May  8 2009 02:12:43
  %ENV:
    PERL5LIB="/usr/local/perls/perl-5.10.0/lib/perl5"
  @INC:
    /usr/local/perls/perl-5.10.0/lib/perl5/⏎
      darwin-2level
```

```
/usr/local/perls/perl-5.10.0/lib/perl5
/usr/local/perls/perl-5.10.0/lib/5.10.0/↵
   darwin-2leevel
/usr/local/perls/perl-5.10.0/lib/5.10.0
/usr/local/perls/perl-5.10.0/lib/site_perl/5.10.0↵
   /darwin-2level
/usr/local/perls/perl-5.10.0/lib/site_perl/5.10.0
.
```

The include path lists the directories that the `use` or `require` directives search for Perl modules, or, in the case of "nested" modules like `File::Basename`, the directories in which the various module trees like File are rooted.

Modifying the include path

If you have modules installed in places other than those listed in the built-in `@INC`, you will have to modify the include path to get Perl to use them.

Under normal circumstances, this won't happen very often. When you build and install modules—either by using the CPAN module or by just unpacking and building them manually—Perl's `ExtUtils::MakeMaker` and `Module::Build` modules automatically know how to put the distribution files in the correct location for your particular installation of Perl. If that's not where you want the module to go, you have to tell them to put it somewhere else (Item 65).

But let's assume you have a module installed in a strange place—say, in the directory /share/perl.

You might be tempted to just modify the include path in your program's source code:

```
unshift @INC, '/share/perl';   # where MyModule.pm lives

use MyModule;                  # WRONG!
```

Unfortunately, this simple approach will not work.

The `use` directive is a compile-time rather than a run-time feature. When `use Module;` appears in your program, it actually means a `require` and an `import`:

```
BEGIN { require 'Module.pm'; Module->import; }
```

Perl executes the code inside the BEGIN block at compile time rather than run time. This means that changes to @INC at run time have no effect on use directives.

Another way around this problem is to put the change to @INC in a BEGIN block of its own:

```
BEGIN {
  unshift @INC, '/share/perl';  # where MyModule.pm lives
}

use MyModule;                     # it works now!
```

Now, the include path is set up at compile time, and use can find the module.

Although this is a workable strategy, there is a better way to control the include path: by using the lib pragma module. To prepend one or more directories to the include path, just supply them as arguments to use lib:

```
use lib '/share/perl';  # add dir /share/perl

use lib qw(              # add more dirs
  /xtra/perl
  /xtra/perl5
);

use MyModule;           # ready to go now ...
```

Aside from improved readability, use lib has one other advantage over explicit changes to the include path. The lib pragma also adds a corresponding architecture-specific autoload path, if such a directory exists. This can result in improved performance if you are using a module that is autoloaded. For example, if the machine architecture is "sun4-solaris," then use lib '/share/perl' adds /share/perl/sun4-solaris/auto if that directory exists.

There are some other ways to control the include path in those cases where use lib isn't appropriate. You can use the -I command line option:

```
% perl -I/share/perl myscript
```

You can also use -I in the shebang line:

```
#!/usr/local/bin/perl -I/share/perl
```

Finally, you can put one or more directory names in the `PERL5LIB` environment variable. On UNIX-like shells, you separate the directories with colons:

```
% export PERL5LIB=/share/perl:/xtra/perl5
```

On Windows machines, you separate the directories with semicolons:

```
% set %%PERL5LIB%%=C:/libs/perl;C:/libs/perl5
```

Use a private library with `local::lib`

Many people are forced to work in situations where they cannot install modules into the standard Perl library directories. Although you can install modules anywhere that you can create files, your home directory is a good place. Simply loading `local::lib` on the command line tells you where it expects to find your modules:

```
% perl -Mlocal::lib
export MODULEBUILDRC="/Users/snuffy/perl5/.modulebuildrc"
export PERL_MM_OPT="INSTALL_BASE=/Users/snuffy/perl5"
export PERL5LIB="/Users/snuffy/perl5/lib/perl5:/Users/↵
    snuffy/perl5/lib/perl5/darwin-2level:$PERL5LIB"
export PATH="/Users/snuffy/perl5/bin:$PATH"
```

Notice that `local::lib` automatically adds the architecture-dependent directories for you. To run your program with your local library directories, you can load it from the command line with `-M`:

```
% perl -Mlocal::lib program.pl
```

You can use `local::lib` in your program and it will add the right directories for you, being a bit more smart than `lib`:

```
use local::lib;
```

You can also automatically install modules into the `local::lib` directories, too (Item 65).

Setting a relative directory

You might set up your application so that the library directories are near the program files. You give your application and libraries to someone, but you don't know where she will put them, so you can't configure `@INC` ahead of time. In that case, you can use the `FindBin` module to locate the program path, and then build off of that to your module directory:

```
use FindBin;
use lib "$FindBin::Bin/../lib";
```

Configuring the include path at compile time

The include path is built in to Perl when you compile it (Item 110). Generally, it derives from the installation prefix specified when you run the `Configure` script:

```
% ./Configure -des -Dprefix=$HOME/localperl
```

Changing the installation prefix allows you to build and install private or alternative copies of Perl for testing or debugging.

Things to remember

- Add your private module directories to `@INC`.
- Use `local::lib` to set up module directories in your home directory.
- Use `FindBin` to add a relative module path.

Item 70. Contribute to CPAN.

CPAN already seems to have a module that does every task, but paradoxically, it's growing faster than ever. Not only do people discover new problems or create interfaces to new libraries, but sometimes even the reinvented wheel is better than the old one. By submitting your code to CPAN, you get quite a lot back.

Contributing to CPAN can fill an entire book on its own, and it has: Sam Tregar's *Writing Perl Modules for CPAN*[1], which you can get as a free download from Apress, LLC (http://www.apress.com/book/view/159059018X). You need only a little bit to get started, though, so we'll give you the basics.

---

1. Sam Tregar, *Writing Perl Modules for CPAN* (New York, NY: Apress, LLC, 2002).

Register with PAUSE

The Perl Authors Upload Server, or PAUSE (http://pause.perl.org/), is the real meat behind CPAN. People upload their modules and programs to PAUSE, which indexes and archives those modules. CPAN then mirrors the files to its own master server.

Start at http://pause.perl.org/. In the menu you see on the lefthand side there is a "Request PAUSE Account" link. Follow that, fill out the form, and PAUSE queues a request for an administrator to see. Every account is inspected by a real person, and most accounts are set up within a day. If you don't get a notice that your account is active, check the *modules@perl.org* archive (http://www.xray.mpe.mpg.de/mailing-lists/modules/). Search for the user name that you requested to see if an admin made any comment about it, or if you see an account setup e-mail. If you didn't get that e-mail, one of the admins can help you access your account for the first time.

Be bold

PAUSE is there for you to upload your distributions. It doesn't judge the quality, the usefulness, or any other aspect of your work. It does check that your namespace will not conflict with one used by someone else, but even then you can still upload: PAUSE just doesn't index the conflicting namespace.

CPAN is purposely designed to allow you to upload very early drafts of code, your experimental scripts, and nuggets of ideas. Its motto might be, "release early and release often." You're not wasting any trees or clubbing baby seals by giving people access to your code as soon as possible.

The sooner that you upload, the sooner you may get help from the rest of the Perl users in the world. If you give your module a development version number (Item 97), you can see the CPAN Testers results without PAUSE adding the distribution to its index.

HTTP file upload

Log in to the PAUSE Web site, choose the "Upload a file to CPAN" menu item, and follow the instructions on the form.

Anonymous FTP

Log in to ftp://pause.perl.org/ as an anonymous user, and put your archive in the incoming/ directory. Once there, return to the "Upload a file to CPAN" item on the PAUSE menu. Go to the bottom of the page to claim your upload. Until you claim it, your module will sit lonely and neglected in incoming/.

Use a command-line tool

The `cpan-upload` tool and the `release` tool from `Module::Release` can handle your upload in a couple of keystrokes without any Web site interaction from you.

Watch the test reports roll in

The CPAN Testers (Item 97) almost immediately see your new upload. These distributed volunteers use their automated testing setups to download your code, run their tests, and send you the results, often within a couple of hours. You can immediately see how well your tests do on platforms that you don't have or might never have heard of. You can control the reports you get by setting your CPAN Testers preferences (https://prefs.cpantesters.org/). It's like having a QA department that you don't have to pay.

Discuss your module

Before you start work on a new module, ask around. There might be a worthy module already hidden in CPAN that does just what you need. Some of the resources in Appendix B can help you find the people who might be able to answer your question.

Many authors like to consider the "three day rule." Any good module idea you have today will still be a good idea three days from now. Following the three day rule gives you a cooling off period after the initial excitement of what seems like a good idea but might get you stuck in a lot of boring work. That doesn't have to keep you from coding for fun, but if you have limited time, it helps you use it wisely.

There are a few things you want to get out of any discussion on a new module:

Am I wasting my time?

It's your time to waste, but you might be satisfied with something that already exists.

Is my interface appropriate?

Before you implement your module, write some sample scripts as if it already exists. However, since it doesn't exist, you can choose any interface you like. Which methods might you need to handle common tasks? Is the interface easy to use, nice to look at, or consistent with the other modules the task might use?

Who can help me?

There's no reason you should do all of the work yourself! Even if you are just coding for fun, sometimes you can have even more fun as other Perlers help you implement your idea, add their own ideas, or spread the word about your wonderful, new creation.

Don't be overly discouraged by feedback you get. People tend to respond in proportion to their annoyance, so the negatives sometime seem to outweigh the positives. Don't discount negative feedback, but you don't have to listen to it (unless it's from the people who sign your checks, and even then you still might win them over). Many now-stalwarts of CPAN started this way.

Welcome to CPAN

That's it! You're now a member of the CPAN author community.

Once you go through the process, you shouldn't be as intimidated as you were before you knew how easy it was. Pay it forward by helping someone else do what you just did.

And, now that you uploaded your first distribution, start thinking what you're going to do for your second one!

Things to remember

- Get a free PAUSE account to upload to CPAN.
- Upload to CPAN early and often to allow people to help you with your project.
- Ask for advice before naming and coding your distribution.

Item 71. Know the commonly used modules.

There are many, many different modules available to Perl programmers. A wide variety of common programming chores has been encapsulated in freely distributed modules available from CPAN. What's available includes e-mail, netnews, FTP, and WWW utilities; graphical and character user-interface tools; Perl language extensions; and database, text processing, mathematical, and image processing utilities. The list goes on from there—and for quite a while!

We can't tell you which modules you should use because we don't know what you are doing. Here's a very short list of popular modules. If your favorite module didn't make it onto the list, send us a note and maybe we can get it into the next edition.

In **App::Ack**, you'll find `ack`, which is a replacement for the command-line `grep`. Learn more at http://betterthangrep.com/.

Catalyst is the most popular Perl Web framework. If you're starting a big Web project, consider using it. There's an active community ready to help you. Get more information at http://www.catalystframework.org/.

CGI::Simple is a drop-in replacement for the CGI portions of the legacy `CGI` module. `CGI::Simple` is lighter-weight, much of this accomplished by dropping the HTML-generation portions of `CGI`.

If you need to work with dates and times precisely, getting all the details of leap seconds, time zones, and durations, **DateTime** is for you.

The **DBI** module is Perl's abstract database Interface. It works with CSV, Sqlite, PostgreSQL, Oracle, ODBC, or any of the other popular (and not so popular) database servers.

For those who don't like to directly use SQL, or who prefer having cross-database SQL automatically generated for them at run time, **DBIx::Class** is an object-relational mapper that is very popular.

E-mail handling can be difficult, but Ricardo Signes and many other people put in a lot of work to make it easy and correct with his **Email** modules. You can send mail, parse mail, handle MIME, and do many other things.

Need to source environment variables from a shell script into your currently executing Perl program? **Env::Sourced** can accomplish this task with a simple `use` statement.

Parsing command line options is easy with the `Getopt` family of modules. **Getopt::Long** handles both the long and short versions of command line arguments and has become a standard for many Perl-based command line programs.

HTML documents are often sloppily structured because of the permissive nature of many Web browsers. **HTML::Parser** is a lenient parser that handles deconstructing real-world HTML documents. **HTML::TreeBuilder** provides more useful features at a higher level.

Image::Magick is a powerful software suite for creating and editing images using the popular library of the same name.

There are several modules that deal with JavaScript Object Notation, and **JSON::Any** pulls them all together under a common interface.

Log::Log4perl is the Perl version of the Java logging library log4j. It handles all of the details of log messages, including which messages to log and where to send them. It makes it easier to turn debugging input on or off on the fly.

LWP (`libwww-perl`) is a powerful set of modules for programming on the Web. For many tasks, the **LWP::Simple** module will do everything that you need with minimal fuss.

If you are scraping the Web or testing Web pages, you need to take a look at **WWW::Mechanize**, which is built on top of LWP. This set of modules makes spidering HTML links on the Web a piece of cake.

If you need to do some heavy number crunching or scientific computing, then the Perl Data Language, **PDL**, is for you. It's a dialect of Perl that's optimized for speedy math, with a natural syntax.

Moose is a next-generation object system for Perl. We wish we could write more about it here, but it really deserves its own book. If you're starting a new work, consider using it as a model across all of your new code. See more at http://www.iinteractive.com/moose/.

POE is a multitasking and networking framework that implements and integrates with event loops. It allows for easy event-driven, cooperative multitasking in Perl programs.

We suspect that historians will look back at the current times and consider Microsoft Excel to be the most useful software ever created. You can read or create Excel files from Perl using one of the **Spreadsheet::ParseExcel** or **Spreadsheet::WriteExcel** modules.

Template::Toolkit is a powerful templating system built in Perl. It integrates well with Web frameworks like Catalyst. See more at http://template-toolkit.org/. You might prefer **Mason** or **Text::Template**. No matter what you choose, templating systems make your program designs much cleaner by moving data out of your code.

Parsing delimited data seems simple enough, but when you start having to worry about embedded delimiters, escape characters, and quoting, it becomes a non-trivial task. **Text::CSV_XS** takes the hassle out of parsing delimited files and does it fast (Item 115). It's important enough to repeat ourselves in another item, even.

There are many ways to parse XML in Perl. **XML::Twig** is one of the more mature systems. It can parse full documents or documents as a stream, has XPath support, and more. See more at http://xmltwig.com/.

XML::Compile uses XML schemas to translate between XML and Perl. It handles all of the alphabet soup of XML, including SOAP and WSDL.

YAML is a whitespace-based configuration language that is popular with many developers. Though it reeks of Python to us, it is still a handy formatting style to know. It did start in Perl, though, so it can't be all bad.

8 | Unicode

The world used to be so simple. Everything fit into 7 bits, and you didn't have to worry about special characters or character sets. Back then, strings were sequences of bytes, and each byte represented its own character. People got used to the idea that bytes and characters were the same thing, and everyone formed really bad habits that still infect programming. We're going to call bytes **octets** instead.

Now you know that characters and bytes aren't the same thing. To get all the fancy characters you need, or even the pieces you need to build new characters, you use the Unicode Character Set (sometimes called just UCS). This book is much too small to go through all of the details of Unicode, but you need to know at least a little to get started.

Unicode maps characters onto **code points**, which are numbers that represent those characters. As the Unicode Consortium says:

> Unicode provides a unique number for every character,
> no matter what the platform,
> no matter what the program,
> no matter what the language.[1]

For example, the letter **k** is U+006B. That's its code point.

Don't think about storage just yet (or ever). That code point number is just floating around. Unicode defines various **encodings** that turn code points into octets, and the other way around. Don't think too much about the octet representation if you can avoid it. Trust Perl to figure out that part for you.

In Perl, instead of just strings, you now have **character strings**, which are sequences of characters, and **binary strings**, which are the old-fashioned strings of octets you already know and love. Perl can deal with each, although sometimes you have to be careful to ensure that Perl treats your data as the right sort of string. Your goal is to always work with the text variety, and let Perl figure out the rest.

---

1. http://www.unicode.org/standard/WhatIsUnicode.html, retrieved January 24, 2010

Not only that, there are different sorts of character strings because there are different **character sets**, such as ISO-8859 (Latin), CP-1251 (Windows), or UCS. At some point, Perl has to store your character string as octets, because that's what computers do. Perl **encodes** the characters as octets. UTF-8 is one possible encoding for UCS, and the one Perl uses internally. Likewise, Perl **decodes** bytes into character strings to go the other way. To see all of the encodings your `perl` supports, try this one-liner:

```
perl -MEncode -le "print for Encode->encodings(':all')"
```

Perl tries its hardest to make most of this encoding and decoding invisible. When Perl knows that it is working with a character string, it does what you expect it to do, mostly. It counts the length in characters, and thinks character-wise with other string operations.

There are times when Perl can't divine the encoding, though. Maybe you typed the characters directly into your source code, read from a file, or fetched a Web page, where none of those sources gave Perl the proper clues. In these cases, you have to give Perl the missing clues explicitly.

Before Perl 5.8, Perl's support for Unicode was quite weak, to put it nicely. Many people have tried to provide better support through modules, but considering that Perl 5.6 was first released in early 2000, we're going to ignore the older versions. If you're using an ancient Perl, you are on your own. Join the modern world!

As of this writing, Perl's Unicode support is still not complete (there's a lot to support to get the 100% seal of approval), but it has most of what you need, and you probably won't miss what's missing.

One final note, though: when we talk about "Unicode" in source, strings, and so on, we're thinking about the UTF-8 encoding, which is what Perl uses internally. If your editor, terminal, and other tools are correctly configured (that's up to you), then that's mostly a matter of your typing the right character.

Item 72. Use Unicode in your source code.

Modern `perl`s let you program with Unicode. You can type it directly into your program source:

```
print 'I need to work on my résumé';
```

There are several things that can go wrong with that bit of code. First, what encoding is your source, really? How is your editor going to save that? You really can't tell just by looking at the characters on the screen. Is it UTF-8, ISO-8859, or something else? Does it even matter how the editor saves it?

Second, even though you save it as UTF-8, the next person who touches the source might not. How does her editor do the right thing with the encoding? Even if it reads it correctly, does it save it correctly?

Lastly, the person who runs your program might neglect to tell `perl` to expect Unicode in the source. How is Perl supposed to know otherwise?

The `utf8` pragma tells Perl to parse the source as UTF-8 (and that's all it does). This example has a Turkish string:

```
use utf8;
```

```
print 'Bu iş kârlı';  # 'This business is profitable'
```

You can even use Unicode in identifiers. This is especially handy for people who keep having to spell out the Greek letters they use in formulas:

```
use utf8;
use Math::Trig;

binmode STDOUT, ':utf8';

my $π = 3.14159265;
my $θ = $π / 2;

printf "cos(θ) is %.2f\n", cos( $θ );
printf "sin(θ) is %.2f\n", sin( $θ );

my $α = atan( 1, 1 ) * 180 / $π;

printf "Angle is %.2f\n", $α;
```

You can't do that with package names or subroutines names, since both of those need to be valid filenames (with roundtrip guarantees). A package name such as `Foo::Bar` translates to Foo/Bar.pm, and `AutoSplit` turns a subroutine name into Foo/Bar/auto/some_sub.al. You might be able to get away with non-ASCII characters in some subroutine names. You might use π as a constant subroutine without an error, for instance, but this is undefined behavior:

```
sub π () { 3.14159265 }

print "π is ", π, "\n";
```

However, if you try to use the snowman character (U+2603), ☃, things probably won't work:

```
sub ☃ () { 'snowman' }
```

The error message is odd, and doesn't immediately lead you to the cause:

```
Illegal declaration of anonymous subroutine ...
```

The utf8 pragma is lexically scoped. If there is only a part of your source where you want Perl to interpret the source as UTF-8, you can enable it within a scope:

```
{
  use utf8;

  print 'Hyvää päivää';  # "Good morning", in Finnish
}
```

Likewise, if you don't want Perl to treat part of your source as UTF-8, you can turn it off within a scope:

```
{
  no utf8;

  print 'Hyvää päivää';  # no guarantees now!
}
```

The utf8 pragma only tells Perl to interpret the source as UTF-8. It doesn't affect the input or output streams, or anything else (Item 73). It also doesn't force your editor or IDE to do anything special, and it doesn't perform any other magic with other tools.

Things to remember

- Use the utf8 pragma to use Unicode characters in your source code.
- Unimport utf8 when part of your source code isn't Unicode.
- Identifiers, except for subroutines and package names, can have non-ASCII characters.

Item 73. Tell Perl which encoding to use.

When you start using Unicode with your old-style programming habits, you're probably going to see warnings about "Wide character in . . . ," where Perl isn't expecting something more than ASCII but gets it anyway. It's fairly easy to fix this. You just have to tell your filehandles what encoding they should expect. Even if you don't see any warning, but your input or output appears to be corrupted, you have to pay attention to how you're telling Perl to treat filehandles.

It's not enough that Perl knows that you used Unicode directly in your program source. When it sends that data to something else, you also need to ensure that the next thing sees the data in the right encoding, too. Perl has to encode your data correctly so the next consumer of the data can decode them correctly.

Setting the default encoding

You can set the encoding for all streams with the `open` pragma. If you want to use the same default encoding for all input and output filehandles, you can set them at the same time with the `IO` setting:

```
use open IO => ':utf8';
```

You can set the default encoding for just output handles with the `OUT` setting:

```
use open OUT => ':utf8';
```

Similarly, you can set all of the input filehandles to have the encoding that you need:

```
use open IN => ':utf8';
```

You can event set the default encoding for the input and output streams separately, but in the same call to `open`:

```
use open IN => ":cp1251", OUT => ":shiftjis";
```

The `-C` switch tells Perl to switch on various Unicode features. You can selectively turn on features by specifying the ones that you want without having to change the source code. If you use that switch with no specifiers, Perl uses UTF-8 for all of the standard filehandles and any that you open yourself:

```
perl -C program.pl
```

You can apply -C more selectively. You can do the same thing as -C by setting the PERL_UNICODE environment variable. It is all detailed in the *perlrun* documentation.

Set the encoding on selected filehandles

For specific filehandles, you can specify the encoding you need with the two-argument form of binmode:

```
binmode STDOUT, ':utf8';


binmode STDIN, ':utf8';
```

You can also do that when you open the filehandle. In the general case, you have to specify it with encoding(...):

```
open my ($out_fh), '>:encoding(UTF-8)', $filename or die;


open my ($in_fh), '<:encoding(koi8-r)', $filename or die;
```

open has a special shortcut for UTF-8:

```
open my ($out_fh), '>:utf8', $filename or die;


open my ($in_fh), '<:utf8', $filename or die;
```

You can specify any encoding that your perl supports:

```
open my ($out_fh), '>:encoding(iso-8859-1)', $file
    or die;
```

Things to remember

- Specify the encodings on all of your filehandles.
- Set the default encoding for all filehandles with the open pragma.
- Use binmode to set the encoding for individual filehandles.

Item 74. Specify Unicode characters by code point or name.

You don't have to type literal characters into your strings. Perl provides a variety of ways for you to get the right character into your data. For characters from 0x00 to 0xFF, you can use the normal Perl syntax, in octal or hex:

```
my $CRLF = "\015\012";
```

```
my $CRLF = "\x0D\x0A";
```

To create literal Unicode code points above `0xFF`, enclose the code point in braces after the `\x`:

```
print "The smiley face is \x{263a}\n";
```

```
print "Watch out for the ",
   "Dread Pirate Fenwick! \x{2620}\n";
```

You might have trouble remembering the code points themselves, so you can use the `charnames` module to use more memorable and recognizable names. Use the double-quotish `\N{NAME}` to stand in for the real character:

```
use charnames qw(:full);
my $arabic_alef = "\N{ARABIC LETTER ALEF}";
```

You can see the list of all the names on the Unicode Consortium's Web site (http://unicode.org/charts/charindex.html), but the list also comes with `perl`, since it needs it to do this magic. Look for the lib/5.n.m/unicore/NamesList.txt file, where the 5.n.m is your particular version of Perl.

Although not as fancy, `chr` and `pack` still work, too, although they are a bit less clear:

```
my $hebrew_alef = chr(0x05d0);
my $georgian_an = pack( "U*", 0x10a0 );
```

These forms work anywhere you have double-quotish interpolation, including the match and substitution operators.

Names from code points

Remember that code points are not necessarily the same thing as the encoding. The fact that you see the octet representation doesn't mean you know the code point. If you know the code point, you can get the name with `viacode`:

```
use charnames qw(:full);
my $code_name =
   charnames::viacode(0x2620);  # SKULL AND CROSSBONES
```

You can use the `Unicode::CharName` module to do the same job. Remember that you need to use `hex` to tell Perl to interpret a string as a hexadecimal number:

```
use Unicode::CharName qw(uname);

# MUSICAL SYMBOL G CLEF OTTAVA BASSA
my $code_name = uname( hex('1D120') );
```

Code points from names

You can go the other way to get the code point if you know the name by using `vianame`, although you probably want to format the number yourself:

```
use charnames qw(:full);
my $code_point = sprintf '%04X',
    charnames::vianame("THAI CHARACTER KHOMUT");
```

Aliases

Those names can be quite annoying. Do you want to type "ARABIC LIG-ATURE UIGHUR KIRGHIZ YEH WITH HAMZA ABOVE WITH ALEF MAKSURA ISOLATED FORM" every time you need it? Us neither. Use aliases instead:

```
use charnames ':full', ':alias' => {
    LONGEST     => 'ARABIC LIGATURE ...',
    OMG_PIRATES => 'SKULL AND CROSSBONES',
    RQUOTE => 'RIGHT-POINTING DOUBLE ANGLE QUOTATION MARK',
    LQUOTE => 'LEFT-POINTING DOUBLE ANGLE QUOTATION MARK',
};

binmode STDOUT, ':utf8';
print "\N{LQUOTE}Hello Perl!\N{RQUOTE}\n";
```

`charnames` already has some aliases, like LINE FEED and CARRIAGE RETURN. If you can't remember what numbers they should be, you're in luck:

```
my $CRLF = "\N{CARRIAGE RETURN}\N{LINE FEED}";
binmode STDOUT, ':utf8';
print "\N{LQUOTE}Hello Perl!\N{RQUOTE}$CRLF";
```

Things to remember

- Translate between numeric representations and names with `Unicode::CharName`.
- Use `charnames` to interpolate characters by name.
- Create aliases for long character names.

Item 75. Convert octet strings to character strings.

In a perfect world, your data would always know what their encodings were, and Perl could figure it out for you. Sadly, that's not the real world. Someone hands you some bytes, Perl doesn't know what encoding it should be, and it's up to you to figure it out. Not only that, you might get data that specifies an encoding that is a lie.

The best advice is to ensure that you properly decode all of your input. That is, you have to take the octets and turn them into a proper character string. Don't trust anything.

Set the encoding

Start with a string of bytes. Take, for example, this long string of hexadecimal numbers:

```perl
my $hex = '4A2761692070617373C3A9206C27C3'
  . 'A974C3A920C3A0205061726973210A';
```

```perl
( my $bytes = $hex ) =~ s/(..)/chr(hex($1))/eg;
```

Perl doesn't know anything about which encoding this string should be. As you are debugging, you can see what Perl thinks of the string with `Devel::Peek`:

```perl
use Devel::Peek;
```

```perl
Dump($bytes);
```

The output shows no special knowledge of the encoding (although we're not giving away the string just yet):

```
SV = PVMG(0x830ce4) at 0x80eb50
  REFCNT = 1
  FLAGS = (PADMY,SMG,POK,pPOK)
```

```
PV = 0x228bc0 "...\n"\0
CUR = 30
LEN = 32
```

In this case, assume that you know that the bytes represent a UTF-8 string. With this prior knowledge, you can use Encode to decode the string to the correct encoding (remember, going from bytes to characters is decoding):

```
use Encode;

my $utf8_string = decode_utf8($bytes);

Dump($utf8_string);
```

Now Dump shows that Perl explicitly knows the encoding and you can see the UTF-8 flag:

```
SV = PV(0x801398) at 0x80ea30
  REFCNT = 1
  FLAGS = (PADMY,POK,pPOK,UTF8)
  PV = 0x259a80 "...\n"\0 [UTF8 "...!n"]
  CUR = 30
  LEN = 32
```

The decode_utf8 is really a convenience subroutine for a couple of other steps. The decode subroutine uses the encoding that you give it:

```
use Encode qw(decode);
decode( 'utf8', $bytes );
```

The decode subroutine does the real work with an object:

```
my $encoding = 'utf8';

my $utf8_string = do {
  my $obj = find_encoding($encoding);
  die qq(encoding "$encoding" not found) unless ref $obj;
  $obj->decode($bytes);
};
```

If you have to decode many strings, you might want to work with the object interface so you don't waste time recreating an encoding object each time you call decode.

Now that you've decoded the input, you can output it. You have to set the right encoding on the output handle, though (Item 73):

```
binmode STDOUT, ':utf8';
```

```
print $utf8_string;
```

The output shows the secret sentence:

```
J'ai passé l'été à Paris!
```

If you run the program through a shell and don't get the text above, there is a good chance that your language or display settings are forcing a character set that is not UTF-8. In our case, we were using iTerm and had to change the terminal preferences to use UTF-8, as well as to set the $LANG environment variable.

Unknown encodings

If you have a string that you know is in one encoding but you need it in another, you can use Encode's from_to. This function changes the contents of the string passed to it.

```
use Encode qw(from_to);
from_to( $string, 'iso-8859-1', 'utf8' );
```

Or, maybe you have a stew of strings with some ASCII, some Latin-1, and some Unicode. Why? Because life is tough sometimes. The fix_latin routine from Encoding::FixLatin will try its best to fix that, although it might not always work, since it has to make some guesses:

```
use Encoding::FixLatin qw(fix_latin);
```

```
my $utf8_string = fix_latin($stew_string);
```

Even if fix_latin appears to work, it might not give you back the string that you need. Since it needs to guess what it sees and can deal with multiple encodings, fix_latin might encounter a sequence of bytes that are valid in more than one encoding, but where each gives a different result.

Command-line arguments

If you take arguments on the command line, your program might receive them in a different encoding based on various session settings that perl can't control. You need to decode the arguments correctly to ensure you get what you want.

First, you can get the correct codeset with the I18N::Langinfo module. The langinfo subroutine knows how to grab various data from the locale. With the CODESET constant, it gets the name of the encoding:

```
use I18N::Langinfo qw(langinfo CODESET);
my $codeset = langinfo(CODESET);
```

Once you have the codeset, you can translate the command-line arguments from whatever they are to Perl's internal encoding:

```
use Encode qw(decode);
@ARGV = map { decode $codeset, $_ } @ARGV;
```

Encoding strings

You can decode any byte sequence that you like, but that doesn't make it a valid character string. For instance, there are certain characters in Unicode called **combining characters** that modify the characters they come after.

Start with this Finnish phrase, which has the bonus of a Swedish name in it. It's a UTF-8 string because the Perl source is in UTF-8:

```
use utf8;


# (Åke is quite a burly guy)
my $phrase = 'Åke on aika körmy';
```

Now you want to turn it into bytes. Use encode:

```
use Encode;
my $bytes = encode( 'utf8', $phrase );

print
  join ':', map { sprintf '%02x', ord($_) }
  split //, $bytes;
```

The byte string looks like:

```
c5:6b:65:20:6f:6e:20:61:69:6b:61:20:6b:f6:72:6d:79
```

The first two bytes in the encoded string are \xc5\x6b, which form the capital A with the ring above it. If you reverse those two bytes, decode with two arguments tries its best, fails, and replaces what it can't decode with the **substitution character** 0xFFFD.

```
my $not_a_with_ring =
  decode( 'utf8', "\x6b\xc5" );  #\x6b\xfffd
```

That's probably not what you want. Now you have a string that isn't the data you expect. Instead, you want to know if there was an error. You can pass decode a third argument that tells it what to do with an invalid byte string. Encode provides four constants that you can use to tell decode how to handle errors:

- FB_DEFAULT replaces invalid sequences with a substitution string.
- FB_CROAK dies immediately on error.
- FB_QUIET stops immediately, leaving the string partially decoded.
- FB_WARN works like FB_QUIET, but with warnings.

Since decode may croak, you can wrap it in an eval to catch the error:

```
my $a_with_ring =
  eval { decode( 'utf8', "\x6b\xc5", FB_CROAK ) }
  or die "Could not decode string: $@";
```

Now you have a way of detecting invalid encodings. If the eval fails, so does your string.

Things to remember

- Use Encode to decode bytes and set encodings on strings.
- Use Encoding::FixLatin to guess what encoding a byte string might represent.
- Decode your command-line arguments before you use them.

Item 76. Match Unicode characters and properties.

Unicode gives you much more flexibility in matching characters with a regex. Instead of the rather limited character classes that you may already know, you can now match not only literal characters, but also *properties* of characters. Unicode characters know a little about themselves.

Match specific characters

Matching a specific character is straightforward. You can match it either by its name or by its hexadecimal value. If you know the code point, you can use that directly in \x{}:

```
if ( $string =~ /\x{263a}/ ) {
  print "I matched a smiley!\n";
}
```

You can use the \N{NAME} syntax directly in your regular expression (Item 74):

```
use charnames ':full';


if ( $string =~ /\N{A_TILDE}/ ) {
  print "I found an A with a tilde!\n";
}
```

You can always use the long names, which specify the script, the capitalization, the letter, various modifying marks, and so on:

```
use charnames ':full';


if ( $string =~ /\N{LATIN CAPITAL LETTER A WITH TILDE}/ )
{
  print "I found an A with a tilde!\n";
}
```

Perhaps you have an Arabic phrase, and you want to know if it has the hamza character. Patrick Abi Salloum supplied this phrase, which he tells us has something to do with a camel crossing a desert:

```
use charnames ':full';

use utf8;
my $phrase = 'ءاجتزا الجمل الصحراء';

if ( $phrase =~ m/\N{ARABIC LETTER HAMZA}/ ) {
  print "I matched a HAMZA!\n";
}
```

Be careful with matching. If you're looking for a grapheme (Item 77), you might be thrown off by the actual combination of characters that make up the grapheme.

Match properties

Inside a regular expression, \p{PROPERTY} matches characters with that property, while its complement \P{PROPERTY} matches characters that don't have that property. For instance, a Unicode character knows whether it is uppercase, title case, lowercase, or none of those (you can see all of the properties in the *perlunicode* or *perluniprops* documentation). This is the Unicode version of the POSIX bracket expressions, like [[:digit:]] and so on.

To match a letter, you can use the Letter property. This matches anything that Unicode considers to be a letter, no matter which language:

```
my ($letters) = /(\p{Letter}+)/;
```

Many properties have shortcut names. Instead of \p{Letter}, you can use \p{L}:

```
my ($letters) = /(\p{L}+)/;
```

The Letter is a class of characters, and you can match specific sorts of Letters. If you want only the uppercase letters:

```
my ($uppers) = /(\p{UppercaseLetter}+)/;
```

```
my ($uppers) = /(\p{Lu}+)/;
```

Similarly, to match a number, no matter which form it comes in:

```
my ($number) = /(\p{Number}+)/;
```

There are quite a, well, number of things that are numbery sorts of characters, most of which you might not expect. See them all for yourself:

```
use utf8;
binmode STDOUT, ':utf8';

foreach my $point ( 0 .. 65535 ) {
  my $string = chr $point;
  next unless $string =~ /\p{Number}/;
  print "$point --> $string\n";
}
```

You probably don't want to match most of those numbers, so there are some extended properties to handle more specific sets:

```
my ($number) = /(\p{ASCIIHexDigit}+)/;
```

Now that you have Unicode, there are a lot more types of whitespace. You can match all of those, perhaps replacing each with a space:

```
$string =~ s/\p{Whitespace}/ /g;
```

Perhaps you want to match only within a certain block of Unicode. If you want something from the Greek block:

```
if ( $string =~ /\p{InGreekExtended}/ ) {
  print "I found some greek!\n";
}
```

Define your own properties

The properties themselves are just special lists of Unicode code points that should match. You can define your own properties, as long as you want to do the work to make that list. You simply define a subroutine that begins with either In or Is, in any package that you like. You then put the full package specification to your subroutine in \p{}.

```
sub MyProperties::IsMyFavoriteLetters {
  return <<"CODE_POINTS";
33
37
62\t6D
CODE_POINTS
}


foreach (qw( 137 Buster XYZ )) {
  if( /\p{MyProperties::IsMyFavoriteLetters}/ ) {
    print "I found my favorite letters in [$_]!\n";
  }
}
```

Since the favorite letters are really [37b-m], the match succeeds for only two of the elements:

```
I found some of my favorite letters in [137]!
I found some of my favorite letters in [Buster]!
```

You can use several sorts of data inside your property definition, including code point ranges, references to existing block properties, references to other similar subroutines, and so on. Those references can include or exclude sets of characters, so you can build up (or take away) just what you need. It's very flexible, and completely explained in *perlunicode*.

Things to remember

- Match Unicode characters by their names.
- Match Unicode characters exactly or by their properties.
- Define custom properties as arbitrary sets of Unicode characters.

Item 77. Work with graphemes instead of characters.

A **grapheme**, which the Unicode glossary (http://www.unicode.org/glossary/) defines as "a minimally distinctive unit of writing in the context of a particular writing system," is what most people consider a character. The programmer dealing with Unicode may see that a grapheme is made up of one or more characters as a matter of implementation. Unicode doesn't have a code point for every possible combination, but it has the idea of a combining character that modifies another character, perhaps to add an accent.

Suppose you want to create the grapheme that is a lowercase "a" with an umlaut (or "diaeresis" to Unicode), *ä*. Unicode has two ways to do that. First, you can use the **precomposed** version that Unicode has already, since it's a common character:

```
use charnames ':full';
my $precomposed =
    "\N{LATIN SMALL LETTER A WITH DIAERESIS}";  # length 1
print "Length of precomposed string is "
    . length($precomposed) . "\n";
```

The other way uses **composite characters** that you combine to create the grapheme. You start with a character and modify it with a combining character:

```
my $composed =
    "\N{LATIN SMALL LETTER A}" . "\N{COMBINING DIAERESIS}";
```

The problem now is that the length of this string is 2, because you used two characters to make the one grapheme:

```
print "Length of composed string is "
    . length($composed) . "\n";
```

Even worse than that, the two strings aren't the same. Perl compares them by characters, not graphemes, rendering the condition in this example false:

```
unless ( $precomposed eq $composed ) {
  print "The strings are different!\n";
}
```

Have you added this to you list of Unicode horrors yet? You can't blindly compare two strings anymore. Logically, the strings are the same even though their representations aren't. A little subroutine to show the characters can help you see what is happening:

```
sub show_chars {
  my $phrase = shift;

  my $string = '';
  foreach my $char ( split //, $phrase ) {
    my $name = charnames::viacode( ord $char );
    $string .= "$name\n\t";
  }

  return $string;
}
```

Now, check your strings with `show_chars`:

```
my $precomposed =
  "\N{LATIN SMALL LETTER A WITH DIAERESIS}";
my $composed =
  "\N{LATIN SMALL LETTER A}" . "\N{COMBINING DIAERESIS}";

print "precomposed:\n\t", show_chars($precomposed), "\n";
print "composed:\n\t",    show_chars($composed),    "\n";
```

The output shows the difference in the strings:

```
precomposed:
  LATIN SMALL LETTER A WITH DIAERESIS

composed:
  LATIN SMALL LETTER A
  COMBINING DIAERESIS
```

Help is on the way, though. You can fix this by normalizing your strings.

Normalizing Unicode strings

There's some good news. To get around the character-grapheme issue, Unicode has the concept of **decomposition**. You can turn the precomposed versions into its parts with `Unicode::Normalize`. It's a non-trivial task that we'll mostly skip here, so suffice it to say that the Normalization Form D (NFD) function takes composed characters and gives back decomposed ones:

```
use Unicode::Normalize;

my $decomposed = NFD($precomposed);
print "decomposed:\n\t", show_chars($decomposed), "\n";
print "Decomposed and composed are the same!\n"
  if $decomposed eq $composed;
```

Now you've turned the single character version into the two character version, and you can compare the strings:

```
decomposed:
   LATIN SMALL LETTER A
   COMBINING DIAERESIS


Decomposed and composed are the same!
```

Graphemes in regular expressions

There's a bit of a bright spot here, though. Regular expressions understand the concept of graphemes. You match a single grapheme, no matter how many characters it uses, with \X:

```
my $composed =
   "\N{LATIN SMALL LETTER A}" . "\N{COMBINING DIAERESIS}";
my ($matched) = $composed =~ /(\X)/;
print "matched:\n\t", show_chars($matched), "\n";
```

The match output shows that the \X matched two characters, just as you expected:

```
matched:
   LATIN SMALL LETTER A
   COMBINING DIAERESIS
```

The \X is really just a shorthand for the combination of two Unicode properties, the "not a mark" and "mark" (?:\P{M}\p{M}*) (Item 76).

Knowing that, you can now get a list of graphemes if you want to work with them individually. There are two easy ways to do that:

```
# separator retention mode
my @graphemes = split /(\X)/, $phrase;


# positive lookahead
my @graphemes = split /(?=\X)/, $phrase;
```

You still have to be careful comparing graphemes, because Perl will compare them character-by-character, which means that you still have the same problem. At least you know that you have a complete grapheme, though.

Things to remember

- Remember that visibly same glyphs can have different representations.
- Decompose precombined characters to normalize your Unicode strings.
- Use \X to match an entire grapheme.

Item 78. Be careful with Unicode in your databases.

Unfortunately, reading this section isn't going to make your life easier because we don't have all of the answers. Different database servers do different things with their data, and these issues aren't something that Perl can fix. Anything that touches or stores your data has a chance to mess up everything.

The DBI module is Unicode transparent. That is, it doesn't care what the data are; it just passes them on to your program. The database driver, the particular DBD, has to handle the details for you. Some of them already support Unicode in their connections:

```
my $dbh = DBI->connect(  # MySQL
  'DBI:mysql:test', 'username', 'pass',
  { mysql_enable_utf8 => 1 }
);
```

```
my $dbh = DBI->connect(  # PostgreSQL
  'DBI:Pg:test', 'username', 'pass',
  { pg_enable_utf8 => 1 }
);
```

Don't be fooled, though. This just tells the driver to assume the data are encoded as UTF-8. The data might not actually be UTF-8 encoded.

You have to ensure that you set up your database schema to handle UTF-8. Some database servers let you set Unicode properties on particular columns, or treat all columns as a particular encoding. However, even if they do that, they might not validate data they put into those records. Pass it an octet string that is malformed UTF-8, and the server may accept it without complaint. When you pull the data out again, the server tells you that it is giving you a UTF-8 string even though that string is invalid (Item 75).

You might also have to consider column lengths in your table. Maybe you set up a `varchar(16)`, but is that really 16 characters, or 16 octets? What happens when you have a name that is 16 graphemes (Item 77)?

The best answer we can give you is a checklist of things to pay attention to. You need to watch the entire round trip.

- If you want a Unicode encoding in your database, ensure that you pass it valid Unicode strings.
- Ensure that the database server stores data as Unicode by checking its various settings.
- Check the data when it comes back to you.

Things to remember

- Set up your database to handle Unicode columns and data.
- The DBI module is Unicode-transparent.
- Enable database Unicode features when you connect to the database.

9 | Distributions

Although anything that you distribute is rightly a "distribution," in Perl that takes on a special meaning to most people. For Perl, a distribution typically refers to a collection of Perl files and supporting files, including a build program that can install them.

Perl distributions are the culmination of many skills and techniques, all wrapped together in a nice package that you can put on CPAN, send in e-mail, put in source control, or do anything else you like with. It could take us an entire book to go through the collected wisdom of regarding putting together your distribution. You'll find some of that advice spread out throughout this book when that advice fits in nicely with another chapter. This chapter has the distribution advice that didn't find a home somewhere else.

There's a lot of opinion that goes into people's distributions, so like bracing and indention styles, there's a lot to debate. There is more than one way to do it (but remember that most of them are wrong).

Item 79. Use `Module::Build` as your distribution builder.

In the beginning was `ExtUtils::MakeMaker` and it was good, well, enough. It took the values from a Makefile.PL and turned them into a Makefile that you used to build the Perl distribution. Coming from the UNIX world, the Makefile poses a problem for other operating systems that don't rely on the same tools. Furthermore, the generated Makefile has to go to great lengths to create portable code.

If someone is going to install a Perl module, you can be pretty sure that he already has Perl. Unlike `make`, Perl is very portable. Instead of dealing with the pain of Makefiles, enjoy the power of Perl instead. Use `Module::Build` instead of `ExtUtils::MakeMaker` when you want to start a new distribution.

The end user's perspective

From the end-users' perspectives, migrating to Module::Build does not require much, if any, change on their part. If they are used to installing your module with ExtUtils::MakeMaker:

```
% perl Makefile.PL
% make
% make test
% make install
```

The sequence to build and install a distribution with Module::Build is similar:

```
% perl Build.PL
% ./Build
% ./Build test
% ./Build install
```

Most people probably won't even notice this if they use cpan or cpanp, which handles the installation for them.

From a module author's perspective

Fortunately, getting started with Module::Build isn't difficult. Say that you have a module called MyModule. The minimal Build.PL file specifies the name of the module, and in which file it should find the version:

```
use Module::Build;
my $build = Module::Build->new(
  dist_name        => 'MyDist',
  dist_version_from => 'lib/MyModule.pm',
);


$build->create_build_script;
```

You can add more information about your distribution. One of the more common additions is requiring prerequisite modules, which you specify either in configure_requires, build_requires, or requires, depending on which part of the process needs the dependency.

Module::Build lets you specify sets of modules that you need for installation via recommends, and modules that can cause issues with your module if they are installed via conflicts:

```
use Module::Build;
my $build = Module::Build->new(
  dist_name           => 'MyDist',
  dist_version_from => 'lib/MyModule.pm',
  requires            => { 'Some::Module' => 1.23, },
  recommends          => { 'Some::Module_XS' => 4.56, },
);


$build->create_build_script;
```

You can even get very precise and exclude a particularly difficult version of a module by specifying strict version requirements:

```
requires =>
{ 'Volatile::Module' => '<= 1.2, !1.3, >= 1.4', },
```

This feature of requirements and recommendations becomes very powerful when you distribute a wrapper module that attempts to unite the interfaces of many similar implementations of a problem space.

Custom actions

`Module::Build` revolves around **actions**, which are similar to build targets in `make`. For instance, when you `./Build test`, you are running the `test` action.

To modify an existing action, subclass `Module::Build` and override the `ACTION_` subroutine related to that action. For instance, to customize the `test` action, you override `ACTION_test`.

Suppose you want to create an action, `critique`, that invokes `Perl::Critic` on your code. Modify your `Build.PL` file to provide a subclass that includes an `ACTION_critique` method:

```
use Module::Build;
my $class = Module::Build->subclass(
  class => "Module::Build::Custom",
  code  => <<'SUBCLASS' );

sub ACTION_critique {
  my $self = shift;
  $self->depends_on("test");
  $self->do_system(qw(perlcritic lib/));
}
```

```
SUBCLASS
my $build = $class->new(
  dist_name => 'MyDist',
  dist_version_from => 'lib/MyModule.pm',
  requires => {
    'Some::Module' => 1.23,
  },
  recommends => {
    'Some::Module_XS' => 4.56,
  },
);


$build->create_build_script;
```

Things to remember

- Use `Module::Build` for new distribution development.
- Subclass `Module::Build` to create new actions.
- Use the `subclass` argument to `Module::Build->new` to customize its behavior.

Item 80. Don't start distributions by hand.

You find yourself writing a fair amount of boilerplate code when you create a new distribution. The first edition of this book used the `h2xs` tool to generate this boilerplate (Item 86). Though `h2xs` will still do the job, it was designed to create the XS glue you needed to connect Perl to C. If you don't need that feature, there are currently better ways to start your distribution.

Begin with `Module::Starter`

Using `Module::Starter` is a simple matter of supplying some arguments to `module-starter`:

```
% module-starter
  --module=Foo::Bar,Foo::Baz \
  --author="John Doe" \
  --email="me@example.com"
Created starter directories and files
```

The `module-starter` program creates the files that you'll find in almost every distribution:

```
./Foo-Bar/Changes
./Foo-Bar/ignore.txt
./Foo-Bar/lib/Foo/Bar.pm
./Foo-Bar/lib/Foo/Baz.pm
./Foo-Bar/Makefile.PL
./Foo-Bar/MANIFEST
./Foo-Bar/README
./Foo-Bar/t/00-load.t
./Foo-Bar/t/boilerplate.t
./Foo-Bar/t/pod-coverage.t
./Foo-Bar/t/pod.t
```

That's quite a bit of work that you don't have to do yourself. With this code, you can navigate to the `Foo-Bar` directory and run a build on your new `Foo::Bar` distribution.

If you prefer `Module::Build` or `Module::Install` to the default `ExtUtils::MakeMaker`, you tell `module-starter` which one you want with the `--builder` command-line option:

```
% module-starter \
    --module=Foo::Bar,Foo::Baz \
    --author="John Doe" \
    --email="me@example.com" \
    --builder=Module::Build
Created starter directories and files
```

You can use a ~/.module-starter/config file to store your repetitive options so that you don't have to type them in every time you run `module-starter`:

```
author: John Doe
email: me@example.com
license: artistic
builder: Module::Install
```

Now you can run `module-starter` with only the `--module` option:

```
% module-starter --module=Foo::Bar,Foo::Baz
```

Plug-ins for `Module::Starter`

After you have created your distribution and seeded it with a few modules, chances are you'll want to add more modules. By default, `Module::Starter` can't do this. However, the `Module::Starter::Smart` plug-in can.

To activate a plug-in, install it and add a line to your ~/.module-starter/ config file. This leaves the basic `Module::Starter` setup in place and adds `Module::Starter::Smart`:

```
plugins: Module::Starter::Simple Module::Starter::Smart
```

From the directory that contains your distribution's base directory, to add another module file you run `module-starter` again:

```
% module-starter --module=Foo::Buzz --dist=Foo-Bar
Created starter directories and files
```

This adds Buzz.pm to your Foo-Bar/lib/Foo/ directory and adds lib/Foo/ Buzz.pm to your MANIFEST. Unfortunately, `Module::Starter::Smart` doesn't add a `use_ok` to your 00-load.t file, so remember to add that manually.

Extending `Module::Starter`

If `Module::Starter` doesn't quite fit your needs, you can easily write a plug-in for it.

Internally, `Module::Starter` loads your listed plug-ins from left to right, dynamically making each plug-in on the left the inherited parent of the module on the right. At the end of the list, it makes `Module::Starter` the final inheritor, and calls `create_distro` on it.

Typically, this means that `create_distro` in `Module::Starter::Simple` is called. This method calls a set of other methods that you can choose to override. For a sample, look at the documentation for `Module::Starter::Plugin::Template`. Whatever plug-in is rightmost in the list of plug-ins wins the battle of inheritance and gets the first say in what the given method does. After it does its work, it can in turn call the method on its parent, continuing the chain of inheritance, or it can hijack the entire method.

In the next example, you can see how to create a plug-in that puts your corporate license in the README file and generates modules that you create with `Module::Starter`.

```
package Module::Starter::Plugin::CorporateLicense;
use subs qw/
  _license_blurb_README_license_module_license/;
sub _license_blurb {
return <<'LICENSE';
This program is distributed under the Nameless
Corporate License
This software is developed as is with little regard
to quality. Should this software eat your homework
or take away your birthday, please call our support
line where we will jerk you around until you give
up.
LICENSE
}


sub _README_license {
  my $self = shift;
  my $year          = $self->_thisyear();
  my $license_blurb = $self->_license_blurb();
return <<"HERE";
COPYRIGHT AND LICENCE
Copyright © $year Nameless Corporation
$license_blurb
HERE
}


sub _module_license {
  my $self = shift;
  my $module = shift;
  my $rtname = shift;

  my $license_blurb = $self->_license_blurb();
  my $year          = $self->_thisyear();
  my $content = qq[
\=head1 COPYRIGHT & LICENSE
Copyright © $year Nameless Corporation
```

```
$license_blurb
];


    return $content;
}
```

Now, add your plug-in to your ~/.module-starter/config:

```
plugins: Module::Starter::Simple Module::Starter::Smart ⏎
    Module::Starter::Plugin::CorporateLicense
```

The next time that you generate a distribution, you'll get your license text instead of the default text.

Use Distribution::Cooker

You might think it is too much work to deal with Module::Starter and its plug-ins to get what you want. Instead, you can start with a distribution setup that you like, and use it as a template for your new distributions. You could even set up that template distribution with Module::Starter.

The dist_cooker program from Distribution::Cooker takes a directory of Template Toolkit templates and processes them, giving you your final distribution. It's really a fancy wrapper around the ttree program:

```
% dist_cooker
ttree 2.9 (Template Toolkit version 2.20)
Source: /Users/Snuffy/.templates/modules
Destination: /Users/Snuffy/Dev/Perl/Foo
Include Path: [   ]
Ignore: [ \b(CVS|RCS)\b, ^#, (\.git|\.svn)\b ]
    Copy: [ \.png$, \.gif$ ]
  Accept: [   ]
  Suffix: [   ]
...
```

The ~/.dist_cookerrc configuration file uses the INI format:

```
[user]
name = Joe Snuffy
pause_id = bdfoy
email = snuffy@example.com
```

```
[license]
perl = 1


[templates]
dir = /Users/Snuffy/.templates/modules
module = lib/Foo.pm
script = bin/script.pl
```

This configuration says the template directory is /Users/Snuffy/ .templates/modules. You can put any files that you want in that directory, and `dist_cooker` will process it. The `dist_cooker` program supplies several templates variables, such as `module` and `module_file`, that you can use without any other setup. Here's a sample README template:

```
You can install this using the usual Perl fashion
perl Makefile.PL
make
make test
make install


The documentation is in the module file.  Once you install
the file, you can read it with perldoc.
perldoc [% module %]
If you want to read it before you install it, you can use
perldoc directly on the module file.
perldoc  lib/[% module_file %]
```

This makes it easy to get the distribution exactly how you want it, and usually that involves almost no code. Less code leads to fewer bugs.

Things to remember

- Use a code generator to do the repetitive, boilerplate work for you.
- Customize your `Module::Starter` output with plug-ins.
- Use `Distribution::Cooker` to create a new distribution from custom templates.

Item 81. Choose a good module name.

Naming your Perl packages well is one of the most important things you can do. Choose a good name and people will naturally find it on CPAN.

Choose a bad name, and your otherwise excellent code might never get a download. Imagine your module going out to CPAN one day. Will people look at your module name and instantly know what your module does? Will its name fit in with everything else that's already on CPAN?

There isn't a set of formal rules, or even their less restrictive little brother guidelines, for naming your packages. Your module can use any name that it likes, but as with all names, a good one goes a long way.

The modules@perl.org (the mailing list for PAUSE admins) and module-authors@perl.org mailing lists can help you choose a good name. Not only are they generally good at names, but they also know quite a bit about what is already on CPAN. They can help you choose a name that puts your module into the right place with all of the other modules.

Naming goals

A module name must accomplish quite a bit in a few characters, and, once chosen, rarely affords the opportunity to change it after people start using it. The name of the module isn't for you; you don't need a name because you created it and understand it. The name is for other people, and those other people don't have any of the context that you do. Your name needs to convey three things: context, key features, and defining characteristics.

Provide context

CPAN is mostly without context other than, "This is something in Perl." We can categorize modules, but that categorization lives outside the module and disappears once someone downloads it, blogs about it, or uses it in code. As a maintenance programmer, what would you think about seeing:

```
use XYZ::WWR::JKL;
```

You might think that's a silly example, but we've seen module names without a single vowel and no recognizable initializations. Even if your name makes sense to you and your industry, does it make sense to everyone else? CPAN is much bigger than any one subject.

The task or the feature the module provides has a context, usually given to it by its author, who created it to scratch some itch. In the author's mind, it's always obvious what the module does and what the name means. Other people don't have that context, and the name needs to provide it.

For example, in the Debian Linux distribution, the package manager is called dpkg. As a name alone, however, that has no meaning to someone who doesn't use Debian. In the context of Debian, it makes perfect sense. In the context of Perl, it means nothing, so people need extra clues.

Almost any abbreviation or acronym is going to be ambiguous. If the first page of Google hits for your initialization isn't about your topic, then you most likely have the wrong name.

Describe key features

Some modules are designed for particular tasks. Other modules perform general sets of tasks. Your name should describe the level of generality. What does an HTML module do? Well, you really can't tell from that name. How about HTML::Parser, HTML::TreeBuilder, and HTML::SimpleLinkExtor? Those names give you more information about what the module can do for you. When you choose your name, you want to show that same kindness to other people.

Distinguish characteristics

Many of the modules on CPAN work toward similar goals in different ways, or work in the same way toward different goals. How many Config and Getopt modules can you find on CPAN? Can you tell what they all do just from the names? If your module is going to live under the same namespace as other modules, how is yours different? Why should people use your module rather than modules with very similar names?

Some naming conventions

CPAN is managed chaos, and many of its conventions have developed over time. These aren't every current convention, and even these might evolve.

App

You can distribute applications as Perl distributions. Typically, those sorts of distributions go under the App namespace, like App::Ack, App::Cpan, and App::Prove. The namespace implies that it's a ready-to-use program rather than a module.

Local

By convention, the top-level Local namespace should never conflict with anything on CPAN. This allows you to be confident that the name you choose under Local isn't going to conflict with anything from the outside world.

Active projects

Some projects, such as Moose, DBI, DateTime, and Catalyst, try to organize the activity under their respective namespaces to ensure everything works together nicely. If you want to add a module to such a project, discuss it on its mailing list.

Names to avoid

CPAN has been around since 1995, and over time the various administrators have discovered or followed certain conventions to make the designed anarchy a bit less chaotic. As an evolutionary process, it is historically inconsistent but modernly optimal. That is, looking at the past as an example might not be the best thing. The fact that other people did it doesn't mean you should do the same.

Top-level namespaces

In general, top-level namespaces are bad, unless one is a nexus for several modules under that namespace, or a fanciful name that describes something more application oriented. You might think that DB is a good name because it's the database portion of your code, but it doesn't say much about what it does. It also happens to be the namespace the Perl debugger uses. Remember, the name should give as much context as possible, and DB certainly doesn't do that (in either case).

That doesn't mean that all top-level namespaces are bad. For frameworks like Moose, Catalyst, or DBI provide a functionality around an idea rather than a particular low-level or general task. They don't live in a hierarchy because they are comprehensive enough to stand on their own.

Net

The Net namespace is one of the most abused namespaces out there. It was originally designed as a home for the code that knows how to talk various defined network protocols, such as FTP, HTTP, NNTP, and so on, but people started using it for code that merely uses the network without knowing anything about it. Modules that interact with Web sites use the network, but they aren't *about* the network, and they have much better homes in `WWW` or `WebService`. If you are implementing a network protocol rather than an application protocol, then `Net` might be for you. Otherwise, it isn't.

Avoid Simple, Easy, Reduced, Tiny

The terms `Simple`, `Easy`, `Reduced`, and `Tiny` are some of the worst parts of the names on CPAN. They all indicate that a module is a variation of another module, but why is that variation interesting? It's usually missing or hiding some features, less flexible than the original, and in most cases, tailored to a particular task the author needed. What is that task, though? Making it easy for you doesn't mean it's easy for the next programmer.

Avoid "API," "Interface," and the like

Your module is an API? No kidding? Don't waste space in your name telling people what they already know. If your code wasn't an interface of some sort, it wouldn't be very useful.

Naming the module after yourself

Many people, lacking other ideas about what their module does, just use their own name. They might have really good names, but that doesn't help anyone figure out what the code does, even if they do attach `Util` to the end. What does `Snuffy::Util` do? Unless those are utilities for manipulating a Snuffy, then it's a waste of space in the module name.

Things to remember

- Use the name of your module to communicate its functionality.
- Avoid vague and nondescriptive names.
- Ask for namespace suggestions on modules@perl.org.

Item 82. Embed your documentation with Pod.

A good many software developers, especially those working on sizable projects, work to coding standards that require them to start off function definitions with block comments that provide key information about that function—overview, inputs, outputs, preconditions, change history, and the like. If they format those embedded comments precisely enough, scripts can parse, extract, and reformat into documentation.

A source file could thus be its own programming reference. This is a good thing, because it allows developers to tweak the documentation each time they tweak the code without having to locate and edit a separate document. Sometimes this is about all the documentation that a developer can manage to do correctly.

Perl source code can contain embedded documentation in **Pod**, or "Plain Old Documentation," format. The Perl parser ignores Pod sections when compiling and interpreting scripts, while other programs supplied with the Perl distribution can scan source files for documentation sections and format them as man pages, HTML, plain text, or any of a number of other formats.

Pod basics

Pod is a very simple markup language designed for easy translation to other formats (text, HTML, etc.). Pod is easily readable in raw form if worse comes to worst, too.

A Pod document consists of paragraphs set off by blank lines. There are three different kinds of paragraphs:

Verbatim text

A paragraph whose lines are indented will be reproduced exactly as it appears—no line wrapping, no special interpretation of escape sequences, no nothing. Translators that can display different fonts will generally reproduce verbatim text in a fixed-width font.

Pod commands

A command is a line beginning with the character =, followed by an identifier, and then some optional text. Currently defined commands, which may not be understood by all translators, include:

- =head1 =head2 (Level 1, level 2 headings)

    ```
    =head1 Understand Packages and Modules.
    =head2 Packages
    ```

- `=item` (An item in a bulleted or numbered list)

  ```
  =item 1 ... a numbered item
  =item * ... a bulleted item
  =item B<NOTE> ... a bolded "other" item
  ```

- `=over N`/`=back` (Indent N spaces/Go "back" from indent)

  ```
  =over 4
  =item * Dog
  =back
  ```

- `=pod`/`=cut` (Beginning of Pod/End of Pod)

  ```
  =pod
  =cut
  ```

- `=for X` (Next paragraph is of format X)

  ```
  =for html
  ```

- `=begin X`/`=end X` (Bracket for beginning and end of format X)

  ```
  =begin comment
  If you can read this, you are using a text translator.
  =end comment
  ```

Filled text

A paragraph that isn't verbatim or a Pod command is treated as ordinary text. Formatters will generally turn it into a justified paragraph, in a proportionally spaced font if possible. A number of special formatting sequences are recognized inside filled text:

- Make *italicized* text with `I<text>`

  ```
  You will be I<very> lucky to have John work for you.
  ```

- Make **bold** text with `B<text>`

  ```
  You will be B<very very> lucky to have Heather ⏎
  work for you.
  ```

- Show inline code with `C<text>`

  ```
  now, add 5 to C<$d[$a,$b]>
  ```

- Enforce non-breaking whitespace with `S<text>`

  ```
  S<foreach $k (keys %hash)>
  ```

- Embed a special character with `E<code>`

  ```
  The less-than, E<lt>, is special in Pod
  This will be a double quote E<34>
  ```

- Make a cross-reference with `L<text>`:

  ```
  L<name>          man page
  L<name/ident>    item in man page
  L<name/"sec">    section in man page
  L<"sec">         section in this man page
  ```

- Mark a filename with `F<lname>`:

  ```
  Be careful not to delete F<config.dat>!
  ```

- Note an index entry with `X<text>`

Note that some Pod formatters will recognize function names (an identifier followed by parentheses) and other special constructs "in context" and automatically apply appropriate formatting to them. In addition, most Pod formatters can convert straight quotes to "smart" matching quotes, doubled hyphens to em dashes, and so forth.

Here is an example Pod file:

```
=head1 My Pod Example
=head2 My 2nd level heading
I<Pod> is a simple, useful markup language for Perl
programmers as well as others looking for a way to
write "Plain Old Documentation." With Pod, you can:
=over 4
=item 1
Create documentation that can be readily translated
into many different formats.
=item 2
Embed documentation directly into Perl programs.
=item 3
Amaze your friends and terrify your enemies. (Possibly.)
=back
```

```
Author: Joseph N. Hall
  Date: 1997
```

When translated—in this case, by my `pod2mif` filter—it yields:

```
Translated Pod file
My Pod Example
My 2nd level heading
Pod is a simple, useful markup language for Perl
programmers as well as others looking for a way to write
"Plain Old Documentation." With Pod, you can:
Create documentation that can be readily translated into
many different formats.
Embed documentation directly into Perl programs.
Amaze your friends and terrify your enemies. (Possibly.)
Author: Joseph N. Hall
  Date: 1997
```

Man pages in Pod

Although you can use Pod for many different purposes, man pages written in Pod should follow certain conventions so that they will resemble other UNIX man pages. Variables and function names should be *italicized*. Names of programs, as well as command line switches, should **bold**.

The man page should have a proper skeleton. The first level headings traditionally appear in CAPITAL LETTERS. The most important of the first level headings, in the traditional order, are:

- NAME—Name of the program/library/whatever.
- SYNOPSIS—Brief example of usage.
- DESCRIPTION—Detailed description, broken into sections if necessary.
- EXAMPLES—Show us how we use it.
- SEE ALSO—References to other man pages, etc.
- BUGS—Things that need a little work yet.
- AUTHOR—Your name in lights.

See the *pod2man* documentation for more information about the layout of man pages.

Things to remember

- POD allows you to embed documentation directly in your Perl code.
- There are three types of POD paragraphs: filled text, verbatim text, and commands.
- Use the common documentation structure that people expect.

Item 83. Limit your distributions to the right platforms.

Most of the time you should endeavor to make your module useful on any operating system and version of Perl, but sometimes that just doesn't work out. Some modules, say `Win32::Process`, can work only on Windows. Perhaps you need to use Perl features that aren't backward compatible. Catch incompatibility problems as soon as possible so you give your users good error messages that tell them what to do.

If you are uploading your work to CPAN, or distributing it internally using the CPAN toolchain, your error message can let the tool know what happened so it can respond appropriately. CPAN Testers has a guide for authors (http://wiki.cpantesters.org/wiki/CPANAuthorNotes) that can help you.

use the right Perl version

The `use` keyword does more than just load libraries. If you give it a Perl version number, it requires that the version of the `perl` interpreter running that code be equal to or greater than the one you specified. If you need to use Perl 5.10 features, say so explicitly:

```
use 5.010;
```

When `perl` tries to compile that statement and finds a version mismatch, it stops the compilation. You should already have this statement in your 5.10 code anyway, since it enables all of the 5.10 features. This feature-enabling aspect of `use` is new to Perl 5.10.

Remember that Perl versions use three places in each of the minor and point portions. People say "Perl 5 10 1" and might write Perl 5.10.1, but inside `perl`, that's 5.010001.

If you need to use an earlier version of Perl, perhaps because you need some external library that works with only a particular `perl`, use the `$]` special variable. Put your check in a `BEGIN` block so your program checks the version as soon as possible.

You can check for a specific Perl version:

```
BEGIN {
  die "This is perl $], but you need 5.008005"
    unless $] == 5.008005;
}
```

You can check that the Perl version must be less than some version, in this case, the entire 5.10 series:

```
BEGIN {
  die "This is perl $], but you need a version"
  . 'less than 5.010'
    unless $] < 5.010;
}
```

You can check that the Perl version is between two versions, inclusively:

```
BEGIN {
  die "This is perl $], but you need between "
  . '5.0006002 and 5.008008'
    unless $] >= 5.0006002 and $] <= 5.008008;
}
```

You can also do this inside your code to let your program follow different paths or load different modules based on the `perl` version.

If you are creating a Makefile.PL or Build.PL, you can specify the Perl version as a prerequisite:

```
# For Build.PL
my $mb =
Module::Build->new( ...,
requires => { 'perl' => 5.008001, }, );

# For Makefile.PL
WriteMakefile( ..., MIN_PERL_VERSION => '5.010001', );
```

Check the operating system

If your code works on only some operating systems, you can check for that, too. If you have to use just standard Perl, you can look in `$OSNAME` (the long version of the `$^O` special variable: see the *perlvar* documentation):

```
use English qw($OSNAME);
   die 'Unsupported OS: You have $OSNAME but '
 . "I need Windows!\n"
   unless $OSNAME eq 'MSWin32';
```

You'll have an easier time using `Devel::CheckOS`, though, since it recognizes *families* of operating systems. The previous example uses a technique that requires you to know the right special string, and that represents only one operating system. The documentation for `Devel::CheckOS` (http://search.cpan.org/~dcantrell/Devel-CheckOS-1.61/lib/Devel/CheckOS.pm) says of the use of that variable: "$^O is stupid and ugly, it wears its pants as a hat"."

```
use Devel::CheckOS qw(os_is);
   die 'OS unsupported! You need Windows to run '
 . "this program!\n"
   unless os_is('MicrosoftWindows');
```

That "OS unsupported" message is important: the CPAN Testers (Item 97) look for it to decide if they should fail your build because it doesn't work, or merely ignore it because it's not targeting their setup. If you don't support their setup, you can also use the `die_unsupported()`. although you don't get to add any extra information to the message:

```
use Devel::CheckOS qw(os_is die_unsupported);
die_unsupported() unless os_is('MicrosoftWindows');
```

To see the list of platform names you can use, try this one-liner:

```
% perl -MDevel::CheckOS -e \
     'print join(", ", Devel::CheckOS::list_platforms())'
```

Some of the names you see in the output may look funny. They actually map to file names, so some operating systems' names lose their special characters or formatting.

Check `perl`'s configuration

When someone compiled `perl` (try it yourself at least once, Item 110), the build process stored all the compilation and configuration directives in the `Config` module. It's the same information you see in the output of `perl -V`.

Suppose that you need a threaded `perl` to run your program. You need to ensure that you have the right `perl` before you start. By loading the `Config` module, you get access to a `%Config` hash that lets you access the values:

```
use Config;
die "You need a threaded perl to run this program!\n"
   unless $Config{usethreads} eq 'define';
```

Perhaps your program needs 64-bit integers. You can check for that in `%Config`, too:

```
use Config;
die 'You need at least a 64-bit perl to run '
   . "this program!\n"
      unless $Config{ivsize} >= 8;
```

Things to remember

- Limit your code to the versions of `perl` under which it should run.
- Limit your program to specific operating systems or a specific Perl configuration as appropriate.
- Use `Devel::CheckOS` to detect the operating system.

Item 84. Check your Pod.

Code isn't the only thing you should test. You also want to ensure that you've done the right thing with your embedded documentation (Item 82). Testing your Pod can find many of the documentation mistakes or omissions. Often, Perl programmers include these as part of their "author tests" (Item 88).

Check for proper Pod formatting

Once you write your Pod, you want it to render properly when someone converts it. Hardly anyone reads raw Pod, and most people probably see it converted to text for their terminals, or as HTML.

From the command line, you can use the `podchecker` tool:

```
% podchecker program.pl
```

It tells you what you messed up:

```
*** ERROR: unterminated C<...> at line 6 in file ⏎
  program.pod
*** ERROR: =over on line 4 without closing =back (at ⏎
  head1) at line 8 in file program.pod
*** ERROR: empty =head1 at line 8 in file program.pod
*** ERROR: =back without previous =over at line 10 in ⏎
  file program.pod
program.pod has 5 pod syntax errors.
```

You can do this from your test suite, too. In t/pod.t, use the example from the Test::Pod documentation:

```
use Test::More;
eval 'use Test::Pod 1.00';
plan skip_all => 'Test::Pod 1.00 required' if $@;


all_pod_files_ok();
```

This is a nice bit of code. It finds all of the files containing Pod and checks those for you. It runs only if you have Test::Pod installed.

Check for Pod coverage

Now that you document your Perl code with Pod, you want to ensure that you document all of it. If you add a new subroutine but forget to add its documentation, you still have work to do. The Test::PodCoverage module can check that for you. Typically, you put this test in t/pod_coverage.t:

```
use Test::More;
eval 'use Test::Pod::Coverage 1.00';
plan skip_all => 'Test::Pod::Coverage 1.00 required'
  if $@;
all_pod_coverage_ok();
```

It complains about any subroutine that you don't document with Pod. It knows how to skip "private" subroutines, whose names conventionally start with underscores (and aren't really private), as well as to skip subroutines that you expressly do not want to document. For example, you can tell it not to complain about subroutines' names that are all uppercase:

```
use Test::More;
eval 'use Test::Pod::Coverage 1.00';
plan skip_all => 'Test::Pod::Coverage 1.00 required'
  if $@;
all_pod_coverage_ok(
  { also_private => [qr/^[A-Z_]+$/], },
);
```

Check your spelling

Perfect spelling is rarely high on the list of priorities for the code that you write. However, having the text in your code spelled properly can give your distributions a little extra polish. Though other people probably won't notice if all of your documentation is spelled correctly, they will notice the times when it is not.

The difficulty in spell checking documentation in Perl is that the documentation is typically maintained in Pod blocks interspersed throughout your code. A standard spell checker calls out many of the code elements, making it more annoying than useful.

`Pod::Spell` is a Pod formatter that helps you spell check your embedded documentation. It parses your code files, ignores anything that it thinks is code, and prints out Pod as plain text so that spellcheckers like `ispell` can easily handle it.

Suppose you have a bit of code with some embedded documentation. Can you spot the spelling mistakes:

```
use warnings
use strict;

=pod
Before using this module, check the compatability the
public API and the local version the library on your
machine. Hopefully the scripability can help you get it
done.
=cut
sub do_something_amazing {
  ...
}
```

The `podspell` utility reduces your file down to just the contents of the Pod blocks:

```
% podspell speling.pl
Before using this module, check the compatability the
public API and the local version the library on your
machine. Hopefully the scripability can help you get it
done.
```

You can now easily run this plain text through spell checking tools. In this case, there are three possible mistakes, and `ispell` suggests possible replacements when it can:

```
% podspell speling.pl | ispell -a | \
    perl -ne 'print if /^[#&]/'
& compatability 3 36: comparability, compatibility, ⏎
  computability
& API 6 61: AI, APE, APT, BPI, DPI, PI
# scripability 57
```

Remembering to spell check is a whole separate issue. If you package your code as a Perl distribution, you can simply add a spelling check to all of your files with `Test::Spelling`. Your t/pod_spell.t file is simple:

```
use Test::More;
use Test::Spelling;
all_pod_files_spelling_ok();
```

Things to remember

- Check your pod format with `podchecker`.
- Check that you've documented all of your methods with `Test::Pod::Coverage`.
- Spell check your documentation with `Test::Spelling`.

Item 85. Inline code for other languages.

Sometimes you need to access software written in a language other than Perl. In the past, this meant that you had to re-write the library in Perl or use Perl's XS mechanism (Item 86) to tie into the library. Re-writing isn't always a reasonable option, and XS can be tricky. Luckily, the *Inline* family of modules makes it simple to interface with other languages.

For instance, there is a considerable number of statistical packages available in Java. With `Inline::Java` you can do things like combining the convenient scriptability and networking ability of Perl with the power of a Java statistical analysis package like *Classifier4J*.

```
use LWP::Simple;
use Inline (
Java => <<'END_OF_JAVA_CODE'
import net.sf.classifier4J.summariser.ISummariser;
import net.sf.classifier4J.summariser.SimpleSummariser;
import net.sf.classifier4J.ClassifierException;
public class MySummarizer {
  private ISummariser summarizer;
  public MySummarizer() {
    summarizer = new SimpleSummariser();
  }

  public String summarize(String input, int sentences)
    throws ClassifierException {
    return summarizer.summarise(input, sentences);
  }
}
END_OF_JAVA_CODE
, CLASSPATH => 'Classifier4J-0.6.jar');
my $input = get(
    'http://www.constitution.org/cons/constitu.txt');
$input =~ s/\[[^]]*\]/ /g; # remove bracketed text
$input =~ s/\s+/ /g; # do some whitespace cleanup
print MySummarizer->new->summarize($input, 1), "\n";
```

In this example, you download a copy the Constitution of the United States, do some minor clean-ups, and pass the text to the `summarize` method that you defined in the `MySummarizer` Java class:

```
% perl summary.pl
All legislative Powers herein granted shall be vested
in a Congress of the United States, which shall consist
of a Senate and House of Representatives.
```

Inlining is useful for more than just using third-party libraries built in other languages. Suppose that you are checking numbers to see if they are prime. If you are brute-forcing it, prime-checking is a very processor-intensive operation. Perl code is likely to be very slow:

```perl
sub is_prime {
  my $number  = shift;
  my $divisor = int( sqrt $number ) + 1;
  while ( $divisor > 1 ) {
    return 0 if $number % $divisor-- == 0;
  }
  return 1;
}


my $prime_count = 0;
my $ceiling     = 1000000;

foreach ( 1 .. $ceiling ) {
  $prime_count++ if is_prime($_);
}

print "There are $prime_count primes under $ceiling\n";
```

When you change your code to use `Inline::C` you can get a substantial speedup:

```perl
use Inline qw(c);
my $prime_count = 0;
my $ceiling     = 1000000;

for ( 1 .. $ceiling ) {
  $prime_count++ if check_prime( $_, int( sqrt $_ ) + 1 );
}

print "There are $prime_count primes under $ceiling\n";
__END__

__C__
int check_prime(int number, int divisor) {
  while (divisor > 1) {
    if (number % divisor-- == 0) {
      return 0;
    }
  }
}
```

```
    return 1;
}
```

The speedup that you get even in this very trivial example is *huge*!

```
% time perl prime.pl
There are 78498 primes under 1000000

real    5m40.985s
user    5m28.979s
sys     0m1.462s


% time perl prime_inline.pl
There are 78498 primes under 1000000

real    0m14.295s
user    0m12.223s
sys     0m0.794s
```

Moving from Perl to C in some cases can really help you out. However, you are even better off searching for a more efficient algorithm that reduces the theoretical run time of your code, even if you are already using C.

Things to remember

- Inline code from other languages to access third-party libraries.
- Improve your Perl algorithm before you optimize by inlining code from another language.

Item 86. Use XS for low-level interfaces and speed.

XS is a glue language that connects Perl to C or C++ code. It takes care of data type conversions and other details for you using a special preprocessor.

With XS, you write functions in C or C++ that you can call from your Perl script. Within XSUBs, the subroutines that make the connection between Perl and C, you have full access to Perl's internals. You can create variables, change their values, execute Perl code, or do pretty much anything that suits your fancy.

Many of the cases that you would have historically pulled out XS for can now be handled more elegantly using the *Inline* family of modules (Item 85). Be sure to check them out for your cross-language integration, too.

An XS module is actually a dynamically loaded, shareable library. Creating one is a complex process fraught with details. Fortunately, with the XS interface you get a bunch of tools that handle most of those details for you. For reasonably simple situations, you need only run x2hs to get a set of boilerplate files; add some Perl and XS code; and run make. There are make targets for building the shareable library, testing it, building a distribution kit, and installing it.

XSUBS provide a handy way to add operating system supported features to Perl—they beat the heck out of syscall. You can also use XSUBS to speed up scripts that are spending a significant proportion of their time in a small number of subroutines. And, of course, you can use XSUBS to add a Perl interface to an existing C or C++ library of your own.

Suppose that you need a subroutine that returns a copy of a list, but with all the elements in random order. In Perl, you might write a Fisher-Yates shuffle:

```perl
sub shuffle2 {
  my @result = @_;
  my $n      = @result;
  while ( $n > 1 ) {
    my $i = rand $n;
    $n--;
    @result[ $i, $n ] = @result[ $n, $i ];
  }
  @result;
}
```

If efficiency is important to your problem, Perl's not always the best tool for a task. You can rewrite this in XS to get the speed of C.

Generating the boilerplate

To start your C implementation of your shuffle, use h2xs to generate a set of boilerplate files:

```
% h2xs -A -n List::Shuffle
Writing List-Shuffle/ppport.h
Writing List-Shuffle/lib/List/Shuffle.pm
Writing List-Shuffle/Shuffle.xs
```

```
Writing List-Shuffle/Makefile.PL
Writing List-Shuffle/README
Writing List-Shuffle/t/List-Shuffle.t
Writing List-Shuffle/Changes
Writing List-Shuffle/MANIFEST
```

The `h2xs` program creates stubs for all of the files that you need to create your C glue.

Writing and testing an XSUB

XS source code goes into files ending with .xs. The XS compiler, `xsubpp`, compiles XS into C code with the glue needed to interface with Perl. You will probably never have to invoke `xsubpp` on your own, though, because it is invoked automatically via the generated Makefile.

XS source files begin with a prologue of C code. A MODULE directive follows the prologue and sets the Perl namespace:

```
MODULE = List::Shuffle PACKAGE = List::Shuffle
```

This indicates the start of the actual XS source. Before you try implementing the shuffle, try simple XSUB that just calls the C standard library `log` function and returns the result:

```
double
log(x)
  double x
```

The return type (`double`) appears first, on a line by itself at the beginning of the line. Next are the function name (`log`) and a list of parameter names (`(x)`). The lines following the return type and function name are ordinarily indented for readability. In this case, there is only a single line in the XSUB body, declaring that x is type `double`.

In a simple case like this, `xsubpp` generates code that creates a Perl subroutine named `log()` that calls the C function of the same name. The generated code also includes the glue necessary to convert the Perl argument to a C `double`, and to convert the result back. (To see how this works, take a look at the C code generated by `xsubpp`—it's actually pretty readable.)

Here is a slightly more complex example that calls the UNIX `realpath()` function (not available on all systems):

```
char *
realpath(filename)
  char *filename
  PREINIT:
    char realname[1024]; /* or use MAXPATHLEN */
  CODE:
    RETVAL = realpath(filename, realname);
  OUTPUT:
  RETVAL
```

This creates a Perl function that takes a string argument and has a string return value. The XS glue takes care of converting Perl strings to C's char * type and back. You don't think about that when you use it in Perl, where it doesn't look any different from any other subroutine:

```
my $realname = realpath($filename);
```

The CODE section contains the portion of the code used to compute the result from the subroutine. The PREINIT section contains declarations of variables used in the CODE section; they should go here rather than in the CODE section. RETVAL is a "magic" variable supplied by xsubpp used to hold the return value. Finally, the OUTPUT section lists values that the XSUB returns. This will ordinarily include RETVAL. It can also include input parameters that are modified and returned as if through call by reference.

These examples all return single scalar values. In order to write shuffle, which returns a list of scalars, you have to use a PPCODE section and do your own popping and pushing of arguments and return values. This is less difficult than it may sound. To get things rolling, insert the following code into Shuffle.xs following the MODULE line:

```
PROTOTYPES: DISABLE
void
shuffle(...)
  PPCODE:
  {
    int i, n;
    SV **array; /* SV is the "scalar value" type */
    SV *tmp;
    /* allocate storage */
    array = New(0, array, items, SV *);
    for (i = 0; i < items; i++) {
```

```
        /* copy input args */
        array[i] = sv_mortalcopy(ST(i));
    }
    n = items;
    while (n > 1) { /* shuffle off to Buffalo */
        i = rand() % n;
        tmp = array[i];
        array[i] = array[--n];
        array[n] = tmp;
    }
    for (i = 0; i < items; i++) {
        XPUSHs(array[i]); /* push result onto stack */
    }
    Safefree(array); /* free storage */
}
```

The `PROTOTYPES: DISABLE` directive turns off Perl prototype processing for the XSUBs that follow.

The strategy here is to copy the input arguments into a temporary array, shuffle them, and then push the result onto the stack. The arguments will be scalar values, which Perl represents internally using the type SV *.

Instead of a CODE block, you use a PPCODE block inside this XSUB to disable the automatic handling of return values on the stack. The number of arguments passed in is in the magic variable `items`, and the arguments themselves are in ST(0), ST(1), and so on.

The SV pointers on the stack refer to the actual values supplied to the `shuffle()` function. You don't want this. You want copies instead, so you use the function `sv_mortalcopy()` to make a reference-counted clone of each incoming scalar.

The scalars go into an array allocated with Perl's internal New() function, and then you shuffle them. After shuffling, you push the return values onto the stack one at a time with the XPUSHs() function, and free the temporary storage you used to hold the array of pointers. If all this seems sketchy, which it probably does, consult the *perlguts* and *perlxs* man pages for more details.

At this point, you can save `Shuffle.xs` and build it:

```
% make
```

You will see a few lines of gobbledygook as Shuffle.xs compiles and the other parts of the build run. If the build worked, next create a test script. Open the test script template t/List-Shuffle.t and add some lines to test your new `shuffle`:

```
# List-Shuffle.t
use Test::More tests => 2;
BEGIN { use_ok('List::Shuffle') }

my @shuffle = shuffle 1 .. 10;
diag "@shuffle";
pass 'shuffled';
```

Run your tests and you should see that your test works, along with some diagnostic output that shows the order in the list:

```
% make test
...
t/List-Shuffle.t .. 1/2 # 4 9 6 1 3 5 7 2 10 8
t/List-Shuffle.t .. ok
All tests successful.
```

Things to remember

- Use XS to create Perl interfaces to C libraries.
- Use an Inline module to create a Perl interface to other languages.
- Use libraries from other languages instead of reimplementing them in Perl.

10 | Testing

Perl has an amazing test culture, and a great set of tools for testing and managing your code. It might even have some of the most widely tested code on the planet, thanks to CPAN Testers (Item 97).

Perl has had a testing infrastructure in place since the first Perl modules came out. The testing craze really took off when Michael Schwern starting pushing testing with the `Test::More` module, which made testing almost trivial. You simply loaded the module and called some convenience functions:

```
use Test::More tests => 2;

ok( $some_value, "The value is true" );
is( $got, $expected, "The values are the same" );
```

The `Test::More` module emits TAP (Test Anywhere Protocol), a simple results format that was started in Perl and has spread to many other languages.

The `Test::Harness` module handled the rest, although you probably didn't notice it doing its job behind the scenes. `Test::Harness` watched the test output and made a summary of it.

The Perl community, led by the Birmingham Perl Mongers, developed the CPAN Testers, which collected these test reports from volunteers as people uploaded modules to CPAN. There are now millions of reports in a publicly browsable database.

Along with that, the practices and techniques of Perl testing have evolved and become more sophisticated. Not only do Perlers test their Perl code, but they also test the details of their distributions, they test the format and spelling of their documentation, and they even test their tests.

Even if you think that tests just create more work for you, after setting up a reasonable test suite you'll spend less time chasing bugs and reading through code, and more time adding features and marking things off of your to-do list. So, don't wait. Let's get started right away.

Item 87. Use `prove` for flexible test runs.

The tests that you write for your code are just Perl programs. Since they are just Perl programs, you can execute them with `perl`:

```
% perl t/my_test.t
```

You do have to be careful about which version of the module under test gets loaded, though. More likely than not, you are developing and testing a module that you have already installed on your system. After all, you wrote the module because you needed to use it, didn't you?

As always, `perl` will search through the paths in `@INC` and will load the first version of the module that it finds. Depending on what is in your search path, this could be the stable version of the module that you previously installed or it could be the development version of the module that you are actually intending to test.

How do you ensure that you always load the development version of the module?

One way is to explicitly include the lib/ directory that your development code is in on the command line:

```
% perl -Ilib t/my_test.t
```

Another option, if you are using build scripts, is to take advantage of the *blib* module. The *blib* module searches your current directory and the next several higher directories looking for the *blib* directory created by your build script, and then adds the first one it finds to the front of `@INC`:

```
% make; perl -Mblib t/my_test.t
```

```
% ./Build; perl -Mblib t/my_test.t
```

After you are sure that you're testing the correct version of your module, you can start running your tests. However, the resulting output of running a test script with `perl` can get out of hand pretty quickly:

```
1..500
ok 1 - testing some code
ok 2 - another test
```

```
ok 3 - let's see if this works
ok 4 - everything should be okay here
ok 5 - checking some functionality
...
ok 500 - this should be looking good
```

Luckily, `perl` comes with a handy program called `prove`. The `prove` command runs your test programs and can interpret their output. Instead of dumping screenfuls of output, `prove` collects the output and provides you a nice summary of what happened. The `-b` switch includes the blib/ directories in `@INC`, just as `-Mblib` does for `perl`:

```
% prove -b t/my_test.t
my_test.t .. ok
All tests successful.
Files=1, Tests=500,   0 wallclock secs ( 0.09 usr  0.01 ⌐
   sys +  0.09 cusr  0.00 csys =  0.19 CPU)
Result: PASS
```

If there is a problem with any of your tests, `prove` gives you more information on just that test:

```
% prove -b t/my_failing_tests.t
my_failing_tests.t .. 1/500
#   Failed test 'checking some functionality'
#   at my_failing_tests.t line 9.
# Looks like you failed 1 test of 500.
my_failing_tests.t .. Dubious, test returned 1 (wstat 25⌐
   6, 0x100)
Failed 1/500 subtests

Test Summary Report
-------------------
my_failing_tests.t (Wstat: 256 Tests: 500 Failed: 1)
Failed test:   5
Non-zero exit status: 1
Files=1, Tests=500,   0 wallclock secs ( 0.08 usr  0.01 sy⌐
   s +  0.08 cusr  0.00 csys =  0.17 CPU)
Result: FAIL
```

If all `prove` did was interpret and summarize the test output, it would still be a valuable tool; however, `prove` does much more.

Randomize test order

One very useful feature of `prove` is its ability to shuffle the order in which it executes your test files. If you have multiple test files, you can pass them all to `prove` along with the `--shuffle` option, and your test files will run in a pseudo-random order. This helps ferret out inter-dependencies between your scripts, such as data from one test file affecting a later test file:

```
% prove --shuffle
```

Another great feature of `prove` is the ability to run tests in parallel. Pass in a `-j` argument followed by a number of tests to run in parallel, and `prove` will run multiple tests at once. This can reduce the real time it takes your tests to run.

`prove` has the ability to save state between runs and use the state from a previous run to help drill down into issues using the `--state` flag.

For instance, you might shuffle your tests and suddenly you experience a test failure. Since a test shuffle changes the order of test execution, you might not be able to recreate the failure easily. However, if you saved state during the shuffle, you can rerun the same shuffle order:

```
% prove --shuffle --state=save
... some failure output...
% prove --state=last t/*t
```

You can also do things such as running only your failing or passing tests from a previous run. You can run your tests in a variety of orders: fastest to slowest, slowest to fastest, or newest to oldest, or just run the tests that have changed since the last time state was modified. You don't have to rerun the entire test suite if you need to investigate certain test failures.

`prove` with other languages

`prove` doesn't really care if your tests are written in Perl, or if you are testing Perl code. It expects test output in the Test Anywhere Protocol (TAP) format that was started in Perl and spread to other languages. You saw an example in the first output example in this Item.

You can just as easily test programs in any other language using the `--exec` argument, as long as the programs emit results in a format understandable by the test harness being used by `prove`. If you want to run your test files with `ruby`, that's easy to do:

```
% prove --exec '/usr/bin/ruby -w' t/*t
```

Things to remember

- Run a single test when you want to focus on its features.
- Use `prove` to selectively run groups of tests.
- Use `prove` to run tests for other languages, too.

Item 88. Run tests only when they make sense.

The default Perl distribution setup puts all of the test files in the t/ directory. The build script typically runs all of the test files every time, although you don't have to do that if you use `prove` instead (Item 87).

Some tests you need just to ensure that you complete all your programming tasks. Other tests you need only for certain situations. With a little bit of test wrangling, you can ensure that tests run only in the situations where they should run.

Author tests

Not all tests deal with the functionality of the code. The most common class of tests that should be filtered is "author" tests. These tests include checks of the embedded documentation (Item 84), tests about the tests (Item 96), and "kwalitee" tests (Item 68), among others. Though important to the quality of your distribution, the failure of any one of these tests shouldn't prevent a person from installing your module.

Use the **TEST_AUTHOR** *environment variable*

A common way to prevent these author tests from running on machines other than yours is to use an environment variable, such as $ENV{TEST_AUTHOR}, to trigger the test:

```
use Test::More;
plan skip_all =>
  'Set $ENV{TEST_AUTHOR} to enable this test.'
  unless $ENV{TEST_AUTHOR};
```

```
eval "use Test::Pod 1.14";
plan skip_all => 'Test::Pod 1.14 required' if $@;

all_pod_files_ok();
```

Beware: TEST_AUTHOR is a fairly common environment variable to set for enabling author tests. Other people developing their own modules might have already set that variable, and they might be surprised when they run your extra tests. Likewise, you might be bitten by the same thing when you run their tests.

You might think that you can fix the unexpected author test problem by checking the value of $ENV{TEST_AUTHOR} for your user name:

```
plan skip_all =>
  'Set $ENV{TEST_AUTHOR} to enable this test.'
  unless $ENV{TEST_AUTHOR} eq 'SNUFFY';
```

However, what if other people, such as your co-maintainers, want to run those tests? Now they have to pretend to be you! That's not very nice.

Use the xt/ directory

Instead of putting your author tests in the same directory as your code tests, you can put them in another directory. Typically this is the xt/ directory (for **extra tests**). You can then run those tests with prove when you need them (Item 87).

If you don't want to risk distributing your author tests and you've put all of them in a separate directory, you can exclude that directory from your distribution with MANIFEST.SKIP, which uses Perl regular expressions to filter files from MANIFEST:

```
^xt/
```

If you don't have your files in a separate directory, you can exclude particular files, although you have to ensure that you now maintain the list yourself:

```
t/pod.t
t/pod_coverage.t
```

Limit tests to the right situations

Skipping OS-dependent tests looks almost identical to skipping author tests, only instead of an environment variable, you rely on the `$^O` variable in Perl:

```
use Test::More;
plan skip_all => 'Skipping Linux-only tests'
  unless $^O eq 'linux';
```

Using `skip_all` skips the entire file. However, you might need to skip only a few tests in the middle of your test file. `Test::More` has special magic that it can use in a block labeled `SKIP`:

```
SKIP: {
  skip 'Skipping Linux-only tests', 2
    unless $^O eq 'linux';

  ok(...);
  is(...);
}

ok( 1 == 1, 'The universe is stable' );

SKIP: {
  skip 'Skipping thread-only tests', 2
    unless $Config{'usethreads'} eq 'define';

  ok(...);
  is(...);
}
```

You can also reuse the concepts that limit your distribution to the right platforms (Item 83) to limit your tests to the right platforms.

Skip tests in an automated environment

The CPAN Testers (Item 97) automatically test any module that you upload to CPAN. This is done programmatically, and usually there is no person monitoring the tests. You probably don't want to run some of your tests in these cases. For instance, if you're creating a graphical interface and expect the user to push a button, the automatic testing process isn't going to work for you. To get around this, use another SKIP block and check the value of the AUTOMATED_TESTING environment variable:

```
SKIP: {
  skip 'These tests needs a real person', 2
    if $ENV{AUTOMATED_TESTING};

  test_start_window();
  test_button_push();
}
```

Things to remember

- Put your author tests into the xt/ directory to separate them from user tests.
- Use a SKIP block to disable tests when they don't apply.
- Disable interactive tests by checking $ENV{AUTOMATED_TESTING}.

Item 89. Use dependency injection to avoid special test logic.

You might want to connect to a production database when your code is on production systems, but to a test database otherwise. Maybe you don't want to send out e-mail when you are running tests in a continuous build (Item 98). No matter what the scenario, the easy (and wrong) thing to do is to add extra conditional logic to your code:

```
my $dbh =
  ($test_mode)
  ? connect_to_mock()
  : connect_to_prod();

if ( not $testing ) {
  send_nag_email();
}
```

We've all done this, even if we don't want to admit it. The code looks harmless, but it actually creates a problem. These conditional branches guarantee that you cannot or will not test some of the code branches, limiting your test coverage (Item 96). This can be the source of some embarrassing errors when you forget to put the test check around code that ends up sending junk e-mail to all of your customers.

Luckily, there are some good solutions for avoiding the problem altogether. **Inversion of control** is one elegant solution—specifically, inverting control through **dependency injection**. As a bonus, dependency injection is a good programming practice even outside of the realm of testing. Once you get the hang of it, you'll start using dependency injection throughout your code base.

In its simplest form, dependency injection constructs dependencies for an object outside of the object itself. Major parts of the functionality come from other objects you create outside of the object of interest.

Here is the constructor for class `Foo` that takes in arguments for a new database handle, creates the handle, caches it, and then returns a new `Foo` object:

```
package Foo;

sub new {
   my ( $class, $dsn, $user, $password, $parameters ) = @_;
   my $self = bless {}, $class;
   $self->{dbh} =
      DBI->connect( $dsn, $user, $password, $parameters );
   return $self;
}
```

To inject the `DBI` dependency instead of constructing it manually, all you need to do is pass an already-constructed database handle:

```
package Foo;

sub new {
   my ( $class, $dbh ) = @_;
   my $self = bless {}, $class;
   $self->{$dbh} = $dbh;
   return $self;
}
```

On the surface this seems like a trivial change, but it makes your code much more flexible. In the first example, you could test the code by passing in valid `DBI` parameters so you log onto a test database of some sort, but that always creates a real database connection. With the second example, you can pass in any type of object for the database handle that you want. It can be a reference to a test database. It can be a mocked object (Item 92). It can be anything that can fake class `Foo` into thinking that it is talking to a live database handle.

Often, people pair up the factory design pattern with dependency injection. You create a factory that constructs and returns the database object for you:

```
package DatabaseFactory;

sub new {
   my ( $class, $dbh ) = @_;
   my $self = bless {}, $class;
   $self->{dbh} = $dbh;
   return $self;
}

sub get_dbh {
   my ($self) = @_;
   return $self;
}

sub set_dbh {
   my ( $self, $dbh ) = @_;
   $self->{dbh} = $dbh;
}

package Foo;

sub new {
   my ( $class, $database_factory ) = @_;
   my $self = bless {}, $class;
   $self->{database_factory} = $database_factory;
   return $self;
}

sub do_something {
   my ($self) = @_;
   my $dbh = $self->{database_factory}->get_dbh();
}
```

For testing, you can create a mock database handle, and you don't have to change anything in your target code:

```
my $dbh     = create_new_mock_database_handle();
my $factory = DatabaseFactory->new($dbh);
my $foo     = Foo->new($factory);
$foo->do_something();
```

This not only adds dependency injection, it also adds an extra layer in your code that allows you to do things such as pooling objects to return from the factory or changing the object at arbitrary times during execution:

```
my $dbh     = create_new_mock_database_handle();
my $factory = DatabaseFactory->new($dbh);
my $foo     = Foo->new($factory);
$foo->do_something();
$factory->set_dbh(
  create_modified_mock_database_handle() );
$foo->do_something();
```

Factories can get clunky quickly. If you are going to be doing a lot of dependency injection and have a large application, check out an inversion of control framework like `Bread::Board`.

Things to remember

- Don't put test versus production logic in your code.
- Construct dependency objects outside the objects that use them.
- Create factories that construct dependency objects.

Item 90. Don't require more than you need to use in your methods.

Even if you are using good dependency injection (Item 89), keep the number of dependencies that you actually need to a minimum. Any more than a couple of dependencies will start to drive you insane and make your code unmaintainable.

Consider a module that checks your car's license to ensure that it hasn't expired. Maybe this Perl code lives in one of those automated cameras on traffic signals. The module doesn't represent the automobile itself, but it can use an automobile object to access the license information:

```perl
package Auto::LicenseChecker;
# Also called City::RevenueGenerator

use DateTime ();

sub new {
  my ( $class, $automobile ) = @_;
  my $self = bless {
    automobile => $automobile
  }, $class;
}

sub check_expired_license {
  my ($self) = @_;
  my $licenseplate =
    $self->{automobile}->get_licenseplate;

  return $licenseplate->get_expiration <
    DateTime->new->now();
}
```

To construct the `Auto::LicenseChecker` object, you passed as an argument an entire automobile object even though you needed only the license plate. Perhaps you had to construct an `Automobile` that required specification of every part before it would give you an object:

```perl
use Test::More tests => 1;

my $automobile = Automobile->new(
  engine          => Engine->new,
  left_front_tire => Tire->new,
  ...
  license_plate   => LicensePlate->new($number),
  ...
);

my $checker = Auto::LicenseChecker->new($automobile);
ok( not $checker->check_expired_license,
  'legal to drive');
```

That's a lot of work, an excessive memory footprint, and too much to consider just to check the expiration date on the plate. Does that camera really care if your car has four tires or an engine? As long as you are going through its intersection, it just wants to figure out which car you are and how to charge you. Instead of giving it the whole `Automobile` object, just give it the license plate object:

```
package Auto::LicenseChecker;

use DateTime ();

sub new {
  my ( $class, $licenseplate ) = @_;
  my $self = bless {
    licenseplate => $licenseplate,
  }, $class;
}

sub check_expired_license {
  my ($self) = @_;
  return $self->{licenseplate}->get_expiration <
    DateTime->new()->now();
}
```

This reduces the amount of setup work you have to do in your test, since you can ignore most parts of the automobile:

```
use Test::More tests => 1;

my $plate = LicensePlate->new($license_plate);

my $checker = Auto::LicenseChecker->new($plate);
ok( not $checker->check_expired_license,
  'legal to drive' );
```

This is another one of those situations where the difficulty in testing signals the difficulty in using the code. If you have to set up too much in your test, you probably have to set up too much in production code, too.

Things to remember

- Give your methods only the information they need.
- Remember that excessive setup in tests means excessive setup in code.

Item 91. Write programs as modulinos for easy testing.

Many Perl programs start off innocently enough as merely a few lines of code that solve the problem of the day. You never think you'll use the code again, so you aren't as careful as you could be. Then somebody finds out about it, asks you to improve it, and eventually you have a massive program that seems to run your entire company. What was once innocent is now a big ball of mud, and it's all your fault.

The problem with this sort of evolution is that it's really hard to compartmentalize the different parts of your program and test them individually. A typical Perl program starts at the beginning and goes to the end. If you want to test one bit, you have to run all of the other parts, too. Anything you do, like printing to standard output or sending warnings to standard error, now becomes a testing problem.

To get around this problem, you can start every program as if it is a module, even though it still acts like a program. This sort of program is known as a **modulino**, or "little module," since it starts off small, just like your innocent program.

The trick is to make your code act like a program when you treat it as a program, but act like a module when you use it as a module. That is, it should run and do its job from front to back when you run it, but not do anything other than compile when you load it as a module.

In its simplest form, you check `caller`. If you loaded the file as a module, there is a higher level to the module, the file that loaded it, and `caller` is true. If you ran it as a program, there is no higher level, so `caller` is false. You use that to decide what to do:

```
package MyApplication::Icelandic;

use warnings;
use strict;
use utf8;

MyApplication->run unless caller;

sub run {
    print "Starf þitt byrjar hér.\n";
}

1;
```

This looks like a typical Perl program, but you put all of the interesting stuff in run, which is like the main routines that you might expect to have in other languages. There's nothing special about the name run; some people like the traditional main, some like activate, and so on. As long as you isolate the executable portion of your module in a subroutine so you delay doing any real work until you are ready, you're constructing a modulino. You have actually gone back a step in language evolution, since Perl was trying to save you the typing by assuming the whole file was your main routine.

Now, as you add to your program, think less about typing out a pile of statements in the run subroutine and more about separating the functionality into separate subroutines.

Continuing with the example, suppose that you now want to test your modulino. The code has some problems that make testing difficult. The run method outputs only to the default filehandle, and it outputs only a single hard-coded message. Though this little chunk of code can do only the one thing, it still largely has the same problems encountered when you test a full program.

You can aid testing by separating the output destination from run. One way to do this involves creating an application object where you can set the output filehandle as one of the attributes:

```perl
package MyModulino;

use strict;
use warnings;

__PACKAGE__->new->run unless caller;

sub run {
  my ($application) = @_;
  print { $application->{output_fh} }
    "Your work starts here\n";
}

sub new {
  my ($class) = @_;
  my $application = bless {}, $class;
  $application->init;
```

```
      $application;
  }

  sub init {
    my ($application) = @_;
    $application->{output_fh} = \*STDOUT;
  }

  sub output_fh {
    my ( $application, $fh ) = @_;

    if ($fh) { $application->{output_fh} = $fh }

    $application->{output_fh};
  }

  1;
```

Now testing is a bit easier. You load the modulino in your test program, construct a new application object, and set the output filehandle to a scalar reference (Item 54):

```
use Test::More tests => 3;

my $class = 'MyModulino';
use_ok($class)
    or die 'Bail out! Could not load module!';

my $application = $class->new;
isa_ok( $application, $class );

my $output_string;
open my ($fh), '>:utf8', \$output_string;

$application->output_fh($fh);

$application->run;
like( $output_string, qr/work/ );
```

Not only can you easily test MyModulino, but you can easily subclass it doing the same thing. You can separate the part of the application that prints the message just as you did with the output filehandle:

```perl
package MyModulino;

use strict;
use warnings;

binmode STDOUT, ':utf8';

__PACKAGE__->new->run unless caller;

sub run {
  my ($application) = @_;
  print { $application->{output_fh} }
    $application->message;
}

# ... same as before

sub message {
  "Your work starts here\n";
}

1;
```

Now you can test the message without going through the rest of the program:

```perl
use Test::More tests => 3;

my $class = 'MyModulino';
use_ok($class)
  or die 'Bail out! Could not load module!';

my $application = $class->new;
isa_ok( $application, $class );

like( $application->message, qr/work/ );
```

When you decide that you need to change the message, you make a very small subclass that provides a new message:

```perl
package MyModulino::Icelandic;

use strict;
use warnings;
```

```
use utf8;

use base qw( MyModulino );

__PACKAGE__->new->run unless caller;

sub message {
  "Starf þitt byrjar hér.\n";
}


1;
```

Things to remember

- Create programs as modulinos for easier testing and subclassing.
- Test your application in pieces.
- Create small subclasses to override features.

Item 92. Mock objects and interfaces to focus tests.

Sometimes you want to test a small part of your code without dealing with the rest of the logic and data that go around it. For these cases, it is often useful to mock, or fake, some parts of the code so you can focus on the feature you're testing and not on every feature that leads up to it.

Say, for instance, that you are testing code that sums a list of numbers. In the real code, these numbers come from a database query:

```
package MySum;

use DBI;

sub sum_values_per_key {
  my ( $class, $dsn, $user, $password, $parameters ) = @_;
  my %results;

  my $dbh =
    DBI->connect( $dsn, $user, $password, $parameters );
```

```
my $sth = $dbh->prepare(
  'select key, calculate(value) from my_table');
$sth->execute();

while ( my ($row) = $sth->fetchrow_arrayref() ) {
  $results{ $row->[0] } += $row->[1];
}

$sth->finish();
$dbh->disconnect();
return \%results;
}


1;
```

You could create a SQLite database for testing (Item 93), but the `calculate()` method call in the SQL makes that difficult, since it's specific to your production database. Although you might consider dependency injection (Item 89), in some cases you need more than that, especially when you don't control the code you need to test.

Using `Test::MockObject`

The easiest thing to do in your `MySum` situation is to mock the database layer. Since the code was poorly written and accesses `DBI` directly, you'll have to create a fake `DBI` object to stand in for the real thing.

Start by creating a "fake" module. You don't want to load `DBI`, so you have to trick Perl into thinking that you've already loaded it. With `fake_module`, you do just that:

```
use MySum;
use Test::More qw(no_plan);
use Test::Deep;
use Test::MockObject;

my $dbi_mock = Test::MockObject->new;
my $sth_mock = Test::MockObject->new;

$dbi_mock->fake_module( 'DBI',
  connect => sub { $dbi_mock } );
```

Once you've tricked Perl into thinking that it has already loaded DBI, you can tell it how to respond to methods. Whenever you call DBI->prepare, you want to return the fake statement handle $sth_mock, and you want disconnect to always return true:

```
$dbi_mock->set_always( 'prepare', $sth_mock );
$dbi_mock->set_true('disconnect');
```

Similarly, you want the $sth_mock object to return some fake data. You assume that the SQL query is going to return what you need; you're not testing the database or the query, but are testing the summing feature:

```
$sth_mock->set_true( 'execute', 'finish' );
$sth_mock->set_series(
  'fetchrow_arrayref',
  [ first  => 40 ],
  [ first  => 70 ],
  [ second => 100 ]
);
```

Now you can call sum_values_per_key. Even though it tries to make a real DBI object, Test::MockObject intercepts this attempt and uses your mocked methods instead:

```
cmp_deeply(
  MySum->sum_values_per_key(
    'dbi:Oracle:testdb', 'user',
    'password', { RaiseError => 1 }
  ),
  { first => 110, second => 100 },
  'sum values'
);
```

You don't always need to fully mock an object in order to get your tests to run. Sometimes simply overriding a method or two will do. For cases like this, use Test::MockObject::Extends to selectively replace methods:

```
use Test::More 'no_plan';
use Test::MockObject::Extends;
use DateTime;

my $dt =
  DateTime->new( year => 1979, month => 10, day => 22 );
```

```
$dt = Test::MockObject::Extends->new($dt);
$dt->set_always( year => 2009 );

is( $dt->year,  2009, 'year overridden' );
is( $dt->month, 10,   'month untouched' );
```

Redefine methods through the symbol table

Sometimes the `Test::MockObject` and `Test::MockObject::Extends` methods can be overkill. You shouldn't be afraid of messing with the symbol table if you have to.

If you need to redefine only the return value of the `year` method in `DateTime`, you can replace the definition of the subroutine. It's best to do this in a small scope to limit your damage. Since this is generally a bad idea for code, Perl will warn you about your replacement. You can turn off the `redefine` class of warnings when that's what you want to do:

```
use Test::More 'no_plan';
use DateTime;

my $dt =
  DateTime->new( year => 1979, month => 10, day => 22 );

{
  no warnings qw/redefine/;
  local *DateTime::year = sub { return 2009 };
  use warnings;
  is( $dt->year,  2009, 'year overridden' );
  is( $dt->month, 10,   'month untouched' );
}
```

Now every call to `year` returns your value of **2009**.

Sometimes you want to keep the original subroutine, just add more code around it. In that case, you can wrap the code but still use the original. Before you redefine the method, you assign the `CODE` part of the typeglob to a variable, so you keep the original definition. In this case, you save it in `$original`, and you can call it again later with `&$original`, using the `&` in the front and no parentheses so it uses the current value of `@_`:

```
use Test::More 'no_plan';
use DateTime;
```

```
my $dt =
  DateTime->new( year => 1979, month => 10, day => 22 );

{
  no warnings qw/redefine/;
  my $original = *DateTime::year{CODE};

  local *DateTime::year = sub {
    my $year = &$original;
    print STDERR "The real year is $year\n";
    return 2009;
  };

  use warnings;
  is( $dt->year,  2009, 'year overridden' );
  is( $dt->month, 10,   'month untouched' );
}
```

Even though you have overridden the method, the output shows that you still called the original one:

```
The real year is 1979
ok 1 - year overridden
ok 2 - month untouched
1..2
```

If you really want to do this sort of thing, you probably don't want to do it by hand; the `Hook::LexWrap` module can take care of all of the details for you.

Overriding Perl built-ins

Sometimes it'll be not modules that you need to mock, but the built-in Perl functions like `time`. If you don't mind overriding the method completely, you can use the `subs` pragma to define your own, and use it in preference to the real one:

```
my $fixed_time = 1234567890;

use subs qw(time);
```

```perl
sub time {
  return $fixed_time;
}
```

```perl
is( time, $fixed_time, 'frozen in time' );
```

If you need to be a little more selective, you can override methods in the CORE::GLOBAL namespace, where Perl keeps the definitions for all of its built-ins. There's a trick to this, though: you have to do it in a BEGIN block before you use it:

```perl
my $fixed_time = 1234567890;

BEGIN {
  *CORE::GLOBAL::time = sub { CORE::time };
}

ok( time > $fixed_time, 'system time' );

{
  no warnings qw(redefine);
  local *CORE::GLOBAL::time = sub { $fixed_time };
  is( time, $fixed_time, 'frozen in time' );
}
```

This can be especially handy when you have to mock code that would normally do something you need to prevent during testing. For instance, you know that `unlink` will delete files, but maybe you want to keep them around so you can see what is in them:

```perl
BEGIN {
  *CORE::GLOBAL::unlink = sub {
    print "Not unlinking @_";
  };
}
```

Now any code that calls unlink calls your version instead.

Things to remember

- `Test::MockObject` allows you to fake classes and methods.
- Redefine a subroutine by assigning to its typeglob.
- Override Perl built-ins through the CORE::GLOBAL namespace.

Item 93. Use SQLite to create test databases.

Code that interfaces with a database management system poses an interesting challenge for testing. A common strategy is to create a test version of the database and connect to it in your tests. You can load the test database with a known set of data, and then write tests against it. Your test code is simple, with minimal-to-no mocked objects (Item 92). The test environment is much more like your production environment. Sounds great, doesn't it?

Connecting to a live test instance of your database is good for integration tests. However, for unit tests that you need to execute repeatedly throughout development, connecting to a test database poses more problems than it solves.

Establishing a connection to a database management system like Oracle or MySQL can be slow enough that it disrupts the flow of your development routine, especially if your tests repeatedly connect and disconnect to the database. A second or two added to the execution time of your test suite can break your train of thought and discourage you from running tests often.

Running multiple tests at once can introduce race conditions. If you're running your tests in parallel or if you run your tests manually while your continuous build is running, you can end up having one test change data that another test depends on. This can cause seemingly random failures that are difficult to track down.

Your broken code might also destroy data in your production database. Accidentally logging in as the wrong user or connecting to the wrong credentials could have you running your tests against a production database and wreaking havoc.

Local test databases

SQLite is not a Perl project but a C-based library that implements a local database. According to the SQLite Web site (http://www.sqlite.org/): "SQLite is a software library that implements a self-contained, serverless, zero-configuration, transactional SQL database engine." That sounds perfect for a test database.

SQLite allows you to interact with a database without the overhead of a full database management system. Since SQLite is a local library, all of your database communication happens locally in the same application space as your tests. There is no network latency, and there is no handshaking.

Suppose that your production code normally connects to MySQL:

```
my $dbh =
  DBI->connect( 'dbi:mysql:my_database', 'user', 'password',
    { other => 'settings' }
  );
```

You need to change only the arguments to `connect` to use SQLite instead:

```
my $dbh =
  DBI->connect( 'dbi:SQLite:database.db', q{}, q{},
    { other => 'settings' }
  );
```

SQLite creates (or reads) a file called database.db. SQLite supports many of the SQL constructs found in popular database management systems. In some cases, when SQLite doesn't support a SQL construct, it at least silently accepts the SQL, so that your code doesn't choke.

You can also create an in-memory SQLite database by not specifying a file name in `connect`. With this setup, you get an empty database for each call to `connect`, and you need to create the tables and fill in the data at test time:

```
my $dbh =
  DBI->connect( 'dbi:SQLite:', q{}, q{},
  { RaiseError => 1 } );


$dbh->do( 'create table test_table '
    . '( id integer, value varchar )' );
```

SQLite is quite handy for testing, but it's not limited to test-only applications. Many open source and commercial tools use SQLite as the data store behind their products. It is a lightweight and proven library that you should definitely look into.

Things to remember

- Don't use production databases to test your code.
- Use SQLite to stand in for production databases during your tests.
- Create in-memory test databases with SQLite.

Item 94. Use `Test::Class` for more structured testing.

`Test::More` provides a great toolkit, but is very lackadaisical on structure. Many programmers dream up their own systems of organization. Sometimes this works, and provides just the right fit. Sometimes this ends up being an exercise in reinventing the wheel poorly. People coming from an xUnit background are typically dismayed at this apparent lack of discipline.

Luckily, the `Test::Class` module provides the structure that will be familiar to anyone who has used an xUnit-style framework. `Test::Class` is an object-oriented testing framework that works in conjunction with other `Test::Builder` modules to provide a level of organization to test code.

As with other xUnit style tests, you create methods in your class that serve as the testing infrastructure:

```
package MyTest;

use base 'Test::Class';  # inherit testing framework
use Test::More;          # no plan needed
use My::Class::Under::Test;

my %test_data = (
  123 => 'hello',
  456 => 'world',
);

sub connect_to_database : Test(startup) {
  my ($self) = shift;
  $self->{dbh} = connect_to_database;
  $self->{insert_sth} =
    $self->{dbh}
    ->prepare( 'insert into test_table (key, value) '
      . 'values (?, ?)' );
  $self->{delete_sth} =
    $self->{dbh}
    ->prepare('delete from test_table where key = ?');
}

sub disconnect_from_database : Test(shutdown) {
  my ($self) = shift;
```

```
  $self->{insert_sth}->finish if $self->{insert_sth};
  $self->{delete_sth}->finish if $self->{delete_sth};
  $self->{dbh}->disconnect    if $self->{dbh};
}

sub insert_test_data : Test(setup) {
  my ($self) = shift;
  for my ( $key, $value ) ( each %test_data ) {
    $self->{insert_sth}->execute( $key, $value );
  };
}

sub create_an_object_to_test : Test(setup) {
  my ($self) = shift;
  $self->{object} = My::Class::Under::Test->new;
}

sub clean_up_after_running_a_test_method : Test(teardown)
{
  my ($self) = shift;
  for my ($key) ( keys %test_data ) {
    $self->{delete_sth}->execute($key);
  };
}

sub do_a_single_test : Test {
  my ($self) = shift;
  is(
    scalar( keys %test_data ),
    $self->{object}->row_count,
    'all data accounted for'
  );
}

sub run_a_fixed_number_of_tests : Test(2) {
  my ($self) = shift;
  isa_ok( $self->{object}, 'My::Class::Under::Test' );
  can_ok( $self->{object}, qw(get row_count) );
}
```

```
sub run_a_dynamic_number_of_tests : Tests {
  my ($self) = shift;
  for my ( $key, $value ) ( each %test_data ) {
    is(
      $test_data{$key}, $self->{object}->get($key),
      "lookup by key $key"
    );
  };
}
```

Each of the test methods is marked with an attribute (which we don't cover in this book, but you can read about in the *perlsub* documentation). Each of these attributes has a special meaning that is fairly easy to deduce, even if you don't know how attributes work:

Test(startup)

Startup methods execute once per run of the test suite and before any of the other methods. You use them for costly operations and to set up data structures that you can use in all of the tests without having to repopulate them.

Test(shutdown)

Shutdown methods execute once per run of the test suite but after all of the other methods. You use these methods for any final cleanup before your test program halts.

Test(setup)

Setup methods execute once before each test method. For example, if you have six test methods, the setup methods execute six times, once for each time, just before a test method. You use setup methods to build data and objects that you need to refresh for each run of the test.

Test(teardown)

Teardown methods are the converse of setup methods. They execute just after each test method and you use them to clean up after each test.

Test[n]

Test methods contain the actual tests to execute. You can declare one test, (`Test`), multiple tests, (`Test(n)`), or an unknown number of tests, (`Tests`).

Now that you've put all of the tests into methods, they don't run unless you call them. The `Test::Class` framework provides a method called `runtests` that handles this for you; all that you have to do is call it.

You can create an extra .t file that does this for you, or use the modulino technique (Item 91) to run the tests when you call the module as a program:

```
__PACKAGE__->runtests() unless caller;
```

This allows you to run your test module directly:

```
% prove test/MyTest.pm
```

One parting note: this example showed tests connecting to a database in order to compactly illustrate all of the hooks in `Test::Class`. You don't have to connect to a production database if you set up a test database or mocks (Item 92).

Things to remember

- Use the `Test::Class` module for xUnit functionality in Perl.
- Add special test methods to your module.
- Run your unit tests normally, or call your module as a program.

Item 95. Start testing at the beginning of your project.

Agile methodologies and test-driven development (TDD) are very popular development practices. Whether you are a staunch advocate of TDD or think that it is just the latest fad, there are some valuable lessons that you can learn. If you don't code with testing in mind, you will have a very difficult time adding tests later in your development cycle.

With true test-driven development, you always write a test first and then write the code necessary to make that test pass. In TDD, you first write a test that runs your not-yet-written code:

```
use Test::More tests => 3;

BEGIN { use_ok('UpperCaser') }

my $uc = UpperCaser->new();
is( $uc->uc('addison clark'),        'ADDISON CLARK' );
is( $uc->uc_first('ella & ginger'), 'Ella & Ginger' );
```

Now you work your way through the error messages emitted from prove (Item 87), coding enough to fix each new error along the way. First, you run the test before the module exists:

```
% prove t/uc.t
#     Error:  Can't locate UpperCaser.pm in @INC
```

The test can't load the module since it doesn't exist yet, so you create the module file, but without adding any code yet. Now the test fails because it can't find the new method:

```
% prove t/uc.t
t/uc.t .. 1/3 Can't locate object method "new" via ↵
  package "UpperCaser" at t/uc.t line 7.
```

You implement new so the test finds the method, but new doesn't do anything yet. The next method fails since it never gets an object:

```
% prove t/uc.t
t/uc.t .. 1/3 Can't call method "uc" on an undefined ↵
  value at t/uc.t line 8.
```

You implement new so it returns the smallest object it can, and now the object can't find the uc method that you haven't yet implemented:

```
% prove t/uc.t
t/uc.t .. 1/3 Can't locate object method "uc" via package↵
   "UpperCaser" at t/uc.t line 8.
```

You fix that, and it fails on the next method call:

```
% prove t/uc.t
Can't locate object method "uc_first" via package "Upper↵
  Caser" at t/uc.t line 9.
```

Finally, you fix that last method call by implementing uc_first as minimally as possible. Since it doesn't yet do its job, you don't get the expected output:

```
% prove t/uc.t
t/uc.t .. 1/3
#   Failed test at t/uc.t line 8.
#          got: undef
#     expected: 'ADDISION CLARK'

#   Failed test at t/uc.t line 9.
#          got: undef
#     expected: 'Ella & Ginger'
# Looks like you failed 2 tests of 3.
```

You make `uc` do what it should, leaving only one method for you to fully implement:

```
% prove t/uc.t
t/uc.t .. 1/3
#   Failed test at t/uc.t line 9.
#          got: undef
#     expected: 'Ella & Ginger'
# Looks like you failed 1 test of 3.
```

And, finally, all of the tests pass when you fully implement `uc_first`:

```
% prove t/uc.t
t/uc.t .. ok
All tests successful.
Files=1, Tests=3,  0 wallclock secs ( 0.03 usr  0.01 sys↵
  + 0.02 cusr  0.00 csys =  0.06 CPU)
Result: PASS
```

After all of the test pass, you have a nice piece of tested code that looks something like:

```perl
package UpperCaser;

use warnings;
use strict;

sub new {
  bless {}, shift;
}
```

```
sub uc {
  my ( $self, $word ) = @_;
  return uc $word;
}

sub uc_first {
  my ( $self, $word ) = @_;
  return join ' ', map { ucfirst } split /\s/, $word;
}


1;
```

This form of development is typically a major change in a programmer's workflow. It guarantees that you have tests for your code. It can also be so intimidating that many people give up after trying it for a few days (or minutes). Don't quit so soon, though!

Even if you don't want to follow TDD, you still should write automated tests for your code. Write these tests soon after developing the code, before you have too much untested work to wrangle. Timing is important, because you are bound to do something that ends up making testing difficult. When it's difficult to test your code, it's also difficult to debug, and probably difficult to use. Testing helps you find those problems before they get too big.

Consider a counterexample, with this bit of code that downloads the main English Wikipedia page and prints out the number of articles currently live:

```
sub print_number_of_wiki_entries {
  my $agent = LWP::UserAgent->new();
  $agent->agent('Mozilla/5.0');
  my $response =
    $agent->get('http://en.wikipedia.org/wiki/Main_Page');
  if ( $response->is_success ) {
    if ( $response->decoded_content =~
      m{>([\d,]*)</a> articles} )
    {
      print
        "There are $1 English articles on Wikipedia\n";
    }
  }
}
```

This is very simple code, and it should be easy to test, right? Unfortunately, there are a few gotchas that make testing a challenge.

First, this subroutine creates a new `LWP::UserAgent` instead of taking it from the argument list, so you can't supply your own user-agent for dependency injection (Item 89).

Second, this subroutine requires an Internet connection as well as access to Wikipedia. To make things even worse, the subroutine prints results directly to standard output, which means that to test the output of the method, you need to somehow intercept the standard output stream (Item 55).

You can avoid most of this if you write the tests first. As you test each bit, you discover these problems and work around them.

Still, since this is a small code block, you can refactor it to be more testable. A quick improvement is simply taking the `print` statement out of the sub-routine and instead having it return a string:

```perl
sub get_number_of_wiki_entries {
  my $agent = LWP::UserAgent->new();
  $agent->agent('Mozilla/5.0');
  my $response =
    $agent->get('http://en.wikipedia.org/wiki/Main_Page');
  if ( $response->is_success ) {
    if ( $response->decoded_content =~
      m{>([\d,]*)</a> articles} )
    {
      return "There are $1 English articles on Wikipedia";
    }
  }
}
```

Now you can test the method with a string comparison:

```perl
use Test::More tests => 1;

like(
  ToughToTestRefactored::get_number_of_wiki_entries(),
  qr"There are [\d,]* English articles on Wikipedia",
  'found number of wiki entries'
);
```

You can also separate the download parts from the data interpretation parts so you do it in two steps:

```
sub get_wikipedia_main_page {
  my $agent = LWP::UserAgent->new();
  $agent->agent('Mozilla/5.0');
  my $response =
    $agent->get('http://en.wikipedia.org/wiki/Main_Page');
  if ( $response->is_success ) {
    return $response->decoded_content;
  }
  return;
}


sub get_number_of_wiki_entries {
  my $html = shift;
  if ( $html =~ m{>([\d,]*)</a> articles} ) {
    return "There are $1 English articles on Wikipedia";
  }
  return;
}
```

Now you can test the download separately from the HTML scraping:

```
use Test::More tests => 2;

my $html = get_wikipedia_main_page();
ok( $html, 'got data back from Wikipedia' );
like(
  get_number_of_wiki_entries($html),
  qr"There are [\d,]* English articles on Wikipedia",
  'found number of wiki entries'
);

my $count = get_number_of_wiki_entries($html);
is( $count, ... );
```

But there is still the pesky network call, which is hard to test if you are offline. Instead of creating your own user-agent, take one that the caller gives you in the argument list:

```perl
sub get_wikipedia_main_page {
  my $agent = shift;
  $agent->agent('Mozilla/5.0');
  my $response =
    $agent->get('http://en.wikipedia.org/wiki/Main_Page');
  if ( $response->is_success ) {
    return $response->decoded_content;
  }
  return;
}
```

Now you can create a mock object (Item 92) to stand in for the real user-agent and avoid the network altogether:

```perl
use LWP::UserAgent;
use HTTP::Response;
use Test::MockObject::Extends;

my $agent = LWP::UserAgent->new();
$agent = Test::MockObject::Extends->new($agent);
$agent->mock(
  'get',
  sub {
    HTTP::Response->new(
      200, '',
      [ 'Content-Type', 'test/html' ],
      'blah <a>123,456</a> articles'
    );
  }
);

my $html = get_wikipedia_main_page($agent);
ok( $html, 'got data back from Wikipedia' );
like(
  get_number_of_wiki_entries($html),
  qr"There are [\d,]* English articles on Wikipedia",
  'found number of wiki entries'
);
```

You've broken the process down into multiple steps, and you've tested them independently. To get back to the single step, you wrap them in another subroutine:

```
sub print_number_of_wiki_entries {
  print get_number_of_wiki_entries(
    get_wikipedia_main_page( LWP::UserAgent->new() )
  ),
  "\n";
}
```

Imagine how much more difficult this process would be if you had to wait a few weeks and after you added a few dozen extra dependencies. Don't create more work than you need: test early.

Things to remember

- Write the tests before you start coding.
- Write just enough code to pass the tests, and then write more tests.
- Refactor your code into digestible parts for easy testing.

Item 96. Measure your test coverage.

It's difficult to track which pieces of your code you've tested and which pieces you still need to write tests for. You can easily see that your tests instantiate your modules and call a few methods, but it is a tedious accounting chore to ensure that you test all methods. To compound the issue, consider the different branches of execution within any given subroutine. Which paths through the code did you execute and which ones did you skip?

Take, for instance, the following module, which has a method with two branches in an `if-elsif` structure:

```
package MyModule;

use warnings;
use strict;

sub do_that_thing {
  my ( $class, $argument ) = @_;
```

```perl
  if ( $argument =~ /x/ ) {
    return 1;
  }
  elsif ( $argument =~ /y/ ) {
    return 2;
  }
  return 3;
}


1;
```

You start testing this module right away (Item 95) and you think you exercise all of the branches:

```perl
use Test::More tests => 2;
use MyModule;
is( MyModule->do_that_thing('xyz'), 1, 'got 1 back' );
is( MyModule->do_that_thing('abc'), 3, 'got 3 back' );
```

You run `prove` (Item 87) and you see that all of the tests pass:

```
% prove -Ilib t/my_module.t
t/my_module.t .. ok
All tests successful.
Files=1, Tests=2,  0 wallclock secs ( 0.03 usr  0.01 ⏎
  sys + 0.02 cusr  0.00 csys =  0.06 CPU)
Result: PASS
```

However, it's not easy to see from those results that you skipped testing an entire branch of the code. You never tested the `elsif` because you didn't give the subroutine any data that would trigger that block. Your test results are only as good as your tests.

Let `Devel::Cover` watch your tests

The solution to this problem is `Devel::Cover`, which can watch your tests as they run, collect statistics, and then present them to you. If the module uses `ExtUtils::Makemaker`, you can activate the coverage test with an environment variable:

```
% HARNESS_PERL_SWITCHES=-MDevel::Cover make test
```

If you are using `Module::Build`, you use the special `testcover` action:

```
% ./Build testcover
```

No matter which one you use, `Devel::Cover` collects its information and puts it in a cover_db/ directory. To process the information, you run the `cover` command. It prints a text summary of the results, which we have slightly mangled to fit on the page:

```
% cover

1..2
Devel::Cover 0.65: Collecting coverage data for branch,⏎
    condition, pod, statement, subroutine and time.
ok 1 - got 1 back
ok 2 - got 3 back
Devel::Cover: Writing coverage database to /Users/jmcadams⏎
    /development/effective-perl-programming/second⏎
    T_edition/esting/code/cover_db/runs/1254690988.30080⏎
    .46156
-------------------------- ------ ------ ------ ⏎
File                         stmt   bran   cond ⏎
-------------------------- ------ ------ ------ ⏎
lib/MyModule.pm              90.9   75.0    n/a ⏎
t/my_module.t               100.0    n/a    n/a ⏎
Total                        96.0   75.0    n/a ⏎
-------------------------- ------ ------ ------ ⏎

   ------ ------ ------ ------
      sub    pod   time  total
   ------ ------ ------ ------
    100.0    0.0   25.7   84.2
    100.0    n/a   74.3  100.0
    100.0  100.0   91.9
   ------ ------ ------ ------


    Writing HTML output to /Users/Snuffy/MyModule/⏎
      cover_db/coverage.html ...
```

The coverage tests break down into several categories:

- Statement coverage—you test every statement in the code.
- Branch coverage—you test each branch (e.g., each block in an `if-elsif-else` structure).

- Conditional coverage—you test each part of each condition (e.g., each side of `$a && $b`).
- Subroutine coverage—you test all subroutines.
- Pod—you document every subroutine with Pod (Item 82).

The text report gives you a summary of each of those types of coverage. `Devel::Cover` also creates several HTML files so you can find the uncovered code. `cover` gives you the path to cover_db/coverage.html at the bottom of its output. You can drill down into code through the HTML pages to see the coverage for each line of code, and decide where to start work to improve your coverage.

As you begin to add more code to your project, your coverage metrics will contain data for files that you really don't care about. For instance, third party modules and test files are normally part of your coverage metrics. In order to avoid this noise in your results, you can pass arguments to `Devel::Cover` to tell it which files to ignore and which to look at:

```
% HARNESS_PERL_SWITCHES=-MDevel::Cover=-ignore,\.t, ↵
   +select,MyModule.pm make test
```

If you want a less noisy command line, you can use the `PERL5OPT` environment variable:

```
% export \
   PERL5OPT=-MDevel::Cover=-ignore,\.t,+select,.*\.pm
% make test
```

Don't leave these options in place, though. `Devel::Cover` adds overhead to the run time of your program, so you don't want to have it execute unless you are explicitly examining code coverage. It also accumulates data, so you'll take up more and more space on disk. To clean out the previously collected data:

```
% cover -delete
```

Hard-to-cover code

Life would be perfect if you could get all coverage metrics to 100%, but sometimes that seems impossible. If you're the exceptionally careful programmer, you might create guard code that checks every possible failure:

```
sub very_careful {
  my ($file) = shift;
```

```
open my ($fh), '<', $file
  or die "Could not open $file\n";

if ( print $fh "Hello there!\n" ) {

}
else {
  warn "Could not print!\n";
  unless ( unlink $file ) {
    die "Could not unlink $file: $!\n";
  }
}

die "Could not close $file: $!\n"
  unless close($fh);
}
```

To achieve full coverage, you now have to create every failure in your tests. You have to ensure the open fails in one test, the print fails in another, and so on. You could try to set up elaborate situations where each of these fails, but you'll probably have an easier time creating mocks and overriding built-ins (Item 92) to test each failure mode.

You might also consider whether you can live with less than 100% coverage or there's another way that you can structure the code so you can test it more easily. Often, hard-to-test code is a sign of unmaintainable or bug-friendly code. Finally, you might consider the economic argument: how much work do you have to do for the benefit you'll receive? Maybe that 99% coverage is good enough while you work on more important things.

Things to remember

- Devel::Cover reports how much of your code you've tested, using several metrics.
- Mock some features to get full test coverage.
- Don't worry excessively about 100% perfect test coverage.

Item 97. Use CPAN Testers as your QA team.

The CPAN Testers (http://cpantesters.org/) is an ad-hoc group of volunteers who automatically and programmatically test every upload to CPAN.

They use a variety of Perl versions, some quite old, and a variety of operating systems and setups. Once they test a distribution, they upload their results, and also send them to the distribution author (Item 68). Some people set up their CPAN toolchains to use `CPAN::Reporter` so they upload test reports for every module that they install.

Although you'll get the most value from CPAN Testers by uploading your code to CPAN (Item 70), you can also use the same tools used by the testers to test your code internally.

Set your CPAN Testers preferences

The output of CPAN Testers is voluminous and sometimes overwhelming, but you can change how and when they notify you. The CPAN Testers allow authors to set preferences for how they receive test reports about their modules (https://prefs.cpantesters.org/). You use the same username and password that you use with your PAUSE account (Item 70). You can set your notification preferences for all of your modules, or set specific, per-distribution preferences.

Use developer versions

You don't have to wait until you have production-ready code to make use of CPAN Testers. By convention, PAUSE considers any version string with an underscore to be a developer version:

```
our $VERSION = '1.001_001';
```

PAUSE does not index a developer version, although it still puts the distribution in your CPAN directory. Since your developer version does not show up in the index files, the CPAN tools such as `cpan` do not install them. However, the CPAN Testers notice the upload, download it directly, and test it. You'll often get test reports within a couple of hours of your upload. This way, you can try something new, upload it as a developer version, and see what happens with CPAN Testers.

Most of the benefit comes from the variety of platforms that CPAN Testers use. You might, for instance, have a tricky bit of C code that needs to use the right types on various platforms and compilers. Rather than test every combination yourself, you upload, and wait for the reports.

One strategy for dealing with version numbers starts developer versions using the last production release. Suppose that last public release was 1.23. Working toward the next public release, you start with 1.23_001, then 1.23_002, and so on. When you are ready to release the next public version, you bump the version to 1.24 and start the process again.

Set up your own smoke tester

You can set up your own continuous integration system (Item 98), but you can also use the same tools that the CPAN Testers use (although you might have to set up your own CPAN if you want to keep your modules off of the real CPAN). The CPAN Testers Smoke Tools page (http://wiki.cpantesters.org/wiki/SmokeTools) gives you the details, but you'll want to check out one of these systems:

- CPAN::Reporter
- CPANPLUS::YACSmoke
- CPAN::YACSmoke
- POE::Component::CPAN::YACSmoke

Once you've installed them, you can configure or modify these tools for your specific needs. If you don't want to send test reports to the public testers' database, you can send them just to yourself. A complete setup is beyond the scope of this book, but CPAN Testers are a helpful bunch. You can get help on their mailing list (*testers@cpan.org*).

Things to remember

- Configure your CPAN Testers notification preferences.
- Use a development version to let CPAN Testers check your development code.
- Set up your own smoke testing tools.

Item 98. Set up a continuous build system.

As you develop your code, you can get tunnel vision and run the tests for only the module that you are currently working on. However, it is not uncommon for changes in one module to cause tests to fail for another. You should periodically run your entire test suite or, even better, have your test suite run automatically on a regular basis.

Continuous integration systems are frameworks that handle the tasks of regularly building your code and executing the tests packaged with that code. These frameworks can range from as simple as locally scheduling a call to `prove` to using a full-featured system like Cruise Control to monitor your version control system and run your test suite on each new commit.

Periodically run `prove`

One of the simplest systems that you can set up is merely to e-mail yourself the results of your test suite running periodically. Just schedule an e-mail of the results of the `prove` command to be sent to you:

```
# in your crontab
prove -I/path/to/code/lib /path/to/code/t/*t | \
    sendmail -t me@example.com -s "build results"
```

Of course, if you don't make changes for a while, you will end up getting the same e-mail over and over again. Also, if you break your build, there might be a long delay before you notice the failure.

Use a pre-commit hook

Consider adding a pre-commit hook to your source control system. This hook can verify that all tests pass before it allows you to commit any changes. Setting up a hook is trivial with most modern version control systems.

With *Git*, for example, you add some code to an executable file named .git/hooks/pre-commit. A few lines of shell code can be used to run `prove` every time you commit:

```
#!/bin/sh
set -e
prove -b t/*t
```

If you use a build system like `ExtUtils::MakeMaker`, you can force *Git* to run your full build and test suite for every commit:

```
#!/bin/sh
set -e
perl Makefile.PL && make test && make realclean
```

Subversion can use identical hooks in a near-identical location, [repo]/hooks/pre-commit, where [repo] is the location of your *Subversion* repository.

Other source control systems that allow for pre-commit hooks can take advantage of a similar setup. Consult the documentation for your version control system to determine the details.

As your test suite grows, running all tests for every commit might get annoying, especially if you commit frequently. You have to make a decision about how much time you and your team are willing to wait to get results in order to keep a functioning build and test suite.

Use Smolder to aggregate test results

Smolder is a good Perl-based option for aggregating your test results. With *Smolder*, you run your tests through `prove` or your regular build script, archive the results, and upload them to the *Smolder* server for analysis and presentation.

To begin running `smolder`, download it from http://sourceforge.net/projects/smolder/ and follow the instructions in the INSTALL file to get the server up and running on your system.

Once you are set up, run your tests through `prove` or your test script, and send the archived results to your *Smolder* server:

```
% prove --archive=/tmp/build.tgz \
  /path/to/tests/t/*t && smolder_smoke_signal \
  --server smolder.example.com --username username \
  --password password --file /tmp/build.tgz \
  --project MyProject
```

The server will display your test results through a nice Web-based interface, track history, and bug you only when something goes wrong.

You can even take advantage of a module like `SmokeRunner::Multi` to monitor branches in your repository, run tests when changes occur, and upload the results to Smolder automatically. This functionality closely mirrors that contained in the popular continuous build system, Cruise Control.

The previous two examples simply run tests against the code on your local disk on a periodic basis. This can be bad because you might have local changes that cause tests to fail, and until they are resolved, your e-mail or build aggregator will report test failure. You could quickly hack something together to automatically check out code from your version control system and run your tests off of that code. But before you start cobbling a system like this together, take some time to look into continuous build systems that monitor your version control system.

Cruise Control

Cruise Control (http://cruisecontrol.sourceforge.net/) is a Java framework that performs continuous integration and testing of your code. With a little modification to your Perl project, you can have it up and running in *Cruise Control* in no time.

Building in Ant

In order for your project to run in *Cruise Control*, it helps if you can build and test it using *Apache Ant*. If your project uses `Module::Build` as a build script, your build.xml file for `ant` would look something like:

```
<project name="myproject" default="all">
  <macrodef name="module.build">
    <attribute name="action" default="build" />
    <sequential>
      <exec executable="/usr/bin/perl"
        failonerror="true">
        <arg value="Build" />
        <arg value="@{action}" />
        <env key='PERL5LIB' path="lib:${env.PERL5LIB}" />
        <env key="PERL_TEST_HARNESS_DUMP_TAP"
          path="/project_dir/target/test-results/"/>
      </exec>
    </sequential>
  </macrodef>

  <target name="all"
    depends="clean, configure, build, test"/>

  <target name="clean">
    <module.build action="clean"/>
  </target>
```

```
    <target name="configure">
      <exec executable="/usr/bin/perl" failonerror="true">
        <arg value="Build.PL"/>
          <env key='PERL5LIB' path="lib:${env.PERL5LIB}" />
      </exec>
    </target>

    <target name="build" depends="configure">
      <module.build action="build"/>
    </target>

    <target name="test" depends="build">
      <module.build action="test"/>
    </target>
  </project>
```

At first, this file might seem intimidating, but it is actually quite simple. All it does is define a project, in this case, *myproject*. It then wraps some build targets for cleaning up, running Build.PL, building your project, and testing your project. The name of the project is up to you. You want to name it something meaningful to you and your team.

You also want to tweak the PERL_TEST_HARNESS_DUMP_TAP environment variable. This variable tells the test harness where to store a copy of the test output. This is where *Cruise Control* will eventually collect information about each test run. This will be a volatile directory, so you probably want to keep it out of your main source tree, or get your version control system to ignore it.

After you finish your build.xml file, you should be able to configure, build, test, and clean up your project using ant:

```
% ant configure
% ant build
% ant test
% ant clean
```

This build.xml file is based on a more robust build.xml found in the documentation of TAP::Formatter::TeamCity. Be sure to check it out if you need more flexibility.

Formatting your output

Getting your project building and testing with ant is a big step, but it isn't the only change that you need to make to your code to get *Cruise Control* to work correctly with your build system. At this point, you could set up *Cruise Control* to know whether your test suite passed or failed as a whole, but that's about it. In order to get *Cruise Control* to interpret your test results and give you test-by-test results, you need to emit JUnit test output XML instead of TAP from your tests.

If you are fortunate enough to be using Module::Build, this is as easy as subclassing Module::Build, overriding a method, and then having your Build.PL file use your subclass.

First, make a subclass that overrides tap_harness_args, and make TAP::Formatter::JUnit the preferred formatter:

```
package MyModuleBuild;
use parent 'Module::Build';

sub tap_harness_args {
  return { formatter_class => 'TAP::Formatter::JUnit' };
}

1;
```

Then, change your Build.PL file to use MyModuleBuild:

```
use MyModuleBuild;

my $build = MyModuleBuild->new(
  module_name  => 'MyModule',
  dist_version => 1,
);


$build->create_build_script;
```

Now when you run ant test, you should see some JUnit XML on your screen and find some XML files in the directory that you assigned to the PERL_TEST_HARNESS_DUMP_TAP environment variable.

If you aren't using Module::Build, it is not as easy to change the output formatter. You might want to change your testing target to just use prove:

```
<target name="test" depends="compile">
  <exec executable="/usr/bin/prove"
    failonerror="true">
    <arg value="--formatter=TAP::Formatter::JUnit"/>
    <arg value="t/"/>
    <env key="PERL_TEST_HARNESS_DUMP_TAP"
      path="/project_dir/target/test-results/"/>
  </exec>
</target>
```

Setting up Cruise Control

Now that you have your project building with `ant` and emitting JUnit test output XML, you are ready to get rolling with *Cruise Control*. The first thing that you need to do is to download and install the framework. Find the download link on its project page.

After you download *Cruise Control*, uncompress the file that you downloaded. Move the resulting folder to wherever you like to store executable files on your system. By default, *Cruise Control* uses this folder to store data, so make sure it has room to grow.

Configure the system by editing the config.xml file in the base directory of *Cruise Control*. Remove the example project and add an entry for your project:

```
<cruisecontrol>
  <project name="myproject">
    <listeners>
      <currentbuildstatuslistener
        file="/cc_dir/projects/myproject/status.txt"/>
    </listeners>
    <bootstrappers>
      <antbootstrapper anthome="apache-ant-1.7.0"
        buildfile="/project_dir/build.xml"
        target="clean"/>
    </bootstrappers>
    <modificationset quietperiod="0">
      <filesystem folder="/project_dir/"/>
    </modificationset>
    <schedule interval="300">
```

```
    <ant anthome="apache-ant-1.7.0"
      antWorkingDir="/project_dir/"
      buildfile="/project_dir/build.xml"/>
  </schedule>
  <log>
    <merge dir="/project_dir/test-results/t/"/>
  </log>
  </project>
</cruisecontrol>
```

Name your project something that you can recognize in the *Cruise Control* interface. Replace /cc_dir with the path to your *Cruise Control*. Everywhere that you see "myproject," replace that with your project name. Everywhere that you see "project_dir," replace that with the path to your Perl source code.

After you get `config.xml` set up, start *Cruise Control:*

```
% ./cruisecontrol.sh
```

You should now be able to navigate to http://localhost:8080 to see your continuous build system in action. Now that you have a basic setup, you can customize *Cruise Control* to better fit your development environment.

Other options

There are many more continuous build systems that you can integrate with your development. `Test::AutoBuild` is a Perl-based system that works well with Perl projects. *Hudson* is another popular Java-based server that can read specially formatted output emitted by `Test::Harness`.

You may be constrained by what your company has already standardized on, or you may be starting from scratch. The important thing is not what system you use, but that you have a system in place.

Things to remember

- Automatically run your tests with a continuous integration system.
- Use a full-featured continuous build system that works with Perl projects.
- Any continuous build system is better than the perfect one that doesn't exist.

11 | Warnings

Perl can be quite helpful in spotting suspicious code and letting you know about it. Most of the debugging skills you may have learned from other languages are just as applicable to Perl. When your program spits out pages and pages of warnings, start with the first ones.

There are several ways to enable warnings. Old-style Perl uses the -w switch on the command line:

```
% perl -w program.pl
```

You can also use command-line switches on the shebang line inside the program:

```
#!perl -w
```

Modern Perl uses the warnings pragma inside the code (Item 99).

```
use warnings;
```

The trick to knowing how to handle the warnings is to figure out not only what Perl is trying to tell you, but when it is telling you. Some problems it can spot just by looking at the code, while for others it has to wait until something questionable happens.

In addition to that, Perl has a wonderful feature called **taint checking** that can track external data throughout your program, and keep your program from passing it to external programs. This feature works to prevent people from feeding bad data to your program to trick it into doing odd things with other programs.

Don't take these warnings for granted; they are indicators of fragility in your program. That doesn't mean, however, that you have to completely solve the source of every warning. Perl has features that let you turn off warnings within a scope. If you understand the warning, accept the risks it indicates, and still need to keep the code the same, you can tell Perl not to complain about it.

Item 99. Enable warnings to let Perl spot suspicious code.

Perl can warn you when it sees something suspicious, whether while it's compiling your code or running it. Warnings are a valuable development tool that you shouldn't ignore. If you aren't used to writing warnings-free code, after a couple of months of Perl's incessant and unflagging harassment, you will start to write better code and see fewer and fewer warnings. Even then, you still should use Perl's warnings.

Perl's warnings are turned off by default for backward compatibility with the quick-and-dirty scripts with which Perl got its start. There are several ways that you can enable warnings. Starting with Perl 5.6, you can enable warnings per file, which is the preferred way:

```
use warnings;  # put this at the top of every file
```

If you haven't added the use warnings line to the files in your project, you can enable all warnings across all files with the -w switch. You can do that on the command line to enable them for one run:

```
% perl -w myscript
```

You can enable them inside a program by appending the -w flag to the she-bang line:

```
#!/usr/bin/perl -w
```

You can selectively enable or disable warnings, too (Item 100).

Compile time warnings

Perl can spot some suspicious problems at compile time. Consider the simple program that has an addition as its single statement:

```
use warnings;
$foo = 1;
1 + 2;
```

When you enable warnings with -w and check your syntax with -c, perl tells you that the addition is useless since you don't do anything with the result, and that a variable you use only once is probably a mistake:

```
% perl -cw program.pl
Useless use of a constant in void context
```

```
Name "main::foo" used only once: possible typo
/home/snuffy/program.pl syntax OK
```

Run time warnings

Run time warnings come from the things that `perl` can't catch by merely examining the source, and as such, are often the most annoying. Consider printing the keys and values for a hash:

```
use warnings;

foreach my $cat ( keys %microchips ) {
  print "$cat --> $microchips{$cat}\n";
}
```

Can you see where the warning might come from just by looking at the code? Neither can `perl`, at least until it starts iterating through a hash that has an undefined value:

```
my %microchips = (
   'Mimi'    => 123,
   'Buster'  => undef,
   'Roscoe'  => 345,
);
```

When `perl` runs into the key for `Buster`, it prints an undefined value and issues a warning:

```
Use of uninitialized value $microchips{"Buster"}⏎
   in concatenation (.) or string
```

Although annoying, that particular warning is less annoying that it used to be. Starting with Perl 5.10, the warning tells you what had the undefined value, in this case `$microchips{"Buster"}`.

Since you can't catch the run time warnings by looking at the source, the best way to catch these is with a rigorous test suite using unexpected data and unusual situations to cover every condition (Item 96).

Get more with `diagnostics`

If you are just starting out with warnings, you're probably going to run into one that you don't understand. Even if you've been using Perl for a long time, you might run into a warning that you haven't seen before. To learn more about a warning, you can look in the *perldiag* documentation to get a detailed explanation of the error. Most of those explanations suggest possible problems that would trigger the warning.

There's an easier way to get the details, though, so you don't have to dig through the documentation. You can use the `diagnostics` pragma to turn the short error messages into the long ones:

```
# use warnings;
use diagnostics;
$foo = 1;
```

The output from the program is much more verbose now:

```
% perl -c program.pl
Name "main::foo" used only once: possible typo ...
    (W once) Typographical errors often show up as unique
    variable names. If you had a good reason for having a
    unique name, then just mention it again somehow to
    suppress the message.  The our declaration is provided
    for this purpose.

    NOTE: This warning detects symbols that have been used
    only once so $c, @c, %c, *c, &c, sub c{}, c(), and c
    (the filehandle or format) are considered the same; if
    a program uses $c only once but also uses any of the
    others it will not trigger this warning.
```

Warnings in production

Enabling warnings in production is a contentious issue, though, so be prepared for some people to scream or jump up and down if you mention this. It's much like bracing style, tabs versus spaces, and Coke versus Pepsi. Decide for yourself which side you are on.

Run time warnings impose a small speed penalty on programs, and it is also not a good idea to present unexpected or spurious warning messages to users. In general, warnings are meant to be seen by developers, not users. You should turn off warnings for application code that is released to the world. Since you can selectively enable warnings and check if they are enabled (Item 100), you can turn them back on when you need to debug your program.

One of the big problems is that the warnings change between versions of Perl. Not only are there new warnings, but there is the chance that some warnings have become fatal that were previously innocuous. Are you willing to take on that risk when you deploy your application?

The people who insist on "all warnings all the time" are probably not the people who have been called in to work in the wee hours of a weekend to find out that an upgrade to `perl` made an otherwise warning-free and working application start spewing new warnings and filling up a disk, despite the facts that the application was still working just fine and no one was monitoring it for warnings.

If you want to leave warnings on, that's fine, but you can also re-enable them any time that you like. It's a completely reversible decision. At the enterprise level, you want to use something like `Log::Log4perl` (Item 113) to record messages from your well-tested, mission-critical code, along with a proper test suite that catches all the warnings before you deploy.

Things to remember

- Check for compile-time warnings with `perl -cw`.
- Enable per-file warnings with `use warnings`.
- Get more information about a particular warning with `use diagnostics`.

Item 100. Use lexical warnings to selectively turn on or off complaints.

Warnings call out code "smells" that aren't serious enough to stop your program, but you still need to pay attention to.

You might not care that `$number` is uninitialized. When Perl converts it to a number, it turns into zero, which is just fine with this addition:

```
my $number;
my $value = $number + 2;
```

However, Perl complains about that when you enable `warnings`:

```
Use of uninitialized value $number in addition (+)
```

You don't really care that `$number` doesn't have a value because the right thing happens anyway. This is a simple example, but you'll run into situations where it's more painful to eliminate the warning rather than just ignore it. In those cases, you can temporarily turn off warnings.

The `warnings` pragma is lexically scoped, so you can wrap the offending code in a block and unimport it temporarily:

```
{
  no warnings;

  my $number;
  my $value = $number + 2;
}
```

There's a small problem with that, though. It turns off all warnings. You might miss other important warnings that way.

The `warnings` pragma groups warnings into categories that you can selectively enable or disable. For the complete list, see the `warnings` documentation. In this case, you can turn off just the `uninitialized` warning:

```
{
  no warnings 'uninitialized';

  my $number;
  my $value = $number + 2;
}
```

Making some warnings fatal

You might hate some problems so much that you want them to be fatal errors instead of warnings. For instance, you normally get a warning when `perl` can't completely convert a string to a number:

```
use warnings;
my $sum = '123buster' + 5;
print "The sum is $sum\n";
```

You get the warning, but `perl` keeps going and gives you an answer:

```
Argument "123buster" isn't numeric in addition (+)
The sum is 128
```

If that should never happen in your code, you can make it fatal:

```
use warnings FATAL => 'numeric';
my $sum = '123buster' + 5;
print "The sum is $sum\n";
```

Now, you only get the warning, because the program stops when you try to add the non-numeric value:

```
Argument "123buster" isn't numeric in addition (+)
```

Use predefined warning categories in your modules

You can issue warnings based on the lexical warnings settings, too. Instead of using `warn` to issue the message, use `warnif` from the `warnings` pragma. You can specify the category of your warning, too:

```
sub create {
  warnings::warnif( 'deprecated',
    'create is deprecated, use new instead' );
  ...;
}
```

If you are using `Carp` (Item 102), you can check that a warning category is enabled before triggering `carp`:

```
use Carp;

sub create {
  carp('create is deprecated, use new instead')
    if warnings::enabled('deprecated');
  ...;
}
```

Although `warnif` respects requests for fatal warnings, there isn't a way for you to check if a particular category of warnings should be fatal before you call `carp`.

Make your own warning categories

Lexical warnings don't stop here. If you find that none of the predefined categories meets your needs, you can define your own and respond to requests for turning them on and off just as if they were predefined categories.

Things to remember

- Disable warnings within a scope with `no warnings`.
- Selectively disable classes of warnings if you know you want to ignore them.
- Promote some warnings to fatal errors.

Item 101. Use `die` to generate exceptions.

Some people have habits left over from the old C-programmer style, where they return a success code after every function. For instance, to signal an error from a subroutine, they might return `undef`:

```perl
sub do_work {
   my $task = shift;

   if ( $task < 0 ) {
      return;  # error, returning undef
   }

   ...;
}
```

This works okay, although you have to do a lot of work to check that their subroutine worked:

```perl
my $value = do_work($task);

if ( defined $value ) {
   print "It worked and I got [$value]!\n";
}
else {
   print "Something went wrong, but I don't know what!\n";
}
```

In case of an error, you know that something went wrong, but you don't know what went wrong. You could `die` when you encounter a problematic scenario, which allows you to give a meaningful error message:

```perl
sub do_work {
   my $task = shift;
```

```
    if ( $task < 0 ) {
      die("Task [$task] should be greater than zero");
    }
    ...;
  }
```

That's not much of change, but it also has another benefit: it forces you to handle the problem, since the program stops otherwise. You can catch this with `eval`. If `do_work` dies, the `eval` catches it and puts the `die` message in `$@`:

```
  my $value = eval { do_work(@tasks) };
  if ($@) {
    # handle the error
  }
```

You have to check `$@` immediately after the `eval`, before anything else has a chance to change it (Item 103).

The `eval-if` idiom acts as you might expect from `try-catch` in other languages, although you can have `try-catch` in Perl, too (Item 103).

It gets even better, though. You can `die` with a reference, which can be an object that represents your error. You might, for instance, have an error-recording module to create your error objects:

```
  sub do_work {
    my $task = shift;

    if ( $task < 0 ) {
      die MyErrors->fatal("Task should be greater than 0");
    }
    ...;
  }
```

When the `eval` fails and you find your object in `$@`, you can deal with it as with any other object. That gives you much more flexibility:

```
  my $value = eval { do_work(@tasks) };

  if ( my $error = $@ and ref $error ) {
    print "I found an error at level ", $error->level, "\n";
```

```
    print "The message was ", $error->message, "\n";
}
```

Calling `die` when you encounter a problem doesn't fit every situation. You don't need to do it explicitly, either, if you use `autodie` (Item 27) to handle errors from Perl built-ins. For more fancy exception handling, use something like `Try::Tiny` (Item 103).

Things to remember

- Use `die` to generate an exception.
- Give `die` a reference or object to pass structured error information.
- Catch exceptions with `eval`.

Item 102. Use `Carp` to get stack traces.

If your code is going to `die` or emit a warning, it's nice if it can give you as much information as possible about what is going on at the time of the failure. One of the most valuable pieces of information is the call stack. Unfortunately, Perl's built-in `die` and `warn` functions don't provide that information.

Here's a series of subroutines that call `randomly_fail`, and some of them call each other. When you run this program, you don't know where it will fail.

```
sub randomly_fail {
    die 'ouch!' if int( rand(100) ) % 10 == 0;
}

sub caller_one {
    randomly_fail();
}

sub caller_two {
    caller_one();
    randomly_fail();
}

sub caller_three() {
    caller_two();
```

```
    randomly_fail();
  }

  while (1) {
    caller_three();
  }
```

When you run the program, you see that it dies (as expected); you just don't know where, or how long the program ran:

```
% perl randomly_fail.pl
ouch! at die.pl line 2.
```

That's not a very informative error message. Of course it died at line 2: that's where you have the `die`. You already know that! It's the same situation with `warn`.

Carp gives you more information

`Carp`, a core module, gives you more useful error messages than `die` or `warn` do. Use `croak` and `Carp` in place of `warn` and `die`, respectively, and you'll get a full stack trace from the perspective of the calling function. The error message tells you not where the code stopped, but one level above that. You find out who called the subroutine:

```
package Bar;
use Carp;
sub fail { croak "Ribbit!" }

package main;

Bar::fail();
```

Although this program stops at line 3, it's really line 7 that caused the problem by calling `Bar::fail`, so that's what `croak` reports:

```
Ribbit! at carp.pl line 7
```

That's the message you get when the caller is in a different package. `Carp` does its work by crawling up the call stack until it finds a package change.

If `Carp` doesn't find a change in packages in the call stack, it gives you a full stack trace. Now you can improve on the first example by changing that `die` to a `croak`:

```perl
use Carp;

sub randomly_fail {
  croak 'ouch' if int( rand(100) ) % 10 == 0;
}

sub caller_one {
  randomly_fail();
}

sub caller_two {
  caller_one();
  randomly_fail();
}

sub caller_three() {
  caller_two();
  randomly_fail();
}

while (1) {
  caller_three();
}
```

Running the program a couple of times shows you the chain of events that led up to the failure for each run:

```
% perl carp.pl
ouch at carp.pl line 4
  main::randomly_fail() called at carp.pl line 8
  main::caller_one() called at carp.pl line 12
  main::caller_two() called at carp.pl line 17
  main::caller_three() called at carp.pl line 22

% perl carp.pl
ouch at carp.pl line 4
  main::randomly_fail() called at carp.pl line 18
  main::caller_three() called at carp.pl line 22
```

If this were an interesting program that you were actually maintaining, you would now have a way to trace the failure.

`confess` always gives a backtrace

You don't have to stay in the same package to get the full stack backtrace. If you change that `croak` to `confess`, you get everything:

```
package Bar;
use Carp;
sub fail { confess "Ribbit!" }


package main;


bar::fail();
```

Now you get the stack backtrace even though the program died in a different package than the caller:

```
Ribbit! at carp.pl line 3
  bar::fail() called at carp.pl line 7
```

This makes `confess` a good debugging tool, but you probably don't want it for production. If you aren't debugging, stick with `croak`. You can turn a `croak` into a `confess` by setting `$Carp::Verbose` to a true value, meaning that you can localize its effect:

```
{
  local $Carp::Verbose = 1;


  Bar::fail();
}
```

If you want to change all `croaks` to `confesses`, you can also just change the `Carp` import:

```
use Carp 'verbose';
```

That way, you code using `croak`, but when you need to debug the program, you selectively and temporarily get the full stack trace.

Things to remember

- Use `Carp` to get information on the code that caused the error or warning.
- Use `confess` to get a full stack backtrace.

Item 103. Handle exceptions properly.

Perl doesn't have a built-in exception handling mechanism, so you have to fake it with `eval` and `if` (Item 101):

```
my $value = eval { die "throw an error"; };
if ($@) {
  warn "I caught an error: $@";
}
```

There's a big problem. You can `die` with any value you like, including a false one. In this case, `$@` is false and the `if` doesn't catch it:

```
my $value = eval { die ''; };
if ($@) {
  warn "I should have caught an error: $@";
}
```

`Try::Tiny` does it right

The right way to do this is best shown in the `Try::Tiny` module. There are several exception handling modules on CPAN, but this one is small and has no problematic dependencies. If you want to do its job with standard Perl, you just have to follow its example.

First, you have to handle `$@` properly. That's trickier than most people think. You need to avoid two problems: you don't want to change the value of `$@` for another `eval` level that wraps you, and you don't want an `eval` that you nest, even if it is hidden behind a function call, to change your `$@`. You start your process by localizing `$@` before you use it. Once you do your `eval`, you immediately save `$@` into your own variable so nothing else changes it. This is a snippet from `Try::Tiny` that shows the meat of the solution:

```
my ( $error, $failed );
{
  local $@;  # protect changes to up level
  $failed = not eval {
    die "throw an error";
    return 1;
  };
  $error = $@;  # protect from changes from below
}
```

```
if ($failed) {
  warn "Caught an error: $error";
}
```

The `Try::Tiny` module handles the boilerplate for you, and gives you the common try/catch syntax:

```
use Try::Tiny;

try {
  die "throw an error";
}
catch {
  warn "Caught an error: $_";
};
```

Notice that the `catch` block ends in a semicolon. It's a Perl statement, just like `eval`. Also, it stores the error in `$_` instead of `$@` (for all the reasons why it had to do the gymnastics earlier).

You can also `die` with a reference (Item 101), and then use the `given-when` syntax (Item 24) to filter the error:

```
use Try::Tiny;
use 5.010;

try {
  die MyError->new(...);
}
catch {
  when ( $_->type eq 'IO' )    { ... }
  when ( $_->type eq 'Fatal' ) { ... }
  default { ... };
};
```

If you want to ignore errors, you simply neglect to catch them:

```
use Try::Tiny;

try {
  die "throw an error";
};
```

Try::Tiny gotchas

Sometimes it looks like you are using `Try::Tiny` when you aren't. This example, which forgets to load the module, is still valid Perl syntax that doesn't complain, even under strictures (Item 3):

```
use strict;

try {
  die "throw an error";  # always dies
}
catch {
  warn "Caught an error: $_";
};
```

Also, since the blocks in `try-catch` are really Perl subroutines, you shouldn't use `return` in them since that would confuse them:

```
try {
  die "throw an error";
  return;  # WRONG!
}
catch {
  warn "Caught an error: $_";
};
```

Things to remember

- Use `eval` to catch errors and examine them in `$@`.
- Handling `$@` is tricky, but `Try::Tiny` does it correctly.

Item 104. Track dangerous data with taint checking.

Taint checking is a Perl run time feature that tracks the flow of data inside a program. Perl marks as "tainted" data that are derived from user input or the outside world in general, such as command-line arguments, environment variables, or file or stream input. You won't be able to pass any of this data to external programs because Perl will stop your program when you try to.

You can enable taint checking with the `-T` switch:

```
% perl -T program.pl
```

You can also enable it on the shebang line:

```
#!perl -T
```

In some cases, such as running under setuid, `perl` automatically turns on taint checking for you.

If you specify `-T` on the command line and try to run the program with `perl` explicitly, you'll get an error:

```
% perl program.pl
"-T" is on the #! line, it must also be used on the ⏎
   command line
```

To give you an idea of how taint checking works, consider a program that takes a glob pattern from the user and passes it to the external `grep` program:

```
#!perl -T
print "Enter a grep pattern: ";
chomp( my $pattern = <STDIN> );
print `grep $pattern *`;
```

If you run this with taint checking enabled, `perl` stops your program before it has a chance to do anything:

```
Insecure dependency in `` while running with -T switch
```

You've gotten the data in the variable `$pattern` directly from standard input, and it could be anything. It is a bad idea to send user input directly to the shell—suppose the user types in something with special characters, such as the `;` that starts a new command:

```
% perl program.pl
enter pattern: ; rm *
```

Under taint checking, you must sanitize your data before you use them with external processes. The only approved way to untaint data is a regular expression match with capture variables. The best way to untaint data is to construct a very specific pattern that matches what you will allow (what Mark Jason Dominus calls the "Prussian Approach"). For instance, if you want people to input only letters, the `.`, and the `*` quantifier in their `grep` patterns, you match only those characters:

```
#!perl -T
```

```
my $tainted_data = <STDIN>;

my $untainted_data = do {
  if ( $tainted_data =~ m/^([a-z.*])$/i ) {
    $1;
  }
  else {
    die
      "The pattern can only contain letters, ., or *!\n";
  }
};


print `grep '$untainted_data' *`;
```

In this example, you fail if the input isn't exactly what you expect. If you miss something that you should have allowed, you don't have a security problem, but you have to adjust your regular expression. The other way around—if you forget to exclude something you should have—you still have a problem. If that's an overly strict approach, you have to decide how strict to be on your own. However, when dealing with external programs, paranoia is a virtue.

You think you've fixed everything, but now when you run the program, you get a different error:

```
Insecure $ENV{PATH} while running with -T switch
```

Perl has to find the `grep` program, so it has to start looking through `$ENV{PATH}`, but that also comes from outside the program so it's tainted as well. When Perl tries to use it, taint checking kicks in and stops the program. To fix this, you can set `$ENV{PATH}` to the empty string, so it's no longer tainted, and use the absolute path to the command that you want (which ensures you get the one that you want):

```
$ENV{PATH} = '';

...;


print `/usr/bin/grep '$untainted_data' *`;
```

You can also set `$ENV{PATH}` to absolute paths, but those directories can't be writeable by the owner or group running your program. That takes a bit more work.

For more information about taint checking, see the *perlsec* documentation or the "Security" chapter in *Mastering Perl*.[1] If you want to add taint checking to existing programs, start with taint warnings (Item 105).

Things to remember

- Use taint checking to prevent external data from affecting external commands.
- Untaint data with a regular expression and captures.
- Inside your program, adjust your PATH environment variable to trusted directories.

Item 105. Start with taint warnings for legacy code.

Taint checking is a Perl development tool that helps you find spots in your program where you pass "untrusted" data to the outside world (Item 104). Once it is enabled, any input that comes from outside of your program is "tainted," including command-line arguments, CGI input, data from files, the values in %ENV, and so on. Perl marks the data with a special flag. Any data derived from tainted values are also tainted, and Perl kills your program when you try to pass those data outside the program.

For older code, turning on taint checking might mean that you don't get back to working code for a long, long time as you track down all of the things that you have to adjust, rewrite, or otherwise work around.

You still want to make your legacy code taint-safe, so Perl supplies the -t switch. It does the same work as its big brother -T, but merely warns when it finds a problem. You can use it on the command line:

```
% perl -t program.pl
```

Or, as with any command-line switch, you can use -t on the shebang line:

```
#!/usr/bin/perl -t
```

Now run the same program with taint warnings instead:

```
#!perl -t

system("ls -l");
```

---

1. brian d foy, *Mastering Perl* (Sebastopol, CA: O'Reilly Media, 2007).

Taint checking issues two warnings instead of dying on the first problem, and still runs the operation:

```
Insecure $ENV{PATH} while running with -t switch...
Insecure dependency in system while running with -t ⏎
   switch...
   ...
```

You enable this on your taint-unsafe legacy code and watch the output logs to identify trouble spots without that much downtime. As you find problems, you can fix them.

In this case, taint checking doesn't like the setting in $ENV{PATH}. The person running the program can set PATH to be anything he likes. As such, the program can't know which ls it will run. You need to set $ENV{PATH} to a list of absolute paths to directories that the owner and group running the script do not have write permissions to. The easy way is not to depend on $ENV{PATH} at all. Instead, specify the path to the command in the system call:

```perl
#!perl -t

$ENV{PATH} = '';  # or '/bin' or other safe directory

system("/bin/ls");
```

Now you've eliminated the two taint warnings.

Once you are confident that you have a safe program, you can promote your code to the full -T. Your program still might blow up on you in rare cases, but at least it shouldn't die on every run, since you've already fixed most of the problems.

Remember, -t is only a tool for bringing legacy code up to snuff. The -t is not a tool for new projects, where you should use -T from the start.

Things to remember

- Be careful with taint-checking in legacy code.
- Use the -t switch to enable taint warnings on legacy code.
- Use -T for full taint-checking on new code.

12 | Databases

Perl's DBI module makes it extremely easy to interact with almost every popular database server (and many not-so-popular ones). Although the mechanics are quite simple and straightforward, there are many higher-level pitfalls.

Database interaction is a specialized topic, since it requires knowledge of a lot more than just Perl. You have to know about the query language, the peculiarities of the database server, and many other extra-Perl things. It's an extremely big topic that deserves a book of its own. However, there are a few things that improve your Perl database experience right away.

We're purposely ignoring some topics, such as KiokuDB, document database systems such as CouchDB, and Object Relational Mappers (ORMs) such as DBIx::Class. All of these topics deserve their own books, too, and they are topics that you should investigate further.

Item 106. Prepare your SQL statements to reuse work and save time.

There are several steps that go into a database query. You construct the query, the database server parses it and figures out how to handle it, the database server handles it, and you get your results. Any one of those steps can be a bottleneck.

Perl's DBI module allows you to make one-shot queries:

```
use DBI;

my $dbh = DBI->connect(...);

my $rv = $dbh->do('DROP TABLE table');

my $array =
  $dbh->selectall_arrayref('SELECT * FROM table');
```

You might quickly convert that `selectall_arrayref` into a loop that makes the same SELECT, but for specific records:

```
foreach my $id (@ids) {
  my $array = $dbh->selectall_arrayref(
    "SELECT * FROM table WHERE id = $id");
}
```

Although that particular query is simple and easy to handle, imagine something much more complex, involving several tables, intricate joins, or sub-selects. Every iteration of that loop starts from scratch, even though most of the details of the query don't change.

If you repeatedly make the same query, although perhaps with different values, after the first query you can skip the steps where you construct the query and the database server parses it and plans how to handle it. In complex queries, those two steps can take up most of the time involved. One colleague constructed a query that took five minutes, much too long for his purposes even though he did everything he could to optimize it. Since he had to call this query several times, his program took a long time to complete. He eventually figured out that 90 percent of that time was just the database planning the query, and once planned, it actually ran very fast. His problem wasn't the query speed at all.

Instead of issuing one-shot queries repeatedly, you can **prepare** a query, which builds and plans the query but doesn't actually execute it. You can reuse this prepared query as many times as you like without having to redo the work to create it. The `prepare` method handles all of the details for you, and you can use placeholders (Item 107) to stand in for the data you fill in later. The `prepare` command returns a statement handle which you store in `$sth`:

```
use DBI;
my $dbh = DBI->connect(...)
  or die 'unable to connect to database';

my $sth =
  $dbh->prepare('SELECT * FROM table WHERE id = ?');
```

Constructing a query with a placeholder allows the database to cache the query. If your database is optimized for caching, it parses the query and stores the execution plan so that subsequent queries use the precalculated execution plan.

When you are ready to run the query, you call the `execute` method on the statement handle, passing the parameters to fill in the placeholders. In the loop, each time you execute the query, the database gets a cache hit and does not reparse the query, making things faster:

```
foreach my $id (@ids) {
  my $array = $dbh->execute($id);
}
```

Preparing multiple statements to handle different situations

Once you prepare a query, you have to use it exactly as-is. If you need to change the number of parameters, the table names, or something else, you need to prepare different queries. You can, however, prepare as many queries as you like and select the appropriate ones when you need them.

Suppose you want to select all of the records for the values in a list. In SQL, you could use `IN`:

```
SELECT * FROM table WHERE id IN ( ... )
```

How many things go into that `IN` list, though? You have to use a fixed number of placeholders in your `prepare` statement. This statement takes exactly two parameters:

```
my $sth = $dbh->prepare(
    'SELECT * FROM table WHERE id IN ( ?, ? )'
    );
```

In your program, though, suppose you need to handle anywhere between 1 and 10 parameters at a time. Since DBI doesn't handle varying parameter counts for you, you have to handle it yourself. Here's a wrapper around a database handle (using dependency injection, Item 89). When you construct a new object in `MyDBI::VariadicPrepare`, it creates several prepared queries. Each queries handles a different number of parameters, and you store each in a statement handle as part of the object hash:

```
package MyDBI::VariadicPrepare::Cache;

sub new {
  my ( $class, $dbh ) = @_;
  my $self = bless { dbh => $dbh }, $class;
```

```
    for my $num ( 1 .. 10 ) {
      $self->{ 'sth_' . $num } = $self->{dbh}->prepare(
        sprintf(
          'SELECT value FROM my_table WHERE id IN (%s)',
          join( ',', ('?') x $num ) )
      );
    }
    return $self;
  }
```

Instead of calling `execute` directly, you provide a wrapper subroutine that selects the correct prepared statement based on the number of parameters:

```
  sub do_something {
    my ( $self, @values ) = @_;
    if ( @values > 10 ) {
      die 'I can only support 10 values or less';
    }
    $self->{ 'sth_' . @values }->execute(@values);
  }
```

This works, but it is ugly. Also, in this specific case, you limited yourself to only ten values for your SELECT statement. To make matters worse, you might never use most of the `prepare` statements you precomputed, potentially wasting a lot of time preparing complex and lengthy statement handles you never use.

Don't worry; there is a better way to do this.

DBI can cache for you

Instead of caching your prepared statements on your own, DBI can do it for you with its `prepare_cached` method. This method does the client-side caching for you, making your code much cleaner and more efficient. You don't have to do any work ahead of time or manage the cache yourself:

```
  use DBI;

  my $dbh = DBI->connect(...)
    or die 'unable to connect to database';
```

```
my $sth = $dbh->prepare_cached(
  sprintf( 'SELECT value FROM my_table WHERE id IN (%s)',
    join( ',', ('?') x $num ) )
);
```

Each time you call `prepare_cached`, DBI searches its statement handle cache. If it finds a matching query that it had already prepared, it returns it. Otherwise, it creates a new statement handle. The first time you create the statement handle, you pay the penalty for the work that DBI and the database server has to do, but you pay only for queries that you actually use.

There's a caveat here, though. If you run two simultaneous queries that use the same statement handle before you `finish` one of them, you can get odd results. The second query replaces the work of the first one. If you want to run simultaneous queries, you have to `prepare` two separate statement handles (thus, you can't use `prepare_cached`).

Not every statement needs a cache

There are cases where preparing SQL statements don't gain you much. If you have a static SQL statement that will be executed repeatedly and doesn't depend on extra parameters, the database should get a cache hit every time the statement is executed. Preparation isn't necessary. These two loops below perform similarly:

```
my $query = 'select count(*) from my_table';

foreach ( 1 .. 100 ) {
  my $array = $dbh->selectrow_array($query);
}

foreach ( 1 .. 100 ) {
  my $sth   = $dbh->prepare_cached($query);
  my $array = $sth->fetchrow_array;
}
```

However, since they have similar performance, you don't have to worry about the odd cases where you cache a query that doesn't need it.

Things to remember

- Save time preparing statement handles by caching them.
- Cache statement handles with `prepare_cached`.
- You don't need to cache every statement, but it doesn't hurt.

Item 107. Use SQL placeholders for automatic value quoting.

Using placeholders for values in your SQL is a good practice that you should follow religiously. SQL placeholders not only make your code faster, but also help protect your code from SQL-injection attacks. It's so easy to do it correctly that you have no excuse not to.

When you are dynamically building SQL statements, there are two major things that can change to make the statements dynamic: the structure of the query itself, and the data values that the query references.

Don't interpolate variables into queries

For a quick program, you might be tempted to write a one-off statement with `selectall_arrayref` that sends a database query and fetches the results:

```
use DBI;

my $dbh->connect( ... );

my $rows = $dbh->selectall_arrayref(
    "select v1, v2 from my_table where id = '$id'"
);
```

This technique has two major drawbacks that should keep you from using it in anything other than the shortest of programs.

First, `selectall_arrayref` creates a completely new query string to pass to the database each time. Since most database management systems search their execution plan caches for exact string matches, there is little chance that you will get any cache hits when you run this query. This can cause some real slowdowns in your code, especially if you have complex queries that take seconds to parse (Item 106).

Second, it's vulnerable to **SQL injection,** where the value of the interpolated variable `$id` contains unexpected but ultimately legal SQL. What if

$id is something like "1' or 'a'='a"? This value effectively short-circuits the filtering logic of the query and causes all data to be returned from my_table. If my_table contains sensitive information, this could spell trouble.

Placeholders for dynamic data values

To include varying data in different calls using the same statement, you can use **placeholders**. You indicate a placeholder with a ? to stand in for data that you'll fill in later.

In selectall_arrayref, you specify the statement with placeholders, the DBI settings for that query (in this example, an empty hash ref), and then the data to use with the query:

```
my $rows = $dbh->selectall_arrayref(
  'select v1, v2 from my_table where id = ?',
  {}, $id );
```

Although different database drivers may handle placeholders separately, this prevents SQL injection. Either the driver sends the data to the server separately from the query, or inserts it into the query with proper quoting and escaping.

More commonly, you'll want to run the same query more than once, so you can prepare it with placeholders, and then execute it with the data for the particular run:

```
my $sth = $dbh->prepare(
  'select v1, v2 from my_table where id = ?');

foreach my $id (@ids) {
  $sth->execute($id);
  ...;
}
```

You can even prepare statements ahead of time and pre-cache them (Item 106).

Creating dynamic SQL elements

Placeholders only insert data values into the query. You can't use place-holders for other parts of the query, such as the table names, for instance.

To use a table name that you decide at run time, you can use DBI's `quote_identifier` to ensure the table name is a valid identifier:

```
my $table = get_table_name();
my $sth   = $dbh->prepare(
  sprintf( 'select * from %s',
    $dbh->quote_identifier($table) )
);
```

This doesn't check that the value in `$table` is an existing table, though. If your database driver supports the `table_info` method, you can check for some existing table names. See the DBI documentation for more details.

Things to remember

- Don't interpolate variables into SQL statements.
- Use placeholders to send data with your queries.
- Placeholders work only for data, not identifiers.

Item 108. Bind return columns for faster access to data.

When you fetch data from a DBI statement handle, you probably assign the values to variables. It's easy to write and the most expedient means when you first implement your database query:

```
use DBI;

my $dbh = DBI->connect(...);

my $sth =
  $dbh->prepare('select one, two, three from my_table');
$sth->execute;

while ( my ( $one, $two, $three ) = $sth->fetchrow_array )
{
  ...;
}
```

This is slightly inefficient, but for a couple of records, this works just fine. If you have to process thousands of records, though, you might notice a slight slowdown. The small inefficiency of copying values into the variables can really add up.

Instead of assigning to new variables, you can **bind** references to your statement handle. This allows the database access layer to directly write the returned data to your variables, cutting one data copy per column per row out of your processing loop. With `bind_columns`, you pass references for all the columns that you select:

```
use DBI;

my $dbh = DBI->connect(...);

my $sth =
  $dbh->prepare('select one, two, three from my_table');
$sth->execute;

my ( $one, $two, $three );
$sth->bind_columns( \$one, \$two, \$three );
while ( $sth->fetchrow_arrayref ) {
  ...;
}
```

Passing a list of references might not be very convenient or readable, so you can also bind the columns one at a time. The `bind_col` method takes a parameter number (counting from 1) and a reference to bind to. You should always call `bind_col` after `execute`:

```
use DBI;

my $dbh = DBI->connect(...);

my $sth =
  $dbh->prepare('select one, two, three from my_table');
$sth->execute;

$sth->bind_col( 1, \my $one );
$sth->bind_col( 2, \my $two );
$sth->bind_col( 3, \my $three );

while ( $sth->fetchrow_arrayref ) {
  ...;
}
```

You have greater control with `bind_col`, too. If you know the data type for the column, you can specify it in the third argument as the attributes for that column. The DBI module exports the `:sql_types` tag that includes constants for the data types:

```
use DBI qw(:sql_types);


$sth->bind_col( 1, \my $one, { TYPE => SQL_DATETIME } );
```

As a shortcut, you can use a scalar as the third argument when the data type is the only attribute:

```
use DBI qw(:sql_types);


$sth->bind_col( 1, \my $one, SQL_DATETIME );
```

Once you bind your columns, you should see some modest performance gains.

Things to remember

- Copying values into variables is slightly inefficient.
- Bind columns to references for faster access to returned results.
- Specify column data types, when you know them.

Item 109. Reuse database connections.

Making a connection to a database is typically a very expensive operation. Avoid making too many connections in your code and cache database connections when possible. This cuts down on the time it takes to make a query as well as preserving connections for other people who may need to connect to the database, too. This can be especially important for high traffic Web sites. Not only do you not want to connect to the database several times in one program, but you also don't want to then run that program several hundred times a minute.

Too many connections

Many programmers don't integrate the database features of their code into the higher level design. Maybe they started their programs as something small and evolved, but they never shed their initial poor decisions. For instance, this example connects to the database only when it needs to make a query, but closes the connection after it makes its query:

```
sub find_value {
  my ($id) = @_;
  my $dbh =
     DBI->connect( $dsn, $user, $password, %options );
  my ($value) = $dbh->selectall_array(
    'select value from my_table where id = ?',
    {}, $id );
  return $value;
}
```

If you call `find_value` only once or twice, you might not notice a problem. If you end up calling it multiple times, your program spends a lot of time setting up database connections when it could be doing something else.

Share database connections

Instead of connecting every time you want to make a query, connect once and store the database handle. How you do this largely depends on what your application needs. You could keep the connection as part of the data:

```
package MyApp::Foo;

sub new {
  my ($class) = @_;
  my $self = bless {}, $class;
  $self->{dbh} = DBI->connect(...);
  return $self;
}
```

When you need to query the database, you take the database connection from the object data:

```
sub find_value {
  my $self = shift;
  my ($value) =
    $self->{dbh}->selectall_array(
    'select value from my_table where id = ?',
    {}, $id );
```

```
   return $value;
 }
```

This can work for short-lived programs, but there's a problem for longer running programs. The database might close the connection after inactivity, the network might have a hiccup, or many other things might cause problems. In your methods, you're trusting that you have an open database connection.

Per-object connections

You can fix this by encapsulating the database handle, which is always a good programming practice. Instead of accessing the object data directly, you call a method to get the database handle. You don't care what that method does or how it does it, as long as it gives you a valid database connection. You can create a `get_dbh` method that uses DBI's `ping` method to check the connection. If `ping` returns false, it tries to reconnect:

```
package MyApp::Foo;

sub connect_to_database {
  DBI->connect(...) or die ...;
}

sub get_dbh {
  my ($self) = @_;

  unless ( $self->{dbh}->ping ) {
    $self->{dbh} = $self->connect_to_database;
  }

  $self->{dbh};
}
```

This still might be a waste of database connections, since you need one for every object.

Per-class connections

If every object in your class should share the same database connection, you can use a class variable to hold the database handle. The mechanics are much like the per-object connection, but you use a lexical variable that the entire class uses:

```
package MyApp::Foo;

my $dbh;

sub connect_to_database {
  DBI->connect(...) or die ...;
}

sub get_dbh {
  my ($self) = @_;

  unless ( $dbh->ping ) {
    $dbh = $self->connect_to_database;
  }

  $dbh;
}
```

Remember that $dbh is a file-scoped variable, so anything in the file can access it, even if you switch packages.

Larger requirements

Sometimes even per-class connections waste resources, and you want to share a connection with the entire application, or even across multiple processes. Very large applications and systems might need much more sophisticated connection management.

The Apache::DBI module shows you how to share a database handle within the same process by providing a wrapper around DBI to handle the connection caching for you. Even if you aren't using Apache, you can adapt its code to your needs. Versions of Apache::DBI before it added Apache2 support might be easier to convert to your specialized needs.

If that's not good enough for you, consider the DBD::Gofer module. It sets up a proxy whose only job is to manage DBI connections. It maintains them in separate processes, giving you flexibility, caching, scalability, throttling, and many other things. Once set up, you modify your call to DBI->connect to tell it to connect to the proxy server that DBD::Gofer sets up:

```
use DBI;

my $normal_dsn = "dbi:...";

my $dbh = DBI->connect(
  "dbi:Gofer:transport=$transport;...;dsn=$original_dsn",
  $user, $passwd, \%attributes
);
```

Be careful with your new data source name: the stuff at the front of the string is for DBD::Gofer. Once it strips off that front part, DBD::Gofer uses the rest of the dsn to make the actual database connection. The "normal," non-Gofer dsn needs to be at the very end.

Once you have the database handle from DBD::Gofer, you use it as you normally would. The rest of the program doesn't care that you are using it, and doesn't even notice it.

Things to remember

- Don't connect to the database every time that you want to make a query.
- Share database connections across objects, classes, or processes.
- Use the DBD::Gofer module as a DBI proxy to share connections.

13 | Miscellany

There were many Items that we couldn't fit into the other chapters, and as with many of the other Items, they are worthy topics that each could deserve much longer treatments. There's no shame in being shepherded into the miscellaneous chapter; some of these are ideas for future chapters. Other items are isolated topics that might be powerful techniques despite their uniqueness. Either way, we think they are important to know.

Item 110. Compile and install your own `perl`s.

Sometimes Perl suffers from its own success. It comes with just about every version of operating systems with UNIX or Linux heritages, including Mac OS X. Many of these systems use Perl as part of their normal operation or provide `perl` as packages. Even then, you can find precompiled `perl`s for most platforms.

Perl on Windows commonly uses precompiled binaries from ActiveState (http://www.activestate.com/), cygwin (http://www.cygwin.com/), or Strawberry Perl (http://www.strawberryperl.com/). People don't have to compile their own `perl`s anymore.

There are many advantages to compiling and using your own `perl`, though. Since many operating systems rely on `perl` for normal maintenance tasks, you want to avoid anything that will break that `perl`. If you upgrade a core module, for instance, an important part of the system may stop working. You probably want to pretend that the system `perl` is not even there.

Also, as a Perl developer, you should install several versions of `perl` so you can test against each of them. It's easy to install and maintain distinct versions. This Item covers the basics, but your system may have additional requirements. The `perl` distribution has several README files that give instructions for particular operating systems.

Compiling your `perl`

To compile `perl`, you'll need a C compiler and the build tools that typically come with it. You'll also need `make` or one of its variants. You don't need any special privileges, and you can install `perl` in your own user directory. This Item assumes you have all of that already worked out.

To start, download the version of `perl` that you want to test. You can find all of the `perl` releases on CPAN (http://www.cpan.org/src/README.html).

Once you unpack your distribution, change into its directory. It's time to choose an installation location. For this example, you'll put all of your `perl`s under /usr/local/perls, and each new installation will get its own subdirectory under that.

The `Configure` script examines your system and prepares the `perl` sources for compilation. The `-des` switches accept all of the default answers and give you terse output. The `-D` switch overrides one of the answers, in this case for `prefix`, which sets the installation location.

```
% ./Configure -des -Dprefix=/usr/local/perls/perl-5.10.1
```

In this case, you've configured the build to install everything under /usr/local/perls/perl-5.10.1. By accepting the defaults, you won't move the `perl` into /usr/bin, so don't be afraid of messing up anything. You should probably do this from an unprivileged account anyway, so your system will stop you from doing anything too bad.

If you want to see everything that you can configure, don't accept any of the defaults; instead, go through the entire process yourself (try it once in your life):

```
% ./Configure
```

After you run `Configure`, no matter which options you've used, you're ready to build the source. Depending on your system, you'll need a `make` variant:

```
% make all
```

When the build completes, you can test it, which might take a while:

```
% make test
```

And finally, you install it. You should see it copy files into the directory you previously specified in `prefix`:

```
% make install
```

After you finish installing that `perl`, try installing another one. You can enable different features, such as threads. You can change the prefix to note the interesting feature of this `perl`:

```
% ./Configure -des -Dusethreads↵
   -Dprefix=/usr/local/perls/perl-5.10.1-threaded
```

Using your `perl`

Once you install `perl`, there's nothing left for you to configure to use it, although you have to use the path to the `perl` you want to use. You can see the default module search path, for instance:

```
% /usr/local/perls/perl-5.10.1/bin/perl -V
```

All of the tools, extra programs, and modules for your new `perl` show up under your `prefix` directory. If you want `cpan` to install modules for this `perl`, you call the `cpan` for that `perl`. It's in the bin/ directory under your prefix:

```
% /usr/local/perls/perl-5.10.1/bin/cpan LWP::Simple
```

Any modules that you install in this fashion go into the library directories for just that `perl`, and do not disturb any other installation. Indeed, that's the point. Remember that when you switch to using another `perl`, you might have to reinstall the modules for that `perl`, too.

If you want to read the documentation, you use the right path to `perldoc` so it searches the correct module path:

```
% /usr/local/perls/perl-5.10.1/bin/perldoc↵
   LWP::Simple
```

If you want to use this `perl` and its tools as your main `perl`, you can add its path to your PATH environment variable. That leaves the system `perl` in place, too. If you want to switch your default `perl`, you just update your path so the shell finds the new default first. Anything else takes care of itself, including the module paths.

You might have some trouble with CPAN.pm or CPANPLUS, since they store their configurations in your home directory (Item 65). Their configurations are per-user instead of per-`perl`. Ensure that you update their configurations for the `perl` that you want to use.

Things to remember

- Install your own `perl` so you don't disturb the system `perl`.
- You can install multiple `perl`s with different configurations.
- Add your preferred Perl's location to your PATH to make it the default.

Item 111. Use `Perl::Tidy` to beautify code.

Consistent formatting is a fundamental attribute of maintainable code. Predictable and repeated patterns in the code make your programs easier for developers to read. Instead of doing the grunt work to beautify your code, you can use `Perl::Tidy` to do it for you.

Start with some code that's not so pretty, and put it in `ugly.pl`:

```
use warnings; use strict;
while(<>) { if(/\d/
) { print "contains number\n"; }
else { print "number-free\n" } }
```

Run `perltidy` on that file:

```
% perltidy ugly.pl
```

The `perltidy` command puts the cleansed source in a file of the same name but with .tdy appended it. Here's the result in `ugly.pl.tdy`:

```
use warnings;
use strict;
while (<>) {
    if    (/\d/) { print "contains number\n"; }
    else         { print "number-free\n" }
}
```

`perltidy` didn't overwrite the `ugly.pl` file, as a safeguard so that you don't lose your original program. Although `perltidy` shouldn't introduce errors, you don't want to rely on that. Be sure to run compilation checks and even unit tests against the beautified code before you get rid of the original (or better yet, use source control).

Alternatively, you can use the -b option to create a .bak file with the original data and modify the code file directly. Using this option can make testing much easier, since you don't have to move files around, but you should still save your original source.

Configuring `Perl::Tidy`

If you want to change formatting style, there are myriad command-line options available. Suppose you want to indent four spaces instead of two, and print to standard output instead of to a .tdy file. With the right options to `perltidy`, you get just that:

```
% perltidy -st -i=4  ugly.pl
```

Your `ugly.pl` is now slightly different (and shown on your terminal):

```
use warnings;
use strict;
while (<>) {
    if  (/\d/) { print "contains number\n"; }
    else       { print "number-free\n" }
}
```

If you don't line that bracing style, you can change it to something else that you like better:

```
% perltidy -st -bl -bli ugly.pl
```

Now the braces for the `while` get their own line:

```
use warnings;
use strict;
while (<>)
  {
    if  (/\d/) { print "contains number\n"; }
    else       { print "number-free\n" }
  }
```

After you find a format that you like, you don't have to waste time typing your configuration options on the command line. Put those options in a .perltidyrc file. One handy way to start that file is to dump the settings of everything:

```
% perltidy -st -bl -bli -dump-options
```

Now you have the settings for everything for that particular invocation, including the default settings:

```
# Final parameter set for this run.
# See utility 'perltidyrc_dump.pl' for nicer formatting.
```

```
--add-newlines
--add-semicolons
--add-whitespace
--backup-file-extension="bak"
--blanks-before-blocks
--blanks-before-comments
--blanks-before-subs
...
```

You can even create a profile that you use for a single project instead of using the same configuration for everything. With the `--profile` switch, you can tell `perltidy` which profile to use:

```
% perltidy --profile=projecttidy ugly.pl
```

You can also override the configuration file location with the PERLTIDY environment variable, as well as creating a global default configuration that you put in /usr/local/etc/perltidyrc or /usr/local/etc/perltidyrc.

If you don't want to use any configuration other than what you specify on the command line, use the `--noprofile` option:

```
% perltidy --noprofile ugly.pl
```

Checking syntax

`Perl::Tidy` can work even if there are some syntax errors in your code, but it cannot get past them all. If `perltidy` gets too confused, it creates a .ERR file that lists the errors.

Here's some broken code that doesn't quote its string properly. It's a syntax error:

```
# b0rk3n.pl
use warnings;
use strict;

print 'I'm broken';
```

When you run `perltidy`, it tells you that it had a problem, and that it puts the errors in a file:

```
% perltidy b0rk3n.pl
## Please see file b0rk3n.pl.ERR
```

And see what is in the .ERR file that was created:

```
5: print 'I'm broken';
          ---^
found m where operator expected (previous token ⏎
   underlined)
5:      hit EOF seeking end of quote/pattern starting⏎
   at line 4 ending in b
```

Although the error was for an unescaped quote delimiter, `perltidy` got confused because it thought the `m` was the start of the match operator. Don't pay too much attention to the error message.

In your test suite

You can create an author test (Item 88) that runs `perltidy` every time you run your test suite. The `Test::PerlTidy` module handles the details for you:

```
use Test::More;

plan skip_all =>
  'Set $ENV{TEST_AUTHOR} to enable this test.'
  unless $ENV{TEST_AUTHOR};

eval "use Test::PerlTidy";
plan skip_all => 'Test::PerlTidy required' if $@;

run_tests();
```

By default, `Test::PerlTidy` uses the standard options. If you want your code formatted with different options, ensure that you have a .perltidyrc file in the root of your distribution or in your home directory.

Things to remember

- Write consistent code to make it easier to read and maintain.
- Use `Perl::Tidy` to standardize code format.
- Set your favorite options in a .perltidyrc file.

Item 112. Use Perl Critic.

Perl is (in)famous for its flexibility and expressiveness. A long-time mantra of Perl programmers is, "There's More Than One Way To Do It" (TMTOWTDI). This flexibility is great; however, sometimes you have to reel it in and follow a few coding standards. Having rules for what is allowed and what isn't can be handy when you are working with a team of other programmers. It can keep people from writing code that is hard to read and make your code base a much more pleasant place. Even when you are working on a project alone, it never hurts to have a few rules in place that keep the look and feel of the code consistent.

Having rules is one thing; enforcing them is another. You can set up agile methods, code reviews, and pair programming, which are all good things but still leave room for human error. What you really need is an automatic system that can review your code and tell you where it is breaking your rules.

Perl Critic is that system. It performs a static analysis of your Perl code and warns you when it can. It doesn't solve all your problems, but it helps you manage them.

On the Web

The easiest way to check your files with Perl Critic is to simply upload them to http://perlcritic.com/. You don't need to install anything, and you can try out Perl Critic before you decide to commit to it. The output you get is similar to that from the other Perl Critic tools you'll see in the rest of this Item.

On the command line

Once you install `Perl::Critic`, you can use the `perlcritic` program directly from your command line.

Here's a short program that will generate some Perl Critic warnings using the default settings:

```perl
package MyPrinter;

sub new {
  bless {}, shift;
}
```

```
sub print {
  print "Hello, World\n";
}


1;
```

Even on simple modules like this, `perlcritic` finds errors. For instance, it warns you that you didn't use `strict` (Item 3):

```
perlcritic MyPrinter.pm
    Code before strictures are enabled at line 3, column 1.↲
      See page 429 of PBP.  (Severity: 5)
```

In the error message, `perlcritic` tells you which line of code has the problem. Additionally, if this problem is one that Damian Conway showed in *Perl Best Practices*[1], you get the relevant page number from that book. Finally, `perlcritic` rates the "severity" of the issue.

There are five levels of policies and corresponding severities, with 5 being the most severe and 1 being the least. You should concentrate on the most severe as your immediate fixes. By default, `perlcritic` shows only level-5 violations. To see lower levels, use the `--severity` switch:

```
% perlcritic --severity 1 MyPrinter.pm
Error: No word lists can be found for the language "↲
  en_US".
Code is not tidy at line 1, column 1.  See page 33 of ↲
  PBP. (Severity: 1)
RCS keywords $Id$ not found at line 1, column 1.  See ↲
  page 441 of PBP.  (Severity: 2)
RCS keywords $Revision$, $HeadURL$, $Date$ not found at ↲
  ine 1, column 1.  See page 441 of PBP.  (Severity: 2)
RCS keywords $Revision$, $Source$, $Date$ not found at ↲
  line 1, column 1.  See page 441 of PBP.  (Severity: 2)
No "$VERSION" variable found at line 1, column 1.  See ↲
  page 404 of PBP.  (Severity: 2)
Subroutine "new" does not end with "return" at line 3, ↲
  column 1.  See page 197 of PBP.  (Severity: 4)
Code before strictures are enabled at line 3, column 1. ↲
  See page 429 of PBP.  (Severity: 5)
```

---

1. Damian Conway, *Perl Best Practices* (Sebastopol, CA: O'Reilly Media, 2005).

```
Code before warnings are enabled at line 3, column 1. ⏎
   See page 431 of PBP.  (Severity: 4)
Subroutine name is a homonym for builtin function at ⏎
   line 7, column 1.  See page 177 of PBP.  (Severity: 4)
Subroutine "print" does not end with "return" at line 7, ⏎
   column 1.  See page 197 of PBP.  (Severity: 4)
Return value of flagged function ignored - print at line ⏎
   8, column 5.  See pages 208,278 of PBP.  (Severity: 1)
```

`Perl::Critic` "themes" policies, and you can include and restrict reported policy violations by theme. For instance, you can apply the policies from *Perl Best Practices* with the `pbp` theme:

```
% perlcritic --brutal --theme=pbp
```

You can also modify themes. Perhaps you want the `pbp` theme, but want to ignore the suggestions that are merely cosmetic (i.e., code formatting) or deal with distribution maintenance. You can adjust the theme directly:

```
% perlcritic --brutal --theme=\
  'pbp && ! (cosmetic || maintenance)'  MyPrinter.pm
```

```
No "$VERSION" variable found at line 1, column 1.  See ⏎
  page 404 of PBP.  (Severity: 2)
Subroutine "new" does not end with "return" at line 3, ⏎
  column 1.  See page 197 of PBP.  (Severity: 4)
Code before strictures are enabled at line 3, column 1. ⏎
   See page 429 of PBP.  (Severity: 5)
Code before warnings are enabled at line 3, column 1. ⏎
   See page 431 of PBP.  (Severity: 4)
Subroutine name is a homonym for builtin function at ⏎
   line 7, column 1.  See page 177 of PBP.  (Severity: 4)
Subroutine "print" does not end with "return" at line 7,⏎
   column 1.  See page 197 of PBP.  (Severity: 4)
```

There are scores more command line options for `perlcritic`. You can restrict or include policies by regular expression, show only a limited number of violations, reformat the output, show code statistics, and more. Any configuration options that you prefer can be stored in a .perlcriticrc file so that you don't have to repeatedly type them. Invest some time in reading the documentation for `perlcritic`.

In the test suite

The command line interface to `Perl::Critic` is nice as long as you remember to use it. You can use `Test::Perl::Critic` to run a static analysis every time you run your test suite. Many people add a t/perlcriticrc file to their distribution so they can adjust the policies just for that distribution. Once you add that file, it's simply a matter of adding the t/perl-critic.t template to your test suite:

```perl
use File::Spec;
use Test::More;

if ( not $ENV{TEST_AUTHOR} ) {
  plan( skip_all =>
    'Set $ENV{TEST_AUTHOR} to a true value to run.' );
}

eval "use Test::Perl::Critic";

if ( $@ ) {
  plan( skip_all =>
    'Test::Perl::Critic required to criticise code' );
}

my $rcfile = File::Spec->catfile( 't', 'perlcriticrc' );
Test::Perl::Critic->import( -profile => $rcfile );
all_critic_ok();
```

Chances are that you are working on a project that already exists, and if you turn on `Test::Perl::Critic` you'll be flooded with too many problems to deal with at once. Instead of stopping all new development to fix your static analysis problems (or scrapping Perl Critic altogether), you can use `Test::Perl::Critic::Progressive`, which warns you only about new problems:

```perl
use Test::More;

eval {
  use Test::Perl::Critic::Progressive
    qw( progressive_critic_ok )
};
```

```
plan skip_all =>
    'T::P::C::Progressive required for this test' if $@;

progressive_critic_ok();
```

`Test::Perl::Critic::Progressive` first takes note of the number of violations in your code, and then on each subsequent run ensures that you have the same number of violations or fewer since the last successful run of the test suite. You get to cap the number of violations that are acceptable in your code base, and to slowly chip away at them over time.

You can even set the step sizes per-policy when you want to reduce some problems faster than others:

```
use Test::More;

eval {
  use Test::Perl::Critic::Progressive
    qw(
      progressive_critic_ok
      set_total_step_size
    )
};
plan skip_all =>
    'T::P::C::Progressive required for this test' if $@;

set_total_step_size( 5 );
progressive_critic_ok();
```

Since the default action of `Test::Perl::Critic::Progressive` merely checks that you have the same or fewer number of violations since your last successful run of the test, you need to force yourself and your team to reduce the total number of violations. To accelerate compliance, you can configure `Test::Perl::Critic::Progressive` with a step amount that complains:

```
my %step_sizes = (
    'ValuesAndExpressions::ProhibitLeadingZeros' =>  2,
    'Variables::ProhibitConditionalDeclarations' =>  1,
    'InputOutput::ProhibitTwoArgOpen'            =>  3,
);

set_step_size_per_policy( %step_sizes );
progressive_critic_ok();
```

Custom policies

`Perl::Critic` is distributed with a large set of policies; however, there are many non-core policies on CPAN that you can integrate into your system based on your own code preferences. There are too many add-on policies to list here, but some notable ones are:

- `Perl-Critic-More`
  A package of many different policies written by the `Perl::Critic` developers.
- `Perl-Critic-Bangs`
  A set of useful policies by Andy Lester that search for code "smells" such as commented-out code and bad variable names.
- `Perl-Critic-StricterSubs`
  Stricter-than-core subroutine rules, for the really masochistic developer.
- `Perl-Critic-Swift`
  Policies that require that you to use UTF-8 encoding declarations in your source and Pod files.
- `Perl-Critic-Moose`
  Criticisms for your Moose-based code.

If you can't find a policy that checks what you need, you can easily write your own policy. Check the `Perl::Critic::DEVELOPER` documentation in the `Perl::Critic` distribution.

Things to remember

- Use `Perl::Critic` to analyze your source code for potential problems.
- Add `Perl::Critic` to your test suite with `Test::Perl::Critic`.
- Use `Test::Perl::Critic::Progressive` to add Perl Critic to an existing project.

Item 113. Use `Log::Log4perl` to record your program's state.

Proper logging can be a powerful debugging and diagnostic tool for your code. At the most basic level, logging can be as simple as using `print` statements:

```
print "The value is [$value]\n";
```

You might even get a little more fancy by controlling that with an environment variable:

```
print "The value is [$value]\n" if $ENV{DEBUG};
```

Easy `Log::Log4perl`

That's indiscriminate and not very flexible. To really harness the power of good logging, you need to use a robust logging framework such as `Log::Log4perl`, which handles all of the details for you. The easiest thing to do is to initialize `Log::Log4perl` with `easy_init`. The `:easy` tag exports variables that represent each of the levels, and subroutines for each level:

```
use Log::Log4perl qw(:easy);
Log::Log4perl->easy_init($ERROR);

INFO 'starting program';

for ( 1 .. 100 ) {
  DEBUG "loop counter: $_";
}

INFO 'program complete';
```

When you run this code, you don't see any output! `Log::Log4perl` ignores the calls to levels below the one you specified in `easy_init`.

`Log::Log4perl` defines several log levels:

- FATAL
- ERROR
- WARN
- INFO
- DEBUG
- TRACE

Each level has its own variable, like `$ERROR`, and a subroutine of the same name. When you initialize `Log::Log4perl`, it will only print the messages from the initialized level or higher. Since you initialized the last example at the `$ERROR` level, you get messages from only the ERROR and FATAL levels. If you want more output, you can change the logging level:

```
Log::Log4perl->easy_init($INFO);
```

Now you get some output, but only from the calls to INFO:

```
2009/10/20 15:47:45 starting program
2009/10/20 15:47:45 program complete
```

You can move the logging level down further:

```
Log::Log4perl->easy_init($DEBUG);
```

Now you get the output from the DEBUG calls, too:

```
2009/10/20 15:48:16 starting program
2009/10/20 15:48:16 loop counter: 1
2009/10/20 15:48:16 loop counter: 2
2009/10/20 15:48:16 loop counter: 3
...
2009/10/20 15:48:16 loop counter: 98
2009/10/20 15:48:16 loop counter: 99
2009/10/20 15:48:16 loop counter: 100
2009/10/20 15:48:16 program complete
```

Object-oriented interface

`Log::Log4perl` also has an object interface, which gives you much more power. You can still use `easy_init`, and after that you can call `get_logger` to get the logging object. The methods have the same names, but all lowercase:

```perl
use Log::Log4perl qw(:easy);
Log::Log4perl->easy_init($DEBUG);

my $logger = Log::Log4perl->get_logger();

$logger->info('starting program');

for ( 1 .. 100 ) {
  $logger->debug("loop counter: $_");
}

$logger->info('program complete');
```

Better configuration

Before long, you'll not like the default logging options that come with `easy_init`, and you'll want to customize your logging. You can call `init` with the name of a configuration file:

```
use warnings;
use strict;
use Log::Log4perl;
Log::Log4perl::init('log4perl.conf');

my $logger = Log::Log4perl->get_logger();

$logger->info('starting program');

for ( 1 .. 100 ) {
  $logger->debug("loop counter: $_");
}

$logger->info('program complete');
```

Since `Log::Log4perl` is the Perl version of Log4j, the configuration file looks a lot like Java configuration files. You can choose an **appender**, which decides where the output goes, and also define your own output format. You configure the `rootLogger` to tell it its level, and which appender it should use:

```
log4perl.rootLogger=DEBUG, Screen

log4perl.appender.Screen=Log::Log4perl::Appender::Screen
log4perl.appender.Screen.stderr=1
log4perl.appender.Screen.layout= ⏎
   Log::Log4perl::Layout::SimpleLayout
```

Running your program again, you see the output in your newly defined format:

```
INFO - starting program
DEBUG - loop counter: 1
DEBUG - loop counter: 2
DEBUG - loop counter: 3

...
```

```
DEBUG - loop counter: 98
DEBUG - loop counter: 99
DEBUG - loop counter: 100
INFO - program complete
```

It gets even better than that, though. You can define multiple appenders at the same time, and you can send output to more than one appender at the same time:

```
log4perl.rootLogger=DEBUG, Screen, Logfile

log4perl.appender.Logfile=Log::Log4perl::Appender::File
log4perl.appender.Logfile.filename=my_program.log
log4perl.appender.Logfile.mode=replace

log4perl.appender.Logfile.layout=PatternLayout
log4perl.appender.Logfile.layout.ConversionPattern= ↵
  [%r] %F %L %c - %m%n

log4perl.appender.Screen=Log::Log4perl::Appender::Screen
log4perl.appender.Screen.stderr=1
log4perl.appender.Screen.layout= ↵
  Log::Log4perl::Layout::SimpleLayout
```

Now, your messages also go to the my_program.log file, which uses its own format:

```
[33] log4perl_object_with_config.pl 8 main ↵
  - starting program
[33] log4perl_object_with_config.pl 11 main ↵
  - loop counter: 1
[33] log4perl_object_with_config.pl 11 main ↵
  - loop counter: 2
[33] log4perl_object_with_config.pl 11 main ↵
  - loop counter: 3
...
[44] log4perl_object_with_config.pl 11 main ↵
  - loop counter: 98
[45] log4perl_object_with_config.pl 11 main ↵
  - loop counter: 99
[45] log4perl_object_with_config.pl 11 main ↵
  - loop counter: 100
```

```
[45] log4perl_object_with_config.pl 14 main ↵
   - program complete
```

You can even create different logging categories and tweak the logging appenders, formatters, and levels per category. You can turn each category on or off independently, and even send their output to different appenders:

```
package MyFirstClass;

use warnings;
use strict;
use Log::Log4perl;

Log::Log4perl::init('log4perlWithClasses.conf');

sub new {
  my $logger = Log::Log4perl->get_logger(__PACKAGE__);
  $logger->debug( 'creating new ', __PACKAGE__ );
  return bless {}, shift;
}

package MySecondClass;

use warnings;
use strict;
use Log::Log4perl;

Log::Log4perl::init('log4perlWithClasses.conf');

sub new {
  my $logger = Log::Log4perl->get_logger(__PACKAGE__);
  $logger->debug( 'creating new ', __PACKAGE__ );
  return bless {}, shift;
}

package main;

my $first  = MyFirstClass->new();
my $second = MySecondClass->new();
```

In your configuration file, you set up each category separately:

```
log4perl.rootLogger=WARN, Screen

log4perl.category.MyFirstClass=ERROR

log4perl.category.MySecondClass=DEBUG

log4perl.appender.Screen=Log::Log4perl::Appender::Screen
log4perl.appender.Screen.stderr=1
log4perl.appender.Screen.layout= ⏎
  Log::Log4perl::Layout::SimpleLayout
```

When set up properly, you get some nice debugging output:

```
DEBUG - creating new MySecondClass
```

Detect the logging level

`Log::Log4perl` also gives you the power to inspect the logging level. Even though `Log::Log4perl` ignores messages from lower log levels, it still has to make the subroutine call, and then inspect its configuration to decide what to do. That can be a waste of time. A great cycle-saver is avoiding costly processing if the output will go unnoticed. You can call `is_debug` to find out if you are at the debugging level:

```
if ( $logger->is_debug() ) {
  for (@big_array) {
    $logger->debug("big array value: $_");
  }
}
```

Each level has a similar method, and `Log::Log4perl` provides other methods you can use to inspect the configuration.

Getting more information

Although this has been the briefest introduction to `Log::Log4perl`, have no fear. The `Log::Log4perl` documentation is excellent, and has many examples for most of the common situations. See the Log4perl project on Source-Forge (http://log4perl.sourceforge.net/). Additionally, you can reuse many of the Log4j examples, since the configurations are very close to each other.

Things to remember

- Use `Log::Log4perl` for powerful and configurable logging in your programs.
- Separate your logging configuration from your code for added flexibility.
- Avoid evaluation if you know that Log4perl will ignore your message.

Item 114. Know when arrays are modified in a loop.

Perl programmers still get bitten all the time because they don't realize when a loop is modifying an array and when it isn't. Let's go ahead and make it simple: `for` loops, `map`s, and `grep`s will modify the underlying array elements if you modify `$_`.

For instance, all of these statements increment the underlying array elements:

```perl
my @array = ( 1 .. 10 );


$_++ for @array;
my @incremented = map  { $_++ } @array;
my @grand_plus  = grep { $_++ > 1000 } @array;
```

You can give the control variable your own name with `for` and `foreach`, and you can modify that variable directly:

```perl
my @array = 0 .. 5;

foreach my $elem ( @array ) {
  $elem++;
}


print "@array\n"; # 1 2 3 4 5 6
```

To make things faster, Perl actually aliases the control variable to the original data instead of copying it. When you modify the value, you are actually modifying the original data.

Things get a little more interesting when you change the array instead of merely changing the elements. This code `pop`s elements off of a ten-item array while you iterate over it:

```
my $sum = 0;
my @array = ( 1 .. 10 );
foreach (@array) {
  pop @array;
  $sum += $_;
}
print "The sum is $sum\n"; # 15 instead of 55
```

Only the first five elements make it into the sum because the other elements disappear from the array. After the first iteration, it is a nine-element array. After the second, it is an eight-element array. This continues until the fifth iteration, when the array becomes a five-element array.

Just as you can remove elements from an array while you are iterating it, you can add elements. This example creates an infinite loop by continually extending the array so the foreach never gets to the end:

```
my $max   = 10;
my @array = ( 1 .. $max );
foreach (@array) {
  print "$_ ";
  push @array, ++$max;
}
```

This loop starts by printing **1**, then **2**, and goes on incrementing until infinity (or at least until all of the memory allocated to the process is consumed).

What about adding elements to the start of an array that you are iterating?

```
my $max   = 10;
my @array = ( 1 .. $max );
for (@array) {
  print "$_ ";
  unshift @array, ++$max;
}
```

This loop will print **1** forever. It seems to perpetually hang at what was the first position in the array, even when values eleven through fifteen are added. But is this really the case? What happens when you stop adding elements to the array?

```
my $max   = 10;
my @array = ( 1 .. $max );
```

```
foreach (@array) {
  print "$_ ";
  unshift @array, ++$max if $max <= 15;
}
```

This code prints **1 1 1 1 1 1 2 3 4 5 6 7 8 9 10**. That's probably not what you were expecting.

The magic of `unshift` and `foreach` working directly on a single array causes some internal memory confusion that leads to unexpected results. You can see similar results when `shift`ing elements off of the beginning of a loop. The code below produces **1 3 5 7 9**, seeming to `shift` every other element off of the array instead of the first element on each iteration.

```
my @array = ( 1 .. $max );
for (@array) {
  print "$_ ";
  shift @array;
}
```

Things to remember

- Don't modify the data in loop control variables.
- `foreach`, `map`, and `grep` can modify the underlying array elements.
- Don't add or remove elements from an array while you iterate over it.

Item 115. Don't use regular expressions for comma-separated values.

The comma-separated values format seems like such an easy format to parse, and don't be embarrassed if you thought so. Everyone has—it's a rite of passage. Most often, the problem is that people haven't encountered all of the perversions of this format.

In its simplest form, you see simple values separated by the comma:

```
my $line = 'Buster,Mimi,Roscoe';
```

That's easy enough to break up into fields by using `split`, or so it seems:

```
my @cats = split /,/, $line;
```

There's a tiny wrinkle when someone leaves some whitespace in the format:

```
my $line = 'Buster, Mimi, Roscoe';
```

Now, is that whitespace part of the value, or it is extraneous padding that you can throw away? You might choose the latter, and adjust your `split`:

```
my @cats = split /\s*,\s*/, $line;
```

Then things get tricky. The source of your data quotes some fields, especially if they have commas in them:

```
my $line = '"Bean, Buster", Mimi, Roscoe';
```

Things aren't so simple, now, are they? Since there is no formal standard, you might run into a record that is spread over more than one line since it has an embedded newline:

```
my $line = '"Bean\nBuster", Mimi, Roscoe';
```

Or maybe there's a field with double quotes in it, which you escape by doubling them up:

```
my $line = '"""Bean""", Buster", Mimi, Roscoe';
```

Almost every single regular expression we've seen to handle CSV has failed in some regard. Instead of wasting your time refining your regular expression to handle more and more absurdities with this format, let the `Text::CSV_XS` module handle it for you. It's going to be faster than anything you write anyway, and it's certainly easier:

```
my $csv = Text::CSV_XS->new( { binary => 1 } )
  or die 'Cannot use CSV: ' . Text::CSV->error_diag;

open my $fh, '<', $file or die "$file: $!";

while ( my $row = $csv->getline($fh) ) {
  next unless $row->[2] =~ m/$pattern/;
  push @rows, $row;
}

$csv->eof or $csv->error_diag;
close $fh;
```

Things to remember

- Don't parse comma-separated values with regular expressions.
- Use the Text::CSV_XS module to parse comma-separated values.

Item 116. Use unpack to process columnar data.

Don't reach for a regular expression or split every time you have to process some lines of text. If your data are in regular, constant width columns, you can use unpack to turn each line into a list of values.

Parse with unpack

Consider how hard you would have to work to process the following text with a regular expression:

```
ID   First Name  Middle   Last Name
 1   brian        d        foy
 2   Joshua                McAdams
 3   Joseph       N        Hall
```

Here, a split on the whitespace wouldn't work because the fields are determined by their positions in the line, not by the type of whitespace or how much (or little) whitespace separates them. In particular, note that one of the names doesn't have a middle initial. That just messes up everything.

The data are formatted consistently. The ID is always columns 1 and 2, the first names are columns 4 to 15, and so on.

You can create a pack format that represents a line:

```
my $format = 'A2 @4 A10 @16 A6 @24 A*';
```

The @ specifier doesn't represent a field. It tells unpack to move to that absolute position before it processes the next part of the format. The A specifier automatically strips any whitespace padding.

Since the data and their headers are in the same columns, you can use the same format to deal with the headers and the data:

```
my $string = <<'COLUMNAR';
ID   First Name  Middle   Last Name
 1   brian        d        foy
```

```
    2   Joshua                  McAdams
    3   Joseph          N       Hall
COLUMNAR

open my ( $fh ), '<', \$string;

my $format = 'A2 @4 A10 @16 A6 @24 A*';

my @headers = unpack $format, <$fh>;

my @names;    # make an array of hash refs

while( <$fh> ) {
  my %hash;
  @hash{ @headers } = unpack $format, $_;
  push @names, \%hash;
}


use Data::Dumper::Names;
print Dumper( \@names );
```

The output shows that unpack extracted the fields and took care of the whitespace for you:

```
@names = (
  {
    'First Name' => 'brian',
    'ID'         => ' 1',
    'Middle'     => 'd',
    'Last Name'  => 'foy'
  },
  {
    'First Name' => 'Joshua',
    'ID'         => ' 2',
    'Middle'     => '',
    'Last Name'  => 'McAdams'
  },
  {
    'First Name' => 'Joseph',
    'ID'         => ' 3',
```

```
        'Middle'       => 'N',
        'Last Name'  => 'Hall'
    }
);
```

Of course, the annoying thing here is counting the columns to get the various @ settings for the fields. It's easier to cheat by guessing at some offsets, trying the unpack, and adjusting until you get them right.

Things to remember

- Don't use regular expressions or split to parse fixed columns.
- Use unpack to parse fixed-width columns.
- unpack with the A specifier automatically handles whitespace padding for you.

Item 117. Use pack and unpack for data munging.

Perl's built-in pack and unpack functions are two of the bigger, sharper blades on the "Swiss Army Chainsaw." Perhaps they were originally intended as ho-hum means of translating binary data to and from Perl data types such as strings and integers, but pack and unpack can be put to more interesting and offbeat uses. For more examples, see the *perlpacktut* documentation.

Packing data

The pack operator works more or less like sprintf. It takes a format string followed by a list of values to be formatted, and returns a string:

```
# "Perl" -- pack 4 unsigned chars
my $packed_chars = pack( "CCCC", 80, 101, 114, 108 );
```

The unpack operator works the other way:

```
my @ints = unpack( "CCCC", "Perl" ) # (80, 101, 114, 108);
```

The format string is a list of single-character specifiers that specify the type of data to be packed or unpacked. Table 13-1 shows selected format specifiers (see pack's entry in *perlfunc* for the rest):

Table 13-1 Selected pack Format Specifiers

Specifier	Description
a	A string with arbitrary binary data, will be null padded.
A	A text (ASCII) string, will be space padded.
h	A hex string (low nybble first).
H	A hex string (high nybble first).
c	A signed char (8-bit) value.
C	An unsigned char octet) value.
s	A signed short (16-bit) value.
S	An unsigned short value.
l	A signed long (32-bit) value.
L	An unsigned long value.
n	An unsigned short (16-bit) in "network" (big-endian) order.
N	An unsigned long (32-bit) in "network" (big-endian) order.
v	An unsigned short (16-bit) in "VAX" (little-endian) order.
V	An unsigned long (32-bit) in "VAX" (little-endian) order.
u	A uuencoded string.
U	A Unicode character number. Encodes to a character in character mode and UTF-8 (or UTF-EBCDIC in EBCDIC platforms) in byte mode.
@	Absolute position.

Each specifier may be followed by a repeat count indicating how many values from the list to format. The repeat counts for the string specifiers (A, a, B, b, H, and h) are special—they indicate how many bytes/bits/nybbles to add to the output string. An asterisk used as a repeat count means to use the specifier preceding the asterisk for all the remaining items.

The unpack function also can compute checksums. Just precede a specifier with a percent sign and a number indicating how many bits of checksum are desired. The extracted items are then checksummed together into a single item:

```
unpack "c4",     "\1\2\3\4";  # 1, 2, 3, 4
unpack "%16c4", "\1\2\3\4";  # 10
unpack "%3c4",   "\1\2\3\4";  # 2
```

Sorting with pack

Suppose that you have a list of numeric Internet addresses—in string form—to sort, something like:

```
11.22.33.44
1.3.5.7
23.34.45.56
```

You would like to have them in "numeric" order. That is, the list should be sorted on the numeric value of the first number, then sub-sorted on the second, then the third, and finally the fourth. As usual, if you try to sort a list like this, the results are in the wrong order (Item 22). Sorting numerically won't work either, because that would sort only on the first number in each string. Using pack provides a pretty good solution:

```
my @sorted_addr =
  sort {
    pack( 'C*', split /\./, $a ) cmp
    pack( 'C*', split /\./, $b )
  } @addr;
```

For efficiency, this definitely should be rewritten as a Schwartzian Transform (Item 22):

```
my @sorted_addr =
  map  { $_->[0] }
  sort { $a->[1] cmp $b->[1] }
  map  { [ $_, pack( 'C*', split /\./ ) ] } @addr;
```

Notice that the comparison operator used in the sort is cmp, not <=>. The pack function converts a list of numbers (e.g., 11, 22, 33, 44) into a 4-byte string (\x0b\x16\x21\x2c). Comparing these as strings produces the proper sorting order. Of course, you could also use Socket, and write:

```
my @sorted_addr =
  map  { $_->[0] }
  sort { $a->[1] cmp $b->[1] }
  map  { [ $_, inet_aton($_) ] } @addr;
```

Manipulating hex escapes

Since pack and unpack understand hexadecimal strings, you can use them to manipulate strings containing hex escapes and the like.

For example, suppose you are programming for the Web and would like to "URI unescape" unsafe characters in a string. To URI unescape a string, you need to replace each occurrence of an escape—a percent sign followed by two hex digits—with the corresponding character. For example, "a%5eb" would be decoded to yield "a^b". You can write a Perl substitution to do this in one line:

```
$_ = "a%5eb";
s/%([0-9a-fA-F]{2})/pack("c",hex($1))/ge;
```

This particular snippet is widespread in some older (and probably broken) hand-rolled CGI scripts. However, it's somewhat obscure looking, and as is the case for many commonly performed tasks in Perl, there is a module designed specifically for the job:

```
use URI::Escape;
$_ = uri_unescape "a%5eb";
```

Dealing with endianness

Computer architectures come in two flavors based on how they store the bytes in a number. In the big-endian representation, the most significant byte comes first, while in the little-endian one, the least significant byte comes first.

Consider the hexadecimal number 0xAABBCCDD. In big-endian representation, the bytes come in the order AA, BB, CC, and DD, so that the byte that holds the biggest part of the number comes first. In little-endian representation, the bytes come in the order DD, CC, BB, and AA, so that the byte that holds the biggest part of the number comes last. There are many endianness tutorials already, so we defer to them for the details.

The problem typically comes up when you have to read from a binary file. You read four bytes, but you have to ensure that the four bytes come out as the right number. If you use the L format, you unpack the bytes according to the local architecture. That may not be right:

```
read $fh, $buffer, 4;
my $number = unpack 'L', $buffer;   # ???
```

Most likely, you have at least an inkling what order the bytes are in, so you can use an unpack format that notes that explicitly.

If you know the order is little-endian, you unpack it with v (for "VAX" order) to get a 32-bit unsigned integer, even if you are on a big-endian system:

```
read $fh, $buffer, 4;
my $number = unpack 'V', $buffer;   # little-endian
```

If the bytes are in big-endian order, you unpack them with N (for "network order"):

```
read $fh, $buffer, 4;
my $number = unpack 'N', $buffer;   # big-endian
```

To see the difference, pack the number 0xAABBCCDD using both orders, and look at the resulting bytes:

```
my $ddccbbaa = pack 'V', 0xAA_BB_CC_DD;   # little
my $aabbccdd = pack 'N', 0xAA_BB_CC_DD;   # big

printf "\$aabbccdd is 0x%s\n",
    join "_",
    map { sprintf '%X', ord }
    split //, $aabbccdd;

printf "\$ddccbbaa is 0x%s\n",
    join "_",
    map { sprintf '%X', ord }
    split //, $ddccbbaa;
```

Even though you packed the same number, you can see in the output that the bytes are in a different order in the actual data:

```
$aabbccdd is 0xAA_BB_CC_DD
$ddccbbaa is 0xDD_CC_BB_AA
```

You can't determine the order of the bytes just by looking at the number unless you already know what that number is supposed to be. If you unpack it with the wrong format, you get the wrong number:

```
my $packed = pack 'L', 137;

printf '%d', unpack 'N', $packed;   # -1996488704
```

You have to decide how to unpack the data to get back to the right number. Usually this means you have to look at the data format definition, or someone has to tell you what the order should be. Once you know the pack order, you unpack with that same order. For this reason, many systems agree to use the network order so both sides know what to expect.

Sometimes the data themselves give you a clue by giving you a byte sequence that represents a known number. For instance, Unicode-encoded files can have a byte-order mark, U+FEFF, that you can inspect to see in which order your architecture translates the sequence. Although the actual order of the bytes is always the same, a little-endian machine turns U+FEFF into the number 0xFFFE.

To play with this idea, you can create your "file" inside a string so you can easily see the byte order. Open a filehandle on the string (Item 54), read two bytes, and then unpack them with the S (16-bit unsigned short) format. To discover the endianness, you can compare the result of your unpack with the numeric value you expect on each architecture:

```
my $string = "\xFE\xFF";
open my($fh), '<', \$string;

read $fh, my( $bom ), 2;
my $unpacked = unpack 'S', $bom;

if( 0xFEFF == $unpacked ) {
  print "Big Endian!\n"
}
elsif( 0xFFFE == $unpacked ) {
  print "Little Endian!\n"
}
else {
  print "What the heck are you?\n"
}
```

Uuencoding

Uuencoding is a way to ASCIIfy data to ensure that it makes it through a 7-bit channel, such as e-mail, without corrupting itself. You spend all that time finding out how to type accented characters and you don't need some mail server messing them up. It's simple to do uuencoding on your own in Perl because pack's u specifier handles the details for you:

```
use utf8;

my $string = <<"HERE";
Can my fiancée, Ms. Sørenson, send you her résumé?
HERE

my $uuencoded = pack 'u*', $string;

print "=begin 644 $filename\n", $uuencoded, "`\n=end\n";
```

Going from the uuencoded text back to the original text is just as easy.
Assuming you have your uuencoded data in a file, you read the file, discard
the header and footer, and then `unpack` the rest:

```
use utf8;

while (<>) {
  last
    if ( $mode, $filename ) = /^begin\s+(\d+)\s+(\S+)/i;
}

if ($mode) {
  open my ($fh), '>:utf8', $filename
    or die "couldn't open $filename: $!\n";
  chmod oct($mode), $filename
    or die "couldn't set mode: $!\n";

  print "$mode $filename\n";

  while (<>) {
    last if (/^(`|end)/i);
    print $fh unpack( 'u*', $_ );
  }
}
```

Things to remember

- Combine data into a single string using `pack`.
- Restore data from a string with `unpack`.
- Use `pack` formats to put data in the right format.

Item 118. Access the symbol table with typeglobs.

You aren't really supposed to know about the symbol table or typeglobs, where Perl keeps track of package variables, named subroutine definitions, and bareword filehandles. For almost anything you might need from the symbol table, you can use lexical variables, references, or object-oriented programming instead. However, sometimes you can't avoid it. You might also encounter the symbol table and typeglobs from time to time in old Perl code, so you should be aware of what they look like and what they do.

In Perl, you can use the same identifier for different variables—for instance, `$foo`, `@foo`, `%foo`, `&foo`, `foo` (as a filehandle), and so on. Perl keeps track of all of the things named "foo" in the symbol table entry for that name.

You can directly manipulate the contents of the symbol table with a construct called a **typeglob**. A typeglob, which might make more sense said as "a glob of types," is an identifier preceded by an asterisk—for example, `*foo`. It represents the symbol table entry for everything with that identifier.

You can use typeglobs to alias names:

```perl
*ren = *stimpy;   # make $ren an alias for
                  # $stimpy, @ren an alias
                  # for @stimpy, and so on.


# Same thing, with an explicit package name.
*main::ren = *main::stimpy;
```

You can localize typeglobs so your change has limited effect:

```perl
$ren = 'hello stimpy';

{
  local *ren = *stimpy;   # $ren, @ren, etc. are local.
  $stimpy = 'yello ren';
  print "$ren\n";         # prints 'yello ren'
}

print "$ren\n";           # still prints 'yello ren'
$stimpy = 'later skater';
print "$ren\n";           # STILL prints 'yello ren'
```

You can change the symbol table hash directly by using a literal string as an identifier (this is different than a soft reference):

```
$main::{'ren'} = $main::{'stimpy'};
local $main::{'ren'} = $main::{'stimpy'};
```

You can pass typeglobs as arguments to subroutines, or store them like scalar values:

```
my @g = ( *foo, *bar );   # Storing typeglobs in an array.
                          # must be package vars!
our ( $foo, $bar ) = ( "ren", "stimpy" );


*s = $g[0];               # Using them.
*t = $g[1];               # Or just (*s, *t) = @g.
print "$s and $t\n";      # Prints "ren and stimpy".
```

You also can alias a single kind of variable, such as only the array or only the subroutine slot, by assigning a reference of the appropriate type to a typeglob. In the code below, you alias the name hello to the subroutine world:

```
sub world { "world\n" }
*hello = \&world;

my $hello = "hello";
print $hello . ", " . &hello;  # Prints "hello, world".
```

If you need to temporarily replace a subroutine definition, you can localize the typeglob and assign a new subroutine definition for that identifier. Perl figures out which slot to use based on the righthand side:

```
sub greet { print "Hello!\n" }

greet();

{
  local *greet;

  *greet = sub { print "How you doing?\n" };

  greet();
}

greet();  # back to normal
```

You can use typeglobs to localize filehandles and directory handles (Item 52) for lexical filehandles, though:

```
sub some_file_thing {
  local *FH;  # FH is local to this subroutine.
  open FH, "foo";
  ...;
}
```

You can also use typeglobs in places where you should ordinarily use references (but avoid doing so unless you have to):

```
sub you { print "yo, world\n" }
&{*yo}();  # Prints "yo, world".
```

Perl also has a "typeglob subscript" syntax, *FOO{BAR}, which allows you to extract individual references from a typeglob:

```
$a    = "testing";
@a    = 1 .. 3;
$sref = *a{SCALAR};
$aref = *a{ARRAY};
print "$$sref @$aref\n";
```

Things to remember

- Perl tracks package variables in symbol tables.
- Alias variables with typeglobs.
- Redefine subroutines by assigning to their typeglobs.

Item 119. Initialize with BEGIN; finish with END.

Perl provides a mechanism, BEGIN blocks, that allows you to execute initialization code at program start-up. Perl also provides a complementary mechanism, END, that allows you to execute code just before normal program termination.

The BEGIN block

A BEGIN block encloses code that is to be executed immediately after it is compiled and before any following code is compiled. For example, you can use BEGIN to initialize a variable that a subroutine will later use. You might also want to make a lexical variable private to a subroutine. You need to define and initialize the lexical variable before the subroutine refers to it:

```
BEGIN {
    my $dow = qw(Sun Mon Tue Wed Thu Fri Sat);

    sub dow {
        $dow[ $_[0] % 7 ];
    }
}
```

If you want to replace part of another module, perhaps because you need to temporarily fix a bug, you need a BEGIN block. You have to ensure that your changes get in before any other part of the code uses the module:

```
BEGIN {
    use Some::Module;

    no warnings 'redefine';
    *Some::Module::some_sub = sub { ... your fixes ... }
}
```

Sometimes you'll want to check the state of your environment before you go on. Some things may not compile correctly if you don't have the right setup. In this case, you check for a threaded perl:

```
BEGIN {
    use Config;

    die "You need a threaded perl to run this!"
        unless $Config{useithreads} eq 'define';
}
```

If you are doing something more interesting, such as connecting to a database, you probably don't want to run that process when you just want to check the syntax, as when you run perl -c. The $^C variable tells you the state of the -c switch:

```
BEGIN {
    if ($^C) {
        print "I'm just checking my syntax with -c\n";
    }
```

```
      else {
        print "I'm getting ready to run, so I should "
          . "get ready\n";
        my $dbh = DBI->connect(...);
      }
    }
```

You might not think you would need to check for -c, but does your editor or IDE show you errors and warnings as you write your program? If so, it's probably running `perl -c` behind the scenes.

You can even have multiple BEGIN blocks. Perl executes them in the order in which you define them, but you'll see more on that in a moment.

The END block

END blocks enclose code that will be executed just as a Perl program terminates under normal conditions. END blocks are useful for cleaning up—getting rid of lockfiles, releasing semaphores, and so forth:

```
END {
  my $program_name = basename($0);
  unlink glob "/tmp/$program_name.*";
}
```

END blocks are executed during any "planned" termination—the end of the script, `exit`, `die`, and so on. Multiple END blocks are executed in reverse of the order in which they were encountered during compilation. This little example shows the BEGIN blocks happening in order of their definition, then the run-time statements, and then the ENDs in reverse order:

```
BEGIN { print "1. I'm first\n"; }
END   { print "6. I'm sixth\n" }
print "4. I'm fourth\n";
BEGIN { print "2. I'm second\n"; }
BEGIN { print "3. I'm third\n"; }
END   { print "5. I'm fifth\n" }
```

If your program exits abnormally, such as from a panic, an uncaught signal, etc., the program just stops, and doesn't get a chance to run its END blocks.

Things to remember

- Use BEGIN blocks to run code at compile time.
- Use END blocks to run code right before program termination.

Item 120. Use Perl one-liners to create mini programs.

Perl's heritage includes the world of system administration, where people like to create their entire programs on the command line. The *perlrun* documentation lists all of perl's command-line options that make this possible, but you'll get only the most popular ones in this Item.

Many of the normal style rules disappear on the command line. Lexical variables, descriptive names, and proper scoping don't matter as much in short programs. Judicious use of default arguments (Items 15 and 16) saves space. Although you shouldn't intentionally make your programs hard to read by making them as short as you can, you don't want to make your one-liners hard to read by making them too long, either.

The -e switch

To specify a program on the command line, you use the -e switch, or the -E switch if you have Perl 5.10 or later and want to enable its optional features. The argument to -e is a string that represents your program. Since you may want to use quotes inside the program text, you might want to use generalized quoting (Item 21) so you don't confuse the shell's quoting (e.g., the Windows cmd wants double quotes around arguments):

```
% perl -e "print qq(Hello World\n)"
```

```
% perl -E "say q(Hello World)"
```

You can add a newline to the end of your output with the -l switch, which means you can often go without the double quoting if you only used the quoting to get the newline:

```
% perl -le "print q(Hello World)"
```

```
% perl -le "print q(The time is ), scalar localtime"
```

To print the module search path, you just have to loop over @INC:

```
% perl -le 'print for @INC'
```

You can still give your script arguments. Remember that `shift` works on `@ARGV` (Item 16) when you use it outside of a subroutine. Here's a one-liner to convert a decimal representation to a hexadecimal one:

```
% perl -e "printf qq|%X\n|, int( shift )" 137
93
```

Once you have a one-liner that you like, you can make it a shell alias so you don't have to do so much typing. If you have to convert number bases often, you might like these bash aliases to translate between binary (b), octal (o), decimal (d), or hexadecimal (h):

```
alias d2o="perl -e 'printf qq|%o\n|, int( shift )'"
alias d2b="perl -e 'printf qq|%b\n|, int( shift )'"
alias h2d="perl -e 'printf qq|%d\n|, hex( shift )'"
alias h2o="perl -e 'printf qq|%o\n|, hex( shift )'"
alias h2b="perl -e 'printf qq|%b\n|, hex( shift )'"
alias o2h="perl -e 'printf qq|%X\n|, oct( shift )'"
alias o2d="perl -e 'printf qq|%d\n|, oct( shift )'"
alias o2b="perl -e 'printf qq|%b\n|, oct( shift )'"
```

If you have to deal with epoch time and want to know what the string version is, that's a similar alias:

```
alias e2t="perl -le 'print localtime( shift )'"
```

The -n switch

The `-n` switch wraps a `while` loop around the program you specify with `-e`. The `while` iterates the lines in the file that you specify:

```
% perl -ne "print" fileA fileB
```

That one-liner program is the same as this full program, where the parts in the `-e` are in the `while` block:

```
while (<>) {
  print;
}
```

This allows you to change the lines of the input to create new output. Suppose that you want to add the line number to each line. You just need to add the `$.` special variable to the output:

```
% perl -ne 'print qq($.: $_)' fileA
```

In that one-liner, you single-quoted it so a UNIX shell wouldn't think that $. and $_ were shell variables. You can change those to double-quotes on Windows, but on UNIX you'd have to escape the $, making things very messy:

```
% perl -ne "print qq(\$.: \$_)" fileA
```

If you want to output only a range of lines, that's easy, too. The flip-flop operator (the .. in scalar context) is false until its lefthand side is true, and it stays true until its righthand side is true. When you give it just numbers, it compares $. to those numbers. This one line prints lines 4 to 7 inclusively:

```
% perl -ne 'print qq($.: $_) if 4 .. 7' fileA
```

If you just want the odd-numbered lines, that's easy, too, with the modulus operator, %:

```
% perl -ne 'print qq($.: $_) if $. % 2' fileA
```

Since the -n wraps your code in while(<>) { and }, you can play some extra tricks on it. It just puts those virtual braces around whatever is in -e, but your entire program doesn't have to be in that while. For instance, you can end the while yourself and start another block. In this example, you use an END block (Item 119) that uses that final parenthesis from -n:

```
% perl -nle '$count++ } END { print $count' *.pl
```

If you typed out that program, you'd get this script, even if it looks a bit oddly formatted:

```
while( <> ) {
    $count++ } END { print $count
}
```

Similarly, you might want to run something once at the start, so you use a BEGIN block (Item 119):

```
% perl -nle '$count++ } \
    BEGIN { print q(Counting ) . @ARGV . q( files) } \
    END { print $count' *.pl
```

The -p switch

The -p switch is like the -n switch, but it automatically prints the value of $_ at the end of each iteration of the loop.

```
% perl -pe 's/buster/Buster/g' fileA fileB
```

The `-p` turns that program into this `while` loop, inserting your code at the top of the loop, but adding a `print` before the end of the loop:

```
while (<>) {
  s/buster/Buster/g;
  print;
}
```

Suppose you want to change all line endings to the UNIX line endings. You just have to supply the part that changes the line, and `-p` handles the output:

```
% perl -pe 's/\012?\015/\n/g' file-dox.txt > \
    file-unix.txt
```

The `-i` switch

The `-i` switch turns on some special magic that lets you process files in-place. When you use `-i`, Perl renames the original file, opens it for reading using its new name, and then opens a new file for writing with the original name. As you read lines from the renamed file, you can change them and write them to the original filename, transforming your file line-by-line. If you want to change all of the colons to tabs, use `-pi`:

```
% perl -pi -e 's/:/\t/' fileA fileB
```

The `-i` switch by itself clobbers the original data. `perl` doesn't keep a copy of the original file. If you want to keep a backup in case things don't work out correctly, you can give `-i` a file extension, such as .old. Now `perl` saves the original data as fileA.old and fileB.old.

```
% perl -pi.old -e 's/:/\t/' fileA fileB
```

You can increment all of the numbers in a file with a global substitution:

```
% perl -pi.bak -e 's/(\d+)/ 1 + $1 /ge' fileA
```

You can increment just the numbers that have non-word characters around them:

```
% perl -pi.bak -e 's/\b(\d+)\b/ 1 + $1 /ge' fileA
```

Or maybe you want to expand all of the tabs into spaces. This one is tricky, because you don't want to simply make every tab a certain number of spaces. You want to just expand a tab until the next tab stop, so you have to do some fancy work to figure out how close to the tab stop you are:

```
% perl -pi -e 's/\t/ q( ) x (4 - pos() % 4) /ge' tabs.txt
```

With the -0 switch, you can specify the input record separator, in either octal or hexadecimal. If you specify 00, you turn on paragraph mode. To rewrap paragraphs, you can turn every run of whitespace into a single space, and then find the first space before 73 characters and turn it into a newline. Before you print $_, you tack on an extra newline to separate paragraphs:

```
% perl -000 -pi.bak -e \
    's/\s+/ /g; s/(.{50,73})\s/$1\n/g; $_.=qq(\n\n)'
```

This example is perfect for the \K, which doesn't include the parts of the pattern before it in the replacement:

```
% perl5.10.1 -000 -pe \
    's/\s+/ /g; s/(.{50,73})\K\s/\n/g; $_.=qq(\n\n)'
```

The -M switch

You can load a module from the command line with -M:

```
% perl -MLWP::Simple -e "getprint 'http://www.example.com'"
```

```
% perl -MFile::Spec::Functions -le \
    'print catfile( @ARGV )' a b c
```

If you want to import a symbol, you start the import list with an equal sign after the module name:

```
% perl -MList::Util=shuffle -le \
    "print for( shuffle(@ARGV) )" a b c
```

If you want to load more than one module, you use more than one -M:

```
% perl -MList::Util=shuffle -MList::MoreUtils=uniq \
    -le "print for( shuffle( uniq @ARGV) )" a b c a h g
```

The -a and -F switches

The -a switch breaks up a line for you and puts the result in @F. By default, it breaks up the line by whitespace. Using the END trick you saw earlier, but this time with for, you can get a word frequency table:

```
% perl -anle '$S{$_}++ for @F } \
    for( keys %S ) { print qq($_ $S{$_})'
```

If you want to sort the list by the number of times you see the word, that's easy, too:

```
% perl -anle '$S{$_}++ for @F } \
    for( sort { $S{$b} <=> $S{$a} } keys %S ) \
    { print qq($_: $S{$_})'
```

That's fine for whitespace-separated words, but what if they are separated by something else—say, colons? The -F switch allows you to change the split pattern that -a uses:

```
% perl -aF: -nle '$S{$_}++ for @F } \
    for( sort { $S{$b} <=> $S{$a} } keys %S ) \
    { print qq($_: $S{$_})'
```

What if you want to count only some of the words, such as the first to third words on each line? In that case, you just use a slice of @F:

```
% perl -aF: -nle '$S{$_}++ for @F[0..2] } \
    for( sort { $S{$b} <=> $S{$a} } keys %S ) \
    { print qq($_: $S{$_})'
```

Things to remember

- Write short programs directly on the command line.
- Back up any files you modify in-place.
- See the *perlrun* documentation for details on all perl switches.

A | Perl Resources

This is just a small book about Perl, and we selected only some of the most valuable topics that we wanted to pass along to the intermediate Perl programmer. The first edition of this book was published when the Perl canon and community were still small. Now both are much larger, and there's a lot more available to you.

Books

We include a short list of book recommendations, but you can find more Perl books at http://books.perl.org/.

- *Learning Perl, Fifth Edition,* by Randal L. Schwartz, Tom Phoenix, and brian d foy (Sebastopol, CA: O'Reilly Media, 2008). This is the canonical book for starting with Perl. You'll get just enough Perl to handle the 80% of the language that you'll use every day.
- *Intermediate Perl* by Randal L. Schwartz, Tom Phoenix, and brian d foy (Sebastopol, CA: O'Reilly Media, 2006). After you go through *Learning Perl*, you're ready for an intensive introduction to references, packages, and modules.
- *Mastering Perl* by brian d foy (Sebastopol, CA: O'Reilly Media, 2007). Instead of teaching you more Perl syntax, this book focuses on using Perl wisely to create robust, enterprise-worthy programs.
- *Higher Order Perl: Transforming Programs with Programs* by Mark Jason Dominus (San Francisco, CA: Morgan Kaufmann, 2005). If you really want to harness the power of Perl's dynamic subroutines, try this mind-bending tome from one of Perl's luminaries. You can download this book for free at http://hop.perl.plover.com/.
- *Object Oriented Perl: A Comprehensive Guide to Concepts and Programming Techniques* by Damian Conway (Greenwich, CT: Manning Publications, 2000). You can learn not only Perl's object oriented syntax, but also a lot of the theory and philosophy of object oriented programming.

- *Network Programming with Perl* by Lincoln Stein (Boston, MA: Addison-Wesley Professional, 2001). Although this book is somewhat dated, the basics of network programming at the low levels haven't changed that much. If you want to understand what the Perl networking modules do behind the scenes, start with this book.
- *Perl Testing: A Developer's Notebook* by Ian Langworth and chromatic (Sebastopol, CA: O'Reilly Media, 2005). Learn more about Perl testing with the advice from this book.
- *Pro Perl Debugging* by Richard Foley and Andy Lester (New York, NY: Apress, LLC, 2005). If you want to know how to use the built-in Perl debugger, this book will show you how to do more than you thought possible.
- *Writing Perl Modules for CPAN* by Sam Tregar (New York, NY: Apress, LLC, 2002). If you're just getting started as a CPAN author, this is a good starting point. It's also available as a free download from Apress, LLC at http://www.apress.com/book/view/159059018X.
- *The Perl Cookbook, Second Edition,* by Tom Christiansen and Nat Torkington (Sebastopol, CA: O'Reilly Media, 2003). Much like this book, *The Perl Cookbook* has many short topics that show you how to accomplish specific tasks.
- *Automating System Administration with Perl: Tools to Make You More Efficient* by David N. Blank-Edelman (Sebastopol, CA: O'Reilly Media, 2009).
- *Perl Hacks: Tips and Tools for Programming, Debugging, and Surviving* by chromatic, Damian Conway, and Curtis "Ovid" Poe (Sebastopol, CA: O'Reilly Media, 2006). Learn some cool tricks and Perl innards, even if just for fun.

Websites

- http://perldoc.perl.org/
  Read the Perl documentation online.
- http://search.cpan.org/
  Find almost everything you need to know about any Perl module.
- http://learn.perl.org/
  Start learning Perl with some of these resources.
- http://perltraining.com.au/tips/
  Find more Perl advice from Perl Training Australia.

- http://pause.perl.org/
  Start your career as a CPAN author at PAUSE, the Perl Authors Upload Server.
- http://www.yapc.org/ and http://yapceurope.org/
  Find out about Perl events and conferences.
- http://www.pm.org/
  Find a Perl user group near you.
- http://www.theperlreview.com/
  The Perl Review publishes articles and other resources for Perl.

Blogs and Podcasts

There are many Perl blogs out there. Most of the good ones are listed in one of the blog aggregators.

- http://perlcast.com/
  Perlcast is a podcast about Perl.
- http://blogs.perl.org/
  This is a Perl blogging service. Get your own account!
- http://planet.perl.org/
  Planet Perl is a Perl blog aggregator.
- http://perlsphere.net/
  Perlsphere is a Perl blog aggregator

Getting help

There are several websites where you can get Perl help.

- http://www.stackoverflow.com/
- http://www.perlmonks.org/
- The beginners.perl.org mailing list at http://www.nntp.perl.org/ group/perl.beginners/ is a gentle place for new Perl programmers to ask questions.
- http://irc.perl.org/
- http://lists.perl.org/ lists many of the Perl mailing lists, many devoted to select topics.

B | Map from First to Second Edition

We restructured the second edition of *Effective Perl Programming*. We removed some chapters, such as "Object-Oriented Programming" and "Debugging," that other books cover much better, and added new chapters for modern topics, such as "Testing" and "CPAN." Of course, we kept and revised quite a number of the original chapters and Items, but shuffled them around a bit.

Table B-1 lists the Items of the first edition in order of appearance in the book and their corresponding Items in the second edition.

Some Items from the first edition do not appear in the second edition. Table B-2 shows the Items that we removed for one reason or another. Possibly they were too outdated to update or were completely eclipsed by a more-modern practice in Perl. Possibly we felt that we couldn't cover the topic adequately within the scope of this book. Maybe we just ran out of time. If we removed an Item that you particularly liked, we apologize—maybe it will make it back into the third edition. Check http://www.effectiveperlprogramming.org/: We're going to post more Effective Perl there and we still might get to cover these items.

Table B-1 Mapping of the Items in the First Edition to Their Positions in the Second Edition

	First Edition		Second Edition		
Item	Chapter	Title	Item	Chapter	Title
1	Basics	Know your namespaces.	5	The Basics of Perl	Know your variable namespaces.
2	Basics	Avoid using slice when you want an element.	11	The Basics of Perl	Avoid a slice when you want an element.
3	Basics	Don't assign undef when you want an empty list.	10	The Basics of Perl	Don't assign undef when you want an empty array.
4	Basics	String and numeric comparisons are different.	6	The Basics of Perl	Know the difference between string and numeric comparisons.
5	Basics	Remember that 0 and " " are false.	7	The Basics of Perl	Know which values are false and test them accordingly.
6	Basics	Understand conversions between strings and numbers.	8	The Basics of Perl	Understand conversions between strings and numbers.
7	Idiomatic Perl	Use $_ for elegance.	15	Idiomatic Perl	Use $_ for elegance and brevity.
8	Idiomatic Perl	Know the other default arguments: @_, @ARGV, STDIN.	16	Idiomatic Perl	Know Perl's other default arguments.
9	Idiomatic Perl	Know common shorthands and syntax quirks.	17	Idiomatic Perl	Know common shorthand and syntax quirks.
10	Idiomatic Perl	Avoid excessive punctuation.	18	Idiomatic Perl	Avoid excessive punctuation.
11	Idiomatic Perl	Consider different ways of reading from a stream.	53	Files and Filehandles	Consider different ways of reading from a stream.
12	Idiomatic Perl	Use foreach, map and grep as appropriate.	20	Idiomatic Perl	Use foreach, map, and grep as appropriate.
13	Idiomatic Perl	Don't misquote.	21	Idiomatic Perl	Know the different ways to quote strings.

440

First Edition			Second Edition		
Item	Chapter	Title	Item	Chapter	Title
14	Idiomatic Perl	Learn the myriad ways of sorting.	22	Idiomatic Perl	Learn the myriad ways of sorting.
15	Regular Expressions	Know the precedence of regular expression operators.	28	Regular Expressions	Know the precedence of regular expression operators.
16	Regular Expressions	Use regular expression memory.	29	Regular Expressions	Use regular expression captures.
17	Regular Expressions	Avoid greed when parsimony is best.	34	Regular Expressions	Avoid greed when parsimony is best.
18	Regular Expressions	Remember that whitespace is not a word boundary.	35	Regular Expressions	Use zero-width assertions to match positions in a string.
19	Regular Expressions	Use split for clarity, unpack for efficiency.	117	Miscellany	Use pack() and unpack() for data munging.
20	Regular Expressions	Avoid using regular expressions for simple string operations.	36	Regular Expressions	Avoid using regular expressions for simple string operations.
21	Regular Expressions	Make regular expressions readable.	37	Regular Expressions	Make regular expressions readable.
22	Regular Expressions	Make regular expressions efficient.	32	Regular Expressions	Use non-capturing parentheses when you only need grouping.
22	Regular Expressions	Make regular expressions efficient.	33	Regular Expressions	Watch out for the match variables.
22	Regular Expressions	Make regular expressions efficient.	38	Regular Expressions	Avoid unnecessary backtracking.
22	Regular Expressions	Make regular expressions efficient.	39	Regular Expressions	Compile regexes only once.
22	Regular Expressions	Make regular expressions efficient.	41	Regular Expressions	Benchmark your regular expressions
23	Subroutines	Understand the difference between my and local.	43	Subroutines	Understand the difference between my and local.
24	Subroutines	Avoid using @_ directly—unless you have to.	44	Subroutines	Avoid using @_ directly unless you have to.

continues

Table B-1 Mapping of the Items in the First Edition to Their Positions in the Second Edition (*continued*)

	First Edition			Second Edition	
Item	Chapter	Title	Item	Chapter	Title
25	Subroutines	Use want array to write subroutines returning lists.	45	Subroutines	Use want array to write subroutines returning lists.
26	Subroutines	Pass references instead of copies.	46	Subroutines	Pass references instead of copies.
27	Subroutines	Use hashes to pass named parameters.	47	Subroutines	Use hashes to pass named parameters.
28	Subroutines	Use prototypes to get special argument parsing.	48	Subroutines	Use prototypes to get special argument parsing.
29	Subroutines	Use subroutines to create other subroutines.	50	Subroutines	Create new subroutines with subroutines.
30	References	Understand references and reference syntax.	58	References	Understand references and reference syntax.
31	References	Create lists of lists with references.	60	References	Create arrays of arrays with references.
32	References	Don't confuse anonymous arrays with list literals.	61	References	Don't confuse anonymous arrays with list literals.
33	References	Build C-style structs with anonymous hashes.	62	References	Build C-style structs with anonymous hashes.
34	References	Be careful with circular data structures.	63	References	Be careful with circular data structures.
35	References	Use map and grep to manipulate complex data structures.	64	References	Use map and grep to manipulate complex data structures.
36	Debugging	Enable static and/or run-time checks.	3	The Basics of Perl	Enable strictures to promote better coding.
41	Using Packages and Modules	Don't reinvent the wheel—use Perl modules.	71	CPAN	Know the commonly used modules.

First Edition			Second Edition		
Item	Chapter	Title	Item	Chapter	Title
43	Using Packages and Modules	Make sure Perl can find the modules you are using.	69	CPAN	Ensure that Perl can find your modules.
44	Using Packages and Modules	Use perldoc to extract documentation for installed modules.	1	The Basics of Perl	Find the documentation for Perl and its modules.
45	Writing Packages and Modules	Use h2xs to generate module boilerplate.	80	Distributions	Don't start distributions by hand.
46	Writing Packages and Modules	Embed your documentation with POD.	82	Distributions	Embed your documentation with POD.
47	Writing Packages and Modules	Use XS for low-level interfaces and/or speed.	86	Distributions	Use XS for low-level interfaces and speed.
48	Writing Packages and Modules	Submit your useful modules to the CPAN.	70	CPAN	Contribute to CPAN.
53	Miscellany	Use pack and unpack for data munging.	117	Miscellany	Use pack() and unpack() for data munging.
54	Miscellany	Know how and when to use eval, require, and do.	25	Idiomatic Perl	Use do {} to create inline subroutines.
56	Miscellany	Don't forget the file test operators.	51	Files and Filehandles	Don't ignore the file test operators.
57	Miscellany	Access the symbol table with typeglobs.	118	Miscellany	Access the symbol table with typeglobs.
59	Miscellany	Initialize with BEGIN; finish with END.	119	Miscellany	Initialize with BEGIN; finish with END.
60	Miscellany	Some interesting Perl one-liners programs.	120	Miscellany	Use Perl one-liners to create mini
Appendix B		Perl Resources	Appendix A		Perl Resources

Table B-2 Items from the First Edition Left Out of the Second Edition

Item number in 1st Edition	Chapter	Title
37	Debugging	Use debugging and profiling modules.
38	Debugging	Learn to use a debugging version of Perl.
39	Debugging	Test things by using the debugger as a Perl "shell".
40	Debugging	Don't debug too much as once.
42	Using Packages and Modules	Understand packages and modules.
49	Object-Oriented Programming	Consider using Perl's object-oriented programming features.
50	Object-Oriented Programming	Understand method inheritance in Perl.
51	Object-Oriented Programming	Inherit data explicitly.
52	Object-Oriented Programming	Create invisible interfaces with tied variables.
55	Object-Oriented Programming	Know when, and when not, to write networking code.
58	Miscellany	Use @{ [. . .] } or a tied hash to evaluate expressions inside strings.

Index

Symbols

livelessons ▶

video instruction from technology experts

- **LiveLessons** allows you to keep your skills up to date with the latest technology training from trusted author experts.

- **LiveLessons** is a cost-effective alternative to expensive off-site training programs.

- **LiveLessons** provides the ability to learn at your own pace and avoid hours in a classroom.

LiveLessons: self-paced, personal video instruction from the world's leading technology experts

- Instructors you trust
- Cutting edge topics
- Customized, self-paced learning
- Learn by doing

4+ HOURS OF EXPERT VIDEO INSTRUCTION

DVD VIDEO & DVD

livelessons ▶
video instruction from technology experts

Perl
Fundamentals

Peter J. Scott

video

Perl Fundamentals includes:

- 1 DVD featuring 4+ hours of instructor-led classroom sessions divided into 15 to 20 minute step-by-step hands-on labs
- Sample code and printed study guide

The power of the world's leading experts at your fingertips!

To learn more about **LiveLessons** visit
mylivelessons.com

informIT.com
THE TRUSTED TECHNOLOGY LEARNING SOURCE

Addison Wesley

PRENTICE HALL

SAMS

Addison
Wesley

REGISTER

THIS PRODUCT

informit.com/register

Register the Addison-Wesley, Exam Cram, Prentice Hall, Que, and Sams products you own to unlock great benefits.

To begin the registration process, simply go to **informit.com/register** to sign in or create an account. You will then be prompted to enter the 10- or 13-digit ISBN that appears on the back cover of your product.

Registering your products can unlock the following benefits:

- Access to supplemental content, including bonus chapters, source code, or project files.
- A coupon to be used on your next purchase.

Registration benefits vary by product. Benefits will be listed on your Account page under Registered Products.

About InformIT — THE TRUSTED TECHNOLOGY LEARNING SOURCE

INFORMIT IS HOME TO THE LEADING TECHNOLOGY PUBLISHING IMPRINTS Addison-Wesley Professional, Cisco Press, Exam Cram, IBM Press, Prentice Hall Professional, Que, and Sams. Here you will gain access to quality and trusted content and resources from the authors, creators, innovators, and leaders of technology. Whether you're looking for a book on a new technology, a helpful article, timely newsletters, or access to the Safari Books Online digital library, InformIT has a solution for you.

informIT.com

THE TRUSTED TECHNOLOGY LEARNING SOURCE

Addison-Wesley | Cisco Press | Exam Cram
IBM Press | Que | Prentice Hall | Sams

SAFARI BOOKS ONLINE

informIT.com
THE TRUSTED TECHNOLOGY LEARNING SOURCE

PEARSON

InformIT is a brand of Pearson and the online presence for the world's leading technology publishers. It's your source for reliable and qualified content and knowledge, providing access to the top brands, authors, and contributors from the tech community.

Addison-Wesley Cisco Press EXAM/CRAM IBM Press. Que PRENTICE HALL SAMS Safari Books Online

LearnIT at InformIT

Looking for a book, eBook, or training video on a new technology? Seeking timely and relevant information and tutorials? Looking for expert opinions, advice, and tips? **InformIT has the solution.**

- Learn about new releases and special promotions by subscribing to a wide variety of newsletters.
  Visit **informit.com/newsletters**.

- Access FREE podcasts from experts at **informit.com/podcasts**.

- Read the latest author articles and sample chapters at **informit.com/articles**.

- Access thousands of books and videos in the Safari Books Online digital library at **safari.informit.com**.

- Get tips from expert blogs at **informit.com/blogs**.

Visit **informit.com/learn** to discover all the ways you can access the hottest technology content.

Are You Part of the IT Crowd?

Connect with Pearson authors and editors via RSS feeds, Facebook, Twitter, YouTube, and more! Visit **informit.com/socialconnect**.

informIT.com THE TRUSTED TECHNOLOGY LEARNING SOURCE PEARSON

Addison-Wesley Cisco Press EXAM/CRAM IBM Press. Que PRENTICE HALL SAMS Safari Books Online

Try Safari Books Online FREE
Get online access to 5,000+ Books and Videos

Safari Books Online

FREE TRIAL—GET STARTED TODAY!
www.informit.com/safaritrial

Find trusted answers, fast
Only Safari lets you search across thousands of best-selling books from the top technology publishers, including Addison-Wesley Professional, Cisco Press, O'Reilly, Prentice Hall, Que, and Sams.

Master the latest tools and techniques
In addition to gaining access to an incredible inventory of technical books, Safari's extensive collection of video tutorials lets you learn from the leading video training experts.

WAIT, THERE'S MORE!

Keep your competitive edge
With Rough Cuts, get access to the developing manuscript and be among the first to learn the newest technologies.

Stay current with emerging technologies
Short Cuts and Quick Reference Sheets are short, concise, focused content created to get you up-to-speed quickly on new and cutting-edge technologies.

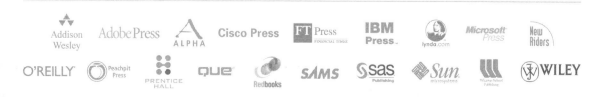

Addison Wesley · Adobe Press · ALPHA · Cisco Press · FT Press FINANCIAL TIMES · IBM Press · lynda.com · Microsoft Press · New Riders

O'REILLY · Peachpit Press · PRENTICE HALL · QUE · Redbooks · SAMS · SAS Publishing · Sun microsystems · Wharton School Publishing · WILEY

FREE Online Edition

Your purchase of **Effective Perl Programming, Second Edition,** includes access to a free online edition for 45 days through the Safari Books Online subscription service. Nearly every Addison-Wesley Professional book is available online through Safari Books Online, along with more than 5,000 other technical books and videos from publishers such as Cisco Press, Exam Cram, IBM Press, O'Reilly, Prentice Hall, Que, and Sams.

SAFARI BOOKS ONLINE allows you to search for a specific answer, cut and paste code, download chapters, and stay current with emerging technologies.

Activate your FREE Online Edition at www.informit.com/safarifree

> **STEP 1:** Enter the coupon code: ADSGTZG.

> **STEP 2:** New Safari users, complete the brief registration form.
> Safari subscribers, just log in.

If you have difficulty registering on Safari or accessing the online edition, please e-mail customer-service@safaribooksonline.com